Language is primarily a tool for communication, yet many textbooks still treat English grammar as simply a set of rules and facts to be memorized by rote. This new textbook is made for students who are frustrated with this approach and would like instead to understand grammar and how it works.

Why are there two future tenses in English? What are auxiliaries and why are they so confusing? Why are English motion verbs hard to use? Why are determiners so important in English? These and many other frequently asked questions are answered in this handy guide.

Student learning is supported with numerous exercises, chapter summaries, and suggestions for further reading. An accompanying website offers further resources, including additional classroom exercises and a chance to interact with the author.

It is the essential grammar toolkit for students of English language and linguistics and future teachers of English as a Second Language.

Thomas E. Payne is an international linguistics consultant for SIL International, and a Research Associate in the Department of Linguistics at the University of Oregon. His previous publications include *Describing Morphosyntax* (Cambridge, 1997) and *Exploring Language Structure* (Cambridge, 2006).

Understanding English Grammar

A Linguistic Introduction

THOMAS E. PAYNE

UNIVERSITY OF OREGON AND SIL INTERNATIONAL

CAMBRIDGE
UNIVERSITY PRESS

CAMBRIDGE
UNIVERSITY PRESS

University Printing House, Cambridge CB2 8BS, United Kingdom

Cambridge University Press is part of the University of Cambridge.

It furthers the University's mission by disseminating knowledge in the pursuit of education, learning and research at the highest international levels of excellence.

www.cambridge.org
Information on this title: www.cambridge.org/9780521757119

© Thomas E. Payne 2011

First published 2011
Reprinted 2014

A catalogue record for this publication is available from the British Library

Library of Congress Cataloguing in Publication data

Payne, Thomas Edward, 1951–
Understanding English grammar : a linguistic introduction / Thomas E. Payne.
    p.   cm.
Includes bibliographical references.
ISBN 978-0-521-76329-5 (Hardback) – ISBN 978-0-521-75711-9 (pbk.)
1. English language–Grammar.   2. Language and languages–Study and teaching.   I. Title.
PE1109.P39 2011
425–dc22   2010020969

ISBN 978-0-521-75711-9 Paperback

Additional resources for this publication at www.cambridge.org/payne

Dedicated to students in the Hanyang–Oregon TESOL
program at Hanyang University, 2004–2009

Contents

Figures

Tables

Preface

The grammar of a language is a dynamic, constantly changing set of habit patterns that allows people to communicate with one another. For some reason, many in academia and language teaching seem to have lost sight of this common sense truth, preferring to treat grammar as though it were an object, outside of human beings in society, consisting of absolute categories and rules. This misperception has led to a deep tension between theoreticians and the practical needs of language teachers, whose students often come to believe that grammar is a tedious classroom subject, to be endured as a kind of rite of passage, rather than a key to the amazing world of human communication.

In recent years linguistics has begun to recognize the importance of language in use to general understandings of human cognition, communication, and culture. This orientation, combined with developments in computational technology, has led to more pragmatic, data-driven, theoretical perspectives as linguists look at the way people actually communicate rather than the ideal systems enshrined in countless textbooks of the last century. This book attempts to bring current linguistic understandings to bear on practical tasks, such as language teaching, learning, and translating. It attempts to balance systematicity with creativity, absolutism with flexibility. It takes into account the fact that grammar is thoroughly human, deeply linked with culture and identity, and stunningly complex.

I hope that this book will promote genuine understanding of English grammar by answering the "why" questions that students often ask, e.g., "Why are auxiliaries so confusing?," "Why does English make such a big deal out of determiners?," "Why are there two 'future tenses'?," "Why do my students have such a hard time using English motion verbs?," and so on. The principle assertion is that grammar can be *understood* and appreciated as a practical system for communication. This perspective has the potential to inspire teachers and students with a genuine enthusiasm for grammar, replacing the frustration often engendered by a more traditional approach.

This book has been written for, and in consultation with, students preparing for careers as English language professionals. Most such students around the world are preparing to teach English as a foreign or second language in TESOL, TEFL, or TESL programs. However, "English Grammar," "The Structure of English," or other similar course titles are taught in a variety of academic programs, including communication studies, journalism, linguistics, and applied linguistics, to name a few. A previous or concurrent course in introduction to linguistics or phonetics would be helpful, but is not strictly necessary as a prerequisite to a course that uses this book.

In the following pages are hundreds of examples from two of the major online corpora of English: the British National Corpus (BNC), accessed via the Brigham Young University interface (Davies 2004), and the Corpus of Contemporary American English (COCA), also accessed via the BYU interface (Davies 2008). Other data come from the Internet (searches by Google), the Internet Movie Data Base (www.imdb.com), contemporary literature, and from personal conversations. Invented examples are used occasionally, and are identified as such.

I have tried to choose examples that will not be offensive or sound biased in any way. However, because the examples are from language in use, they represent how people actually talk and write. For that reason some readers may question my use of examples that contain words and names that reference specific genders, socially defined groups (like football teams or political parties), products, or even specific well-known people, events, and situations. I ask the reader to please understand that the focus of the book is understanding English grammar. The examples illustrate linguistic points, and have not been chosen according to any political or other "agenda."

There is also a website available to support the use of this book (see www.cambridge.org/payne). On this website you will find several resources for teachers and students, including:

- an opportunity to interact with the author.
- additional classroom exercises and solutions.
- additions and emendations to the text.
- references to additional resources as they become available.
- errata.

I sincerely hope this website will contribute to the continuing value of the text to anyone interested in understanding English grammar.

Acknowledgements

I am very grateful to the many people who contributed thoughts and opinions that have shaped this book. These include, but are not limited to, the faculty and students of the University of Oregon Department of Linguistics, the Hanyang–Oregon TESOL program at Hanyang University, Seoul, Korea, and the Canada Institute of Linguistics at Trinity Western University in Langley, British Columbia. I would also like to especially thank the following individuals who read and commented on earlier drafts of various portions of this work, or helped me work through the arguments in some way. These include (in alphabetical order) Colleen Ahland, Michael Ahland, Brian Butler, Genie Chung, Martin Endley, Lee Engdahl, Hae Kyung Kim, Kent Lee, Daryn Ma, Diane Majors, Arlyne Moi, Oddvar Moi, Rick Nivens, Soyeon Park, Barbara Partee, Emma Pavey, Doris Payne, Warren Payne, Jaime Peña, Ron Ross, and Fernando Zuñiga. I would also like to thank Mark Davies for help with the corpora. I'm very sorry if I have left anyone out. In a very real sense this book is written for the students who make all this work worthwhile.

Typographical conventions and abbreviations

Typographical conventions

In the body of the text, **italics** are used to cite a word or other form as a linguistic expression, e.g., the phrase *a linguistic introduction*. Very occasionally italics are used for emphasis in the text. In examples, italics are used to draw attention to the part of the example that is in view.

An **asterisk** in front of a form usually means that the form is not a grammatical structure of English, e.g., **knowed*. An asterisk is occasionally used to indicate that the form is a hypothetical historical reconstruction that is not directly attested in any documents, e.g., the Indo-European root **ank-*.

The **frowny face** symbol indicates that a form is grammatical, but not coherent in the context provided, e.g., *Where are you going? ☹I AM going.*

All upper case letters usually indicate abstract features rather than actual words. For example:

Semantic features: The verb *feed* combines the semantic features of ENABLE and EAT.
Semantic roles: The semantic roles of AGENT and PATIENT.
Cover terms in formulae and diagrams: The regular past tense pattern is [VERB]+ *-ed*.
Linguistic abbreviations in examples from other languages: NOM, ACC, etc.
Occasionally, particularly in Chapter 15, all upper case letters are used to indicate contrastive stress, e.g., *BILLY pushed Johnny off the veranda.*

Initial upper case letters are used for syntactic functions, e.g., Modification/ Modifier, Inflection, Complement, Head. This distinguishes syntactic functions from syntactic categories, e.g., noun, verb, noun phrase, clause.

Small caps are used for technical terms at their first occurrence. These terms all appear in the glossary. For example: *The verb* be *is notoriously* SUPPLETIVE *in English.*

Abbreviations

1SG	First person singular (*I, me*)
2SG	Second person singular (*you*)
ACC	Accusative case
ADJ	Adjective
AdjP	Adjective phrase
ADV	Adverb
AdvP	Adverb phrase
ART	Article
AUX	Auxiliary
BNC	British National Corpus (Davies 2004)
C	Complement
CAUSE	Causative
COCA	Corpus of Contemporary American English (Davies 2008)
CONJ	Conjunction
CP	Complement phrase
CSE	Contemporary Standard English
CTP	Complement-taking predicator
D	Determiner
DAT	Dative
DECL	Declarative
DP	Determined noun phrase (or determiner phrase)
GP	Genitive phrase
GR	Grammatical relation
H	Head
Incorp	Incorporated element
INF	Infinitive
INFL	Inflection
IP	Inflected verb phrase (or inflectional phrase)
L1	The first language a child acquires – the "mother tongue"
L2	Any language learned after L1 is acquired.
MKR	Marker of comparison
MOD	Modifier
N	Noun
NICE	Negation, Inversion, Code (tag questions), and Emphasis
NOM	Nominative case
NP	Noun phrase
O	(Direct) Object

OC	Object Complement
OV	Object+Verb constituent order
P	Preposition
PAST	Past tense
PDQ	Predeterminer quantifier
POSTP	Postposition
PP	Prepositional phrase
PREP	Preposition
PRES	Present tense
PRO	Pronoun
Q	Quantifier
S	Clause (also "Subject" in Chapter 2)
SC	Subject Complement
SLL	Second language learner
SR	Semantic role
STD	Standard of comparison
TAM	Tense, Aspect, and Mode
V	Verb
VO	Verb+Object constituent order
VP	Verb phrase

Introduction

The harmony between thought and reality is to be found in the grammar of the language ... Uttering a word is like striking a note on the keyboard of the imagination.

Ludwig Wittgenstein (1981[1958])

Language gives form to thought. Thought itself is hidden, internal, intangible, whereas language seems to be external, physical, exposed for all the world to see and hear. But is it really? Certainly the noises we make when we communicate using spoken language are "external" in that they are physical modifications of the mind–external environment in the form of complex sound waves moving through air. But the noises themselves are not the essence of our language. We often think in language without overt expression. When we write, we say we are writing "in a language," even though the medium is visible marks (or pixels) rather than noises. Signed languages used by the deaf are still languages, though they don't rely on sounds at all. The forms of language are certainly not random, like the sound of water tumbling over rocks in a stream. Regardless of the form it takes, language is governed by complex underlying patterns. If there were no consistent patterns, people would not be able to communicate with one another, and, after all, language is all about communication. It is the harmony between underlying patterns and external expression that is the essence of language.

So where do these patterns that constitute a language exist? Some would argue that they exist in the minds of individuals. But if they are purely mind-internal and individual, how can two individuals ever "understand" one another? Somehow the linguistic patterns in one person's mind must match, more or less closely, the patterns in another person's mind in order for communication between minds to take place. Therefore, others would argue, the patterns that give structure to the noises and other gestures people make when they communicate in a language exist "out there" in a community. In this view, being born into a community exposes an individual to patterns of communication that automatically and unconsciously become part of that person's way of being, like the culture-specific ways in which people walk, eat, or dress. The fact is that any human with common mental, emotional, and physical capacities and needs, participating in a community with other humans, develops patterned communicative behavior of the sort we call "language" in all parts of the known universe.

Imagine for a moment a community of ten people living on a remote island, each person being a native speaker of a different language, and none of them having any knowledge of any of the languages spoken by the other nine. What do you think would happen over time? Would they all just retreat from one another, and never communicate? Hardly likely, given the social nature of human beings. Would they each just speak their own language, and expect everyone else to understand? That doesn't seem like a very efficient solution either. Would they all somehow agree to learn one of the languages, and use that one all the time? Or is there some other possibility? I expect that eventually certain patterns would begin to emerge in the communicative behavior of the inhabitants of this hypothetical community. Such patterns may be a combination of gestures, grunts, and words from the ten native languages, but they would be uniquely adapted to the situations in which the people in this community find themselves. Recurring situations would call for recurring communicative acts – requests for goods, offers of assistance, expressions of facts, emotions, etc. Eventually, a new and unique system of communicative habit patterns would develop, especially suited to the needs of that particular community. Children born into the community would naturally begin using that system, and eventually lose all concept of their parents' original native languages, though the language of the community would bear traces of all ten original languages.

Of course, such a pristine situation for the development of a new language never exists in reality. However, this thought experiment does represent reasonably well some of the forces that shape real languages: a need to communicate in a specific historical, geographic, and social context, plus the physical and cognitive equipment it takes to cultivate a system that we can call a human language. Thus, the conditions that give rise to language are both external and internal to individual minds. The individual habit patterns that arise become part of the shared ways of being and cultural heritage of a community.

What is "English"?

This question is actually harder to answer than it may seem at first. I've just characterized a language as unconscious habit patterns that arise naturally in human communities. At the beginning of the third millennium of the Common Era (CE), there are literally thousands of communities around the world in which community members speak "English." Are all the sets of communicative habit patterns that have arisen in all of these communities really "the same"? Not by any means. In fact even the patterns employed by one individual speaker vary considerably from time to time and place to place. This variation is multiplied when compounded among all the members of a community, and then compounded again from one community to the next. In fact, a language is never *one thing*. For this reason, it is impossible to "capture" any language within the pages of a book. A language is a constantly changing and infinitely variable symbolic system. Trying to describe it explicitly is like trying to describe a river. Every river rises and falls with the seasons, and its path changes from year to year. Sometimes it may be calm and gentle, while other times raging and violent. A large river has tributaries and rivulets that contribute to its character. Sometimes it is hard to tell whether a particular rivulet is part of the "mainstream" or not. Nevertheless, in spite of all this variation and change, you know when you've come to the bank of a river. You have a general idea where you are going if you are floating down a river, and you can probably map a river's course in a general way that remains stable in its broad outlines over time.

Like a river, a language varies dramatically and is constantly changing. However, there are certain generalizations that do seem to hold constant over most of the speech varieties that have been called English at any given point in time and space. In this book, I will attempt to describe and explain a good portion of these generalizations. I will use several terms to refer to the subject matter of this book. The most general term is simply *English*. When I use this term, I am referring to generalizations that seem to hold across most, if not all, the symbolic systems known as "English" around the world in about 2010 CE. Of course, as the author of this text, I have not investigated all of these varieties myself, and so some of the claims and examples may be controversial. However, I have tried to base all claims on empirical evidence from naturally occurring "English" discourse.

Sometimes I will use the term "Old English" to refer to the major language spoken in the southern British Isles before the Norman Conquest in 1066 CE (see Chapter 1), and "Middle English" to refer to the language spoken and written in the same area between 1066 and the time of William Shakespeare, about 1500 CE. "Modern English" technically refers to the language of Shakespeare's plays and all later varieties. However, from the time of Shakespeare on, English began to be carried around the world by British sailors, armies, missionaries, and settlers, and so became vastly more fragmented than it had ever been in its earlier stages. It is therefore even more difficult to characterize "Modern English" in any coherent way than it is to characterize Old English or Middle English (though those varieties are challenging enough). For this reason, I'll sometimes use the terms "Englishes" or "Modern Englishes" to refer to the many varieties known as "English" at the time this book is being written.

Sometimes I will use the terms "spoken English" or "written English" when contrasting features that vary depending on the medium. As a linguist, my preference is to consider spoken language to be primary, and written language to be secondary. For this reason, spoken or VERNACULAR forms may sometimes appear in this book. These may include unconventional spellings, like *gonna*, or *wassup*, to non-standard morphological and syntactic constructions, like *He just bees himself*, or *I'm all, like, "thanks a lot."* When such forms are used in examples, they are meant to illustrate important points about the functions, history, or development of English.

Sometimes the term "Contemporary Standard English" (or CSE) will be used to refer to an international "Standard" English that is prevalent at the beginning of the third millennium. This would comprise the written standards of Great Britain, the USA, Canada, and other countries around the world in which English is the acknowledged majority language. Of course, these countries are independent speech communities themselves, and as such have their own standard written and spoken varieties, just as communities within these countries have their own standards. Certainly, however, most of the variation in English occurs in countries where English is not the MOTHER TONGUE (i.e., the first language) of most of the population, yet serves as a LINGUA FRANCA, or language of wider communication, among speech communities that have different mother tongues. This would include notably South Asia, and the ANGLOPHONE countries of Africa, Asia, and the Pacific. Each of these countries, and regions within them, have their own variety of English. For example, Standard Filipino English is very different from Standard Indian English, and both are different in their own ways from international CSE, as represented in internationally marketed dictionaries and pedagogical grammars. In countries where English is neither the majority language nor a *lingua franca*, such as Korea, Japan, and Mexico, people have their own ways of speaking, teaching, and writing English. In this book, I will try to be as honest as possible about variation when it exists, but will focus on the commonalities among all of these varieties commonly known as "English."

2   What is a linguistic perspective?

There are many possible perspectives one might take toward the shared habit patterns that make up a language. When a language has been written for a long time, such as Chinese, Kurdish, Korean, Arabic, Xibe, Italian, Tamil, English, and hundreds of others, traditions develop that tend to influence the perspective people take toward their language. Usually such traditions arise among an educated, literate few who have a strong sense of history, respectability, and correctness. Just as there are venerated traditions in art, so there are venerated traditions in grammar and other aspects of language usage. Since the literate few usually control educational systems, these venerated traditions lead to deeply ingrained ideas concerning what is "proper" usage, and what language varieties are "better" than others. This is sometimes called a "prescriptive" perspective on language, because it consists of prescriptions of how one ought and ought not to speak.

Yet, most people in the world do not think very much about the "proper" way to speak their language at all. They simply use it. By about the age of six years, most people are perfectly fluent native speakers of one or more languages. They apparently effortlessly learn the categories and patterns that constitute the grammar of their language entirely subconsciously. Speakers simply concentrate on their need to communicate with others – and the language of their social environment becomes the most readily available and natural tool for doing this. From this perspective, different people speak differently simply because they exist in different social environments, with no sense that one environment is inherently "better" than any other. Judgments about what is correct and incorrect only arise when communication breaks down. For example, people who must communicate across environments, such as those who want to sell goods in many different communities, must adjust their speech to the patterns of their clients or risk losing business because of miscommunication. We may call this approach a "pragmatic" perspective on language.

In this book, we will be taking a "linguistic perspective" on the grammar of English. A linguistic perspective does not deny the value of knowing the prescriptive norms of a speech community, especially communities with long literary traditions. After all, the "standard" variety of a language is a legitimate variety, and anyone who wishes to interact effectively in the community who uses that variety must be aware of its peculiarities and norms. At the same time, a linguistic perspective affirms the essentially pragmatic, or "functional," nature of language – namely, that language is a means to an end for most people. Communication is unquestionably the major intended result of language in use. For this reason, it makes sense that the structures of language can be described and insightfully *understood* in terms of the essential property of language as a tool for communication.

A linguistic perspective recognizes that language consists of elements of form, such as words, phrases, and clauses, that people employ to "mean," "express," "represent," or "refer to" concepts they wish to communicate with others. Although linguists often imply that the linguistic forms themselves express concepts, this must be taken as a shorthand way of saying that speakers *use* linguistic forms (among other tools) to accomplish acts of expressing, referring, representing, etc. (Brown and Yule 1983:27ff). For example, a WORD is a linguistic element. Its form is just a complex gesture, either vocal or via some other medium, that produces an effect in the external environment. What makes the form a *word* rather than just a random "noise" is that it is produced intentionally in order to express some idea. When used by a skilled speaker, words can combine into larger structures, such as

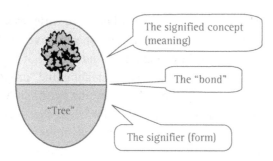

Figure 1 The form–meaning composite

PHRASES, CLAUSES, SENTENCES, and DISCOURSES, including conversations, speeches, arguments, textbooks, and other highly complex communicative acts. While the forms of language may aid in the formulation of concepts, or may constrain the concepts that can be expressed, the forms themselves are logically distinct from the concepts that might be communicated.

Langacker (1987), building on Saussure (1915), describes linguistic units as consisting of form–meaning composites. The upper half of the diagram in Figure 1 represents the meanings, concepts, or ideas expressed in language, while the bottom half represents the linguistic forms. The line across the center represents the relationship, or the BOND between the two. Various terms can be used to refer to the components of this composite. Terms associated with the top half include "meaning," "semantics," "signified," "function," "conceptual domain," and "content." Terms associated with the bottom half include "structure," "form," "sign," "signifier," and "symbol." The idea is that every symbolic act consists of some external *form* that represents or stands for some internal (or "underlying") *concept*.

As a typographical convention, in this book I will use all capital letters when referring to meanings, and lower case letters when referring to forms. For example, TREE refers to the meaning of the English word *tree*, whereas *tree* refers to the word itself.

In ancient times, philosophers who thought about language often considered words to be inherently connected to their meanings. Of course, the language of the philosopher (Sanskrit, Greek, or Latin) most closely represented the "true" meanings of words. In more recent times, linguists have tended to emphasize the ARBITRARINESS of linguistic form. That is to say, there is no necessary connection between the form of a symbol and its meaning. The noise spelled *tree* in English certainly has no inherent connection to the range of concepts that it can express. Indeed, even in closely related languages, such as German and French, very different noises (spelled *baum* and *arbre* respectively) express essentially the same range of concepts. Even more recently, linguists are beginning to notice that linguistic signs are arbitrary to a certain extent, but that they are also MOTIVATED by factors such as understandability, ICONICITY (including SOUND SYMBOLISM), and economy.[1] It seems that somewhere there is a balance to be struck between arbitrariness and motivation of the bond between form and meaning.

While the notion of the form–meaning composite is most easily described using an example such as *tree*, a linguistic perspective considers all linguistic units to be form–meaning composites. This also includes meaningful parts of words (BOUND MORPHEMES) and syntactic constructions (see Chapter 4 on morphology and Chapters 7 and 8 on syntax). Everything a speaker knows about his or her language can be thought of as an IDEALIZED form linked to a range of plausible intended meanings.

Linguists assume that the bond between a sign and a signified concept is intentional. That is, language users *intend* to establish a link between form and meaning – they consciously *want* their utterances to be understood. From this it follows that the forms used to represent concepts will be structured so as to make the link obvious, within limits of cognition and memory. This is not to deny the possibility that certain aspects of language may actually have no relation to the concepts expressed or may even serve to *conceal* concepts. However, we make it a working assumption that in general language users want and expect linguistic forms to represent concepts to be communicated. Therefore, the bond between form and meaning is *motivated by* (i.e., makes sense in terms of) the desire of speakers to make their messages understandable.

In any symbolic system, there must be consistency in the relationship between the symbols and categories or dimensions in the symbolized realm. We do not live in a "Humpty Dumpty world" where words mean anything we want them to mean (Carroll 1872). In order to communicate with others, we have to count on the probability that words and other structures in our language mean approximately the same thing to other people as they do to us. Ideal symbolic systems (e.g., computer "languages") maximize this principle by establishing a direct, invariant coding relationship between every form and its meaning or meanings. However, real languages are not ideal symbolic systems in this sense. They exist in an environment where variation and change are normal. New functions appear every day in the form of new situations, concepts, and perspectives that speakers wish to express. Vocal and auditory limitations cause inexact articulation and incomplete perception of utterances. These and many other factors lead to variation in the form of language, even in the speech of a single individual. The bond between form and meaning in real language is neither rigid nor random; it is direct enough to allow communication, but flexible enough to allow for creativity, variation, and change.

A linguistic perspective, then, views any language as a large set of form–meaning composites employed by a community of speakers to accomplish communicative work. As we will see in the course of this book, this perspective provides a consistent way, not just of describing, but also of *understanding* the various structures and patterns that make up the language. I hope to convince the reader that English is not simply a list of rules to be memorized. It is a dynamic, ever-changing, and complex tool kit used to express the kinds of ideas human beings need to express in their day-to-day lives. As with any tool kit, the forms (the tools) that make up a language "make sense" in terms of their functions, though they are not precisely determined (or mathematically "predicted") by those functions.

Viewing language as a tool kit has profound consequences for all kinds of applications. Whether you are planning to contribute to linguistic theory, document one of the many unwritten languages of the world, prepare educational materials, translate or interpret between languages, teach, or learn to speak a second language, you will profit greatly from a perspective that considers language as a tool for communication.

Conceptual categories

Every language categorizes the universe in its own unique way. This truism is obvious to anyone who has tried to learn a second language. In fact, one could go a step further and say that each individual person categorizes the universe in a unique way. A good part of the art of human communication involves figuring out how our individual categorization scheme compares with the schemes of people we are trying to communicate with, whether we are speaking the "same language" or not. For example, when learning Korean, speakers of English are likely to be perplexed when they find that Korean has at least two pronouns that correspond to each first and second person subject pronoun of English. Here are the two systems compared:

(1)

English Subject pronouns

	Singular	Plural
1st person	I	we
2nd person	you	you

(2)

Korean Subject pronouns:

	Singular	Plural
1st person	저 [ʧɔ] or 나 [na]	저희 [ʧɔhi] or 우리 [uri]
2nd person	당신 [taŋʃɪn] or 너[nɔ]	당신들 [taŋʃɪndɯl] or 너희들 [nɔhidɯl]

It turns out that Korean pronouns are *categorized* differently than English pronouns are. There is an additional distinction in these Korean pronouns that just isn't made categorically in English. This is the distinction between formal and informal speech. Here is a better chart of the Korean pronouns:

(3)

Korean Subject pronouns

	Formal		Informal	
	Singular	Plural	Singular	Plural
1st person	저 [ʧɔ]	저희 [ʧɔhi]	나 [na]	우리 [uri]
2nd person	당신 [taŋʃɪn]	당신들 [taŋʃɪndɯl]	너[nɔ]	너희들 [nɔhidɯl]

English speakers trying to learn Korean tend to have a very difficult time remembering when to use one or the other of the two possibilities for each of these pronouns. This is because for English speakers, the distinction between formal and informal speech is not ingrained in their cognitive habit patterns. Now, this isn't to say that English speakers can't *understand* the difference between formal and informal speech, or even that they can't make a distinction that is similar to the Korean use of informal and formal pronouns when speaking or writing English. It's just that this distinction is not a deeply ingrained *conceptual category* for English speakers. They must adjust their mental framework in order to speak Korean at all fluently. Such mismatches between conceptual categories in different languages are common in vocabulary, grammar, and patterns of conversation.

The word "category" is a very useful and common word in linguistics. We can define the term CONCEPTUAL CATEGORY in a technical way to describe some specific element of meaning that speakers of a language pay special attention to grammatically. This will help us understand how languages differ in the ways they express ideas, and therefore help us understand many of the problems that second language learners of Modern English have in assimilating English grammatical patterns.

In order to be a conceptual category a particular element of meaning must underlie some structural pattern. It does not need to be a perfectly consistent or regular pattern, but there needs to be a pattern. For example PAST TENSE is an element of meaning that speakers may express when they use any English verb. There is an expectation that verbs in English can be "tweaked" morphologically (often with the ending -*ed*) if the event being described occurred prior to the time the verb is uttered. The particular pattern for expressing past tense varies considerably from verb to verb, but every verb has a past tense form.[2] New verbs that come into the language also must be assigned a past tense form. This is evidence that a recurring pattern exists, and therefore past tense is a conceptual category in English.

In order to clarify the notion of conceptual category, it may help to contrast conceptual categories with other possible meaning elements that are never categories in any language, and with some that are categories in some languages, but not others. For example, I do not believe there is any language in the world that includes an expectation that verbs should be grammatically marked for the altitude above sea level of the event described by the verb. Such a language is conceivable, because this meaning element can probably be expressed in any language: *We slept at 2000 meters* or *they ordered rice and dal at sea level*. However, I doubt whether any language has a recurring grammatical pattern (prefixes, suffixes, a set of AUXILIARIES, etc.) that regularly shapes clauses for this precise parameter of meaning.

In addition to elements of meaning that are not conceptual categories in any language, there are also elements of meaning that are categories in some languages but not in others. Formal vs. informal speech, as illustrated in (3) above, is one example. Another is "location downriver." This is not a conceptual category that is relevant to the grammar of English, though in many languages in the riverene areas of South America it is. The reason that location downriver is not a category that is relevant to English grammar is that there is no regular expectation that clauses involve *grammatical* indication that an action happens "downriver" from the place of speaking. Certainly English speakers *may* specify that an action occurs "downriver" by enriching the clause with additional material, e.g., *He went fishing downriver*. However, without the adverb *downriver* in this example, no assertion is made as to where the event occurred: *He went fishing*. The event described by this clause could have happened anywhere, including downriver from the place of utterance or any other conceivable reference point. In Yagua (a language spoken in the rainforest region of Peru), however, there is a set of about ten verb suffixes that orient the location of the event to the location of the other events in the discourse, including one that means "downriver" (glossed DR in the following example):

(4)   Naada-rãáyãá-*mu*-yada   'They two danced around downriver.'
       they.2-dance.around-DR-past

If none of the suffixes in this set are used, the implication is that the event happened in a neutral location, normally at the same place as the other events in the particular discourse. Therefore, we want to say that *location* describes a set (or PARADIGM) of conceptual categories in Yagua, similar to the way *tense* describes a set of conceptual categories, past and non-past, in English.

The important ideas to keep in mind at this point are:

- A conceptual category exists when there is an *expectation of patterned behavior* – a recurring relationship between variation in form and variation in meaning.
- The conceptual categories of one language do not necessarily match the conceptual categories of even closely related languages. Sometimes one language will have a conceptual category or paradigm of conceptual categories that is totally missing in another language. Other times, conceptual categories may be similar in two languages, but they may be different enough that communication is impaired if the categorial system of one language is imposed on the other.

The expression of conceptual categories

There are three broad EXPRESSION TYPES, or ways of expressing conceptual categories in all languages. These can be described as LEXICAL EXPRESSION, MORPHOLOGICAL EXPRESSION, and SYNTACTIC (or ANALYTIC) EXPRESSION. Each of these expression types in English will be discussed in more detail in the following chapters. Lexical expression is discussed in Chapter 3, morphological expression in Chapter 4, and various kinds of syntactic expression in later chapters. In this section I would like to bring together these three broad types in order to compare and contrast them, and give a few examples of each type.

Lexical expression

Lexical expression is any formal expression of a conceptual category which simply must be memorized, rather than constructed according to a pattern. For example, the past tense of the verb *go* is expressed lexically in English because there is no way a language learner could ever guess that the form is *went* based on any pattern that is relevant to any other verbs in the language. This is just something that must be learned outright; therefore it is a lexical property of the verb *go*.

There are three subtypes of lexical expression. The first subtype, represented by the difference between the bare form and the past tense form of the verb *go*, is sometimes called STRONG SUPPLETION, or simply SUPPLETION. Suppletion in this sense means that in order to express a conceptual category, one root is replaced by an entirely different root. The verb *be* is notoriously SUPPLETIVE in English:

(5)   Bare form: Past tense: Present tense:
       be   was/were   is/am/are

The forms of this verb are completely distinct from all other verbs in the language. There is no way language learners (either children learning their first language or second language learners) could guess what these forms would be, even if they knew the patterns for all other verbs. The forms of *be* must be committed to memory as individual items that are part of the LEXICAL ENTRY for the verb *be*. Therefore, strong suppletion is a type of lexical expression.

The second type of lexical expression is called WEAK SUPPLETION. This is substitution of one root for another that is similar to the first, but which still cannot be derived by any recurring pattern. For example, the forms of the English words *buy* and *bought* "feel" like they are related – they both start with *b*. However, there is no regular pattern (or *rule* of grammar) that creates one of these from the other, in the way that the regular past tense rule creates, for example, *called* from *call*. How do we know there is no pattern that relates *buy* and *bought*? There are two ways: first, there are no other pairs that can be related in exactly the same way. Yes, there are past tense verb forms that sound like *bought* (e.g., *brought* and *thought*), but the bare forms of these verbs are *bring* and *think*, not **bruy* and **thuy*,[3] which is what they would have to be if they were subject to the same (non-existent) pattern that derived *bought* from *buy*. The second way we know there is no rule that relates *buy* and *bought* is that other verbs that sound like *buy* do not logically fall into the same pattern. So, not only is it UNGRAMMATICAL, but also not even logical to think of the past tense of *cry* as *crought*, or *die* as *dought*, etc.[4] Therefore, the IDIOSYNCRATIC (apparently random) formal variation that expresses the past tense must be listed in the lexical entry for the verb *buy*. It cannot be guessed from the form of the verb itself. Therefore it constitutes lexical expression.

Finally, the last subtype of lexical expression is sometimes termed ISOMORPHISM. This is where a regular, expected adjustment in meaning is accomplished by *not* changing the form at all. For example, the past tense of the verb *hit* is *hit*. The bare stem is used, with no -*ed* added. This is a fact about the verb *hit* that just has to be memorized. It cannot be guessed (or "predicted") by applying a rule; therefore it is lexical expression. The lexical entry for the verb *hit* has to specify, among many other things, that the past tense is simply *hit*.

Why would we call past tense formation for the verb *hit* an "expression" at all when the word does not change its form? Why don't we just say that past tense is not expressed for this verb? Aren't there a lot of other meaning components that have no overt expression? For example, a sentence like *John is working* leaves much information out, some of which may be expressed grammatically in some languages. He may be working upriver or downriver, during the day or at night, with an axe or with his hands, etc. If we say that *hit* expresses past tense lexically, would we want to say that all of these other notions (and many more) are also expressed lexically in English? I don't think so.

What makes the past tense of the verb *hit* in English an expression is that we *expect* all English verbs to have a past tense form. The fact that *hit* doesn't change the way many other verbs do is meaningful. You may say that there is a "conspicuous absence" of a past tense marker for the class of verbs to which *hit* belongs. There is no analogous expectation that English verbs should express whether the action takes place upriver or downriver, at night or during the day, with hands or with an axe.

In summary, the three subtypes of lexical expression we will be considering in this book are:

* (Strong) Suppletion – replacing one stem with a completely distinct one
* Weak suppletion – replacing one stem with a randomly similar one
* Isomorphism – no overt structural change.

Morphological expression

Morphological expression consists of patterned variations in form that accomplish variations in meaning by altering the shapes of words. For example, the difference between the noises spelled *call* and *called* follows a regular pattern. Someone who knows most of the verbs of English could guess the correct past tense form by constructing the form *called* by adding *-ed* to *call*. This pattern applies to many verbs in English, and its function is to allow English speakers to express the past tense. There is no need to memorize both *call* and *called* (as well as *stall* and *stalled*, *walk* and *walked*, etc.) as members of one long list of words that are not related to one another in any way. Instead, all you need is a rather shorter list of individual verbs, plus one morphological pattern (or "rule") that says "add *-ed* to form the past tense."

There are four types of morphological expression in English. These will be discussed in much more detail in Chapter 4. Here I will simply list the types, and give some examples.

- PREFIXATION involves the addition of a word piece (a prefix) to the beginning of a stem. For example, *un-* is a prefix, as in *untie*. Sometimes several prefixes can be attached to one stem. An example of this would be a word like *anti-disestablishment*. This word has at least two prefixes, *anti-* and *dis-*.
- SUFFIXATION involves the addition of a word piece (a suffix) to the end of a stem. The tense marker spelled *-ed* is a suffix. There also may be more than one suffix on a word. The word *establishments* has two suffixes, *-ment* and *-s*.
- STEM CHANGE is a change in shape that does not involve the addition of any prefix or suffix. For example, the difference in form between *sing* and *sang* cannot be called AFFIXATION (a cover term that includes prefixation and suffixation) because there is no specific word piece that has been added to the stem. Rather, the stem vowel has just changed from *i* ([ɪ]) to *a* ([æ]). One might ask how this is different from "weak suppletion" described above. The difference is that *sing* and *sang* can be related by a pattern ("change *i* to *a* to form the past tense") that applies to several other verbs like *drink/drank, sink/sank, sit/sat,* etc. On the other hand, weak suppletion such as the difference between *buy* and *bought*, applies only to one verb, and therefore just has to be memorized (see Chapter 3 for further discussion).
- STRESS SHIFT does not directly change consonants and vowels. Rather, it consists of a difference in STRESS. For example, the difference between some nouns and verbs is expressed by a change in stress. This difference is not indicated in the English spelling system, so I will place a stress mark in these words to show the difference between, for example, *convért* (a verb) and *cónvert* (a related noun).

Syntactic expression

Finally, syntactic expression involves the arrangement of words in a phrase, or a combination of separate words. Syntactic expression is also called ANALYTIC EXPRESSION or PERIPHRASTIC EXPRESSION. For example, word order is very important for expressing grammatical relations in English. If you change the order, chances are you are going to change the meaning in a significant way:

(6)   Zarina taught Aileron.
      Aileron taught Zarina.

These two invented sentences obviously mean very different things. The important function of expressing who is acting and who is being acted upon is expressed syntactically, by the order of words in English.

Another kind of syntactic expression is when whole words are combined to express a specific conceptual category. For example, the common future tense of English is expressed syntactically, as in *I will call*. The shape of the verb *call* does not change in the future tense; rather a separate word, *will*, is added. Therefore linguists may say "future tense is a syntactic construction in English," or "future tense is expressed syntactically." The other way of expressing future tense is by a combination of syntactic and morphological expression:

(7)   I am going to call./I'm gonna call.

Because the separate words *am* (a form of *be*), *going*, and *to* are added to the bare verb, we can say that this future tense is also an instance of syntactic expression. In addition, the auxiliary *go* must take the suffix *-ing*. This is a morphological pattern; therefore expression of the "gonna future" is morphological as well as syntactic.

The triad of lexical, morphological, and syntactic expression is relevant to many different functional tasks in any language. Some tasks that are typically accomplished by, say, morphology in one language, may be accomplished by syntactic expression in the next language. For this reason, it is important for English language professionals to be aware of the difference between conceptual categories and the various means that languages have of expressing them.

Discourse is a play

The next theoretical principle we will discuss is based on a metaphor that has proven particularly useful in several theoretical and empirical approaches to discourse and communication. This metaphor is summarized as "discourse is a play." The idea is that a person who intends to communicate an idea is like the director of a play. The speaker has an image in mind, and uses linguistic tools to encourage some audience to create a similar image in their minds. That mental image can be thought of as a "scene" with actors, props, and activities interacting in potentially complex ways. The scene may be an actual or fictional series of events occurring over time, in which case we may say that the discourse produced is NARRATIVE. Or the scene may involve a description of some concrete thing or abstract idea, in which case the speaker engages in EXPOSITORY discourse.

Sometimes a speaker will use language to describe ways the speaker would like the audience to behave. This would be called HORTATORY discourse. In any of these discourse types (or GENRES), as well as several others, linguistic tools are used to "set the stage," bring actors "onto stage," change "scenes," change the "perspective" of a scene, etc. Such images form the content of linguistic communication, and can insightfully be understood as the DISCOURSE STAGE.

Much research on discourse production and comprehension has used some form of this metaphor to formulate hypotheses and claims about how people communicate. For example, Minsky (1975) used the term FRAMES to refer to stereotyped situations within which knowledge is categorized and stored in memory. For example, the word *restaurant* evokes a "frame" in the audience's mind that consists of tables, chairs, servers, food, a bill, etc. Once a speaker mentions a restaurant, the audience automatically knows that these items are "on stage," and available for use in expressing the particular message the speaker has in mind. Schank and Abelson (1977), building on Schank (1972), introduced the notion of SCRIPTS. Whereas a frame is a static set of entities in a particular arrangement, such as a restaurant, a script is a potentially dynamic series of events and situations, e.g., the process of sitting down, ordering, and dining at a restaurant. Fillmore (1976, 1977) suggested that verbs activate SCENES in the minds of language users. Lakoff's (1987) notion of COGNITIVE MODELS is an extension and elaboration of this notion of scene. What frames, scripts, scenes, and cognitive models have in common is that all are idealized mental images, "pictures" if you will, that the human mind uses to categorize, store, and communicate experience and knowledge.

The metaphor of discourse as a play helps us understand English grammar in a number of ways, many of which will become apparent in the following chapters. One example is the use of the so-called articles. The articles (*the*, *a/an*, *some*, and zero) are particularly frustrating for many second language learners (SLLs), since the notions they express are really quite "exotic" from the point of view of most of the languages of the world. However, when interpreted in terms of the "discourse stage," they make a lot more sense. While there are many apparent exceptions and special cases, in general the "indefinite articles," *a/an* (singular), and *0/some* (plural), function when a speaker wants to bring a participant or notable prop onto the discourse stage for the first time. The "definite article," *the*, on the other hand, is used for participants that the speaker believes the hearer can already identify. Let's look at a text from the movie *The Curious Case of Benjamin Button* (Roth 2008; quoted in the IMDB). Since this is a quote from a movie, it may be particularly easy to imagine this as a scene being enacted on a stage. In this excerpt, the articles *a* and *the* are given in bold:

(8)   A woman in Paris was on her way to go shopping, but she had forgotten her coat – went back to get it. When she had gotten her coat, **the** phone had rung,

so she'd stopped to answer it; talked for a couple of minutes. While the woman was on the phone, Daisy was rehearsing for a performance at the Paris Opera House. And while she was rehearsing, the woman, off the phone now, had gone outside to get a taxi. Now a taxi driver had dropped off a fare earlier and had stopped to get a cup of coffee. And all the while, Daisy was rehearsing. And the cab driver, who dropped off the earlier fare; who'd stopped to get the cup of coffee, had picked up the lady who was going shopping, and had missed getting an earlier cab. The taxi had to stop for a man crossing the street, who had left for work five minutes later than he normally did, because he forgot to set off his alarm. While the man, late for work, was crossing the street, Daisy had finished rehearsing, and was taking a shower. And while Daisy was showering, the taxi was waiting outside a boutique for the woman to pick up a package, which hadn't been wrapped yet, because the girl who was supposed to wrap it had broken up with her boyfriend the night before, and forgot.

As you can see, *a/an* and *the* are very common words! The very first phrase in the excerpt employs the indefinite article. This is because an important character, *a woman*, is being introduced for the first time onto the discourse stage. The next article is *the*, used with *phone*. Now, a phone has not been mentioned yet, but the use of *the* instructs the hearer that a phone must be already on stage as part of the context. We can assume, then, that "the phone" is the phone in the woman's apartment, since she had apparently gone back to her apartment to get her coat. Once an apartment scene is evoked, it is reasonable to identify a phone, since apartments often have phones. Similarly "the street" mentioned twice toward the end of the text is treated as identifiable because of the scene evoked by terms like "Paris" and "taxi" – in a city like Paris there are streets, and taxis drive on streets. This pattern of indefinite articles identifying new participants, and definite articles referring to participants that are identifiable from the context, is maintained throughout this text. In the last two lines, two other participants are treated as identifiable because of the context – *the girl* and *the night before.* The girl can be introduced with *the* because she is identified by the relative clause … *who was supposed to wrap it.* The package, and the fact that it needed to be wrapped was already mentioned. If you have a package that needs to be wrapped, you can assume that there must be a person who is supposed to wrap it. So in this context, a person can be treated as identifiable because of her potential relationship to the package which is already on stage. The relative clause following *the girl* simply identifies the girl as that person. Finally, *the night before* is identifiable because for any given day or night, there is always one unique *night before.* There can be no question of WHICH night before is referred to.

The functions of articles and other determiners is discussed in more detail in Chapter 15. For now, this is but one small example of how the metaphor "discourse is a play" can help us understand the choices that speakers make when engaging in conversation. The use of grammar is largely a matter of making such choices automatically and in a way that is consistent with patterns that are established in the community.

3   Form, meaning, and use

Another helpful perspective on "grammar" is provided by Diane Larsen-Freeman (1997). Speaking to students and teachers in applied linguistics, Larsen-Freeman views grammar as involving three interrelated dimensions – form, meaning, and use. Grammar teaching involves not just teaching the grammatical structures (forms), but also the meanings that grammatical structures express, and the appropriate contexts in which they may be used. This proposal has become quite influential in the field of language teaching, and provides a point of intersection between a linguistic perspective and the interests of English language professionals. At various points throughout this book, it will be useful to refer back to this framework, as different topics impinge more directly on the form, the meaning, or the use of particular structures and functions.

The essence of Larsen-Freeman's proposal is that grammatical structures are not isolated from their meanings or their uses. "Learning grammar" is not just a matter of learning arbitrary, boring, and unconnected rules, but rather it is learning how to accurately, clearly, and fluently express meaning in particular contexts. Every grammatical form, according to Larsen-Freeman, has a meaning and a use dimension, as well as its obvious structural features. One example is the passive voice construction. We may talk about the structural adjustments necessary to convert an active voice clause into the passive voice; namely, change the verb to a past participle form, add a form of *be*, and put the object into the subject position. But one hasn't really *learned* the passive construction if this is all one learns. Language learners need to understand the effect the passive construction has on the meaning expressed by the clause, and when it is appropriate to use the passive in discourse. In terms of meaning, the passive presents the situation as a process undergone by a PATIENT, while the active may present the same situation as an action accomplished by an AGENT. As for usage, the passive is used in a number of contexts, e.g., when the speaker wishes to downplay the responsibility of an AGENT, when the PATIENT is the more topical participant in the discourse, etc. Studying the meaning and use of grammatical structures provides answers to such questions as "Why does English grammar have two voices at all? How do the different voices help speakers communicate?"

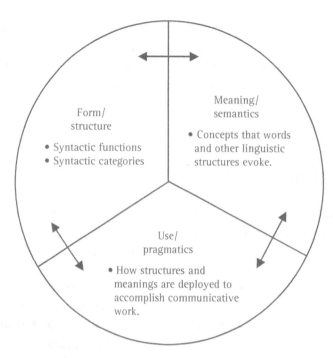

Figure 2 The interrelationships among form, meaning, and use

In terms of linguistics, Larsen-Freeman's form–meaning–use diagram may be adapted as indicated in Figure 2. The arrows indicate interrelations among the three dimensions.

In the previous section I used the image of the form–function composite to describe the relationship between grammatical structures and their functions. From that point of view, meaning and use both belong to the domain of function. Linguistic forms are tools that fulfill or serve functions, including expressing meanings and adapting meanings to particular contexts of use.

As we will see beginning in Chapter 7, within the formal domain there are SYNTACTIC CATEGORIES, such as nouns, verbs, noun phrases, prepositional phrases, etc., and there are SYNTACTIC FUNCTIONS, Subject, Object, Complement, etc. These all belong to the domain of form. They constitute the structural framework that supports the intended communicative function of discourse. The use of the term syntactic *function* as a part of the domain of *form* may seem confusing, but this is standard in the community of scholars that think and write about grammar and grammar teaching, so it is helpful to understand these terms as they are used.

One way of understanding the notions of syntactic category and syntactic function, and how these structural notions are distinct from meaning and use, is by analogy with the structure of a corporation. The staff of a corporation are qualified to perform various job categories (accountant, keyboardist, engineer, designer, etc.). These are the job categories staff members as individuals are specifically prepared to fill, but these characteristic jobs are independent of people's working relationships with other staff members in the organizational structure of the company. For example, one engineer may function as the *manager* of a department with other engineers being *assistant managers*, *team members*, etc., of that department. People who belong to other job categories, e.g., receptionists, accountants, may also be members of the same department. These employees would be *co-workers* to each other, but all would be *supervisees* of the manager. In addition to such internal relationships, each department has a particular role that helps fulfill the task of the corporation as a whole (verifying accounts, designing new products, selling products, etc.). Finally, the company itself must function within the larger society – it must meet some need, otherwise it would go out of business!

Syntactic categories are like the characteristic job categories that staff members are individually qualified to fulfill. Syntactic functions are like the relationships among staff members in the organizational structure of a company. Both of these are structural notions, even though one of them is labeled *function*. Separate from both of these is the concept of meaning. Meaning is like the purpose of a corporate department, and use is like the role of the whole company in the community.

All of these notions are interrelated, but are defined independently of one another. Sometimes, for example, it may serve the needs of the corporation for an engineer to function as a communications specialist for a while, perhaps to develop technical users' manuals for other staff members. Anyone who has worked in an organization for very long knows that people are not always working in jobs for which they are uniquely qualified. So in language there is never a precise one-to-one relationship between syntactic category and syntactic function, between syntactic function and meaning, between meaning and use, or between use and syntactic categories and functions. There may be strong *tendencies* (e.g., engineers usually do engineering work) but there are seldom invariable correlations. For example a word that is (or seems to be) basically a noun, whose major function is to refer to persons, places, or things, may function as a predicator or as a modifier at times, e.g., *trash* in *we trashed our television*, or *trash truck*. Similarly, a structure that is formed like a question, may be used in a conversation as a kind of polite command: *Can you open the window?* These kinds of examples of "mismatches" among form, meaning, and use will be discussed in detail in the following chapters.

I hope that this analogy and the others presented in this introduction will help readers understand the general perspective taken in this book. At various points throughout the text I will refer back to the notions of form, meaning, and use, as well as to the metaphors of the discourse stage and the form–meaning composite. Understanding English grammar involves understanding the formal structures, the meanings they evoke, and the uses to which people apply them in communication.

Summary

In summary, in this book we will view English grammar as a thoroughly practical and thoroughly human tool for communication. Grammar does not have to be a list of arbitrary rules and impenetrable facts. Rather, it is one major way in which human communities define themselves and make sense of their experience. The focus of this book will be on *understanding patterns* rather than *memorizing rules*. It will also *describe* the ways those patterns are actually employed in various types of discourse rather than *prescribe* proper usage. Central principles recurring throughout the book include:

(1)   Any language, English in particular, is the product of a historical process.
(2)   Language variation is normal and to be expected.
(3)   Communication involves the construction and comprehension of mental "scenes."
(4)   Language is a very human and very efficient *tool for communication.*
(5)   Meaning is expressed and inferred holistically, making use of all levels of linguistic structure and context simultaneously.

This approach draws on insights emerging from recent scholarship in Cognitive Linguistics (Langacker 1987, 1991, Lakoff 1987, Croft and Cruse 2004, *inter alia*), Construction Grammar (Goldberg 1995, Fillmore and Baker 2001, Croft 2002, *inter alia*), and recent approaches to Applied English linguistics (Larsen-Freeman 1997).

I believe that the general movement in the field of applied linguistics and language pedagogy is toward more "communicational" or "functional" approaches. I see this as more than just a passing trend, but as a permanent deepening and maturing of scholarship in the field. It is a positive sign that linguists and language educators are learning from each other and drawing on each other's areas of expertise more than has traditionally been the case.

1 History

Language is the archives of history.
Ralph Waldo Emerson

Variation and change are facts of every language. There are many reasons for variation: geographic isolation causes people who live in different regions to speak different varieties of a language; sociocultural isolation results in different groups of people, defined by ethnicity, vocation, social class, age, gender, and many other variables, speaking different varieties. People who speak different languages interact with each other and "borrow" sounds, words, and grammatical features from one another, thus changing their languages by the addition of these borrowed features. New functions appear every day in the form of new situations, concepts, and perspectives that speakers wish to express. Also, some forms and functions become archaic, and gradually cease to be employed in the language of everyday life. Styles and mannerisms simply change. These and many other factors lead to variation in the form of language, even in the speech of a single individual. Across time and space, this variation results in the splintering of a language into different varieties, and eventually distinct "daughter" languages. This process is the topic of historical and comparative linguistics.

Often change is equated with deterioration, as though at some early stage the language exists in an ideal state, and as subsequent generations of speakers introduce changes, the language successively degenerates. In the English tradition, we revere the language of Shakespeare, or the King James Bible, and deplore the "sloppy" or "illogical" ways in which younger people speak. Funny thing though – our parents said the same thing about how we speak! And their parents said the same thing about them, *ad infinitum*. Will Shakespeare's parents probably said the same thing about him and his generation. If language change were equivalent to degeneration, by now we would all be speaking in grunts and whistles!

From a linguistic perspective, variation and change are normal and to be expected. After all, like any tool, people adapt their language to suit the purposes for which they use it. Young people don't necessarily speak "worse" than their elders – they just use the language differently, in totally appropriate ways for their social contexts. The ways of being for one group of people are different from the ways of being of any other group, and consequently the ways of communicating within different groups are also different.

Like any language, English has a complex and layered history. The concept of a uniform language being passed down from generation to generation, changing little by little at every stage is a bit simplistic to describe the intricate, convoluted, and sometimes sordid history of the language we now know as Modern English. It is perhaps more useful to think of the history of contemporary English as a "tapestry" consisting of various interwoven "threads." The threads represent the various influences on English over the centuries. In looking at this tapestry from the vantage point of the twenty-first century, four threads emerge as being particularly salient. In this chapter we will concentrate on these. Of course, there are many other threads, and some of these will be mentioned below also. However, understanding the four major threads will help the English language professional make sense of several otherwise perplexing features of Modern English.

The four threads we will consider are: the Celtic thread, the Anglo-Saxon (Continental Germanic) thread, the Scandinavian (Northern Germanic) thread, and the Latin (Romance) thread. All of these threads originate within a very large family of languages known as Indo-European, so it is appropriate to consider English to be an Indo-European language (Jones 1798). However, Celtic, Germanic, and Romance are very distinct subfamilies of Indo-European; therefore Modern English is a tapestry woven with threads from quite distinct sources.

1.1   The Celtic thread

The first historical records concerning human populations of the Atlantic Archipelago (the modern-day British Isles) are Roman characterizations of the Celts. It is known from archeological evidence that the islands were inhabited as early as the Paleolithic Age (the Old Stone Age, up to 2.5 million years ago). It is also known that several waves of immigration or invasion occurred for thousands of years before the Celts arrived, all originating on the mainland of Europe. However, nothing is known about the languages of these pre-Celtic peoples, and there is no evidence of their languages influencing the Celtic or other threads that led to the development of Modern English. This doesn't mean that these prehistoric languages *did not* eventually influence Modern English, but only that there is no concrete *evidence* of their influence. It is fairly uncontroversial, however, that Celtic tribes began to arrive about 600 BCE (Before the Common Era), and that the peoples who inhabited the islands prior to that time were not Celtic (Baugh 1963).

Figure 1.1 Ogham inscription

Modern Celtic languages still spoken in the islands include Irish, Welsh, Scottish Gaelic, Cornish, and Manx Gaelic. Another Celtic language, Breton, is spoken in Brittany, in France.

The Roman legions invaded Celtic Britain in the year 55 BCE, fragmenting Celtic society, and driving many to retreat into the northern and western reaches of the islands – the areas now known as Scotland, Ireland, Cornwall, and Wales. Unfortunately, most of what is known about the early Celts comes from reports of the Roman conquerors, since the Celts themselves did not (at least in the earlier years) write anything down. Before Christianity arrived in the fifth Century CE (the Common Era), writing was a magical art to most Celtic tribes. Only the Druids, a highly educated and powerful social class, wrote anything down, and mostly that was for ritual and magical purposes – not for recording history. Therefore, the historical accounts that survive are very one-sided in favor of the Romans, emphasizing the barbarity and disorganization of Celtic society. Archeological evidence, however, suggests a highly organized, albeit fragmented, society that took art, music, and religion very seriously. "Fierce," even "barbaric," may be accurate characterizations of the Celtic interactions with their enemies, but certainly they were no worse than the Romans, who routinely tortured and beheaded vanquished combatants and non-combatants alike.

From the fifth through the tenth centuries CE a fairly standard writing system called Ogham was used in many of the Celtic areas of Britain. Most of what is now known about Ogham comes from stone inscriptions. It is believed that Ogham was also written on other materials, such as tree bark and animal skins, but of course only the stone inscriptions have survived to the present day. Currently there are about 400 Ogham inscriptions throughout Ireland, Scotland, and the west coasts of England and Wales. Most of these are grave markers, which are often circular or triangular in shape (Figure 1.1).

Of the four threads in our tapestry of the English language, the Celtic thread is probably the least influential in shaping the character of Modern English. Nevertheless, Celtic is a significant thread for a couple of reasons. First, any discussion of the history of England or the English language would be remiss in not mentioning the Celts. After all, the quintessentially English monarchs of the house of Tudor from Henry VII (1457–1509) to Elizabeth I (1533–1603) were of Celtic (Welsh) ancestry ("Tudor" is an Anglicization of the Welsh surname *Tewdwr*). Second, while traditional scholarship maintains that the Celtic languages had little impact on English, there is a recent and growing body of research that attributes some significant and unusual grammatical features of Old English to Celtic influence. While it is true that very few vocabulary items in Modern English can be traced to early contact with the Celts, these unusual grammatical constructions are impossible to explain in terms of any of the other threads. The following is one brief example.

In Modern German, as in all the other Germanic languages (except, oddly, English), to form a yes/no question from statement (1a), you simply invert the subject and the verb, as in (1b):

(1) a. Ich   mag   Zucker.   'I like sugar.'
         I   like.1SG   sugar
     b. Magst   du   Zucker?   'Do you like sugar?'
         like.2SG   you   sugar

The sentence corresponding to (1b) is strictly ungrammatical in English:

(2) *Like you sugar?

Instead, a "dummy" auxiliary, *do* (*did* in the past tense), must be inserted in order to express a yes/no question. The rest of the sentence maintains the normal English Subject-Verb-Object order:

(3) Do you like sugar?   Did you like sugar?

Where did this rather odd feature of English come from? It apparently didn't come from Old German or Old Norse, since none of the other modern descendents of these languages have this feature. Well, it just so happens that something very similar occurs in Celtic languages. The following are some examples from modern Irish Gaelic. In (4a), the statement shows Verb–Subject–Object order, which is very common among the Celtic languages. The yes/no question in (4b) shows the presence of an obligatory "dummy" auxiliary *an* in the present tense, while (4d) illustrates the past tense form, *ar*, of the same auxiliary. The rest of the sentence shows the normal Irish Verb–Subject–Object order:

(4) a. Díolann   sé   siúcra.   'He sells sugar.'
         sell.PRES   he   sugar

b. *An*   díolann   sé   siúcra?   'Does he sell sugar?'
    AUX.PRES   sell.PRES   he   sugar

c. Díol   sé   siúcra.   'He sold sugar.'
    sell.PAST   he   sugar

d. *Ar*   díol   sé   siúcra?   'Did he sell sugar?'
    AUX.PAST   sell.PAST   he   sugar

This feature is very common among the Celtic languages, and has a very ancient pedigree (i.e., it is *not* borrowed from English). Thus Celtic influence is a possible source of modern English "DO insertion" and other "periphrastic DO" constructions (Filppula *et al.* 2008:49–59), which taken together give English a decidedly non-Germanic "flavor."

While this is circumstantial evidence for a Celtic influence, an increasing number of scholars are exploring and arguing for this connection. The more general tendency for English to invert subject and auxiliary (rather than subject and verb) in many interrogative, negative, and emphatic clauses, and to insert "dummy" auxiliaries in such structures, distinguishes English from all other Germanic languages. While a Modern German speaker feels rather "at home" learning to speak Swedish, Norwegian, Danish, Dutch, or Frisian, this feeling of kinship is not so strong when learning English. There is a very real possibility (some would say probability) that this distinctiveness of English is at least partially a result of Celtic influence (see Filppula *et al.* 2008 and MacWhorter 2009).

1.2   The Anglo-Saxon thread

The term *English* derives from the Indo-European root **ang-/*ank-*meaning "bent" or "crooked" (Klein 1966:75).[1] In the fourth century of the Common Era, the term *Angli* (the Bent Ones) was used by the Romans to refer disparagingly to a minority Germanic people of North Western Europe. This feisty minority, along with several other groups including the Saxons, Jutes, and Frisians, began invading the Atlantic Archipelago as early as 365 CE (Higham 1994:118–45). This coalition of Germanic groups is usually referred to collectively as the "Anglo-Saxons."

At that time, the Archipelago had recently been a Roman colony known as Brittania, but was largely inhabited by Celtic-speaking peoples (see Section 1.1 above). It was fortuitous for the Germanic-speaking invaders that the Roman Empire was in serious decline by the beginning of the fifth century, and Rome had already abandoned most of the Archipelago. The Celts that remained, at least in the South and East, had been deprived of weapons and knowledge of warfare by their Roman overlords for 400 years or so. This made it possible for the Germanic-speaking barbarians (as they would have been called by the Romans) to conquer much territory without serious opposition. According to tradition, in 449 one of the Celtic groups actually invited the Anglo-Saxons to help them in their wars with their Celtic cousins the Picts and the Scots (Higham 1994:111).

The language spoken by the Continental Germanic peoples who settled Britain in the fifth century eventually came to be known as *Englisc*, and later *English*. Of course, as is true of any complex speech community, there existed much variation from place to place and time to time during this whole period. Nevertheless, it is convenient to think of roughly the second half of the first millennium of the Common Era (~500–1000 CE) as being the Old English period. Indeed, the first written records in English come from this period, and include such famous texts as *Caedmon's Hymn*, *Beowulf*, and the *Anglo-Saxon Chronicle*.

The following is an excerpt from an epic Anglo-Saxon poem called "The wanderer." This poem illustrates an epic style of oral literature that was probably recited by bards who wandered the countryside and provided entertainment at local homes, inns, and pubs by singing bawdy songs and reciting long poems such as this one. *The Wanderer* was not written down until about 960 CE, though it undoubtedly existed for many years before that in oral form (Krapp and Dobbie 1936). This poem embodies the Anglo-Saxon thread of the emerging tapestry of English:

Anglo-Saxon original	Modern English translation
Oft him anhaga	Often the solitary one
are gebideð,	finds grace for himself
metudes miltse,	the mercy of the Lord,
metudes miltse,	the mercy of the Lord,
geond lagulade	must for a long time
longe sceolde	move by hand [i.e., rowing]
hreran mid hondum	along the waterways,
hrimcealde sæ	(along) the ice-cold sea,
wadan wræclastas.	tread the paths of exile.
Wyrd bið ful aræd!	Events always go as they must!
…	
Hwær cwom mearg?	Where is the horse gone?
Hwær cwom mago?	Where the rider?
Hwær cwom maþþumgyfa?	Where the giver of treasure?
Hwær cwom symbla gesetu?	Where are the seats at the feast?
Hwær sindon seledreamas?	Where are the revels in the hall?
Eala beorht bune!	Alas for the bright cup!
Eala byrnwiga!	Alas for the mailed warrior!
Eala þeodnes þrym!	Alas for the splendour of the prince!

In his novels, J.R.R. Tolkien, who was a linguist and a scholar of Old English, drew heavily on imagery and language from the Anglo-Saxon and Scandinavian (see Section 1.3) periods of English history. For example, in *The Two Towers*, the hero Aragorn sings a song of the country of Rohan (itself a portrait of Anglo-Saxon England), which begins "Where now the horse and the rider? Where is the horn that was blowing?" (Tolkien 1965 [1954]:142). Aragorn's song clearly echoes this section of *The Wanderer*.

There are three letters in this text that will not be familiar to Modern English readers. The letters ð and þ indicated voiced and voiceless interdental fricatives, very similar to the first consonants of Modern English *then* and *thin* respectively. The Modern English alphabet represents these two sounds (and others!) with the same digraph, *th*. The third unfamiliar letter is the digraph æ, which represents a low, front vowel such as the vowel in the modern English words *fat* or *bat*. For some reason the modern English writing system no longer distinguishes these important sounds.

1.3 The Scandinavian (Northern Germanic) thread

From the late eighth through the eleventh centuries (~750–1100 CE) Northern Germanic peoples from Scandinavia began arriving in the Atlantic Archipelago, first as invaders known as "Vikings," then as colonists and settlers.[2] Scandinavian settlements were established in many areas of what is now Northern England, Scotland, and Ireland. In fact, a large area of Eastern England, from London to Scotland, was governed by Danish kings from 878 until 954. This region was known as the Danelaw. To this day, many people in the Danelaw regions and other areas in the Northern and Eastern British Isles trace their ancestry to Scandinavia. Place names with elements such as *-by* (Grimsby, Appleby, etc.), *-thorp*, *-throp* (Northrop, Scunthorpe, etc.), *-kirk*, *kirk-*, *kir-* (Ormskirk, Kirby, Kirkham, etc.), and many others all derive from Scandinavian roots, and were probably settled by Danish or Norse colonists in the ninth and tenth centuries (Hadley 2006:1–27).

In the ninth and early tenth centuries, there were many wars and skirmishes between the Danish and Anglo-Saxon inhabitants of the Archipelago. It was actually by a very slim margin that King Alfred of Wessex (the only English king to earn the title "The Great") successfully defended the English (i.e., Anglo-Saxon) throne against the Danes. If it were not for his legendary skill as a military leader and zeal as English patriot, Modern England could very well have become a Scandinavian country, with the majority language becoming a Scandinavian variety, similar to modern Danish or Norwegian. What we know today as "English" may have become a kind of regional minority dialect.

Over the years and centuries, as the Scandinavian immigrants fought, traded, intermarried, and simply lived among the Anglo-Saxon and Celtic natives, their languages became interwoven into the rich tapestry now described as English. Hundreds of words in modern English entered the language from the languages of the Danish and Norse settlers before, during and after the Danelaw period. Here I can mention only a few. In particular, one-syllable words that contain the sequence *ski-* are almost certainly of Old Norse origin. These include such modern English words as *skirt, skit, ski, skid, sky, skip, skin, skill,* etc.

Since Anglo-Saxon and Old Norse were both Germanic in origin, many pairs of words in the two languages came from the same Germanic root. However, since the communities had been isolated from each other for at least 500 years by the time the Vikings started arriving in England, normal sound change and semantic change had already taken place such that several such *cognate* pairs had come to sound different and to mean slightly different things. Some of these pairs of words with similar sound and similar meanings have survived into modern English. These include such pairs as: *shirt* (Old English) and *skirt* (Old Norse), *bath* (OE) and *bask* (ON), among many others. Thus the vocabulary of English was enriched significantly by the addition of hundreds of synonyms or near synonyms.

There is another important respect in which English began to change because of contact with Scandinavian languages. This is the fact that the complex system of OE noun inflections began to break down. This probably arose out of the necessity for people who spoke quite different languages (Anglo-Saxon and Old Norse, or Danish) to communicate with each other over day-to-day matters. Consider the following forms of the phrase meaning "the king" in Old English (Baugh 1963):

(5) a. sē cyning   "the king" (Nominative case, singular)
    b. ðone cyning   "the king" (Accusative case, singular)
    c. ðæs cyninges   "of the king" (Genitive case, singular)
    d. ðǣm cyninge   "to the king" (Dative case, singular)

(6) a. ðā cyningas   "the kings" (Nominative, accusative plural)
    b. ðāra cyninga   "of the kings" (Genitive plural)
    c. ðǣm cyningum   "to the kings" (Dative plural)

What a complicated system for a second language learner to learn! Every time you'd utter a noun, you'd have to know the gender (masculine, feminine, or neuter), the number (singular or plural), the case (nominative, accusative, genitive, or dative), and which of two "declension classes" a noun may occur in (the so-called "strong" vs. "weak" declensions). When multiplying out these possibilities, the result is forty-eight possible forms for each noun, not even considering many "irregular" forms. Now, this level of complexity is not at all problematic for children learning a language as their mother tongue. Indeed, several languages present more complicated systems of noun inflection than this. However, for a second language learner, this presents a big challenge. As anecdotal evidence, I will risk a personal story: I remember that when I was learning Spanish as an adult, it was difficult for me, as a native English speaker, to remember the genders of nouns and to express them correctly, since Modern English nouns are not generally categorized for gender. Yet, apart from irregular forms, Spanish allows only four possibilities for each noun: either masculine or feminine, and singular or plural. Maybe I was a particularly poor language learner, but if four possibilities can be problematic, imagine how difficult it would be to manage forty-eight possibilities!

As tends to happen all over the world when a language is used for communication between groups of people who speak different native tongues, the word structure of English tended to simplify. A Danish immigrant who wanted to trade with English settlers may have said something like "I want buy two horse," ignoring many inflectional distinctions. While this would have sounded odd to Anglo-Saxon ears, in the right context it would have communicated perfectly well. The pragmatic function of language as a tool for communication is not necessarily impeded by such simplifications. Since there was still no real "standard" English at the end of the first millennium, and most speakers were not literate anyway, many such simplifications over time became incorporated into the language of the majority. By the time of Chaucer (*ca.* 1343–1400), simplification of the noun inflections was almost complete. There was still more complexity in the plurals than there is in Modern English, but the system of genders and cases had pretty much been scrapped.

1.4   The Latin thread

In considering the influence of Latin on English, it may be more appropriate to talk about the Latin "threads" rather than "thread," since Latin influences have impinged on the development of Modern English from a number of different directions and at different times throughout its history. First and most generally, it is hard to overestimate the impact of the Roman Empire on English, and on all the other languages and cultures of Europe for that matter. For practically the entire history of English from the ancient Celts to the twentieth century, the discourse of science, literature, art, politics, and the Christian religion has been conducted either in Latin, or with strong influence from Latin. In this general sense, all the languages of Europe have been strongly affected by the dominance of Latin in areas of life that involve writing.[3] In fact, the text you are reading at this moment is in the Modern English alphabet, which itself is based most directly on Latin (even the type font I am using is called "Times New *Roman*"!). Throughout Europe (and North Africa), as more people became literate, Latin began to have more and more influence on the spoken languages as well. The modern "Romance Languages" (French, Spanish, Italian, Sardinian, Portuguese, Catalan, Gallego, Occitan, Provençal, Rheto Romance, among others) are descendents of the regional varieties of Latin that were used as spoken *lingua francas* (languages of wider communication) during and after the Roman period.

However, in addition to the general "pan-European" influence of Latin as the language of writing, English was particularly affected by Latin because of a very significant series of events that happened early in the second millennium. In January of 1066 CE, the King of England, Edward II (the Confessor), died without a clear heir. This threw the kingdom into turmoil at a very crucial point in history. The main contender for the Crown was Harold Godwinson, the Earl of Wessex (note the English spelling of "Harold"). However, two others, both of whom were distant cousins of Edward, were also waiting in the wings for a crack at the English throne. One was King Harald III of Norway (note the Scandinavian spelling), and the other was William II, Duke of Normandy in what is now France. Both Harald and William began to poise their armies for an invasion in support of their claims, Harald in the North and William across the English Channel in Normandy.

The day after Edward II died, Harold Godwinson was crowned king at Westminster Abbey. Within a few months, both Harald and William began to invade from different directions. It was a bad time for the English for a number of reasons, and on October 14, 1066, English and Norman armies met at the famous Battle of Hastings in Southern England. Although the armies were roughly evenly matched in numbers, the Normans had enough tactical advantages to carry the day. At that battle, the new king Harold Godwinson was killed, paving the way for William II of Normandy to be crowned William I of England on Christmas Day, 1066. Soon William dealt with the Norse threat by paying Harald III a large sum in gold, effectively ending Norse aspirations in the British Isles. Thus began what is known as the Norman period in English history.

The Norman period lasted for over 300 years, and had a tremendous effect on English society, culture, and language. William I introduced a single Roman-based legal system that extended throughout what is now Modern England, and instituted the structure of local governments based on Shires, which is still recognized to this day. Here I will only briefly consider the impact of the Norman period on the English language.

Norman French (a Romance language) became the language of court and the nobility, while local language varieties continued to be used by the common people. Little by little the nobility also began to use a version of Old English deeply infused with French vocabulary.[4] This "mixed language" became a kind of *lingua franca* for the entire population, most of whom spoke sometimes mutually unintelligible varieties of Old English, Celtic, and Scandinavian tongues. Thousands of words came into the English language from French at that time, many of them from semantic domains having to do with courtly activities (*court, sovereign, royal, princess, throne, scepter, crown*, etc.), and other "high class" pursuits (*bureaucracy, money, bribe, dine, retire, tour, leisure, relax, luxury, inherit*, etc.). The impact of Norman French on the English language is so great that scholars have given a distinct name to the majority language as spoken in Southern England beginning about 1066 – Middle English.

As just mentioned, since Norman French was the language of the nobility, French vocabulary tends to occur in semantic domains having to do with "refined," scholarly, or upper-class activities, whereas Anglo-Saxon vocabulary tends to occur in more mundane semantic domains. This added an entirely new, even larger number of synonyms or near synonyms to the layers of Anglo-Saxon and Scandinavian vocabulary that had already permeated the majority language of the day. In most near-synonymous pairs, the Old English word represents the same concept as the Old (Norman) French word, but with a different connotation. This is particularly clear in the domain of food – barnyard terms used for foods and items having to do with food preparation are Anglo-Saxon, while the more refined terms used at the table are from French. The following is a very short list of some of the modern pairs of words with similar meanings beginning with the kitchen vocabulary. Thousands of pairs like this could be listed, but this will be enough to provide a sense of the sociolinguistic connotations of Anglo-Saxon vs. French vocabulary which continue to permeate the mindset of English speakers throughout the modern world:

(7)   Mundane (Anglo Saxon)   Refined (Norman French)

Mundane (Anglo Saxon)	Refined (Norman French)
chicken	*poultry*
cow	*beef*
calf	*veal*
pig	*pork*
sheep	*mutton*
meal	*repast*
board	*table*
eat	*dine*
dish	*plate*
cup/mug	*glass*
cupboard	*cabinet*
pot	*vase*
die	*expire*
dog	*canine*
fall	*cascade*
funny	*comical*
ship	*vessel*
spit	*expectorate*
sweat	*perspire*
talk/speak	*lecture*
walk	*perambulate*

Contemporary influences

In addition to thousands of Scandinavian and French borrowings, many other lexical items have since entered English through the various languages that have enriched the British, North American, and other cultures around the world for which some variety of English is the major language. Here are a few examples:

(8)	Word	Source
	algebra	Arabic
	boondocks	Tagalog
	canoe	Carib
	chocolate	Nahuatl (Aztec)
	moccasin	Algonquian
	mumps	Icelandic
	nark	Sanskrit
	pajamas	Farsi (Persian)
	safari	Swahili
	shamrock	Irish
	silk	Chinese
	silo	Spanish
	taboo	Austronesian (possibly Tongan)
	thug	Hindi
	tobacco	Carib
	totem	Ojibwa
	yoghurt	Turkish

This list is but a taste of the wide range of vocabulary that has been incorporated into English from other languages over the centuries. The actual list is potentially infinitely long for the following reason: most speakers of English at the beginning of the Third Millennium have learned English as a second language. For these speakers, their first language is a rich and natural resource for additional vocabulary items as needed. It would be impossible to list all of the "non-English" words that are used every day by multilingual speakers in conversations that are otherwise essentially English. Some of these words become part of a localized Standard English used in a particular country or region of a country (e.g., *pakka*, meaning "legitimate" or "proper" in Indian English, or *unu*, meaning "you plural" in Jamaican English), while others are simply used as needed ("for the nonce"), but never catch on to become established lexical items. A few (such as those listed in (8) above) may work their way into international standard English, and begin to appear in well-respected and internationally marketed dictionaries and other publications. But overall, the vocabulary of English is a constantly expanding collection of meaningful units, open to contributions and suggestions by any and all peoples who consider themselves to be English speakers. The relatively new English word, *wiki*, comes to mind as a pointed example and an apt description of the grass roots nature of the vocabulary of English.[5] The current meaning of *wiki* is something like "a self-regulating body of knowledge built by numerous, often anonymous, individuals." Certainly, Modern English is exactly this – a *wiki*-language!

1.6   The genius of English

Two consistent themes that transcend all of the threads that make up the tapestry of modern English are: (1) decreasing morphological complexity and (2) increasing vocabulary. Another way of putting this is that for centuries English has progressively become less dependent on complex inflections of individual words (morphology) for expressing nuances of meaning, while at the same time proliferating its vocabulary. This heritage has endowed Modern English with a character that lends itself to adoption as an international *lingua franca* – the morphological simplifications (instigated by second language learners as described above) make the basic sentence patterns relatively easy to learn, while at the same time the many layers of vocabulary allow speakers to express the kinds of fine nuances usually associated with languages that are structurally much more complex.

Modern English is at its very roots a language created by and for second language learners. From the Vikings to the Norman French to the many nationalities that use English in the current era, individuals have learned English as a foreign language, and have adapted it to suit the special communicative needs of their communities. This legacy as a "mixed" language has resulted in a tradition of openness and flexibility that seems to permeate the spirit of Modern English. One piece of evidence for this is that there is no "English Academy" that defends the purity of the language, as there is for French, Spanish, and many other major languages of the world. Indeed, such an academy would have nothing to defend, since English has been "impure" ever since the Bent Ones first stepped onto the Atlantic Archipelago! It is true that many people have strong opinions as to what variety of English or which usages are "best" or "proper"; however there is no universally accepted board of standards. In short, no one "owns" English. It belongs to the world, and will continue to be shaped and molded by generations of speakers in all parts of the world whose main goal is to communicate effectively with individuals and nationalities they find themselves in contact with.

Summary

In this chapter the history of the English language is described as a "tapestry" consisting of four major threads, and many other less central influences. The major threads are:

- The Celtic thread
- The Anglo-Saxon thread
- The Scandinavian thread
- The Latin thread

Because of this heritage as a "mixed" language and a language of wider communication, the history of English has been characterized by a tendency for morphology to simplify, syntax to rigidify, and vocabulary to multiply. This fact has served speakers of English well, as layers of vocabulary added over the years allow speakers to express fine nuances of meaning, while maintaining a grammatical system that is fairly transparent, and learnable by second language speakers.

FURTHER READING

The definitive work on the history of English is undoubtedly Hogg (2001). In addition, several recent works approach the topic from different perspectives. McCrum *et al.* (2002), and Bragg (2006) are the companion volumes for two major television documentaries, both of which provide entertaining and well-researched popular introductions to the history of English. Van Gelderen (2006) focuses on internal rather than external change. Brinton and Arnovick (2006) concentrate on processes of language change from a broader theoretical perspective, including generative theory and grammaticalization theory. Machan (2009) looks more specifically at sociolinguistic forces that have shaped the history of English since King Alfred the Great. Finally, MacWhorter (2009) embeds strong arguments for the Celtic influence on Modern English within an engaging overall history of the language. Lass (1995) is a detailed discussion of the history of English spoken in the Old English period from a linguistic perspective.

Exercises

1. Find two 100-word excerpts on the Internet, one from a technical manual, and the other from a children's story. In both excerpts, underline all the words that are of Latinate origin (through French or directly from Latin) and circle all words that are of Germanic origin (Scandinavian and Old English). You should be able to determine the origins of most words just given the information in Chapter 1. However, a dictionary that includes etymological details (e.g., American Heritage 2006) will be helpful to check your hypotheses and identify problematic words.

As you compare the relative number of circled and underlined words in the two excerpts, what do you observe? Can you explain the pattern that seems to emerge in terms of the history of English?

2. Old English (by Taylor Meizlish, Lee Engdahl, and Tom Payne). Here are some Old English sentences (reconstructed based on a West Saxon ideal) followed by their translations in random order.

   Part A: Match the translation of the Old English by placing the correct letter after the Old English sentence.

   1. Se dola mann siehþ þone gōdan mann _____
   2. Glæd mann siehþ þā hreowcearigan ierþlingas _____
   3. Þes reþa cyning siehþ þā glædan freondas _____
   4. Stedefæste menn seoþ þā gōdan menn _____
   5. Swift cyning siehþ swiðferhðe brimliðendas _____
   6. Se nehsta geþeahter siehþ swiftne swicdoman _____
   7. Glæade ierþlingas seoþ lustbærne neorxena wang _____

   Modern English translations in RANDOM order:

   a. A glad person sees the troubled farmers.   e. Glad farmers see pleasant paradise.
   b. Steadfast people see the good people.   f. The foolish person sees the old person.
   c. This fierce king sees the glad friends.   g. A swift king sees brave seafarers.
   d. The last counselor sees swift betrayal.

   Part B: Based on what you have learned in part A, translate the following into common Modern English.

   Se cyning seihþ hreowcearigne neorxena wang.
   Þā lustbæran geþeahteras seoþ þisne stedefæstan brimliðend.

   Part C: Now translate these sentences into Old English.

   Good kings see a fierce farmer.
   This steadfast person sees the last paradise.

   Part D: Some of the words in this exercise have survived into Modern English, while others have not. Sometimes a word form has survived, but the meaning has changed. For each word in this exercise, try to determine whether there is a formally similar related word in Modern English. List the words with their Modern English equivalents (if any), indicating whether and how the meanings have changed over the years.

   Examples:

OE word	Related modern word	Meaning change
seoþ	sees	– none –
nehsta	next	In OE this meant 'last.'
brimlið	end	– none –

2 Typology

Dylan Hunt, there are three types of people in the universe: those who can count, and those who can't.

Flavin (Alan Scarf) in TV drama *Andromeda* (2004)

Every language has its own character, or "spirit." Part of learning to speak a second language fluently is developing a sense of the ways it tends to form words, combine words into phrases and sentences, and express ideas. Speaking a language like Korean, for example, in which the main verb usually comes at the end of a clause, is a very different experience from speaking a language like English, in which the main verb is more comfortable resting somewhere in the middle of the clause. Similarly, someone who is used to speaking English, a language in which major grammatical relations like Subject and Direct Object are expressed by the order of words, must reset their cognitive framework in order to speak Russian, a language in which grammatical relations are mostly expressed by word endings. These and many other features pertain to the TYPOLOGICAL CHARACTERISTICS of a language, i.e., what "type" of language it is according to various features of form, meaning, and use. Understanding what type of language English is, especially as it compares to one's mother tongue, or the mother tongues of one's students or clients, can be very useful to any English language professional (see Ramat 2002 for several case studies).

A TYPOLOGY is simply a division of some range of phenomena into types. To "typologize" something is to group its parts into types. We often hear jokes, such as the one at the beginning of this chapter, that purport to typologize people into two or more groups according to some parameter. Linguistic typologists are linguists who group languages into well-defined and useful types. But a typology is only useful when it makes "predictions" about several characteristics of the items being typologized. For example, suppose we were to typologize motorized vehicles. Which of the following do you think would be the most meaningful typology, A or B?:

- Typology A: bus, van, automobile, tractor ...
- Typology B: red ones, green ones, silver ones, white ones ...

If you know that a motor vehicle is a bus, what else do you know about it? Quite a lot actually – it is probably a large vehicle, with lots of seats, designed primarily to carry people. Its identity as a bus reflects its general character, rather than just some isolated feature. If, on the other hand, you know a motor vehicle is silver in color, there is not much else you can guess about its characteristics. Therefore, typology A better summarizes the basic character of each type of motor vehicle, because it reflects "clusters" of structural and functional characteristics that tend to go together.

Turning to a linguistic example, we could say that there are two kinds of languages in the world – those that have the sound [r] and those that don't. However, knowing whether a language has an [r] is not likely to have many repercussions in other parts of the language; therefore this is not a particularly interesting or useful typology. However, there are several other linguistic typologies that have been very helpful to people interested in understanding the characters of individual languages, and of the human mind in general. In this chapter we will consider three major linguistic typologies, and will situate English within these typologies. These are MORPHOLOGICAL TYPOLOGY, CONSTITUENT ORDER (or SYNTACTIC) TYPOLOGY, and SEMANTIC (or LEXICAL) TYPOLOGY. These typologies are important because they identify *clusters* of properties. They define the general character of any language, and therefore have broad application in many areas of language usage, as well as language teaching and learning. Second language learners of English who come from language backgrounds that are different typologically in any of these respects will have problems if they try to view English as a kind of "code" for their first language. Understanding the typological characteristics of English can help teachers and other English Language professionals understand the problems such students face, and give them a few helpful tips and exercises that will enable them to conceptualize and incorporate into their own INTERLANGUAGE the "essence" of English, and achieve a level of fluency that may otherwise be out of reach for them.

2.1   Morphological typology

MORPHOLOGY is the study of shapes. Morphology in linguistics has to do with the shapes of words, and how speakers may change the shapes of words in order to express meaning. Central to the concept of morphological typology is the notion of a MORPHEME. A morpheme is the smallest linguistic unit that can be used to express meaning. For example, the word *unreasonable* consists of three morphemes, *un-*, a PREFIX meaning "not," *reason*, the ROOT of the word, and *-able*, a SUFFIX indicating

Figure 2.1 The index of synthesis (from Comrie 1989)

the function of this word as an adjective. Each of these parts contributes something to the meaning of the whole word. Furthermore, each of these parts cannot be further divided into smaller meaningful parts, e.g., the *rea-* part of *reason* does not express a meaning itself. Therefore, each of the three parts is a minimal form or shape that expresses meaning – a morpheme. Morphemes, including their types and subtypes, will be discussed in more detail in Chapter 4. In this section we will consider a framework for comparing languages in terms of their general morphological character, and will situate Modern English within this framework.

Early linguistic typologists recognized three morphological types of languages: (1) ISOLATING languages, (2) AGGLUTINATING languages, and (3) INFLECTIONAL or FUSIONAL languages. In this section we will see that English is a fairly isolating language, though it has some agglutinating and fusional characteristics thanks to the many other languages that have contributed to its typological character over the centuries. Comrie (1989) proposed two "indices" or parameters for measuring the morphological typology of a language. These parameters are the INDEX OF SYNTHESIS and the INDEX OF FUSION. In the following two sections, each of these indices will be discussed and illustrated in English.

Synthesis

The index of synthesis has to do with how many morphemes tend to occur per word. This index defines a continuum from isolating (or ANALYTIC) languages at one extreme to highly POLYSYNTHETIC languages at the other (see Figure 2.1).

A strictly isolating language is one in which every word consists of one and only one morpheme. Many languages of East Asia, in particular the Sinitic (Chinese) languages, come close to this extreme. English is predominantly an isolating language, although not nearly as isolating as, for example, Mandarin. Here is an invented English sentence in which every word consists of only one morpheme:

(1)   My brother will go to the store after dinner.

Notice that some of these words have more than one SYLLABLE (a phonetic "pulse" of air), and some of those syllables may look like morphemes. For example, the words *brother*, *after*, and *dinner* all end in -*er*, which is a morpheme in words like *opener* (a thing for opening) and *smarter* (more smart). However, in this sentence, the -*er* syllables express no meaning of their own – they are just parts of the roots

Table 2.1 **The personal pronouns of English**

Pronouns		Case			
		Nominative	Accusative	Possessed	Possessor (Genitive)
1st person singular:		I	me	mine	my
2nd person singular:		you	you	yours	your
3rd person singular:	Masculine	he	him	his	his
	Feminine	she	her	hers	her
1st person plural:		we	us	ours	our
2nd person plural:		you	you	yours	your
3rd person plural:		they	them	theirs	their

brother, after, and *dinner.* In fact, it's probably true that these *-er* syllables are each related historically to one of the *-er* morphemes, but in the contemporary language, they do not express a meaning in these particular words. So, for example, most Modern English speakers do not think of *after* as meaning "more aft," or *dinner* as being "a thing for dining" though these are the likely origins of these words. In each case the root and the suffix have by now been LEXICALIZED together into a single linguistic unit (see Chapter 3 for a discussion of lexicalization).

Notice also that at least one word in this sentence has several meaning components, but still can be considered one morpheme. This is the pronoun *my*. One could say that *my* expresses the ideas of 1st person (the speaker), singular (rather than plural), and genitive (or possessive) case. Since these are three separate meaning components, shouldn't there be three morphemes? Well, the problem is there is no consistent pattern (or "rule") that relates the form *my* to other 1st person forms, other singular forms, or other genitive forms. It is not the case, for example, that the *m-* means 1st person, and the *-y* means singular + genitive, or something like that. If you change any of the three components that define this pronoun, you must change the pronoun to something altogether different, e.g., *your, our,* or *I*. Therefore, the pronoun itself is one morpheme that expresses three distinct meaning components.[1]

Example (1) illustrates the general isolating character of Modern English. As mentioned in Chapter 1, however, prior to the Norman Conquest at the beginning of the second millennium, English was much more polysynthetic, with nouns expressing a rich case, number, and gender system. Remnants of this stage are still present in the personal pronouns, illustrated in Table 2.1.

The pronouns in Table 2.1, like most small words with grammatical functions, come from Anglo-Saxon (also known as Old English) or Old Norse. In Old English (OE), all nouns, determiners, adjectives, and pronouns were marked for case (nominative, accusative, genitive, and dative). In Modern English, the only trace

Figure 2.2 The index of fusion (from Comrie 1989)

of the case system on ordinary nouns is the -'s ending, as in *John's house.* This reflects the OE genitive case. Other than this, the case system has been lost in nouns and noun phrases, but is mostly still intact in the pronoun system. The accusative and dative cases of pronouns were already very similar in OE, and have completely fallen together into the generic "accusative" case of Modern English.[2] Also, several forms that were distinct in OE, e.g., 2nd person singular and plural, nominative and accusative, are no longer distinct. But still, it is clear that the case system is much more viable in pronouns than in ordinary noun phrases.

The pronoun system, then, illustrates a remnant of a more synthetic stage of the English language. Contemporary English, however, leans more toward the isolating or "analytic" type.

Fusion

A second index of morphological typology that Comrie (1989) introduced was the index of FUSION. This describes the degree to which units of meaning are "fused" into single morphemes. In a highly fusional language (sometimes called "inflectional"; but since this has other connotations, we will use the term "fusional") one morpheme can simultaneously express several meanings, e.g., the personal pronouns illustrated above. At the other extreme are languages in which most morphemes express only one meaning. These are called AGGLUTINATIVE languages (see Figure 2.2).

While there is no quantitative method for precisely locating any language on the index of fusion, English is probably more agglutinative than fusional, e.g., in *anti-dis-establish-ment-ari-an-ism* each morpheme has a specific and fairly straightforward meaning. But then, such words are all of Latin origin.

Examples of fusion in English include "strong" verb forms, such as *sang, thought,* and *drove,* and certain noun plurals such as *feet* and *mice.* The word *sang* is the past tense of the verb *sing.* However, the part that means past tense cannot be strictly separated out from the root. You might say that the past tense and the root are simply "fused" together in one form. This contrasts with a form like *walked,* where the part that means past tense (*-ed*) can be cleanly distinguished from the root, as though it is "glued" on. A word like *feet* also exhibits fusion. The root is *foot,* and to form the plural you change the vowel, rather than glue on a separate piece. For this reason we say that these forms are *FUSional* (pieces *fused* together) rather than *agGLUtinative* (pieces *glued* together in a sequence).

Table 2.2 Spanish verb inflections – an example of a relatively synthetic language

	Present	Past perfective	Past imperf.	Simple future	Conditional
1 sg	amo	amé	amaba	amaré	amaría
1 pl	amamos	amamos	amábamos	amaremos	amaríamos
2 sg	amas	amaste	amabas	amarás	amarías
2 pl[3]	amáis	amasteis	amabais	amareis	amaríais
3 sg	ama	amó	amaba	amará	amaría
3 pl	aman	amaron	amaban	amarán	amarían

Table 2.3 English verb inflections – an example of a relatively isolating language

	Present	Past perfective	Past imperf. (progressive)	Simple future	Conditional
1 sg	love	loved	was loving	will love	would love
1 pl	love	loved	were loving	will love	would love
2 sg	love	loved	were loving	will love	would love
2 pl	love	loved	were loving	will love	would love
3 sg	loves	loved	was loving	will love	would love
3 pl	love	loved	were loving	will love	would love

For the most part, however, individual word pieces in English can be separated fairly clearly from one another, and each piece pretty much expresses one meaning component. In comparison to many other languages, then, the morphology of English tends to be fairly agglutinative. However, since English is also fairly isolating, not a lot of communicative work is accomplished via morphology. For example, major grammatical relations like Subject and Object are expressed syntactically via word order, rather than by case marking morphology on nouns, or rich AGREEMENT marking on verbs. Even verbal categories like tense and aspect (see Chapter 12) tend to be expressed syntactically in English. Yes, there is one tense morpheme, usually spelled -ed, for past tense, and one tense/agreement morpheme, -s, that means 3rd person, plus present tense. But these are relatively minor morphological expressions in comparison to the robust morphologies of languages such as Spanish, Russian, Hungarian, and many others.

To illustrate this contrast, let's compare Spanish and English verb forms. In Spanish, much of the tense, aspect, and person marking is expressed morphologically on verbs. Consider the partial paradigm for the regular Spanish verb *amar*, "to love," given in Table 2.2.

Just looking down the columns of Tables 2.2 and 2.3, we see much more variation in word shapes in Spanish than in English. In Spanish, the verb has a different shape for just about every person and number category of Subject. This is true for every single column of Table 2.2. In English, on the other hand, the only variations are in the first and third columns, and these are very minimal. In column 1 of Table 2.3 the 3sg form has an -*s* on the end, and in column 3, the 1sg and 3sg forms of the auxiliary is *was*, while the other forms of the auxiliary in column 3 are all *were*. Then looking across the columns of both tables, we see that the different tense, aspect, and modal categories represented by the five columns are all expressed morphologically in Spanish – each category by a different verb ending. In English, however, only the past tense is expressed purely morphologically, by the addition of one suffix, -*ed*. Present tense is expressed by the bare form of the verb, while imperfective (or progressive), future, and conditional are all expressed analytically by the addition of an auxiliary. The progressive in English also involves the suffix -*ing*, so there is a bit of morphology involved there as well.

Tables 2.2 and 2.3 illustrate the difference between a language that expresses important conceptual categories (such as tense and identity of the Subject) *synthetically* – by changing the shape of the verb, and one that expresses roughly the same conceptual categories *analytically* – by putting together separate words. Linguists would say that Spanish is a more *synthetic* language than English. English, in turn, is more synthetic than a language like Classical Chinese, for which a verb doesn't vary in shape at all. Important conceptual categories like person and number of the Subject, aspect, and mode in Chinese are all expressed analytically.

The morphological variation in Tables 2.2 and 2.3 represents INFLECTIONAL MORPHOLOGY of verbs. Most of the morphological variation in English tends to be DERIVATIONAL, rather than inflectional. In other words, most of the ways of shaping words to express meanings in English involve building (or "deriving") new words out of roots and affixes. This is much more common for English words of Latin than Germanic origin, since Latin was more synthetic than Old English or Old Norse were. A more detailed discussion of the differences between inflectional and derivational morphology, and a list of the most common derivational morphemes is provided in Chapter 4 (see especially Table 4.1 and the discussion thereof).

2.2   Constituent order typology

For many years linguists have noticed that discourse tends to be divided into CLAUSES. The notion of a clause seems so intuitive, so central to our conception of language that it is almost impossible to imagine a theory of language that did not include it. A clause is simply one or more noun phrases combined with a PREDICATING ELEMENT, usually a verb phrase of some sort, to express a complete information unit (a "thought"). Sometimes the noun phrases and predicating element are called CONSTITUENTS, because they are the parts that "constitute" a clause. Constituent order is sometimes also described as word order.

Individual languages tend to structure their clauses in characteristic ways: some languages tend to place the predicating element at the end, others at the beginning; still others place it somewhere in the middle. Finally many languages seem to place the predicating element just about anywhere. Among the noun phrases in a clause, an important distinction has traditionally been drawn between Subject (S) and Object (O).[4] From this point of view there are six logically possible orders of constituents in a clause that contains a Subject, an Object, and a Predicating element (V for "verb"). These are: SOV, SVO, VSO, VOS, OSV, and OVS. Languages can often be described according to which of these orders is typical, or "basic." More recently, the assumption that Subject and Object are indeed the universal categories relevant to the ordering of nominal elements in a clause has been seriously questioned (see D. Payne 1992, Mithun 1992, Dryer 2007, *inter alia*). Nevertheless, this typology is a useful starting point for understanding the functions of constituent order and the general syntactic "character" of any language.

Joseph Greenberg (1963) investigated thirty randomly selected languages in terms of their basic constituent orders. Among the results of Greenberg's study was the observation that there is a major distinction between languages in which the verb comes before the Object and languages in which the verb comes after the Object. These can be described as VO and OV languages respectively. The position of the Subject (S) seems to be less typologically significant. Several syntactic characteristics tend to correlate with these two fundamental language types – in many ways, they are "mirror images" of one another. Furthermore, the languages of the world seem to be fairly evenly divided between those that can be classified as OV and those that can be classified as VO. There are also many that defy either of these classifications, but those that *can* be classified according to this typology are pretty evenly distributed between these two orders. In other words, one order does not appear to be more "natural" than the other.

Before discussing the correlations observed by Greenberg, we need to define a few terms. ADPOSITION is a cover term for words that are typically called PREPOSITIONS and POSTPOSITIONS in particular languages. Prepositions precede noun phrases, while postpositions follow them. Here are some examples of adpositions from English and Japanese (an OV language):

(2) English: in   [the village]
                PREP   NOUN PHRASE
     Japanese: 村   に   'in the village'
               mura   ni
               village   in
               NOUN   POSTP

An AUXILIARY is a small word that combines with a verb to express the tense, aspect, and/or mode of a clause. Sometimes auxiliaries are called HELPING VERBS. Auxiliaries

Table 2.4 **Summary of Greenberg's universals (from appendix 2 of Greenberg 1963)**

Parameter	Correlation	
	VO	OV
Basic Main Clauses	Object follows verb (English, French, Chinese, Tagalog, Arabic, etc.)	Object precedes verb (Japanese, Korean, Hindi, Mongolian, Tamil, etc.)
Adpositions	Prepositions	Postpositions
Genitive (possessor) and possessed Noun	Possessor follows noun	Possessor precedes noun
Noun and Modifier	Modifier follows noun	Modifier precedes noun
Relative Clause and head Noun	Relative clause follows head noun	Relative clause precedes head noun
Comparatives	Adj-Mkr-Std	Std-Mkr-Adj
Inflected Auxiliaries	Auxiliary precedes verb	Auxiliary follows verb
Question particles	Clause-initial	Clause-final
Question words	Clause-initial	Clause-initial or elsewhere
Affixes	Prefixes and suffixes	Suffixes

in English come before the word that expresses the Predicating element of the clause. A few examples of auxiliaries are given in italics in (3):

(3)   I *am* singing.
      I *will* sing.
      I *might* sing.
      I *have* sung.

A COMPARATIVE CONSTRUCTION is a clause that compares some item, the Subject, to another item, the standard, according to some property, usually expressed in an adjective. Comparative constructions also contain a MARKER OF COMPARISON, that marks the clause as a comparative. Examples of comparative constructions in English, with these parts labeled, are given in (4):

(4)	**Subject**		**Adjective**	**Marker**	**Standard**	
	My brother	is	taller	than	my sister.	
	She	walks	faster	than	he	does.

Now we are ready to summarize the syntactic correlations observed by Greenberg for VO and OV languages. It is important to recognize that Greenberg simply observed certain correlations, as represented in Table 2.4. He did not attempt to provide a reason for (i.e., to "motivate") those correlations, or even to test them for statistical significance. Nevertheless, Greenberg's work stimulated the field of typological linguistics and continues to be very influential.

Not every language fits this "Greenbergian Typology" perfectly. In particular, recent work has shown that the correlation between order of Object–verb and Modifier–noun are actually fairly random – there are many languages that don't conform to Greenberg's observations in this respect (Dryer 1988). The strongest correlations are in adpositions, auxiliaries, and comparative constructions:

(5)

		VO	OV
a.	Adpositions:	Prepositions	Postpositions
b.	Auxiliaries:	AUX + VERB	VERB + AUX
c.	Comparatives:	ADJ-MKR-STD	STD-MKR-ADJ

The first two of these parameters, in particular, are very central to the basic clause structure of any language. If you speak a language with prepositions, it takes quite a bit of mental effort to internalize the use of postpositions, and vice versa. This is also true for the placement of auxiliaries in relation to main verbs.

The following examples compare English with Japanese according to each of these parameters. I think you'll see how the two languages are to a large extent mirror images of one another.

(6)

Japanese:[5]   English:

Main clauses:

SUBJECT	OBJECT	VERB		SUBJECT	VERB	OBJECT
太郎は	犬を	見た。		Taroo	saw	a dog.
Taroo ga	inu o	mita.				
Taroo NOM	dog ACC	saw				

(7)

Relative clauses and Head Noun:

	REL-CLAUSE		HEAD			HEAD	REL-CLAUSE
太郎は	[肉を	食べた]	犬を	見た。	Taro saw the dog [that ate the meat.]		
Taro ga	[niku o	tabeta]	inu o	mita.			
T. NOM	meat ACC	ate	dog ACC	saw			

(8)

Adpositional phrases:

	NP	POSTP				PREP NP
太郎は	[窓	から]	犬を	見た。	Taroo saw a dog [from the window.]	
Taroo ga	mado	kara	inu o	mita.		
T. NOM	window	from	dog ACC	saw		

(9)

Comparative clauses:

SUBJ	STD	MKR	ADJ		SUBJ	ADJ	MRK	STD
犬は	[猫	より	大きい。]	The dog is bigger than the cat.				
Inu ga	neko	yori	ookii.					
dog NOM	cat	than	big					

(10)   Auxiliaries:

	VERB	AUX		AUX	VERB
私は	眠って	いる。	I	am	sleeping.
watashi ga	nemu-tte	iru.			
I	NOM sleep-INF	am			

It should be clear from these examples that if you speak one of the many OV languages of the world, there are several respects in which you must "invert" your language reception and production processes in order to understand and speak a VO language such as English. I should also reiterate that these correlations do not just apply to Japanese. Japanese is simply one example of a language that exhibits all of the characteristics that are common among OV languages. Not every OV language has exactly the same constituent order patterns that Japanese does, but, as Greenberg first pointed out in 1963, there are definite tendencies.

2.3   Lexical typology

We've now seen how English compares to other languages in terms of its morphology (the way words are shaped) and syntax (the way words combine to form phrases and clauses). Another area that is difficult for many second language learners of English, and therefore in need of attention by English language professionals, is the lexicon (see Chapter 3). In particular, functions performed by morphology or syntax in many languages are often expressed by different vocabulary items (or LEXEMES) in English. LEXICAL TYPOLOGY is the subfield of linguistics that studies the way languages tend to combine meaning components into lexical packages, such as nouns and verbs. In this section, we will look at English verbs in terms of the characteristic ways that they combine, or "package," meaning components. We will concentrate on characteristics of the English lexicon that are quite different from those of most other languages. Let's start with a basic example, and then discuss some specific parameters that are known to be particularly tricky.

English tends to combine the meaning component of CAUSATION[6] with other concepts in individual verbs. For example, an English verb like *feed* combines the meanings EAT and ENABLE or CAUSE. In other words, *feed* in some sense means ENABLE TO EAT. In some languages, the notion of FEED is expressed with a verb that means EAT, with some extra morphology or another verb added. One of the many languages that does this is Korean:

(11)   a.   닭은   쌀을   먹었다.   'The chicken ate rice.'
            tak-eun   ssal-eul   meok-eoss-ta
            chicken-NOM rice.grain-ACC eat-PAST-DECL

b. 나는　　　닭에게　　　쌀을　　　　먹였다.　　'I fed the chicken rice.'
na-neun　tak-eykey　ssal-eul　meok-y-eoss-ta
1SG-NOM　chicken-DAT　rice.grain-ACC　eat-CAUSE-PAST-DECL

Notice that the verb (which comes at the end of the clause in Korean) is almost the same in both of these examples. The only difference is that in (11b) there is an extra -*y* in the verb. This -*y* is what expresses the difference between EAT and ENABLE to EAT, and is called a MORPHOLOGICAL CAUSATIVE. This is one fairly common way in Korean of changing a verb, V, into another verb that means "CAUSE/ENABLE/ALLOW to V." English does not have a morphological causative, or much of a morphological anything! Instead it tends to rely on its rich vocabulary to express causation, as in the difference between the verbs *eat* and *feed*.

We must remember that English, largely because of its history as a "mixed" language, has a very robust and well-developed lexicon, but rather pathetic morphology. Many concepts that are expressed morphologically in other languages are expressed by distinct words in English. This is a "habit pattern" that English speakers have become accustomed to, such that it has become part of the implicit mindset involved in speaking English. English speakers have a very difficult time understanding morphological processes like causatives when learning Korean, gender when learning Spanish, or case when learning Russian, because these categories simply are not expressed morphologically in English. Similarly, individuals from these language backgrounds often have difficulty sorting out the various lexical choices that English provides. Pairs of verbs such as *borrow/lend*, *buy/sell*, *teach/learn*, *eat/feed*, *show/see*, and many others are related semantically in ways that are often expressed morphologically in other languages.

In the following sections we will see some other respects in which the lexicon of English is structured differently from that of many other languages. Much of the following discussion is based on work by the psycholinguists Leonard Talmy (2007) and Daniel Slobin and colleagues (Slobin 2006, Lemmens and Slobin 2008).

Manner and motion

Another respect in which the vocabulary of English differs significantly from many other languages is that there is a large set of verbs that combine the concept of MANNER with the concept of MOTION (see, e.g., Slobin 2006). For example, a verb like *run* expresses both a manner of movement (quickly, in a hurried way), with motion to or from some location. The specific path of motion is usually expressed in a prepositional phrase. So in English it is very common and natural to say ...

(12)　He ran to the store.
　　　He's running away from the police.
　　　She ran through the crowd of people.

This same observation holds for dozens or hundreds of verbs in English, such as the following:

(13)   The bird flew out the window.
       We rushed him to the doctor.
       The farmer trucked his crop to town.
       She grabbed it off the shelf.
       He jammed it in his pocket.
       We pushed through the crowd of people.
       They boated around the island.
             motored
             sailed
             floated
             rafted
             hydroplaned
             soared
             rocketed
             inner-tubed
             splashed
             careened
             bounced
             rolled
             hobbled
             scurried
             etc.

In many languages, it is less common for a verb that expresses motion to simultaneously express the manner of motion as well. Rather, the motion is normally expressed in one verb and the manner of motion in another constituent; either another verb, a prepositional phrase, or an affix on the verb. Let's take Spanish as our example this time. While most of the English sentences in (13) have direct Spanish counterparts, it usually sounds more natural in Spanish to express the manner of motion with one constituent (a verb or prepositional phrase), and the movement itself with another. The following are some examples that make this contrast clear (thanks to Ronald Ross and Jeanina Umaña for consultation on these examples):

(14)   a.   *El muchacho nadó através del río.   'The young man swam across the river.'
      b.   El muchacho cruzó el río nadando.   'The young man crossed the river swimming.'
      c.   *Lo patearon fuera de la cantina.   'They kicked him out of the bar.'
      d.   Lo sacaron de la cantina a patadas.   'They removed him from the bar with kicks.'
      e.   *Cojeó fuera de la cantina.   'He limped out of the bar.'
      f.   Salió cojeando de la cantina.   'He left limping from the bar.'

The verb *nadó* "he/she swam" in (14a) expresses a manner of motion, but neither the motion itself nor the path. The verb *cruzó* "crossed" in (14b) combines the concepts of motion and path (motion in a path that crosses a river), while the manner is expressed in a separate verb form, *nadando* "swimming." This is a much more natural collocation in Spanish than (14a) is. On the other hand, *swim* in English may express motion as well as manner. The phrase *to cross a river*, in English implies some "unmarked" manner, probably walking over a bridge. If a more specific manner is required, other verbs that combine motion and manner become more likely, such as *swim, wade, paddle*, etc. In other words, *He swam across the river* sounds more natural to an English ear than *He crossed the river swimming*, while in Spanish the reverse is true. A similar story can be told for the transitive Spanish verbs *patearon* "they kicked" and *sacaron* "they removed" in comparison to the English verbs *kick* and *remove* in examples (14c) and (14d). *Sacaron* describes the caused motion of an object along a path leading out of an enclosed space. The normal way of expressing the idea of *sacar* plus a manner in English is to express the motion and manner with a single verb, and the path with the post-verbal particle *out*: *They kicked/threw/pushed/motioned/transferred* (etc.) *him out of the bar*. The same is true for the Spanish verb *salió* "went out" in example (14f). This verb describes intransitive motion along a path leading out of an enclosed space. English has the motion + path verb *to exit*, but this is a rather odd verb with very limited uses. The normal way of expressing the idea of *salió* in English is to express the motion with either the neutral motion verb *go*, or a verb expressing manner, such as *limp*, and the path separately with the post-verbal particle *out*: *He went out*; *He limped out*.

In summary, it is a general typological property of the vocabulary of English motion verbs that they often express manner as well: *run, swim, fly, rush, walk, hurry, shoot, spew, wiggle, sashay, dance, drive*, and dozens more are translated as manner only in other languages, but can directly express manner + motion in English. Therefore, English can be called a MOTION + MANNER language. Spanish, on the other hand, has been called a MOTION + PATH language, because ordinary motion verbs in Spanish are much more likely to incorporate the meaning component of path than manner. This is but one typological characteristic that has very specific impact on the way teachers present English grammar in ESL and EFL courses.

Causation

The Korean sentences and their English translations given in (11) above illustrate how English expresses the notions of CAUSE and EFFECT in one verb. The meaning of the verb *feed* involves the idea that someone does something (the CAUSE) to cause or enable someone or something else to eat (the EFFECT); the verb *feed* is completely distinct from the verb *eat*. In contrast, the Korean way of expressing the idea of CAUSE TO EAT is to start with the verb root meaning EAT, and add a causative suffix. In this section we look at some more examples of this phenomenon, and a related phenomenon that also illustrates the fact that English has a tendency to express the meanings of CAUSE and EFFECT together in individual verbs.

In addition to *eat* and *feed*, there are several other pairs of verbs in English in which one verb expresses an idea, and the other verb expresses that same idea, but with the added notion of CAUSE. Here are a few more such pairs:

(15)   He learned Spanish.
      We taught him Spanish.   *teach* = CAUSE TO LEARN
      They saw the pictures.
      Sarah showed them the pictures. *show* = CAUSE TO SEE
      The chicken died.
      The farmer killed the chicken.   *kill* = CAUSE TO DIE
      The shoe fell.
      The director dropped the shoe.   *drop* = CAUSE TO FALL

There is a related phenomenon whereby one verb has both a causative and a non-causative sense. In other words, some verbs can be used both intransitively and transitively, and the TRANSITIVE usage is the causative of the INTRANSITIVE. Here are some examples of this phenomenon. The subscript i, as in $grow_i$, refers to the intransitive sense of the verb *grow*, while the subscript t, as in $grow_t$, refers to the transitive sense of this verb:

(16)   The tomatoes are growing in my garden.
      I'm growing tomatoes in my garden. $grow_t$ = CAUSE TO GROW$_i$
      The ice is melting.
      They are melting the ice with salt. $melt_t$ = CAUSE TO MELT$_i$
      The city has changed.
      The new mayor has changed the city. $change_t$ = CAUSE TO CHANGE$_i$
      The child is bathing.
      I am bathing the child. $bathe_t$ = CAUSE TO BATHE$_i$

Not every verb that can be used both transitively and intransitively functions in this way, and we will see some that don't in the next section on PERSPECTIVE. Among the world's languages, however, it is relatively uncommon for the same verb to express both intransitive and causative senses. Most languages would make *some* structural difference between *grow* and *cause to grow*, *melt* and *cause to melt*, etc. The difference may be morphological, as in Korean, Japanese, Indonesian, and most of the languages of South and Central Asia; or it may be syntactic, formed by combining two or more verbs, as in many other languages of Asia and Europe. West Africa is one area of the world where several languages (at least of the Gur and Chadic families) seem to have even more verbs of this type than English does, though this is a matter of ongoing research (see Payne and Jing-Schmidt 2009).

There is a very small class of verbs in English for which the causative and the non-causative forms are similar, but not identical. Here are all the examples I can think of. Perhaps you can think of others:

(17)   The book is lying on the table.
        She is laying the book on the table.   *lay* = CAUSE TO LIE
        The cup rises.
        I raise the cup.   *raise* = CAUSE TO RISE
        That tree is going to fall.
        Bunyan is going to fell that tree.   *fell* = CAUSE TO FALL
        This book just sits on my shelf.
        She sets the book on the shelf after reading it.   *set* = CAUSE TO SIT

These examples may be considered to illustrate weak suppletion (see the Introduction). That is, the causative and non-causative forms of these verbs seem to be related, but there is no way to guess which verbs belong to this category, and therefore "predict" what the causative or non-causative forms may be. One has to just memorize these forms outright.

Perspective

There is one other major respect in which the lexical typology of English verbs differs from that of many other languages. In this section we will see yet again that the rich vocabulary of English makes up for its relative lack of morphological resources for accomplishing communicative work.

We can define perspective in terms of the metaphor "discourse is a play" described in the Introduction. Consider the English verbs *buy* and *sell*. Fillmore (1976) describes these verbs as evoking the same scene in the minds of English speakers; Fillmore calls this the "commercial transaction" scene. In any commercial transaction there are certain participants. These are:

(18)   a.   money
        b.   goods
        c.   a person who starts out with the money and ends up with the goods.
        d.   a person who starts out with the goods and ends up with the money.

A commercial transaction is defined as an event in which goods and money exchange hands. Well, if both *buy* and *sell* evoke the same idealized scene, what is the difference in meaning between them? Consider the following two English sentences, both of which could describe the same scene in some real or imagined world:

(19)   a.   I bought a car from Abelardo for $200.
      b.   Abelardo sold me a car for $200.

The difference, according to Fillmore (1976), is a matter of perspective. For the verb *buy* the person who ends up with the goods (the "buyer") is in primary perspective, while the other three participants are "downplayed" in some way. In terms of the discourse stage metaphor, for (19a) "I" and the car are on center stage, with "I" being primary and the car secondary. Abelardo and the money are on "side stage." In (19b), on the other hand, Abelardo is in primary perspective, while I, the car, and the money are downplayed. If the speaker wishes to put the goods in primary perspective, the verb *cost* can be used.

(20)   a.   This car cost me $200.

In many other languages, the same verb is used for all of these perspectives, the difference being expressed by the construction in which the verb appears. Here are some examples from Tagalog, one of the major languages of the Philippines:

(21)   a.   Binili ko ang kotse mula sa Abelardo.   'I bought a car from Abelardo.'
      b.   Nabili ako ng kotse sa Abelardo.   'I sold a car to Abelardo.'

Tagalog (or Filipino) is a language that uses the same verb root, *bili*, to express both the ideas of BUY and SELL. The difference in perspective is expressed via different morphology on the verb. In (21a), the INFIX *-in-* is sometimes called a "Goal Focus" marker because it expresses the idea that the GOAL, i.e., the car, is the main participant in the clause. (21b), on the other hand, has the prefix *na-*, which indicates "Actor Focus," because it expresses the idea that the ACTOR, "I," is the main participant in the clause. The verbs *buy* and *sell* in English accomplish essentially the same task of focusing on different participants.

The verbs *borrow* and *lend* are also verbs that express different perspectives on essentially the same event. Many languages use the same verb for these two ideas, but in different constructions. Here are some examples from Dutch, a language that is genetically closely related to English:

(22)   a.   Hij   leende   me   een   dollar.   'He lent me a dollar.'
          he   lend.PAST   me   a   dollar
      b.   Ik   leende   een   dollar van   hem. 'I borrowed a dollar from him.'
          I   borrow.PAST a   dollar from him

In these examples the same verb, *lenen* in its base form, translates as English *lend* when the person who receives the dollar is the Direct Object, but *borrow* when the person who receives the dollar is the Subject, and therefore in primary perspective.

Finally, here are some examples of one verb in German that translates as two verbs in English, depending on perspective.

(23) a. Er raubte meine Tasche.   'He stole my handbag.'
      b. Er beraubte mich meiner Tasche. 'He robbed me of my handbag.'

In these examples, we again see the same verb root, *raub*, that translates as English *steal* when there is no prefix, but as *rob* when the prefix *be-* occurs.[7] In both of these examples, the thief is in primary perspective. With *raubte*, the item stolen is the Direct Object, and is therefore in perspective to some degree. With *beraubte*, the person who has something stolen from them is the Direct Object, and therefore is being portrayed as more central to the communicative event than the item stolen. Again we see that a job that is accomplished morphologically in one language is accomplished by distinct verbs in English.

There are dozens of pairs of English verbs that express different perspectives on essentially the same scene. A few of these include:

(24) own/belong
      bequeath/inherit
      frighten/fear
      please/like
      realize/dawn on
      say/tell
      see/appear
      replace/substitute
      consist/comprise
      etc.

In other languages, such concepts are often expressed by one verb in different constructions, or with different morphological patterns. Of course, there are morphological and syntactic ways to adjust the perspective of a situation in English as well, but it does seem to be the case that English speakers are particularly prone to rely on their lexicon for this purpose. In Chapter 13 we will discuss the ways English speakers can adjust the perspective of a clause by using syntax and morphology.

In this section, I have tried to show that it is a general *typological* property of English that its rich lexicon lends itself to many communicative jobs, such as the expression of manner, causativization, and perspectivization. This fact has many consequences for the English language professional. In particular, when translating or learning English verbs, it is very important to understand the perspectives that each verb can present. Verbs seldom translate exactly from one language to the next, and second language learners of English are often confused by the wide range of verbs available that seem to express the "same idea."

Summary

In this chapter we have discussed the linguistic typology of Modern English – what type of language it is in comparison to other languages of the world. We looked at three typological dimensions, and made the following observations:

- Morphological typology. English is a fairly isolating language, meaning most words are fairly simple in structure, having only one or two morphemes. More complex words tend to be of Latinate origin, and much of the morphological complexity in such words is not fully integrated as "live" patterns in Modern English, though some is.
- Constituent order typology. English is a "VO" (Verb + Object) language, and has many of the characteristics linguists expect VO languages to have, based on research by Joseph Greenberg (1963) and others. Second language learners of English whose L1 is an OV (Object + Verb) language (roughly half the languages of the world) in many ways must "invert" their grammatical habit patterns when communicating in English.
- Lexical typology. Because of the history of English as a "mixed" language and *lingua franca*, it has developed a very robust vocabulary (lexicon). We have seen that in English there is a greater tendency than in most languages to incorporate the meaning components of MANNER OF MOTION, CAUSATION, and PERSPECTIVE into the meanings of particular verbs. Verbs with complex packaging of meaning components are often difficult to assimilate into the interlanguage of second language learners, and can lead to serious miscommunication when used inappropriately.

In summary, English is a language that does relatively little communicative work with morphology, preferring to rely on its rich lexicon and relatively rigid syntax to accomplish many jobs that other languages are more likely to accomplish with morphology or by combining separate words.

FURTHER READING

Linguistic typology is by its very nature a cross-language field of inquiry. For this reason there is little or no research that focuses specifically on the typological characteristics of English alone. Rather, there are general works on linguistic typology, and several works that compare and contrast English with particular other languages, e.g., English and German (Hawkins 1994), English and Japanese (Nayuki 2009), and many others. Comrie (1989) is the leading introductory account of morphological and syntactic typology from a cross-language perspective. Croft (2003) approaches some of the same topics from a more "constructionist" perspective. Basic research on semantic or lexical typology are Talmy (2007) and Lemmens and Sloben (2008). Further work on how different languages approach the notions of space and motion is found in Levinson (2003). The studies in Ramat (2002) provide excellent illustrations of the potentials of linguistic typology for helping identify the loci of interference phenomena and to formulate hypotheses in second language learning research.

Exercises

1. The following examples are actual utterances produced by second language learners (SLLs) of English. Many of these exhibit features of the speakers' "interlanguage" (Selinker 1972), i.e., their emerging grammar of English that is still highly influenced by their first language, or L1. Describe how each utterance differs from Standard English (CSE), and explain the differences in terms of the typological characteristics of English described in Chapter 2. Can you guess what type of L1 background the speakers come from? The differences may have to do with morphological, syntactic, or lexical typology. Some examples may illustrate multiple L1 influences. The first example is done for you.

   a. Are the table nights included with the bedroom set?
      Answer: In the noun phrase "the table nights" the Modifier, *night*, follows its head, *table*. In CSE these would be reversed: *the night tables*. The speaker's L1 probably normally places Modifiers after their nouns in noun phrases.
   b. My friend went crossing the river this morning.
   c. My friend her boyfriend saw today.
   d. She rose her hand.
   e. Look the window out!
   f. We wanted playing tennis that weekend.
   g. My son walking to school.
   h. They came my house.
   i. My relatives for dinner came.

2. Typological characteristics of Korean and English
   The following are some ordinary examples extracted from Korean newspaper articles. These examples are presented both in the standard Korean writing system, and in one common Roman transliteration (letter-by-letter transcription). Morpheme-by-morpheme GLOSSES and free translations into English are also provided.

   Just looking at these examples, what can you say about the morphological, syntactic, and lexical typology of Korean? Because of the typological differences between Korean and English, what kinds of challenges do you think Korean speakers may face when it comes to learning English? Note that the focus of this exercise is NOT the writing systems, but the typological properties of the languages (Korean and English) themselves.

   a. 경찰들이   건물   밖에서   살인범을   뒤쫓았다
      gyeongchal-deul-i geonmul bakk-eseo sarin-beom-eul dui-jjoch-ass-ta
      police-PL-NOM   building outside-LOC murder-NZR-ACC after-chase-PAST-DECL
      'The police chased the murderer out of the building.'

b. 초기   청동기   시대의   유물은   자기편이
    chogi   cheo-tong-gi   sidae-eui   yumul-eun   jagi-pyeon-i
    early   blue-copper-tool   age-GEN   relic-TOP   porcelain-piece-SUB
    'As for relics of the early Bronze Age, many porcelain pieces

    많이   출토되어왔다.   그러나,
    manhi   chulto-doy-eo-wa-ss-da   geureona
    many   excavate-PASSIVE-DUR-come-PAST-DECL   but
    have been excavated; but

    이번에는   청동   불상이   출토되어
    i-beon-e-neun   cheong-dong   bul-sang-i   chulto-doy-eo
    this-time-LOC-TOP   blue-copper   Buddha-icon-NOM   excavate-PASSIVE-and
    this time a bronze Buddha icon was excavated and

    학계의   관심을   모으고있다.
    haggye-eui   gwansim-eul   moeugo-iss-da
    academia-GEN   interest-ACC   attract-PRES-DECL
    is attracting the attention of academia.'

3 | The lexicon

We don't just borrow words; on occasion English has pursued other languages down alleyways to beat them unconscious and rifle their pockets for new vocabulary.

Booker T. Washington

In Chapter 2 we discussed how English compares to other languages in terms of morphology, syntax, and lexicon. One conclusion of Chapter 2 was that the lexicon of English is one of its richest resources for expressing meaning. English language professionals will do well to study the lexicon carefully, as many tasks performed by morphological and syntactic means in other languages are expressed by lexical choices in English.

In linguistics, the lexicon of a language is normally defined as a network of all the individual pieces of information a person must have stored in memory in order to speak the language. While there is much variation in theoretical approaches to how such information is represented in the mind, there is general agreement that the lexicon consists at least of the set of basic units, or form–meaning composites, that make up a language – the storehouse of raw materials used to construct communicative utterances. The lexicon is sometimes contrasted with morphology and syntax, which, in some approaches, are distinct components of grammar consisting of structural patterns for constructing new utterances. If the lexicon is the storehouse of raw materials, the morphology and syntax (or MORPHOSYNTAX) are the building codes for combining those raw materials into meaningful utterances.[1]

3.1 Characteristics of items in the lexicon

The best examples of units (or "items") in the lexicon are *basic*, in that they are not made up of other form-meaning composites. Rather they exist in memory as wholes. For example, *cat* is a LEXICAL ENTRY, or LEXEME, in my internal mental lexicon of English. It is a particular form – the noise transcribed phonetically as [kʰæt] – associated with an idealized meaning, consisting of a general image, plus a network of meaning features that make up the concept of *cat* as I have experienced it in my life history. The form *cat* cannot be broken down into smaller meaningful parts, i.e., the individual phonetic pieces, [kʰ], [æ], and [t], or combinations thereof are not themselves associated with meanings. Therefore *cat* is a basic, indivisible form–meaning composite.

The form *cats*, on the other hand, is a combination of two form–meaning composites – *cat* and *-s*. The latter is the conventional spelling for the form–meaning composite that, when attached to a noun root, expresses the notion of "plural" – more than one. Therefore *cats* is not, traditionally speaking, an item in the lexicon. It is an ASSEMBLY composed of two distinct units, combined by a regular morphological pattern.[2]

3.2   The boundaries of the lexicon

One of the major ways that linguistic theories differ is in what they include and what they exclude from the lexicon. We can very generally describe the different theoretical approaches in terms of a continuum extending from a very "narrow" view at one end, to a very "broad" view at the other. In this book we will take a rather broad view, based loosely on work by Fillmore 1977, 1992, Langacker 1987, 1991, 2008, Goldberg 1995, Croft 2002, and others. However, we will also try to be consistent with the way most linguists and applied linguistics professionals view the lexicon as compared to the rest of grammar. Individual theoretical approaches fall somewhere in between the extremes of the continuum illustrated in Figure 3.1. In the extreme broad view the notion of "lexicon" becomes so broad as to disappear altogether – everything anyone needs to know in order to speak a language is in the lexicon, so there is no need to posit a lexicon as distinct from the rest of grammar!

While all approaches to the lexicon consider basic word forms, such as *cat*, to be lexical entries, many approaches also consider meaningful parts of words to be

"Narrow" view	"Broad" view
The lexicon is a very distinct "component" or "module" of grammar. It consists of a stored list of indivisible forms only. The lexicon is distinct from the morphology and syntax.	All grammar consists of "stored" knowledge about a language, including roots, affixes and syntactic structures (or constructions). There is no "lexicon" that is distinct from morphology and syntax.

Figure 3.1 Linguistic approaches to the lexicon

lexical entries as well. For example, the *-ed* part of a word like *walked* can mean PAST TENSE. This is a form–meaning composite that everyone has to know in order to know English; therefore *-ed*, according to some approaches, must be in the lexicon of English. Notice, however, that not just any *-ed* means "past tense," but only those instances of *-ed* that are attached to meaningful stems used as verbs. Therefore, it may be more accurate to say that the *pattern* of a stem followed by *-ed* means "past tense" in the lexicon of English. This may be represented in a formula such as (1):

(1) $[\text{VERB}]_{\text{past tense}} \rightarrow \text{STEM} + \text{-}ed$

The formula in (1) may be read as "To express a verb in the past tense, add the suffix *-ed* to a stem." This is one way of representing on paper the unconscious pattern in the minds of all English speakers that allows them to express the past tense of many verbs. Therefore this formula may be considered (part of) the lexical entry for the past tense morpheme.

Once you start to include patterns such as (1) in the lexicon, it is a slippery slope to a broad view that includes all kinds of morphological and syntactic patterns. For example, (2) is a syntactic pattern of English:

(2)   PREPOSITIONAL PHRASE → PREPOSITION + NOUN PHRASE

This pattern specifies that there is class of structures called PREPOSITIONAL PHRASES that consists of any member of a class of items called PREPOSITIONS and any member of a class of items called NOUN PHRASES. This idealized pattern gives rise to a whole range of actual linguistic utterances, for example:

(3)   in the house
       under the bed
       with a hammer
       down the rabbit hole
       through the mystical forest inhabited by strange beings and fraught with
       unfathomable dangers
       etc.

The phrases in (3) are not in the lexicon. Rather, they are composed of other units that *are* in the lexicon. The pattern in (2) is one of those units, if we take a very broad view of the lexicon (see, e.g., Langacker 1987). Furthermore, prepositional phrases are functionally as different from other kinds of phrases (like verb phrases or noun phrases – see Chapter 7) as nouns, verbs, and adjectives are different from each other. Therefore, according to very broad approaches to the lexicon, the construction illustrated in (2) expresses meaning and therefore should be considered a memorized lexical item.

Under narrower views abstract syntactic patterns such as (2) are not considered part of the lexicon. Rather, they are part of a quite distinct component of grammar, called SYNTAX. Under this view, the lexicon can be thought of as a mental dictionary of all the MORPHEMES (roots and other meaningful pieces of words). Syntactic patterns, such as (2), then, are not part of the lexicon.

The feature common to all approaches to the lexicon is that it consists of a structured network (or list) of memorized units (or lexemes), each of which must be learned on its own. Patterns such as (2) are themselves (unconsciously) memorized units that allow speakers to create potentially unique structures. Thus under a broad view patterns themselves may be items in the network that constitutes the lexicon, but the specific structures produced by those patterns are not. The difference between lexicon and morphosyntax, then, is "the difference between what speakers need to know outright, vs. what they can figure out based on what they already know" (Fillmore *et al.* 1988:501). It must be kept in mind, however, that this difference is not always absolute and clear. In the next section we will discuss the notion of lexicalization, or the continuous process by which linguistic structures become items in the lexicon of a language.

3.3 Lexicalization

As outlined above, many theoretical approaches to grammar propose that there is in fact no strict "boundary" between what is lexical and what is morphological or syntactic. There is good evidence that certain complex pieces of language are stored in memory and accessed in exactly the same way as individual words and smaller pieces are. But how does anything become a unit in the knowledge network we call the lexicon of a language? The one-word answer to this question is "frequency." We all know that when we need to commit something to memory, we sometimes repeat it over and over to ourselves. Items that are used repeatedly become automated, habitual "units" in the mind. Once something becomes a unit, a speaker doesn't have to "construct" it afresh each time it is needed – it just appears automatically as one coherent piece. Sometimes words like "entrenchment" or "ingraining" are used to describe the process by which a form becomes part of a person's internalized lexicon.

We should never underestimate the power of frequency in producing complex behavior. Think of a gymnast performing a balance-beam routine. To most of us, it is almost unbelievable what young, Olympic level gymnasts can do on a 10 cm wide beam. I'm sure I could barely walk the length of one without falling off, yet they can perform handsprings, cartwheels, and many other complex acrobatic moves in an amazing display of grace and balance. What makes this possible? Frequency. Gymnasts practice their moves literally thousands of times in training until every nuance of movement becomes "second nature." A well-trained gymnast doesn't have to think about the contraction of every muscle. Rather, she exercises habituated psycho-motor "routines" called up from unconscious memory as unified wholes, and performs them without contemplation or hesitation.

Speaking a language is something like that. We don't think of it as being quite so amazing as what a gymnast does, simply because everyone does it. Yet, speaking also involves very complex psycho-motor behaviors requiring great precision. Performed by a fluent speaker, these behaviors are executed apparently effortlessly in smooth and unified order. Just as frequency allows people to habitualize complex behaviors such as gymnastics routines, so frequency allows people to habitualize (overlearn, entrench, routinize, or automate) the units and recurring patterns that constitute the lexicon and morphosyntax of a language.

But what kinds of units and patterns are used frequently? There is a one-word answer to this question as well – "usefulness." Think for a moment of the lexicon as a set of tools designed to accomplish particular jobs. A good mechanic is very familiar with his or her tools. The most useful tools in any toolkit are used over and over again to accomplish many different tasks, or perhaps one task that is very common. These are the tools that are the most well-worn, showing signs of use by having worn out handles and dulled ends. They are also the ones that the mechanic knows best, and that therefore can be adapted for use in a number of different tasks. Every toolkit also contains tools that are seldom used. These are the ones that are designed to perform very specific, but possibly less common, tasks. Routines associated with such tools may not be as well entrenched in the mechanic's "lexicon" of regular activities. The mechanic may have to pay more attention to the use of an unfamiliar tool in order to make sure that it accomplishes the intended task; its use may not be "second nature."

A similar pattern occurs in communication. The common units are those that are most useful for expressing the kinds of meanings that people ordinarily need to express. These are the ones that are the easiest to call up from memory. They also tend to show signs of being worn down by constant use and by having unusual or "irregular" morphological properties. Think about it. What are the most useful, frequently used verbs in English? The verbs *go* and *be* should certainly top your list. In addition to being very small (two sounds each), having been worn down by centuries of constant use, they also happen to be the most "irregular" verbs in the language, displaying very odd morphological behavior in comparison to most other verbs:

(4)

	"Regular" pattern	GO	BE
Bare form:	walk	go	be
Past tense:	walked	went	was/were
Present, 3SG:	walks	goes	is
Present, other:	walk	go	am/are
Past participle:	walked	gone	been

The verbs *go* and *be* are extremely frequent in discourse, both because they express very useful concepts that people often need to express, but also because they have been adapted to serve a number of extended functions, principally as auxiliaries (see Chapter 11). Another way that these particular verbs are being adapted to new functions is that both of them can currently be used as quotative verbs, i.e., verbs introducing direct speech:

(5)   "Then he *goes* 'wassup with that?' And I'*m* all 'Thanks a lot!'" (from an Internet blog)

As you can see, *go* and *be* are very useful verbs that show all the signs of wear and tear one would expect of tools that are frequently used. The same is true, though perhaps to a lesser extent, of other common verbs such as *do* and *have*, as well as certain words from other major word classes. There is a growing literature on GRAMMATICALIZATION that discusses this process in great detail from a cross-language perspective (see, e.g., Traugott and Heine 1991).

In addition to individual words, certain assemblies of lexical items, such as *goodbye*, *dog-eat-dog*, or *stirfry* are so useful, and are used so often, that they become entrenched in the collective memory of a speech community as "chunks," i.e., inseparable units, and so effectively become individual words. This process can be diagrammed as follows:

(6)   X+Y ... +N = Z

That is, any number of distinct items combine to form one *lexicalized* unit, Z. The longer a lexicalized assembly exists in a language, and the more frequently it is used, the more likely it is that speakers will "forget" the original pieces that made up the assembly in the first place. This has happened, for example, with the extremely common word *goodbye* (or even just '*bye*). This word was originally a sentence – *May God be with thee*, but currently most English speakers have no concept of the original parts of this utterance. It's absurd to imagine that modern English speakers construct this phrase using the pieces *may*, *god*, *be*, *with*, and *thee*, plus the syntactic patterns of English each time they use it. They simply use it as a unit in their mental lexicon.

Goodbye is an extreme case of lexicalization of a syntactic assembly, but there are many more that are not as far along in the lexicalization process. For example, a compound such as *mainstay* is not as lexicalized as *goodbye*, since it is reasonable to suppose that most English speakers can still recognize that this form consists of a combination of the words *main* and *stay*. However, English speakers don't use this expression only when they refer to a "stay" (a physical prop or brace) that is "main." It currently means any principle part of something, as in the following examples from the British National Corpus (BNC):

(7)   torture ... was the *mainstay* of the Stasi method.
       Surere had mentioned the protection of innocence as the *mainstay* of his creed.
       Americans are the *mainstay* of my business.

While the relation of the parts *main* and *stay* to this usage is fairly obvious, still it is not likely that English speakers unconsciously construct the form *mainstay* from these individual parts each time they use it. In fact, the word *stay* as a noun meaning "prop" or "brace" (one example in the BNC – in a quote from Robert Frost) is far less common than the compound *mainstay* (134 examples in the BNC). The stress pattern on this word also confirms the fact that it is treated as a unit. If it were a noun phrase referring to a "stay" that is "main," both parts would receive word stress – *máin stáy*. In the compound, however, only the first element receives word stress, exactly as one would expect for a two-syllable noun. In Chapter 4, compounding as a morphological process will be discussed in more depth. In this section, the important point is that complex assemblies can become established in the lexicon as units over time, and this is a major way that items enter the lexicon of any language.

In summary, it must be understood that because every language is constantly undergoing natural change, the boundaries of the lexicon are "fuzzy," or "flexible" – forms and assemblies are always subject to varying communicative pressures, and are at various points on the road to lexicalization. Useful assemblies, even quite complex ones like *May God be with thee*, race toward status as lexical items with great speed and energy, while less useful ones, for example *green cow*, are hardly likely ever to become fully lexicalized. Unless someone coins this phrase to describe some new and useful cultural concept (maybe an environment-friendly source of milk?), it is forever destined to be constructed afresh each time someone finds a use for it in a conversation.

Though the boundaries of the lexicon are constantly changing, a reasonable way of deciding whether a form is established as a lexical item or not is to look it up in a good dictionary. Good dictionaries will include entries for well-established expressions like *stirfry*, *dog-eat-dog*, and *domestic partner*, as these are useful terms that are common enough that they have taken on meanings that could not have been predicted based on the meanings of the individual parts. And, after all, the main characteristic of units in the lexicon is that they are particular forms associated with particular meanings.

Lexicalization and second language learning

The notion that complex assemblies can become established as lexical items has profound implications for second language learning. For example, complex expressions like those in (8) are so useful and common that second language learners may profit by treating them almost as individual words, rather than constructing them as needed ("for the nonce") out of the individual pieces. These kinds of structures have been referred to as "power tools" in the second language learning literature (Orwig 2009):

(8) a. Let's take a look at NOUN PHRASE
     b. There's INDEFINITE-NOUN-PHRASE   LOCATIONAL-PREPOSITIONAL-PHRASE
     c. I wanna VERB-PHRASE
     d. NOUN-PHRASE BE gonna VERB-PHRASE

Each of these templates could give rise to expressions such as the following (and an infinite number of others) respectively:

(9) Let's take a look at *another example | the next slide | Mr. Phelps* ...
     There's *ants in the syrup | a monkey wrench on the table* ...
     I wanna *hold your hand | solve this problem | write a chapter* ...
     They're gonna *build a new bridge | offer their condolences* ...

From a second language learner's point of view, such common and useful lexicalized expressions are indeed analogous to power tools for accomplishing the work of becoming proficient in a second language. For example, "I'm looking for –" can be committed to memory in the same way as any vocabulary item, but with a blank left to be filled in by other items, similar to the way a verb might be learned with a blank left for its subject and inflectional information. Then drills can easily be constructed in which different NPs, of increasing complexity, can be inserted in the blank.

Expanding the lexicon

The lexicon of any language, in particular of English, is "open ended" for a couple of reasons. First, as described in Chapter 1, languages routinely BORROW (or "steal" depending on one's perspective) words and other units from other languages. English seems particularly good at this, possibly because most English speakers in the world are (and always have been) multilingual,[3] and so the vocabularies of other languages have always been rich resources for expressing new concepts in English. The fact that English is particularly permeable to such influences is probably due to the history of English as a *lingua franca* for over 1500 years, and the lack of an "English Language Academy" to defend the language against outside influences.

Another way that words can enter the lexicon is by being COINED. Occasionally, entirely new words are simply invented. Even more occasionally, such invented words "catch on" and become a part of the lexicon of at least a large subset of speakers. About the only documented examples of this invention of new words out of nothing are the word *nerd*, which was first used in a children's book by "Dr. Seuss" (Theodore Seuss Geisel) called *If I ran the Zoo* (Seuss 1950), and *googol*, a very large number, coined by a nine year old, Milton Sirotta, in 1938 (American Heritage 2006). More often however, coining refers to new words created out of other words or parts of other words that already exist. Such coinings fall into various categories. Here is a representative sample of some fairly recent additions to the lexicons of many English speakers, categorized according to the type of coining they represent:

> CLIPPINGS are abbreviated versions of useful longer words, usually with a special new sense: *fax* (facsimile), *zine* (magazine), *cords* (corduroy trousers), *detox* (detoxification), *gym* (gymnasium), *gas* (gasoline), *gator* (alligator), *phone* (telephone), *flu* (influenza), *abs* (abdominal muscles), *bike* (bicycle or motorcycle).

> COMPOUNDS consist of two or more words combined into one lexical item to express a new, useful, and specific idea (see Chapter 4 for discussion of compounding as a morphological process): *mallrat, road rage, snail mail, soccer mom, audiophile, date rape, etc.* Compound words can also be "clipped" (see above): *halfcaf* (half caffeinated), *op art* (optical art), *op ed* (opinion+editorial), *sci-fi* (science fiction).

> BLENDS are like compounds, but the words are combined in such a way that one or more syllables of each word are blended, and the result is one word; *Japanimation* (Japanese animation), *fantabulous* (fantastic fabulous), *brunch* (breakfast lunch), *televangelist* (television evangelist), *emoticon* (emotion icon), *screenager* (screen teenager), *blog* (web log).

> ACRONYMS are words consisting of the initial letters of words in a useful phrase: *Imho* (in my humble opinion), *dweeb* (dim-witted eastern-educated bore), *radar* (radio detecting and ranging), *wasp* (white, Anglo-Saxon protestant), *lol* (laughing out loud), and many more.

In addition to these new words that arise out of old words or parts of words (including letters), many coinings simply involve new usages for preexisting words or catchy phrases. Some examples of these include:

> Words: *awesome* (very good), *threads* (clothes), *wheels* (a car), *artsy* (cleverly artistic).

> Phrases: *once-in-a-lifetime* (very rare), *do-or-die* (very important), *go bananas* (react in a highly emotional manner), *basket case* (very mixed up, or crazy state of mind), *beef up* (strengthen), *chat up* (get someone to talk, perhaps about something important, by approaching them in a casual manner), *be on the same page* (have the same presuppositions), etc.

In summary, there is literally no end to the creative ways that people may construct words in English when it suits their conversational goals. Considering the fact that there are so many highly specific contexts and semantic domains in which people communicate, it is not unreasonable to conclude that the lexicon of the English language is potentially infinite in size.

3.4 Classes in the lexicon

Full lexical words and grammatical functors

The biggest division within the lexicon of any language is the distinction between FULL LEXICAL WORDS and GRAMMATICAL FUNCTORS. Full lexical words may be roots, but they also may be complex stems and useful phrases that have become *established* through the process of lexicalization described earlier. The word "functor" is a rather odd term, but it is useful for describing smaller categories of lexical items that include affixes (see Chapter 4), clitics, and certain well-defined classes of free morphemes such as pronouns, prepositions, auxiliaries, conjunctions, and particles.

As you will soon see, most distinctions that linguists make are not absolute but describe the ends of a CONTINUUM, with many intermediate possibilities. This is the case with the distinction between full lexical words and grammatical functors. There are very good examples of full lexical words, and very good examples of grammatical functors, but there are also many examples of items that have some properties of full lexical words and some properties of grammatical functors. This is because every language is in the process of change. As items in the lexicon of a language undergo normal change over time, they often start out as full lexical words and become grammatical functors (rarely the reverse). Since at any given stage of a language there are units at various points on this path, some units may not be easily classified as belonging to one class or the other. Nevertheless, it is useful to try to classify the lexical items of English between full lexical words on the one hand and grammatical functors on the other. First I will present a few examples of grammatical functors and full lexical words, and then give a chart of the characteristics of both groups. Figure 3.2 illustrates the path of historical change from full lexical words to grammatical functors.

Grammatical functors include elements that occur in relatively small sets (or PARADIGMS), such as pronouns (*I, me, you, we, us, she,* etc.), auxiliaries (*be, might,*

Figure 3.2 The diachronic path from full lexical word to grammatical functor

Table 3.1 **A comparison of full lexical words and grammatical functors**

Full lexical words	Grammatical functors
Tend to be larger in form.	Tend to be smaller in form.
Occur in relatively open classes – it is fairly easy to add new members to a class of lexical words, via BORROWING from other languages, innovation of new terms, etc.	Occur in relatively closed classes. It is difficult to add new members to classes of grammatical functors.
Occur in relatively large classes.	Occur in relatively small classes. There are only a few items in each class of grammatical functors.
Tend to have broad and RICH meanings, such as "Alice," "frumious," or "evaluate." Lexical words express many semantic features.	Tend to have specific and narrow meanings, such as "feminine, singular" or "past tense."
Tend to stand on their own as FREE morphemes.	Tend to BIND to other items, i.e., they tend to be CLITICS or affixes (see Chapter 4).
Take PRIMARY WORD STRESS.	Are either always unstressed, or take word stress only for special pragmatic purposes, such as contrast.

should, could, etc.), prepositions (in, on, of, under, etc.) and affixes, such as the past tense -ed, and the plural -s. They also tend to have fewer sounds than full lexical words, and are usually unstressed. Full lexical words, on the other hand, tend to be larger than grammatical functors in that they usually have more sounds, and take their own PRIMARY WORD STRESS. They also belong to larger classes; e.g., there are many more nouns in the lexicon than there are pronouns. This is because it is much easier to add a full lexical word to the vocabulary of any language than it is to add a grammatical morpheme; in other words full lexical words occur in OPEN CLASSES. Some examples of full lexical words in English are *rabbit, fall, open,* and *ramification*. Finally, sometimes it is said that full lexical words have a high degree of SEMANTIC CONTENT, or LEXICAL CONTENT, in comparison to grammatical functors. For example, a word like *rabbit* evokes a rather complex image with many semantic features: long ears, pretty fur, wrinkly nose, quickness, and many more. A pronoun like *she*, on the other hand, evokes exactly four features, some of which are more "grammatical" than semantic, namely 3rd person, singular, feminine, and nominative case. These characteristics of the two general categories of lexical items are summarized in Table 3.1.

Word classes

Within the categories of full lexical words and grammatical functors, there are several distinct "classes" of entries. A WORD CLASS is simply a group of lexemes that have similar sets of morphosyntactic (form), semantic (meaning), and discourse pragmatic (use) properties (see Section 5.1 for a discussion of these three kinds of properties). Entries that possess all the properties that characterize a particular word class are called the PROTOTYPES for that class (Coleman and Kay 1981). However, classes usually contain entries that lack some of the properties, and are therefore less than prototypical examples of the word class. There also may be lexemes that don't seem to fit into any particular word class.

Traditionally, word classes, or "parts of speech," such as nouns, verbs, prepositions, etc., are considered to be classes in the lexicon. They have sometimes been called "lexical classes," or "lexical categories." Recently, however, many linguists have come to question whether word classes, even the major ones – noun, verb, adjective, and adverb – are really lexical classes at all (see, e.g., Hopper and Thompson 1984). Rather, word classes may be categories of positions in syntactic structures. Let's look at some examples of how words may be assigned to word classes because of their use in syntactic structures.

Most people would say that a word like *trash* is a noun. Certainly it can function as a noun in syntactic structures.

(10)   Please take out the *trash.*   (Head of a Object noun phrase)
All this *trash* in the hallway is a disgrace!   (Head of a Subject noun phrase)

However, this form can also function as a verb or an attributive Modifier:

(11)   We *trash*ed our television.   (Transitive verb)
The *trash* truck came today.   (Modifier of a Subject noun)

Looking at this same idea from another perspective, any nonsense word will be understood as a noun when it occurs in the position of a noun in clause structure, and a verb when it occurs in the position of a verb:

(12)   Please pass me the *blick.*   (Noun)
We *blicked* the home team.   (Transitive verb)

Even though there is probably no lexical item *blick* in English, and we have no idea what it might mean, in these contexts we know it can be a noun or a verb. This shows that categories such as noun and verb arise in context, and are not necessarily inherent to individual words.

I once asked a group of students to try to think of nouns in English that can't be used as verbs. It took a while, but looking around the classroom, they eventually came up with *television, door, desk,* and *window.* OK, I agreed; I couldn't imagine a context in which these particular lexemes could be used as verbs. Later, however, I did Internet searches for the forms *televisioned, doored, desked,* and *windowed,* wondering whether there might possibly be uses of these forms as verbs. Sure enough, there are dozens of coherent examples on the Internet. Here are a few:

(13)   You still owe me for the hip replacement from when you *doored* me in New York!"
(zebrameat.com/z2/features/pilney_jackieo.html)

To *door* someone means to open a car door in their path as they are riding a bicycle. This seems to be a fairly common usage that has lots of independent examples on the Internet. Example (14) illustrates two uses of the verb form *televisioned*:

(14) a. The partly *televisioned* national military parade was organised by the Hame military district in the city of Lahti, Finland. (commons.wikimedia. org/wiki/File:NSVT_(2).JPG)

      b. I *televisioned* into ABC last night for the special announcement, checking to see if I am the new "The Bachelor." (humor.about.com/ library/blog.htm)

Most of the examples of this verb are in the past participle, as a synonym for *televised*, i.e., to be broadcast via television, as in example (14a). There are too many independent examples of this usage for it to be a mistake. There are also a few examples of the past tense, as in example (14b). This novel usage of the PHRASAL VERB *to television into X* seems to mean "to tune a television to program X."

Here is a fairly typical example of *desk* used as a verb:

(15) "New York cop *desked* after tasered man dies." *Montreal Gazette*, Nov. 1, 2008.

The verb *to desk* X means "to assign X to a desk job," or "to put X away in a desk." Finally, example (16) illustrates the form *window* used as a verb:

(16) "[This command] returns the shift size used *to window* the incoming speech signal." From cmusphinx.sourceforge.net.

The transitive verb *to window X* apparently is a term understood by computer programmers to mean "to open X in a separate application window."

So lexical vocabulary items in English are notoriously "shifty" in terms of their class membership. As discussed in Chapter 2, this seems to be a general typological feature of English. In most cases speakers seem to have an intuitive sense of what the "basic" word class of an item is, and if that item can function as a member of a different class, the "unusual" or "non-basic" usage may be considered derivative of the basic usage (see Chapter 4 on derivation). However, few studies have tried to objectify speakers' intuitive judgments by, for example, looking at how particular stems are actually used in any of the large English corpora, such as the British National Corpus (BNC) or the Corpus of Contemporary American English (COCA). The fact seems to be that lexical items are forms associated with particular meanings (i.e., they are form–meaning composites), but speakers may use them in any way they find reasonable and useful in the context of actual communication. This fact is consistent with the perspective that views linguistic units as tools that accomplish tasks – most tools designed for a particular task may be used to perform others. For example, a screwdriver may be used as a pry-bar, an ice-pick, or even a "pencil" in the right context (e.g., on a sandy surface). So, word stems can be called upon to express meanings and fill functions that may not be their expected or "normal" usages.

As for grammatical functors, they too may "shift" word class, but apparently not as easily as lexical vocabulary items can. For example, the word *for* is one of the most common prepositions, yet it can be used as a conjunction meaning roughly the same thing as *because*. The following is a conversational example from the BNC:

(17)   it used to be kind of famous, *for* they all, they all came here.

This is an older, respectable use of *for* that is listed in all good dictionaries. However, in the present day it is hardly ever used in conversation, except when quoting well-known texts.[4] In the present day, *for* is mostly used as a preposition.

Words may also shift their usages between major and minor classes. For example, several words can function as conjunctions, a minor word class, and adverbs, a major class:

(18)   I've never seen you *before.*   *before* as adverb.
       Before I leave, I have one thing to say.   *before* as subordinating conjunction.

       They haven't arrived *yet.*   *yet* as adverb.
       she eats nothing, *yet* I never saw her look better   *yet* as coordinating conjunction.

Prepositions and conjunctions may even be used as nouns:

(19)   We left it *behind* the barn.   *behind* as preposition.
       Yeah, shot in the *behind* by an arrow.   *behind* as noun.
       No *ifs*, *ands* or *buts* about it.   *if, and,* and *but* as nouns.

Any good dictionary will list the various uses of multifunctional forms like *for*, *before*, and *behind* as subentries. This is usually easier to do for grammatical functors than for lexical vocabulary, probably because the classes of grammatical functors are more closed and static, and their meanings are relatively fixed and categorical. As mentioned above, lexical vocabulary items have richer (more detailed) semantic content than grammatical functors, and the classes are open to new members. This probably makes them more open to new usages as well, and hence rather "slippery" when it comes to documenting all their common uses in a dictionary.

The point is that word classes are not necessarily given once and for all in the lexicon. It may even be more appropriate for these classes to be thought of as syntactic functions that can be filled by any stem that happens to express a meaning that a speaker considers appropriate in a particular context. While stems do intuitively seem to have basic, or "normal," uses, most stems in the lexicon can function as more than one word class in the crucible of actual language in use.

Having provided a rather extended "disclaimer" concerning the classification of the lexicon into discrete word classes, we are in a position to simply list and briefly describe eight word classes (or parts of speech) that are often proposed for Modern English. The classes of nouns, pronouns, verbs, adjectives, and auxiliaries are only introduced briefly here, since they are described in more detail in Chapters 5, 6, 10, and 11. We also recognize a ninth class, particles, but the syntactic properties of forms that have been called particles are so varied that there is little that can be said of them *as a class*. Therefore, these will not be mentioned here, but rather will be described independently as needed in subsequent chapters. The remaining classes (adverbs, prepositions, and conjunctions) are presented and exemplified in some detail below, since they are not dealt with in specific chapters later in the book. However, discussion of the specific syntactic and semantic functions of prepositions and conjunctions will be postponed until later chapters.

Nouns

The class of NOUNS includes words that typically refer to entities that have clear boundaries and are easily distinguished from their environments, e.g., *tree, king, mausoleum*, etc. These are concepts that tend not to change very much over time, and which can be referred to repeatedly in discourse as the *same thing*. For example, a storyteller may refer to one character in a story as *a queen*. From then on the same character may be freely mentioned, sometimes as *the queen*, other times as *she, the king's wife, the princess' mother, the tyrant*, etc. In context, each of these expressions could be understood as making mention of the queen. Hopper and Thompson (1984) describe this property of prototypical nouns as DISCOURSE MANIPULABILITY. The morphological and syntactic properties of nouns, as well as several subclasses of nouns, such as abstract nouns and mass nouns, and the use of noun phrases in discourse will be discussed in more detail in Chapter 5.

Verbs

The best examples of VERBS are words that describe visible EVENTS that produce changes in the world, e.g., *die, run, break, cook, explode*. The morphosyntactic properties of verbs, as well as several subclasses of verbs, will be discussed in more detail in Chapter 6.

Adjectives

An ADJECTIVE is a word that refers to an attribute, such as color, size, shape, temperament, or other PROPERTY CONCEPTS. When we think of adjectives, most of us think of Modifiers of nouns within noun phrases, such as the following:

(20)   *green leafy* vegetables
         big fat companies

This can be called the ATTRIBUTIVE FUNCTION, and is certainly one of the major functions of adjectives, though syntactic elements of several other categories can also function in this way (see Chapter 10 on Modification).

   Another major function of adjectives is to contribute to the main meaning of a predicate, as in the following examples:

(21)   None of us is *perfect* forever.
         My holiday became *very long*.
         Are you *sick*?
         The salad dressing smells *bad*.

This is sometimes called the PREDICATIVE FUNCTION of adjectives.

   While words of many classes may function as Modifiers (see Chapter 10), English fairly clearly has a grammatically distinct class of adjectives. This is because words that refer strictly to property concepts for the most part have none of the grammatical properties of nouns, verbs, or other major word classes. For example, properties of verbs in English include: (a) the ability to take past tense inflection (22a), and (b) agreement with a 3rd person singular Subject in the present tense (22b). Properties of prototypical nouns include: (c) the ability to take plural marking (22c), and (d) the ability to head noun phrases that take articles, modifiers, and quantifiers (22c) and (22d). Adjectives, like *sick*, have none of these properties (22e through 22h).[5]

(22)   a. He *sang* all evening.   e. *He *sicked* all evening.
         b. She *sings* every morning.   f. *She *sicks* every morning.
         c. We saw thirty-five *patients*.   g. *We saw thirtyfive *sicks*.
         d. The *patient* is sitting on the sofa. h. *The *sick* is sitting on the sofa.

This is good evidence that English has a fairly well defined word class of adjectives.

   The concepts that are expressed by adjectives can be subdivided into the following types of properties:

(23)   AGE (*young, old ...*)
         SPEED (*fast, slow, quick ...*)

VALUE (*good, bad ...*)
HUMAN PROPENSITY (*jealous, happy, clever, wary ...*)
DIMENSION (*big, little, tall, short, long ...*)
SHAPE (*round, square ...*)
COLOR (*black, white, red ...*)
PHYSICAL CHARACTERISTICS (*hard, heavy, smooth ...*)
NATIONAL ORIGIN (*Japanese, Hungarian, English ...*)

We will have much more to discuss about the general function of Modification, including subtypes of adjectives, in Chapter 10.

Adverbs

Any full lexical word that isn't clearly a noun, a verb, or an adjective is often considered to be an ADVERB. Semantically, forms that have been called adverbs cover an extremely wide range of concepts, and they have correspondingly varied syntactic properties. For this reason they cannot be identified as a group in terms of individuation or any other well-defined semantic parameter. Also, sometimes adverbs function on the clause or discourse level, i.e., their semantic effect (or SCOPE) is relevant to entire clauses or even larger units rather than just to phrases or individual words (see Chapter 10 on Modification at different levels of structure). There is no separate chapter on adverbs in this book, partly because there is no *one thing* that unites all the various types of words that have been called adverbs. Rather, they represent a very disparate conglomeration of full lexical words, and even some particles and conjunctions with very different semantic, morphosyntactic, and discourse pragmatic properties. The following are examples of various semantic types of adverbs in a number of contexts.

(24)   MANNER ADVERBS (the way in which some activity is carried out):
He left for work five minutes later than he *normally* did.
And if only one thing had happened *differently* ...
They *quickly* prepared the papers and left.
I *eagerly* await her arrival.

(25)   TIME ADVERBS (the time when some activity happens, or the frequency with which it happens):
That was *then*, this is *now*.
Yesterday, love was such an easy game to play.
We'll see each other *tomorrow*.
They *just* finished running the Boston marathon.
It is *frequently* easier to be honest when you have nothing to lose.
Arrogance and self-awareness *seldom* go hand in hand.

(26) EXTENT ADVERBS (the degree to which some variable quality is asserted):
I can *hardly* hear.
They didn't *fully* understand.
I believe whatever doesn't kill you, *simply* makes you stronger.
The driver was *momentarily* distracted.
The paper's *slightly* psychic.
Your vital signs indicate you're being *somewhat* less than honest.
We heard a *very* large crash.
He's *just* a high-schooler.
It's *about* three feet long.

(27) EPISTEMIC ADVERBS (how likely or possible some situation may be, or how the speaker obtained the information):
I *certainly* hope not.
In your last house you *clearly* had a level of security that I'm not used to.
Evidently Julliard has heard of you.
Apparently she got one step ahead of us.
Mr. Bregman, you are *possibly* the stupidest criminal I have ever met.
A man in your position would *surely* have acquired life insurance.
He was *definitely* amusing to hang out with.

(28) LOCATION ADVERBS (the place where a situation occurs):
It is *here* that alternative approaches are discussed and weighted.
Tell me about being *over there*, gramps.

(29) HEDGING ADVERBS (disclaimers of responsibility):
This woman *sort of* knows my situation.
I'd eat, *like*, a piece of bread all day.
And once you start having children . . . *I mean*, 13-year-old twin girls can be difficult.
We were talking *kind of fairly* casually about that . . .

A speaker may use a hedging adverb when making a guess, clarifying, or just giving a general sense of some situation, rather that asserting something as definite fact. Hedging adverbs "protect" the speaker from possible charges of uttering false information.

As mentioned above, nouns, verbs, adjectives, and adverbs are together sometimes referred to as the major word classes. This is because they are large and open classes of full lexical words. The other four or five classes are closed, relatively small, and consist of grammatical functors (see above). For this reason they are sometimes called "minor" classes. This does not mean they are unimportant, but only that they tend to have fewer members than the major word classes, they tend to be "smaller" in every way, and they are not as open to new members as the major word classes are.

Auxiliaries

Auxiliaries are sometimes considered to be a subclass of verbs. Indeed, some of them (*be*, *have*, *do*, *need*, and *dare*) can also function as main lexical verbs. The other auxiliaries do not have many properties of lexical verbs at all, and it is usually clear when a given form is functioning as an auxiliary or a lexical verb. Therefore, when one form, e.g., *do*, functions sometimes as an auxiliary and other times as a lexical verb, this can be considered an instance of "class shifting," as described above. We do not say, for example, that conjunctions are a subtype of prepositions because some forms, e.g., *for*, *as*, and *except* can function in both roles. Similarly, it is not necessary to consider auxiliaries to be a subclass of verbs simply because certain auxiliaries can also be used as full lexical verbs. Auxiliaries constitute a closed, rather small set of grammatical functors that play a very key role in English syntax. All English language professionals and second language learners will do well to study auxiliaries carefully, and attempt to develop an intuitive sense of how they are distinct from lexical verbs, and from one another. We will have a lot more to discuss about the types and syntactic properties of auxiliaries in Chapter 11. It is worth emphasizing that auxiliaries are the "pivot point" of English clausal syntax, and in many ways are the key to understanding English grammar.

Prepositions

Prepositions are grammatical functors that precede determined noun phrases (DPs)[6] to specify the SEMANTIC ROLE of the DP to the rest of the clause. They include words like *above*, *at*, *in*, *of*, *with*, *around*, *on*, *under*, *beside*, *through*, *inside*, *before*, and *opposite*. Several kinds of semantic roles are expressed by prepositions, many of which are described in Chapter 6. In general, the syntactic function of prepositional phrases is OBLIQUE. Chapter 7 discusses the distinction between semantic roles and syntactic functions in some detail. Some prepositions are made up of more than one piece, including *out of*, *by means of*, *in spite of*, *instead of*, *up to*, *up against*, *on top of*, *upon*, etc. Many prepositions also function as post-verbal particles, as in *get in*, *pick up*, *switch off*. These PHRASAL VERBS are discussed in more detail in Chapter 6.

Pronouns

Pronouns are ANAPHORIC words, which means that they are tools that speakers use to refer to (or "mention") participants and props on the discourse stage. They are sometimes treated as a special subclass of nouns, because pronouns distribute like DPs (see Chapter 7) in phrases, clauses, and discourses. The various types of pronouns and their functions are discussed in Chapter 5 on participant reference.

Conjunctions

Conjunctions are grammatical functors that serve to connect words, phrases, or clauses to form complex constructions. Subtypes of conjunctions include the following:

- COORDINATING CONJUNCTIONS conjoin two units that are "equal" in terms of their syntactic status, i.e., they must be of the same word class or PHRASAL CATEGORY, and they must have the same syntactic function (see Chapter 7 on syntactic functions). There are about six words that can function as coordinating conjunctions in CSE. These are: *and, but, or, for, then*, and *yet*. There are also three or four complex coordinating conjunctions, *either ... or, neither ... nor, and yet*, and *and then*. Coordinating conjunctions always occur in between the two structures that are conjoined (see the examples below).

- SUBORDINATING CONJUNCTIONS conjoin two units that may have distinct syntactic or discourse functions. The unit that follows a subordinating conjunction is DEPENDENT in some way on the other unit (dependency is discussed in more detail in Chapter 14). Subordinating conjunctions include: *after, because, although, if, before, since, though, unless, when, now that, even though, only if, while, as, whereas, whether or not, since, in order that, while, even if, until, so, in case*, etc.

In the following examples, the conjunctions are in italics, and the syntactic categories that they conjoin are indicated to the right:

(30) Coordinating conjunctions joining words:

The section on health *and* safety could be quite large.	Nouns
... femininity, innocence *and yet* sensuality.	
Future tapes will provide information on wine *and then* meat.	
neither they *nor* we have got any right to be content.	Pronouns
She can *neither* walk *nor* talk.	Verbs
we'll just kick back *and* eat *and* eat.	
common, *but* simple design problems ...	Adjectives
It turned blue *then* black.	
What the commissioner alleges is *neither* known *nor* admitted.	
It's *either* now *or* never.	Adverbs
Head north-east *then* east to enter a small wood.	
You'll be chauffeur-driven to *and* from Birmingham.	Prepositions

(31) Coordinating conjunctions joining phrases:

a handsome boy *and* lovely girl	NPs
that's *either* two years *or* a year between them.	DPs
It was so near, *yet* so far.	AdjPs
She seldom barked *but* would often growl.	IPs
She would bark furiously *and* growl ferociously.	VPs
They're either in the cupboard *or* under the sink.	PPs

(32)   Coordinating conjunctions joining clauses:
You can't live with them, *and yet* they're everywhere.
Keep quiet *or* you'll be shot.
These are the Oscars *and* this is my dream.

(33)   Subordinating conjunctions joining non-clausal elements (not common):
day *after* day, month *after* month, year *after* year ...
The congress is seen as a sort of unfortunate *if* necessary check and control on the presidency.

(34)   Subordinating conjunctions joining clauses:
The shape and style only evolves *as* the metal is worked.
Because these are biologically active compounds, they don't follow the simple chemical processes ...
If I'm with you, I'm in trouble.
Listen, *while* you're grabbing the Rambaldi manuscript, *if* you happen to see a sandwich ...
We're not gonna join any men's club *unless* there's like, chicks in it.
While everyone else was agin', I was gettin' younger ...
When you were my age, you were sick.
So tell me, *after* defending this country for 150 years and four wars, how would you like to really serve your country?

3.5   Conclusion: the lexicon and language learning

Anyone who learns a second language spends a great deal of time working on vocabulary. However, memorizing lists of vocabulary items (or piles of vocabulary cards) out of context is of little value in developing one's personal lexicon of a language. Packing words into the mind by brute force in this way is like trying to become a master mechanic by amassing a huge collection of tools. Yes, a mechanic needs tools, but the way to become proficient with those tools is to practice using them to accomplish real work. When someone is learning to be a mechanic he or she uses only a few tools at a time. The apprentice mechanic becomes proficient with a few tools used to accomplish relatively simple and useful tasks before moving on to attempt more difficult tasks with more complex and more specialized tools. Just having the tools in your toolbox does not guarantee that you know how to use them any more than having a book on your bookshelf guarantees you understand the content of that book. You have to read the book in order to learn its content, and you have to use a word for it to become a part of your internal lexicon.

The main idea to be gleaned from a linguistic perspective on the lexicon of a language is that items are committed to the lexicon to the extent that they are useful and frequent in actual communication. We learn a vocabulary item by needing it often and using it appropriately. This is as true for syntactic structures as it is for individual words. The way this happens in a second language classroom is through what are sometimes known as "fluency building" activities (see, e.g., Celce-Murcia *et al.* 1996:290). These are activities which attempt to replicate actual communication situations as closely as possible within the constraints of a second language classroom.

My rather audacious opinion is that a second language is not really a classroom subject – no one ever learned to speak a language by reading a book or taking a class. A second language is learned by doing, similar to riding a bicycle or skiing. If you want to learn to ride a bicycle, you don't check out a book from the library! You get on a bike, you fall down a few times, but you keep trying until you can keep your balance. You may be wobbly at first, but if you work hard enough you can start to use your bicycle to accomplish actual work, like getting to class on time. While learning a second language is not really a classroom subject, I will say that a second language class can be useful as a way of "priming the pump" for second language learning. And I suppose there are classes in how to ride a bicycle as well – but the *best* classes would be those that give you lots of practice! To return to an earlier metaphor, a few tools are needed in order to get started in the process of becoming a master mechanic. Similarly, brute memorization of a few words and structures at a time may be helpful in giving SLLs something to build their emerging fluency on. However, appropriate use of those words and other tools should become well habitualized before additional, more complex tools are added to the student's repertoire of usable linguistic units. A second language classroom, therefore, can be useful to the extent that it can be thought of as a "hothouse" for fluency building. An hour of class is an intense time of focus on particular structures, both learning new structures and beginning to incorporate those structures into the usable lexicon through fluency building activities. However, it can never be a substitute for using the language to accomplish actual communicative work in real contexts.

Summary

Traditionally, the lexicon of a language is equated with vocabulary. Most linguistic approaches consider the lexicon to be a storehouse of "raw materials" for constructing words, phrases, and clauses. A continuum exists between "narrow" and "broad" theoretical approaches to the lexicon. In a narrow view, the lexicon is distinct from other components or "modules" of linguistic knowledge, such as morphology and syntax. In a broad view, all linguistic knowledge, including knowledge of conventionalized morphological and syntactic structures, is stored in the same way; therefore there is no necessary distinction between the lexicon and other kinds of linguistic knowledge. The approach taken in this book is a rather broad view in which the boundaries of the lexicon are quite "flexible." There are very good examples of lexical categories and lexical processes, and there are very good examples of morphosyntactic patterns, but there also may be many cases that fall somewhere in between. The conceptual distinction between "lexicon" and "morphosyntax" is useful for understanding much of the theoretical literature, and for outlining lessons in grammar.

The structure of the lexicon is discussed in Section 3.4. The major categorial distinction is between full lexical words and grammatical functors. Within each of these large categories, there are subcategories known as word classes. Under full lexical words are the major word classes:

- Nouns
- Verbs
- Adjectives
- Adverbs

Under the heading of grammatical functors the following word classes fall:

- Auxiliaries
- Prepositions
- Pronouns
- Conjunctions

Nouns, verbs, adjectives, auxiliaries, and pronouns are only mentioned briefly, as they are dealt with in more depth in subsequent chapters (nouns and pronouns in Chapter 5, verbs in Chapter 6, adjectives in Chapter 10, and auxiliaries in Chapter 11). The other classes, adverbs, prepositions, and conjunctions are described in some detail in this chapter. A ninth class, particles, is mentioned but not discussed, as there are very few properties that characterize particles *as a class*. Rather, individual particles are mentioned and discussed as they arise in the course of discussion in later chapters.

Finally, a section on the lexicon and language learning discusses the importance of focusing on lexical learning through fluency-building exercises in ESL and EFL classrooms.

FURTHER READING

The FrameNet lexical database (http://framenet.icsi.berkeley.edu/) is an excellent online resource for the lexicon of English. It is based on frame semantics and supported by evidence from English as it is actually used. As of January 2010, this database contains more than 12,000 annotated lexical entries from all word classes. Broad views of the lexicon are discussed in the extensive Cognitive Grammar literature, notably Langacker (1987, 1991, 1995, 2008). Other extreme broad views may be found in Construction Grammar (Croft 2002) and Head Driven Phrase Structure Grammar (Sag *et al.* 2003). Extreme narrow views of the lexicon can be found in recent versions of Generative Grammar (Radford 2004). Lexical Functional Grammar (Bresnan 2001) is a good example of an intermediate approach.

Exercises

1. Find a coherent English paragraph of approximately 150 words on the Internet, and print it out double spaced. Underline all the full lexical words, and circle the grammatical functors in the paragraph. Describe any problems that you encounter as you make your decisions.

2. In Chapter 3, the expressions *green cow*, *domestic partner*, *mainstay*, and *goodbye* are given as examples of degrees of lexicalization: *green cow* is not lexicalized at all, *domestic partner* is somewhat lexicalized, *mainstay* is very lexicalized, while *goodbye* is extremely lexicalized. The following English expressions represent different degrees of lexicalization. Arrange them on a scale from least to most lexicalized, and give the reasons for the arrangement you propose. A good dictionary may be helpful as you solve this exercise. Note: There may be more than one "correct" solution. The main part of the exercise is the reasons you give for putting these expressions in a particular order.

   a. alphabet
   b. Santa Claus
   c. tumble weed
   d. corn bread
   e. o'clock
   f. elephant garlic
   g. portable patio furniture
   h. high school
   i. ATM
   j. vis-à-vis

3. How do you think the following words entered the lexicon of English? They may be derived from more basic roots and affixes, borrowed from other languages, or they may have been "coined." If a word is a coining, indicate the type of coining as described in Chapter 3, and give the source if possible. Try to determine your answer before you look the words up in a dictionary, though a good dictionary will be necessary for some of the words.

   Example: diesel   This is a coining based on the last name of the inventor of the "Diesel" engine.

   a. chic
   b. savvy
   c. to text
   d. crap
   e. jumbo
   f. thingy
   g. polythene
   h. van
   i. jogathon
   j. sandwich
   k. to SMS
   l. hullabaloo
   m. the chunnel
   n. to coin (a word)
   o. dyslexia
   p. xerox
   q. guestimate
   r. scuba
   s. Japan-gate
   t. britcom
   u. psycho
   v. walkie-talkie
   w. bonfire
   x. nostril

4 Morphology – the shapes of words

I ascribe a basic importance to the phenomenon of language ... To speak
means to be in a position to use a certain syntax, to grasp the morphology
of this or that language, but it means above all to assume a culture,
to support the weight of a civilization.

Frantz Fanon (1952)

Morphology in linguistics is all about the shapes of words. Every language has certain consistent patterns by which the shapes of words can be adjusted to express ideas. In this chapter we will discuss the word structure of Modern English, beginning with definitions of some basic concepts in morphology, and how they apply to English. Following this, the distinction between derivation and inflection will be outlined, and a brief overview of derivational categories in English presented. Inflectional categories are discussed in more detail in the discussions of nouns, verbs, and auxiliaries in Chapters 5, 6, and 11.

4.1 Some basic concepts in morphology

The first term that needs to be defined in any discussion of morphology is the notion of WORD. What is a word? This question is not as easy to answer as it might seem at first. See Dixon and Aikhenvald (2002) for an in-depth, cross-linguistic approach to this question. One possible definition of a word is "the smallest structural piece that can be surrounded by pauses." In practice, however, this definition quickly breaks down. For example, pauses may occur between any two syllables, whether we intuitively think of them as two words or not. Imagine someone being asked to pronounce the sentence *his emotional response is understandable* very slowly. Pauses may occur in any number of places (indicated by /):

(1) a. / his / emotional / response / is / understandable /
    b. / his / emo / tional / response / isun / derstand / able /
    c. / his / e / mo / tion / al / re / sponse / is / un / der / stand / a / ble /

While (1a) may seem intuitively more "natural" than (1b), and (1b) more reasonable than (1c), still the judgments are subjective. There is nothing ungrammatical or dysfunctional about (1b) or (1c). Therefore, this definition does not provide a truly objective way of identifying words.

Another characteristic that helps in the definition of word for English is the fact that English has a well-defined STRESS SYSTEM. As mentioned in Chapter 3, full lexical words all have one PRIMARY WORD STRESS. That is, one syllable is pronounced with slightly higher pitch and greater volume than the others (in the following examples, primary word stress is indicated with an acute accent over a vowel letter):

(2) **One syllable words**   **Two syllable words**
    spéak   básic   ascríbe
    tíme   lánguage   assúme
    wáits   cértain   suppórt

In addition, full lexical words with more than two syllables often have a SECONDARY WORD STRESS (in the following examples, secondary word stress is indicated with a grave accent over a vowel letter):

(3) **Three syllable words**   **Longer words**
    áptitùde   phenómenòn
    stímulàte   morphólogỳ
    ádvertìze   cìvilizátion

The stress patterns of English are described in any good introduction to English phonetics, phonology, or pronunciation (see, e.g., Celce-Murcia *et al.* 1996:131ff.). Even grammatical particles like pronouns, auxiliaries, and prepositions can take stress if they are being contrasted with something else. In the following examples contrastive stress, which is generally stronger than ordinary word stress, is indicated by capital letters:

(4) She put the book ON the table, not UNder it.
    THEY will fail, while WE succeed.
    We WILL reach our goal.

The ability to take primary word stress or contrastive stress is a property that is almost impossible for most affixes (a cover term for prefixes and suffixes); though of course this isn't entirely true either, since speakers may "bend" their language in any way they want to if it suits their communicative needs. Intonation is one respect in which any language is quite "bendable":

(5) ?He printED the documents, not WILL print them.
    The fish is flopPY, not flopPING. (Attested in a recent personal conversation.)

So probably the best way of defining a word for English is the smallest unit of language that can be surrounded by pauses and can take primary stress. This definition does have some problems, as we will see in particular when we discuss compounding in Section 4.2, but will work well for us most of the time.

It is important to note that the writing system does not directly give us evidence for words or the boundaries between words. As mentioned in the Introduction, this book treats English as primarily a spoken phenomenon. The writing system can be useful for generating hypotheses, confirming independently verified hypotheses, or calling others into question, but the writing system does not directly constitute evidence for or against linguistic analyses.

Next, we need to define the components of words, known as MORPHEMES. In linguistics, the classic definition of a morpheme is a minimal structural shape or piece that expresses meaning. Some words consist of just one morpheme. For example, the word *dog* cannot be divided into smaller meaningful pieces (e.g., the *d-* at the beginning does not itself express a meaning). Therefore *dog* is a morpheme – a minimal shape. Some words, on the other hand, are made up of more than one morpheme. The word *dogs*, for example, consists of two morphemes: *dog*, which expresses the main lexical meaning of the word, and *-s*, a grammatical morpheme which expresses the meaning of plurality (more than one).

For English, the definition of a morpheme as the "minimal structural piece that expresses meaning" works well most of the time. However, there are some morphemes that don't fit this definition exactly. These are morpheme types that we will call STEM CHANGE and STRESS SHIFT, and will be described in detail in the following section.

4.2   Types of morphemes

A FREE MORPHEME is a minimal shape that can be used in discourse with no other forms attached to it. For example, the form *flex*, as in *flex your muscle*, is a fully pronounceable and usable word on its own. Most roots in English (see below) are free morphemes. A BOUND MORPHEME is a morpheme that must be attached to some other morpheme in order to be used naturally in discourse. Bound morphemes can be ROOTS, AFFIXES, or CLITICS.

A ROOT is a morpheme that expresses the basic lexical meaning of a word, and *cannot be further divided* into smaller pieces. Roots are the only morphemes in English that are subdivided into free and bound subtypes. FREE ROOTS are those that have a pronounceable and meaningful "bare form," i.e., a form that has no other morphemes attached to it (like *flex* or *dog*). A BOUND ROOT is a root that has no pronounceable and meaningful "bare form" – another morpheme is required in order for it to be a fully understandable word. For example, the form *struct* in

Table 4.1 **Free and bound Latinate roots**

sect	form	duce	fer	spect
resect	reform	reduce	refer	respect
transect	transform	transduce	transfer	transpicuous
insect	inform	induce	infer	inspect
	deform	deduce	defer	despicable
prosect		produce	proffer	prospect
		introduce		introspect
section	formation	conduction		inspection
		seduce		suspect
				spectator

English is a root because it expresses the basic meaning of many words and cannot be divided into smaller meaningful parts. However, because it cannot be used in discourse without a prefix and/or a suffix being added to it, as in *construct*, *structure*, and *destruction*, it is a bound root.

Struct is an example of a root that descends from Latin. There are many such bound roots in Modern English, simply because so much of the vocabulary, particularly in literary, religious, technical, and scientific domains, comes from Latin. Sometimes it is difficult or impossible to say whether a given form qualifies as a root in Modern English or whether it is just a relic from an earlier time. If it were a "live" root for Modern English speakers, we would expect it to have certain characteristics:

1. Reasonably competent English speakers should be able to infer, i.e., guess with evidence, the meanings of new words constructed using the root plus common derivational affixes (see below for a discussion of derivation vs. inflection).
2. English speakers should be able to infer the general meaning of the root itself.

For example, consider the words in Table 4.1. Each column represents words based on a particular Latin root. Can you infer what the meanings of the five roots are just based on the meanings of the complex English words? Check your answers in this endnote.[1] *Sect* and *form* are free roots in English, so competent speakers and hearers can fairly confidently assign meanings to these roots, and in some cases each of the complex forms, even if they have never heard them before. However, the other three roots, *duce*, *fer*, and *spect*, are all bound roots, and although they can appear with some of the same prefixes and suffixes as do *sect* and *form*, the meaning relationships among the various forms are not at all straightforward. If you do not know Latin, it is probably impossible to guess the meaning of *duce*, for example, just given the meanings of the eight English words in column 3. Similarly, even if you know the English words *sect* and *form*, you probably couldn't guess the meanings of *insect, prosect,* and *inform* if you had never learned them individually. You could construct them from their parts, but you could not be sure that you understood the standard meaning in Modern English. For this reason it is doubtful whether *duce, fer,* and *spect* can be thought of as Modern English roots at all. Rather they are Latin roots, many forms of which have descended into Modern English already assembled into complex words. Those complex words have undergone natural semantic and phonological shifts over the years, such that most current speakers (except those who have studied Latin) have lost track of what the original roots might have meant.

There are other bound roots in English that are not descended from Latin (or Greek). These include *huckle-*, as in *huckleberry; cran,* as in *cranberry; dreg*; and the noun *clothe* (as in *clothes*).[2] The first two only occur compounded with *berry* and in certain family names (*Huckleby* and *Cranston,* for example), while the last two appear most often with the plural *-s* ending, though they both occasionally appear in the singular:

(6) So Jay drifted next door for her *dregs* of brandy. (101 BNC examples)
      His main companion is the pathetic *dreg* of society, Ratso Rizzo. (4 BNC examples)
      My *clothes* have always stayed on except when I have a bath, (6949 BNC examples)
      Without his fedora his hairline was receding, and the *clothe* was wrong on him (2 BNC examples)
      There's only one *clo* in the dryer! (heard spoken by a 5-year-old child – 0 BNC examples)

The use of *clothe* or *clo* as singular forms is obviously a BACKFORMATION from *clothes*, pronounced in relaxed speech as [kloᵒz]. Similarly, *dreg* may be backformed from *dregs*. Prototypically, *dregs* refers to the residue at the bottom of a container of liquid after the liquid itself has been poured off. It is a negative term referring to the least desirable part of the liquid. The expression *dregs of society* is a metaphorical extension of this basic meaning, referring roughly to "undesirable people left behind by the mainstream of society." It is a fairly simple logical step, then, to refer to one such person as a "dreg of society."

Affixes in English can be PREFIXES, SUFFIXES, and one SUPRAFIX. A prefix is a meaningful part of a word that is added to the beginning of a root. For example, the *un-* part of *unflex* is a prefix. It changes the verb *flex* into a different verb that means the opposite of *flex*. A suffix is a meaningful part of a word that is added to the end of a root. For example, the *-ible* part of *flexible* is a suffix. It changes the verb *flex* into an adjective that means something like "having the ability to flex."

A suprafix is a regular morphological process that does not directly involve consonants and vowels, but simply adjusts the shapes of words by changing some

Table 4.2 **A few noun–verb pairs that illustrate "stress shift"**

Noun form	Verb form
cónflict	conflíct
cónvert	convért
cráckdown	crack dówn
désert	desért
énvelope	envélop
fóllowthrough	follow thróugh
hándout	hand óut
íncrease	incréase
íntercept	intercépt
ínterchange	interchánge
íntrovert	introvért
óverhang	overháng
óverride	overríde
pérmit	permít
présent	presént
próduce	prodúce
próject	projéct
récord	recórd
réject	rejéct
úndercut	undercút
úpset	upsét

AUTOSEGMENTAL feature such as pitch, tone, or stress. There is only one suprafix in English, and this is a process that involves a shift in stress. This morphological pattern in English distinguishes certain noun forms of some multisyllabic verbs. The meaning of the noun is usually something like "a product that results from the action described by the verb," though there is quite a bit of variability and idiosyncrasy. The structural pattern is easily stated as follows:

(7)   Word stress on the verb shifts to the first syllable of the noun form.

Table 4.2 illustrates some of the words and phrasal verbs that follow this pattern. Since English spelling does not indicate stress, stress marks are added to the examples in Table 4.2.

There are dozens of pairs of forms like those in Table 4.2; however, the process does not apply to all multisyllabic verbs. In particular, verbs that don't naturally result in a "product" mostly don't fall into this category. Some that come to mind include *include, infer, confer, remain,* and many others. Even some verbs that do logically result in some kind of product, such as *review*, don't fall into this category – the product of an act of reviewing can be described as a *reviéw*, as in *book reviéw*. If *review* were a verb that underwent stress shift, the noun form would be *réview, with stress on the first syllable. So, while this is a regular and consistent pattern, it is not totally productive.

Along with this stress shift, certain vowel quality changes also occur. In particular, VOWEL REDUCTION occurs in unstressed syllables. A few of these pairs are given in example 8 in phonetic transcription to illustrate this point:

(8) conflíct [kʰənflíkt]   cónflict [kʰánflɪkt]
     rejéct   [ɹidʒékt]   réject   [ɹíʲdʒɛkt]

Notice that the vowel in the first syllable of these words is pronounced slightly differently when it is unstressed. The first vowel in *conflict* is pronounced [a] when stressed, and schwa [ə] when unstressed. The first vowel in *reject* is pronounced [íʲ] when stressed, and [i] when unstressed. These vowel variations are consistent with the regular pronunciation patterns for stressed and unstressed syllables throughout the language (see, e.g., Celce-Murcia *et al.* 1996:109 for a clear discussion of vowel reduction in English), and are therefore a consequence of the stress shift. They do not of themselves constitute the morphological process that expresses the difference between these nouns and verbs. Furthermore, the stress shift itself reflects the fact that nouns and verbs generally follow different stress patterns in English. These stress patterns are quite complex, and full of "exceptions." Nevertheless, English speakers do seem to follow different "rules" when stressing nouns vs. verbs in general – not only for pairs such as those illustrated in Table 4.2.

Clitics are grammatical functors (see Chapter 3) that attach phonologically to some other word, but which distribute more freely than prefixes or suffixes. The word a clitic attaches to is known as its HOST. For example, the articles *a* and *the* are clitics because they normally, unless stressed for special emphatic purposes, attach phonologically to whatever word that follows. This is evident by the stress pattern and certain pronunciation rules that cross the boundary between the article and the host that follows, but which don't cross boundaries between separate words. Consider the phonetic transcriptions of the English phrases below:

(9) a. [ðiʲǽpl̩]   'the apple'
     b. [ðədɔ́g]   'the dog'

First, these expressions normally follow the stress pattern of single words, taking only one stress. Second, the vowel of *the* is fully pronounced as [íʲ] when appearing before a vowel-initial word (9a) and reduced to schwa [ə] when appearing before a consonant-initial word (9b). Furthermore, the article *a* takes a final [n] when appearing before a vowel, and takes no [n], but instead reduces to [ə], when appearing before a consonant:

(10) a. [ənǽpl̩]   'an apple'
      b. [ədɔ́g]   'a dog'

These processes do not cross boundaries between separate words:

(11)   [géˢlə ǽpɬ]   'Gala apple'   Not: *[géˢlənǽpɬ]   '*galan apple'
        [síli dɔ́g]   'silly dog'   Not: *[sílədɔ̀g]   '*silla dog'

Therefore, we can conclude that *a* and *the* CLITICIZE, or phonologically attach to the word that follows. Notice that the writing system does not reflect this linguistic reality. For good reasons these clitics are written as though they are separate words. However, from a linguistic perspective they are clearly attached. What makes them clitics, rather than prefixes, is the fact that they function at the phrase level, i.e., they attach to the beginning of a noun phrase rather than simply to a noun (see Chapter 7 on phrase structure). As such, their host is whatever word happens to come first in the noun phrase, regardless of its word class:

(12)   the dog   Cliticized to the Head noun
        the big dog   Cliticized to a Modifier
        the two big dogs   Cliticized to a numeral
        the very big dog   Cliticized to an adverb

Because the articles cliticize to the beginning (the left side in writing) of their hosts, they can be called PROCLITICS. One additional piece of evidence that the indefinite article forms a word with the host that follows is the case of the indefinite determiner *another*. This word is transparently constructed of the indefinite article plus the post-determiner *other*. When the quantifier *whole* is added to this complex, the result is often to break *another* before the *n*:

(13)   It opens up *a whole nother* list of people. (From a television interview)
        Which is *a whole nother* story. (From a magazine article)

Speakers of British English will be comforted to know that there are no examples of this usage in the BNC. However, there are 14 examples in the COCA – 8 in the spoken corpus and 6 in the written corpus. This is in comparison to about 350 examples in the COCA of *a whole other*. We can conclude that this is primarily an American English phenomenon, but that, counter to common assertions, it is not at all limited to the spoken language.

Another interesting illustration of the difference between clitics and affixes is the case of the genitive -*'s* vs. the plural -*s*. These forms are usually pronounced the same (though see below for some variation), but have very different functions and different morphological behaviors. The -*'s* ending can be described as a clitic, because, like *a* and *the*, it functions at the phrase level, and therefore attaches to a host of any word class that happens to occur at the end of a genitive noun phrase. The difference between -*'s* and the articles is that -*'s* is an ENCLITIC – it follows its host:[3]

(14)   the queen's crown   Cliticized to the Head of a genitive DP
                                       (*the queen*).

       the queen of England's crown   Cliticized to the Object of a modifying
                                       prepositional phrase.

       the queen who reign's crown   Cliticized to a verb.
       the queen I think highly of's crown   Cliticized to a preposition/particle.

The plural -*s*, on the other hand, is a suffix. It always appears on the Head of the plural noun phrase:

(15)   the queens
       the queens of England
       the queens who reign
       the queens I think highly of

Another respect in which genitive -'*s* and plural -*s* differ structurally is in the way they affect the pronunciation of certain roots. In most cases, these two bound morphemes have the same set of ALLOMORPHS (variant pronunciations), conditioned by the same phonological contexts:

(16)   After a vowel or voiced,   Genitive   Plural
       non-sibilant consonant,
       the pronunciation is [-z]:   [voᵂlvoᵂz] 'Volvo's'   [voᵂlvoᵂz] 'Volvos'
                                      [dɔgz]   'dog's'   [dɔgz]   'dogs'
                                      [tʰʲiʧɚz]   'teacher's' [tʰʲiʧɚz]   'teachers'
                                      [wɪŋz]   'wing's'   [wɪŋz]   'wings'

       After voiceless stop
       consonants, the
       pronunciation is [-s]:   [kʰæts]   'cat's'   [kʰæts]   'cats'
                                      [dɛsks]   'desk's'   [dɛsks]   'desks'

       After sibilant consonants,
       the pronunciation is [-ɨz]:[4] [wáʧɨz]   'watch's'   [wáʧɨz]   'watches'
                                      [búʃɨz]   'bush's'   [búʃɨz]   'bushes'
                                      [kʰɨsɨz]   'kiss's'   [kʰɨsɨz]   'kisses'
                                      [wéʤɨz]   'wedge's'   [wéʤɨz]   'wedges'

The cases which distinguish -'*s* from -*s* are when the singular form ends in a voiceless *f* [f] or *th* [θ] sound. For many such words, the word-final sound remains voiceless in the genitive case but may become voiced in the plural:

(17)   Genitive   Plural   Proportion in BNC[5]
       'wife' [waʲf]   'wife's' [waʲfs] 'wives' [waʲvz]   1867/1   V/F
       'half' [hæf]   'half's' [hæfs]   'halves' [hævz]   349/11   V/F
       'roof' [ɹuᵂf]   'roof's' [ɹuᵂfs] 'rooves' [ɹuᵂvz]   5/658   V/F

'truth' [tʰɹuᵂθ] 'truth's' [tʰɹuᵂθs] 'truths' [tʰɹuᵂðz]
'path' [pʰæθ]   'path's'   [pʰæθs]   'paths'   [pʰæðz]
'oath' [oᵂθ]   'oath's'   [oᵂθs]   'oaths'   [oᵂðz]

This is yet another, albeit small, piece of evidence that the genitive -'s is a different kind of morpheme than the plural -s. This evidence is consistent with the hypothesis that -'s is a phrase-level clitic, while -s is an inflectional suffix.

The final type of morpheme we will discuss is sometimes called STEM (or root) CHANGE. Rather than adding a "chunk" of form, or a different stress pattern to an otherwise stable stem, stem change simply adjusts the shape of the stem by changing the quality of a vowel and in some cases adding a consonant. Some Germanic (mostly Anglo-Saxon) nouns form their plurals, and certain Germanic verbs form their past tenses and/or past participles, in this way. The following noun plurals and verb past tenses illustrate this phenomenon:

(18) Nouns   Verbs

Bare stem	Plural	Bare stem	Past tense
goose	geese	sing	sang
mouse	mice	bring	brought
louse	lice	catch	caught
tooth	teeth	begin	began
foot	feet	break	broke
crisis	crises	choose	chose
		drive	drove

Table 4.3 gives a few more examples of stem change as a morphological process. The three columns of this table represent three sets of verbs that follow three different stem change patterns. These provide important insight into the distinction between lexical expression and morphological processes.

In the Introduction I described (strong) suppletion and weak suppletion as lexical means of expressing conceptual categories. For instance, I described the past tense of the verb *go* (*went*) as an example of strong suppletion, and the past tense of *fall* (*fell*) as an example of weak suppletion. Why don't we say that the past tenses of *dive*, *grow*, *drink*, and all the rest of the verbs in Table 4.3 are also examples of weak suppletion? Aren't the past tenses of these verbs as different from their roots as *fell* is from *fall*? Well, not exactly. The difference is that for these verbs there is at least a bit of a *pattern*. Remember that morphological processes are *patterned* variations in the shapes of words. "Patterned" means that a consistent change in form results in a consistent change in meaning across multiple forms. The fact that there are several examples in each column of Table 4.1 indicates that there is at least a little bit of such patterned consistency within each column. The columns

Table 4.3 Stem change as a morphological process: the past tenses of some minor class verbs

'drink' class	'dive' class	'grow' class
drink/drank	dive/dove	grow/grew
sink/sank	drive/drove	know/knew
sing/sang	strive/strove	throw/threw
ring/rang	ride/rode	blow/blew
sit/sat	write/wrote	
swim/swam	smite/smote	
stink/stank	weave/wove	
shrink/shrank	shine/shone	
spit/spat	stride/strode	
sit/sat	rise/rose	

indicate morphologically defined classes of roots that follow the same pattern. Suppletion, on the other hand, is variation that applies only to one form and therefore must simply be memorized. Suppletive forms cannot be constructed on the basis of a root plus some consistent pattern. Rather each suppletive form must be committed to memory itself, as a separate word.

Another piece of evidence for the existence of a morphological pattern is that innovative or nonsense words may logically fit the pattern. For example, I once heard a child say the following:

(19)   I brang my new toy.

This example shows that the child unconsciously applied the past tense formation pattern for verbs in the *drink* class to the verb *bring*. This is a totally understandable "mistake," since *bring* fits the pattern for the other verbs of this class perfectly. The fact that the innovative verb form *brang* is totally logical and understandable to fully competent English speakers proves that there is a pattern for this class of verbs – the past tenses are not just memorized as individual words.

The major (most common) pattern for forming the past tense in Modern English is the one that adds a suffix usually spelled -*ed* to a stem. This is the pattern that newly coined verbs are usually assigned to, e.g., *emailed, faxed, googled, texted*, etc. Sometimes the major class is called "regular" and the minor classes called "irregular." Most linguists don't like to use these terms because it makes it sound like there is something "wrong" with verbs that happen to exhibit a minor morphological pattern. As we've seen, the minor classes do follow patterns, but they are just not as widespread as the major pattern is. If any verbs are "irregular," it would be the ones that exhibit true suppletion, such as those illustrated in Table 4.4.

Table 4.4 **The past tenses of some "irregular" (suppletive) verbs**

Strong suppletion	Weak suppletion
go/went	choose/chose
be/was	come/came
	eat/ate
	fly/flew
	get/got
	have/had
	lose/lost
	run/ran
	teach/taught

For the verbs in Table 4.4, the past tense forms could not be "predicted" based on any patterns that apply to any other verbs – they just have to be memorized as distinct words. Some of the weakly suppletive past tense forms seem to bear traces of one of the patterns that apply to other verbs. For example, the past tense of *fly* (*flew*) is similar to past tenses of verbs in the "*grow* class" of Table 4.3. However, the roots of verbs in the *grow* class all end in *-ow* (phonetically [o$^{\omega}$]), rather than *-y* ([a^{j}]). Therefore a speaker who knows the verb *fly* and is trying to guess its past tense form would not associate it with the pattern for the *grow* class, and so could not "predict" what the past tense form should be. The best guess would be that it goes into the major class, *flied.

For many years some scholars have called all verbs that form their past tenses by changing a vowel STRONG VERBS, and those that form their past tenses by adding *-ed* WEAK VERBS. This terminology stems from the fact that in Old English most verbs formed their past tenses by changing a root vowel (a process sometimes called ABLAUT). The "strong" pattern was the most common or regular one. However, as soon as Norman French vocabulary started to overrun Old English in about 1066 CE (see Chapter 1), many verbs came into the language that did not lend themselves to the past tense pattern for most native English verbs. Therefore, a Germanic minor past tense pattern involving a [-t], [-d], or [-θ] suffix became the norm for words entering the language from French. For the past 1000 years or so this "weak" pattern has been gaining in popularity to the point that by Shakespeare's time the weak pattern had become the major pattern. Even today forms with *-ed* are still taking over verbs that previously followed a strong pattern. For example, forms like *dived, hanged,* and *weaved* exist alongside the older forms *dove, hung,* and *wove.* It may seem ironic to call the major pattern the *weak* pattern, and a host of minor patterns collectively as the *strong* pattern, but that's the way the terminology has evolved.

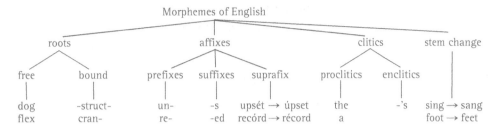

Figure 4.1 Summary diagram of types of morphemes in English, with examples

This concludes the discussion of types of morphemes in English. Figure 4.1 summarizes the definitions presented so far in the form of a tree diagram. A few representative examples of each type are given at the bottom of the figure.

4.3   Derivational vs. inflectional morphology

English exhibits an important distinction between DERIVATION and INFLECTION. Sometimes you will hear or read about derivational and inflectional *categories* (as subsets of conceptual categories), derivational and inflectional *morphology*, or derivational and inflectional *processes*. These terms are all roughly analogous, and simply reflect different perspectives on the same general reality. As with most distinctions in linguistic terminology, the difference between derivation and inflection is actually a continuum, with very clear cases at the extremes, and many intermediate cases falling somewhere in between. In the following sections we will discuss these two general types of morphological processes.

4.4   Morphologically complex structures and the notion of derivation

The basic form of a word can be called its STEM. A stem may consist of just a root, as described above, or it may be morphologically complex, i.e., it may consist of a root plus one or more other morphemes. Morphemes added to roots to create new stems are called DERIVATIONAL MORPHEMES, because they create or "derive" new stems from simpler ones. Often a new stem created by derivational morphology belongs to a different word class than the original stem, but sometimes not. The important characteristic of derivational morphology (sometime termed DERIVATIONAL PROCESSES) is that it derives stems with significantly different meaning from the stem they are attached to. This is in contrast to INFLECTIONAL MORPHOLOGY (INFLECTIONAL PROCESSES or INFLECTIONAL CATEGORIES) which do not create new stems, but rather simply adjust the shape and meaning of a given stem to adapt it to a particular syntactic and discourse context. Inflectional morphology is described in more detail below, and in the chapters on Participant reference (Chapter 5), Actions, states, and processes (Chapter 6), and Time and reality (Chapter 12).

Derivational processes tend to be less PRODUCTIVE than inflectional processes. A productive process is one that applies to every stem of a certain class, and which can be used to create new stems that may never have been created or conceived of before. For example, the derivational suffix spelled -*able* or -*ible* forms an adjective from a transitive verb. The adjective then refers to the property of being able to be an object of the action described by the verb stem:

(20) **Verb**   **Adjective**
       paint   paintable
       drink   drinkable
       climb   climbable
       flex   flexible
       sink   sinkable
       reduce   reducible
       love   lovable

I can't think of a good transitive concept (one that involves a PATIENT or UNDER-GOER) for which the verb cannot occur with -*able* or -*ible*, can you? Even some intransitive concepts allow it, such as *live* → *livable*. The form *livable* refers to the property of a location where someone may comfortably live, even though *live* is not a transitive verb:

(21)   This apartment is very *livable*.   *They lived this apartment.

However, most verbs in their intransitive senses do not comfortably appear with this suffix (no examples of the following words occur in the BNC):

(22)   *fallable
       *bleedable
       *dieable
       *flowable
       *seemable

Because the class of forms to which -*able*/-*ible* can be applied is very well defined (transitive verbs), and because it contributes the same meaning component each time it applies, we can say that this is a very productive derivational affix.

Other derivational affixes aren't nearly as productive as this, and, as you might guess by now, there is a whole range of possibilities between very productive derivational morphology, such as -*able*/-*ible*, *un*-, and a few others, and those which are very *non-productive*, or idiosyncratic. An example of a form that is fairly idiosyncratic is the suffix spelled *-th* or *-t*. It derives an abstract noun from certain adjectives that express dimensions, as in the following examples:

(23) | Adjective | Abstract noun |
|---|---|
| wide | width |
| long | length |
| broad | breadth |
| high | height |
| deep | depth |
| heavy | heft |
| ? | girth (the circumference of something or someone) |
| ? | weight (related to *weigh*, which is not often an adjective in Modern English) |

There are at least two respects in which this morpheme is less productive than *-able* and *-ible*. First, it does not apply across the board to all adjectives, or even all adjectives of dimension:

(24) | Adjective | Abstract noun | |
|---|---|---|
| tall | tallness | *tallth |
| big | size/bigness | *bigth |
| heavy | heaviness | *heavith |
| low | lowness | *lowth |

Second, it doesn't have the same phonological effect each time it appears. There is usually a change in the root vowel that is not predictable based on other phonological patterns of the language. Also, in the case of *height*, *heft*, and *weight*, the suffix is a *-t* ([t]) rather than a *-th* ([θ]). For these reasons, the abstract noun forms in example (23) have to be learned individually, rather than being predictable based on their parts. It is doubtful whether new forms (such as the starred forms in example (24)) would logically be constructed by children or second language learners based on this pattern. Nevertheless, we still have a sense of relation between *wide* and *width*, *deep* and *depth*, etc., and there is some consistency to the pattern across a fairly well-defined class of roots.

One final example will complete a characterization of the continuum of productivity. There is a VESTIGIAL (a remnant left over from an earlier state) derivational process that forms a transitive stem from an intransitive root by changing the vowel (stem change). This process is not obvious in standard spelling, so phonetic transcriptions as well as the spellings are given in example (25):

(25) | Intransitive | Transitive (causative) | | Example |
|---|---|---|---|
| fall [fal] | fell | [fɛl] | 'They felled the tree.' |
| rise [raʲz] | raise | [reʲz] | 'She raised her glass.' |
| lie [laʲ] | lay | [leʲ] | 'He laid the book on the desk.' |
| sit [sɪt] | set | [sɛt] | 'I set the camera down.' |

There is really very little consistency in these forms, and I don't think anyone would claim that this constitutes any kind of a live pattern. Nevertheless we do see some intriguing clues that these intransitive and transitive verbs are related morphologically as well as semantically. All of the transitive verbs have the same consonants as the intransitive forms, and they all have a front, mid root vowel ([e] or [ɛ]). However, there is no hint of productivity in this vestigial pattern. First, there is no coherence to the class of verbs to which the pattern applies. Yes, they are all intransitive verbs, but *most* intransitive verbs are not subject to the pattern. Within the set of intransitive verbs, there is nothing in particular that sets these verbs apart from all the others. Second, the pattern is inconsistent. It's not the case, for example, that a particular vowel X always changes into another vowel Y. Third, it is highly doubtful whether innovative forms could ever be constructed based on this pattern. Can you imagine the transitive form of *cry*, for example, being **cray*?

(26)   *He crayed the baby.   (Trying to mean "He made the baby cry.")

I don't think so. So this is an example of a potential derivational process that is so non-productive that linguists would not classify it as a process at all. From the point of view of Modern English, *fall* and *fell*, *rise* and *raise*, etc., are just distinct verbs. The fact that there is any consistency at all is because at one point in history there was a productive morphological causative pattern. However, this pattern is so buried in history that it has no real existence in the internalized system of categories and patterns we call English grammar today.

A few derivational processes of English

Having given a definition of derivational processes, and outlined a continuum of productivity between very productive and very non-productive derivational processes, we are in a position to simply list some of the major derivational processes in English. A few of these will be discussed in more detail in subsequent chapters. These are given in Table 4.5.

Compounding

I grew up in a suburb of Los Angeles, California, called *Eaglerock*. To this day, when I hear this name pronounced as one word (with primary stress on *Eagle* and not on *rock*) I think of the place where I grew up. I do not think of an eagle, or a rock any more than students at Stanford think of their University as stepping stones across a river (a *stone ford*), or residents of Washington imagine their state as a ton of laundry! Where I live now, in the US State of Oregon, there is a place up the MacKenzie River called *Eagle Rock*. When I hear this phrase (with primary stress on both words), I do think of a rock. The phrase evokes an image of a large

Table 4.5 **Some derivational affixes of English**

Affix	Example basic roots	Derived stems	Meaning
-age	bag verb marry store short use drain out	baggage (N) verbiage (N) marriage (N) storage (N) shortage (N) usage (N) drainage (N) outage (N)	Noun describing a collection of noun ROOT, or abstract/collective noun referring to something that results from action described by verb ROOT.
-ance	perform import insure	performance (N) importance (N) insurance (N)	An action or abstract quality described by ROOT.
-en	black cheap dead	blacken (V) cheapen (V) deaden (V)	To take on or cause something to take on the property described by adjective ROOT.
en-	large fold dear	enlarge (V) enfold (V) endear (V)	To cause something to take on a property, or undergo a process described by ROOT.
-er	sing open	singer (N) opener (N)	Agent or instrument that accomplishes verb ROOT.
-esque	statue Roman Python	statuesque (Adj) Romanesque (Adj) Pythonesque (Adj)	The most salient property associated with ROOT.
-ful$_1$	fruit success watch	fruitful (Adj) successful (Adj) watchful (Adj)	A property characterized by ROOT.
-ful$_2$	mouth spoon car	mouthful (N) spoonful (N) carful (N)	A quantity measured by ROOT.
-hood	neighbor child false priest	neighborhood (N) childhood (N) falsehood (N) priesthood (N)	(Usually) abstract noun associated with ROOT.
-ish	green Scot fool squeam	greenish (Adj) Scottish (Adj) foolish (Adj) squeamish (Adj)	A property that is, or almost is, the main property of ROOT.
-ity	conform secure active	conformity (N) security (N) activity (N)	Abstract noun associated with ROOT.

Table 4.5 (*cont.*)

Affix	Example basic roots	Derived stems	Meaning
-less	end power tire	endless (Adj) powerless (Adj) tireless (Adj)	Lacking ROOT.
-ly	slow month	slowly (Adv) monthly (Adj/Adv)	Do in the manner or time frame described by ROOT.
-ness	aware sick forgive	awareness (N) sickness (N) forgiveness (N)	The state associated with ROOT.
-ous	bulb fame danger	bulbous (Adj) famous (Adj) dangerous (Adj)	Adjective associated with noun ROOT.
re-[6]	assign draw	reassign (V) redraw (V)	Do verb ROOT over again.
-ship	friend hard professor	friendship (N) hardship (N) professorship (N)	Abstract noun describing a state, situation, or quality associated with ROOT.
-tion	educate act create	education (N) action (N) creation (N)	Abstract noun
un-	tidy employ tie	untidy (Adj) unemploy (V) untie (V)	The opposite, negation, or reversal of ROOT.

rock with eagles perched on it. These examples illustrate the difference between phrases and COMPOUND WORDS, or simply COMPOUNDS.

COMPOUNDING is a derivational process that involves combining stems to form new stems. Here are a few more examples:

(27)   bláckbird
       píckpocket
       scárecrow
       hómework
       fóotball
       stírfry
       kíckstart
       science-fiction writer

In the examples above, it is impossible to identify one part as the root and the other as an affix. *Black* and *bird* are both roots that clump together morphologically to form a stem. The new stem, *bláckbird*, expresses an idea that is more than simply the combination of the meanings of the two roots – this word does not refer to any bird that happens to be black, but rather to a specific species of bird. Even though this word is formed out of two roots, it functions just like other noun stems in the language. The same is true of all the other compounds listed in (27).

What does it mean for roots to "clump together morphologically"? We are not talking about spelling. Remember that spelling may or may not reflect how forms "clump together" in speech (cf. the discussion of clitics earlier in this chapter). In fact, the spelling of compound words is one rather contentious issue among English language professionals. There is much variation, and not much consensus. Sometimes compounds are written as one word, *fundraising*, hyphenated, *fund-raising*, or as two separate words, *fund raising*. Sometimes the word class of the compound determines how it is most likely to be spelled. So the verb *to fund raise* tends to be written with the roots separate, while related nouns tend to be written as one word, *fundraiser*, *fundraising*. But there is variation even here. Since this book takes a linguistic perspective, we will look at the linguistic evidence for calling any two roots that are adjacent to each other a phrase versus a compound word. Linguistic evidence always derives primarily from the spoken language.

Linguistic criteria for identifying a compound are structural and semantic. The structural criteria provide evidence that the two forms have "clumped together morphologically" in speech:

- Compounds exhibit a stress pattern characteristic of single words. As discussed at the beginning of this chapter, a word in English receives one primary stress. Longer words may receive secondary and possibly tertiary stress. If *Eágle* and *Róck* each receive primary stress, then they must each be a separate word, and the expression is a phrase. But *Eágleròck* receives only one primary stress on *Eagle*, and a secondary stress on *rock*. This is one piece of evidence that this is treated as one word in the speaker's internal grammar, and is therefore a compound.

- Sometimes compounds exhibit unusual word order, e.g., the compound *fúndraiser* consists of a noun plus a verb where the noun represents the Object rather than the Subject of the verb (a person or event that *raises funds*). Normally Objects follow the verb in English.

- Compounds may undergo MORPHOPHONEMIC PROCESSES characteristic of single words, e.g., the compound word *róommate* can be pronounced with a single *m*, whereas normally if two *ms* come together accidentally, both are pronounced, e.g., *some mice* will be understood as *some ice* if both *ms* are not pronounced.

- Finally, compounds can function like single words for inflectional and derivational affixation. For example, *to can open* is hardly a verb, **I can opened all evening.* But with the instrumental *-er* suffix the compound *can open* is treated exactly as though it were a verb stem, *can opener*, following the pattern of *slicer, grinder*, etc. Another example is *stirfry*. This compound is composed of two verb roots, *stir* and *fry*. However, the forms of this word follow the regular pattern for major class verbs: *stirfries, stirfried, stirfrying*. The two verbs are not inflected separately – **She stirred fried the vegetables.*

Continuing on this theme, a sentence like *She stirred and fried the vegetables* does not mean the same thing as *She stirfried the vegetables.* This illustrates semantic evidence for compounding. The dominant semantic property of compounds is that the meaning of a compound is either more specific or entirely different than the combined meanings of the words that make up the compound. For another example, in American English the compound word *windshield* can't be used for just any shield against wind, but only for those specific objects made of transparent material used in vehicles of various sorts. So while a line of trees along a farmer's field can for the nonce be called a *wind shield* (though the technical term is *shelter belt*), it cannot be called a *windshield*.

Some compounds contain one root which is not an independent word, e.g., *huckleberry, cranberry*, etc. In fact, sometimes neither part is a contemporary independent word, at least not one that can be related to the meaning of the whole compound, e.g., *chipmunk, magpie, somersault, mushroom*, and *grapenuts*.

Compounding is probably more prevalent than many people realize. For example, consider the following:

(28) a. Énglish téacher
　　　 b. Énglish tèacher

In example (28a) both stems take word stress, whereas in (28b) only the first stem takes primary word stress. The second takes secondary stress, as though this is one, four-syllable noun. There is also a difference in meaning between these two examples. Example (28a) refers to any teacher, perhaps a *máth tèacher*, who happens to be from England, while (28b) refers to a teacher of any nationality who happens to teach English. This would be a person who "English-teaches" as though *to Énglishtèach* were a verb. Therefore (28b) can be identified as a compound.

Compounds can have internal structure of their own. For example, *lighthouse* is a compound. *Housekeeper* is also a compound. Someone who keeps a lighthouse is a *lighthouse keeper* (29a). Someone who does light housekeeping is a *light housekeeper* (29b). The structure of these expressions are very different from one another, and can be diagrammed as boxes within boxes as follows:

(29)   a. | lighthouse | keeper |

      b. | light | housekeeper |

Conversion or "zero derivation"

In Chapter 3 we discussed the propensity for words in English to be "shifty" in terms of their word class membership. Sometimes this shiftiness is described as a derivational process that is expressed by "zero" morphology, or "zero derivation." This phenomenon is also referred to as "conversion" (Huddleston and Pullum 2002:1640 ff). Take, for example, the English tendency to use what seems to be a noun root as a verb. For some nouns such derivation seems natural, regular, and standard, such as *chair* (*to chair a meeting*), *table* (*to table a motion*), etc. Other nouns don't seem to lend themselves as easily to such derivation, e.g., *television*, *desk*, *door*, or *window*. Yet, as we have seen in Chapter 3, given the right context, these, and possibly all other nouns, may function perfectly well as verbs.

The very term "conversion" implies that stems inherently belong to one class and are "changed" or "converted" into some other class. This view makes some sense when an overt morpheme is added to a stem to form a new, more complex stem, e.g., the suffix *-er* changes (converts) a verb into a noun. However, in the case of "zero derivation," this view can be called into question. How do we know which form is "basic" and which one is "derived"? And does it really matter? Some quick searches on the BNC and COCA reveal that some words, e.g., *break*, *scoop*, and *pinch*, are used in fairly equal proportions as nouns and as verbs. In fact *scoop* is used slightly more often as a noun in the BNC (160 to 156 examples), but more often as a verb in the COCA (1213 to 1004 examples). Does this mean that *scoop* is basically a noun in British English and a verb in American English? Perhaps. But really, what difference does that make to most English teachers and learners? The fact is that *scoop* is a form–meaning composite that can be used in various syntactic structures as a noun, a verb, and possibly other classes as well depending on the communicative needs of the speaker. There is no particular reason to posit a "derivational process" that shifts it from one category to another.

4.5   Phonosemantics and contextual meaning

In Chapter 3 I claimed that the lexicon of any language, in particular of English, is actually potentially infinite in size. One reason for this is that new words can be created (derived) for particular purposes and assigned meanings just based on the context in which they occur. This is sometimes referred to as CONTEXTUAL MEANING. All words derive meaning from their contexts to a certain extent, e.g., in the following example, the word *bank* can have two meanings depending on the situation:

(30)   Let's try another bank.

In the context of fishermen looking for a good place to fish, it means one thing. In the context of people who are tired of the institution where they keep their money, it means something else. This is sometimes called LEXICAL AMBIGUITY because the two different interpretations are both associated with the same noise, [bæŋk]. This ambiguity is resolved when the utterance is situated in a more specific context. There is no particular reason to treat one of the meanings as "basic" and the other one as derived from the first by some kind of conversion process. For some reason, however, when the same noise functions sometimes as a noun and sometimes as a verb, this is not considered ambiguity resolved by context, but rather derivation or conversion:

(31)   You can bank on that!

In this example, because the noise [bæŋk] follows a pronoun, *you*, and an auxiliary, *can*, it must be interpreted as a verb, and conventionally the verb *bank* expresses a meaning that is similar to the verbs *depend* or *rely* – quite distinct from either of the meanings of this word as a noun. Again, since it is the context (this time the syntactic context, rather than the situational context) that leads the hearer to infer the intended meaning, this can be considered as an example of ambiguity resolved contextually as well.

So far we have seen that lexical ambiguity can be resolved via situational or syntactic context. One way of looking at this is to say that words can derive at least some of their meaning from their contexts. Occasionally words can be invented by speakers "on the fly," i.e., special purpose words that derive *all* of their meaning from the context in which they appear. In such cases, PHONOSEMANTIC PROCESSES can help hearers infer the specific meanings intended by speakers. These are processes whereby stems are created by combining sounds from other words that seem to fit the specific meaning intended by the new word. This process is particularly obvious with so-called onomatopoeic words and word pieces. For example, if a thing *thumps* when it falls, what kind of a thing is it, and what kind of surface is it hitting? What if it *thuds, crashes, tinkles, kachunks, kerblunks,* or *galoomps*? The first three of these words are fairly well established in English and appear in most dictionaries, but the last three, and potentially many more, could be made up on the spot by speakers looking for a word with exactly the right sound to express the kind of impact they want to describe.

Lewis Carroll's famous poem, *Jabberwocky* (Carroll 1872), is an excellent example of how words can be endowed with meaning entirely based on the context and their sound. The poem starts out with the following verse:

'Twas brillig, and the slithy toves
Did gyre and gimble in the wabe;
All mimsy were the borogoves,
And the mome raths outgrabe.

Even though many of the words in this verse are nonsense in Standard English (even in 1872), in context we can infer a lot about the linguistic structure, and even develop a rough image of the scene being described. For example, we know that *brillig* probably refers to a time, because it is preceded by *'twas*. We also know that *toves* is a plural noun that refers to something that can perform actions (probably persons or animals of some sort), because they *did gyre and gimble*, and these words obviously refer to actions. We also know that *wabe* must describe a place where *gyring* and *gimbling* may occur. *Slithy* and *mimsy* must be Modifiers that describe properties of the *toves* and *borogoves* respectively.

The overall impression one gets from this verse may be something like strange creatures acting in some kind of special state or condition. We wait expectantly for the second verse to help fill in the gaps in our mental scene.

This example is from a famous author, but we don't have to study great literature to see how words can acquire their meanings from their contexts. Everyday conversation will easily suffice. For example, I once heard the following sentence in an actual conversation:

(32)   My dog just snerdled under the fence.

I don't find the verb *snerdle* in any of my dictionaries, and it does not occur in any of the corpora. Yet, this sentence is immediately understandable, in context, to anyone who is a fluent speaker of English. We know *snerdle* must be a verb, because it has a Subject (*my dog*) and takes the past tense ending *-ed*. These are structural features of this sentence. Because the sentence has these structural features, we can make a very good guess about what the function, i.e., the *meaning* of the sentence might be. Because we know something about dogs and fences, and we know about verbs that start with *sn -* (*snot, snort, sniff, snuff, snore, snicker,* etc.), and verbs that end in a PLOSIVE CONSONANT plus *-le* (*wiggle, waddle, fiddle, jiggle, juggle, sidle, bubble, whittle, giggle,* etc.), we can develop a very specific mental image based on this sentence. Dogs are very "nose-oriented" creatures, and they are prone to escape from behind fences. These contextual facts, plus the phonosemantic facts that: (a) verbs that start with *sn-* tend to describe actions involving the nose; and (b) verbs that end in plosive consonants plus *-le* express small repetitive motions, we can guess what the meaning of *to snerdle* might be – namely "to dig one's way out from under a fence by moving one's nose back and forth repeatedly," or something like that. You may even say that the speaker provides a meaning for the verb *snerdle* by using it in exactly this context. It would be quite difficult to guess what this word means apart from its use in a specific communicative context. If this new verb fills a functional gap in the vocabulary of English, it may catch on to the point where it may even begin to appear in dictionaries. This kind of inventiveness characterizes every language on earth, and is one way that new words are added to the vocabulary of any language. English seems to be particularly rich in its propensity to create and employ words based on context plus phonosemantics.

4.6   Conclusion

In conclusion, while Modern English makes little use of inflectional morphology in comparison to many other languages of the world (e.g., Spanish, Russian, Hindi, and hundreds of others), it has inherited several derivational processes, mostly from Latin, which allow speakers to augment the already robust lexicon with a wide variety of new word forms. Derivational morphology is thus a kind of "turbocharger" for the lexicon, giving speakers a powerful boost in performance that more than compensates for the diminished power of the inflectional system.

Summary

In this chapter we have discussed the word structure of English. First some basic terms in linguistic morphology, such as *word, morpheme, root, stem, bound,* and *free* were introduced. Then inflectional and derivational morphology in English were characterized – inflectional morphology is variation in word structure that adds highly important conceptual categories (such as plurality or tense) to a word's basic meaning, or adapts a word to its specific syntactic environment. Derivational morphology is variation in word structure that creates new word stems out of other pieces. Finally, we discussed how meaning depends partially or completely on context.

FURTHER READING

Matthews (1991) is a classic textbook on linguistic morphology in general. The articles in Spencer and Zwicky (1997) provide in-depth treatment of specific topics, e.g., inflection, derivation, compounding, and productivity, by leading researchers in the field. Carstairs-McCarthy (2002) is a lively introduction to some of the same morphological questions treated by these other works, but at a more elementary level using exclusively English data. Finally, Plag (2003) is a thorough compendium and textbook on word-formation processes in English.

Exercises

1. Divide the following English words into morphemes. Label each morpheme as a root, prefix, or suffix (do not worry about the distinction between root and stem at this point). There may be some interesting, controversial, and tricky examples here, but they will provide some good points to ponder and discuss:

   Example: re|analyze|s pref-root-suf

a. heaviness	h. rejection	o. understand
b. silly	i. enlighten	p. different
c. linguistic	j. rationalistically	q. unnaturally
d. universal	k. walked	r. remittance
e. dirty	l. overemphasized	s. pitifully
f. neighborhood	m. inequality	t. indecipherable
g. untitled	n. readable	u. incomprehensibilificationalism

2. Compound words (adapted from Finnegan 1994:110). Find a passage of about 200 words in an English language newsweekly, such as *Time* or *Newsweek*, or a similar Internet website. Make a list of all the compound nouns and verbs (if any) in the passage. Remember that not all compounds are written as one word.
   A. Identify the word class of each part of each compound.

   Example: "scarecrow" scare = verb, + crow = noun.
   B. Choose five of the compounds, and explain the relationship between the meaning of the parts and the meaning of the compound.

   Example: Scare + crow. A scarecrow is a thing that scares crows. The noun "crow" is the PATIENT of the verb "scare."

3. As mentioned in Chapter 4, English regular plural and genitive endings have three allomorphs (variant pronunciations), [-z], [-s], and [-ɪz]. Imagine that you have just heard the following words used as singular nouns in English. For each word, which of the three regular allomorphs would probably occur in the plural and genitive singular forms? Careful! For some words the plural and genitive allomorphs may be different.

a. shunk	e. hamin	i. ranath
b. snafe	f. parall	j. jollont
c. wug	g. skaze	k. kafu
d. contash	h. nad	l. lonitong

   Now imagine you've heard these words used as the bare forms of verbs. For each one, which regular past tense allomorph would you expect, [-t], [-d], or [-əd]?

5 Participant reference

> When you are a Bear of Very Little Brain, and you Think of Things, you find sometimes that a Thing which seemed very Thingish inside you is quite different when it gets out into the open and has other people looking at it.
>
> *Winnie the Pooh* (Milne 1956 [2001]:102)

Participant reference is the functional domain of referring to or mentioning Things in the mental world of discourse. The relationship between referring expressions and participants is illustrated in Figure 5.1. If I am talking about an old fox, the image that appears in my mind is the REFERENT and I may use any number of referring expressions to mention that referent; I may use a determined noun phrase, *an old fox*, a pronoun, *it*, *he*, or any number of other linguistic forms. Which form I use depends on a number of factors, including the precise nuances of meaning I want to express, the syntactic context, and my judgments concerning the version of the discourse stage that my hearers have already built in their minds.

In context, almost any gesture can serve to refer to something a speaker wishes to mention; a glance, a nod of the head, a pointing finger, elbow, or lips can serve the function of "setting up" or referring back to a character on the discourse stage. Referring to participants is such an important communicative function that every language has well-oiled grammatical means of accomplishing it. Specifically linguistic referring strategies include several types of pronouns, nouns, noun phrases, and conspicuous silences, or "gaps," in clause structure. These conventionalized referring expressions, including how they tend to function in English discourse, constitute the subject matter for this chapter.

5.1 Properties of nouns

The category of NOUN is a word class in the lexicon and a syntactic category in syntactic structure. All entries in the lexicon have three interrelated sets of properties. First, the basic meanings associated with a particular word are its SEMANTIC

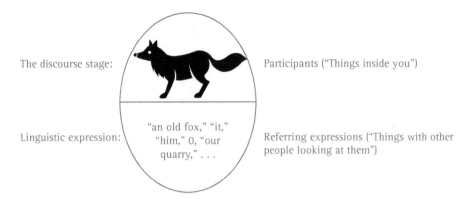

The discourse stage:

Participants ("Things inside you")

Linguistic expression:

"an old fox," "it," "him," 0, "our quarry," . . .

Referring expressions ("Things with other people looking at them")

Figure 5.1 Nouns and discourse referents

PROPERTIES. Second, the ways a word's shape can be changed to express nuances of meaning, and the ways it fits into syntactic constructions can be called its MORPHOSYNTACTIC (MORPHOLOGICAL and SYNTACTIC) properties. Third, words have characteristic uses in communication. These can be called a word's DISCOURSE PRAGMATIC PROPERTIES.

These three kinds of properties – semantic, morphosyntactic, and discourse pragmatic – reflect the three dimensions of grammar independently described by Larsen-Freeman (1997) as meaning, form, and use respectively. They all affect one another in significant ways, and for that reason are sometimes difficult to tease apart. However, these sets of properties are logically distinct from one another, and understanding the various properties of lexical items will go a long way in helping anyone understand English grammar (see Figure 5.2).

Semantic properties of prototypical nouns (meaning)

In order to understand how words are used, we have to understand what they mean. The mental images evoked by words to a large extent determine their morphosyntactic and discourse pragmatic properties (see Dixon 2005, for a thoroughly semantically based approach to English grammar). The problem with meaning, however, is that it is not itself entirely distinct from form and use. Words like *tree* or *fox* may seem to evoke particular images out of context, but what about a word like *slide*? What comes to your mind when you hear a phrase like *a slide*? If you have young children, you may think of a piece of playground equipment; if you are a trombonist, you may think of a major part of your instrument; if you are a photographer, you may think of photographic transparencies; if you are a laboratory technician … I think you get the idea. The meanings of words out of context are only very vague images, sometimes called SCHEMATA (singular SCHEMA, Langacker 1987). Schemata are sparse collections of properties and relationships

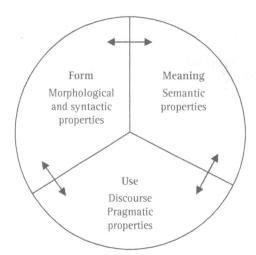

Figure 5.2 Properties of lexical entries

that may not resemble any discourse world referent very closely at all. The word *slide* out of context evokes no more than a bare image of something moving linearly against something else. This rather stark schema is simply a tool that can be used for building more specific images in particular contexts. Some would say that a word really doesn't evoke any image *until it is used to communicate an idea*. From this point of view, words are assigned specific meanings only in context. Whether or not I am a trombonist (I'm not), I know what a trombone slide is, and in the right context will understand an expression like *the slide is sticky* to refer to the slide on a trombone.

When I use a word like *slide* as a linguistic example, I'm not referring to any discourse world item (except "the word 'slide' "). The word is "decontextualized," cited out of context. The only way a reader may understand an expression like "the meaning of the word *slide* " is to recall (subconsciously, of course) actual situations in which people have used this form, and extract from those situations a generalized ideal "meaning." So meaning itself arises out of the interplay between structure and use.

Philosophers and linguists have debated the nature of meaning for centuries, so I don't think we are going to resolve the issue here. This is an important debate, however, and I encourage English language professionals to become familiar with it as a means of deepening and broadening their perspective on language and language teaching. A couple of good places to start would be Lakoff and Johnson (1999) or Katz (1990). For our purposes, we will think of words as "having" or "expressing" idealized meanings. We must take this as a shorthand way of saying that *speakers* have meanings, and *speakers* express meanings. They *use* words to help them express specific meanings in particular contexts.

As mentioned in Chapter 3, the idealized meanings that prototypical nouns help speakers express tend to be clearly BOUNDED or INDIVIDUATED concepts, like *tree*, *fox*, *stone*, *mausoleum*, etc. That is, concepts referred to by nouns tend to have clear boundaries, and be recognizable as individual Things. These are also concepts that tend not to change very much over time, i.e., they are TIME-STABLE (Givón 2001:44). The semantic properties of nouns are the basis for the schoolbook characterization of a noun as a word that refers to a person, place, thing, or idea. Of course, this is not a *definition* of noun, since there are many words that refer to time-stable, bounded, individuated concepts, but are not always nouns. Consider the italicized words in the following sentences:

(1) The constable *towered* over her.   STOOD VERY TALL
     It recognizes abnormal cells, destroys them or *walls* them off.   ISOLATES
     It was the third one that really *floored* me.   SURPRISED
     They *grassed* it *over* for a playground.   PLANTED GRASS ON
     Time and again we have *been treed* by bears.   CHASED UP A TREE
     This whole street we see now which looks pretty well *treed* will be almost clear-cut a year from now.   LINED WITH TREES
     The dire light and dark shadows *foxed* him.   CONFUSED, MISLED

The words *tower*, *wall*, *floor*, *grass*, *tree*, and our friend *fox* are usually thought of as describing pretty time-stable concepts, yet they do not always function as nouns in syntactic structures such as these. Furthermore, there are words that refer to time-UNstable concepts, like *fist*, *sincerity*, and *weather*, yet commonly do function as nouns. So semantic properties alone do not absolutely determine whether a word is a noun or not, but the best (or prototypical) examples of nouns do tend to exhibit the semantic properties of time-stability, boundedness, and individuation.

Morphosyntactic properties of prototypical nouns (form)

The ways the forms of words are adjusted to express nuances of meaning are its morphological properties, and the ways words enter into constructions with other words are its syntactic properties. Together these are a word's structural, or morphosyntactic, properties.

Consistent with the general character of English, nouns are relatively simple morphologically. While there are several rather idiosyncratic derivational processes that nouns can participate in (see below), about the only inflectional categories that are expressed with any regularity on nouns are singular and plural.[1] Derivational morphology that may create new nouns is described in Chapter 4.

For nouns that describe things that can be counted (see below for a discussion of countable and non-countable concepts), plurality is usually expressed morphologically:

(2)   **Singular**   **Plural**
    tree [tʰɹɨʲ]   trees [tʰɹɨʲz]
    cat [kʰæt]   cats [kʰæts]
    slide [slaʲd]   slides [slaʲdz]
    fox [fɔks]   foxes [fɔksɨz]

The systematic differences in word shape between words in the first column and words in the second column of example (2) correlates with a difference in meaning between singular and plural, so this is a morphological pattern. It is a live (or "productive") pattern because new nouns that enter the language may be assigned a plural form based on this pattern.

Singular and plural can also be expressed lexically, but there are no syntactic plurals in English. The lexical plurals involve WEAK SUPPLETION (non-systematic variation in form) or ISOMORPHISM (see the Introduction). The word *person* and its plural *people* may be the only case of STRONG SUPPLETION (complete variation in form) expressing plurality, though this is debatable. *People* is actually a kind of COLLECTIVE PLURAL, like *cattle*, *vermin*, and *swine*, and it coexists with the contrasting regular plural *persons*. We will have more to say about collective plurals and similar constructions later in this chapter.

A number of weakly suppletive plurals in English are a result of Germanic ablaut processes. These must be considered lexical, i.e., memorized outright (see Chapter 3) in modern English because there is no evidence that a live morphological pattern is involved for any of the classes of forms. In fact, most of these "classes" seem to involve only one singular/plural pair:

(3)   **Weakly suppletive plurals in English**
    mouse/mice, louse/lice   *but not*:   grouse/*grice, spouse/*spice
    goose/geese, tooth/teeth   *but not*:   moose/*meese, booth/*beeth
    foot/feet
    die/dice
    woman/women [wɪmən]

The suffix -*en* is another reflex of a Germanic plural that appears in a few words.

(4)   ox/oxen
    child/children
    brother/brethren

This is very irregular, however, since in *children* and *brethren* there are additional sound changes beyond just the addition of a suffix. And, of course, for most speakers *brethren* is archaic having been replaced by the regular *brothers*. This would be considered an example of a lexical process (weak suppletion), since there is no evidence that this is a live morphological pattern of modern English.

More common are classes of weakly suppletive plurals consisting of words that are of relatively recent borrowing from Latin. There is actually some evidence that the contrast between the ending -*us* in the singular and -*i* in the plural is becoming a morphological pattern of English, rather than just a reflex of a morphological pattern of Latin. What do you think? Consider the following pairs of forms:

(5)   alumnus/alumni
      cactus/cacti
      focus/foci
      fungus/fungi
      nucleus/nuclei
      octopus/octopi
      radius/radii
      stimulus/stimuli

Now that you've read this list of singular/plural pairs, think quickly of what the plurals of these nonsense nouns might be: *calamus, toblus, contarus*. If you answered *calami, tobli*, and *contari*, then your internal morphology has a pattern that says "change -*us* at the end of a singular noun to -*i* to form the plural of that noun." If you came up with *calamuses, tobluses*, and *contaruses*, then -*us* to -*i* is still a lexical process for you; you have just memorized the forms in (5) as individual "irregular" nouns. Many such plurals, in fact, exist alongside regularized forms such as *cactuses, focuses*, and *hippopatamuses*.

Other examples of "irregular" plurals in English stemming from regular morphological processes in ancient languages include the following. This is not by any means an exhaustive list, but it illustrates the major classes. There remain individual weakly suppletive forms such as *corpus/corpora* and *schema/schemata*:

(6)   analysis/analyses   erratum/errata   index/indices
      axis/axes   datum/data   appendix/appendices
      basis/bases   ovum/ova   matrix/matrices
      crisis/crises   symposium/symposia
      ellipsis/ellipses   colloquium/collquia   alga/algae
      emphasis/emphases   vertebra/verebrae
      neurosis/neuroses   criterion/criteria
      oasis/oases   phenomenon/phenomena
      synthesis/syntheses

Finally, there is a group of nouns that includes mostly animal names for which the plurals are isomorphic with (have the same form as) the singulars. These include *fish, sheep, deer, buffalo, elephant, bison*, and *elk*. Most of these also have counterparts with the regular -*s* plural (*buffaloes, elephants*). When there is a regular plural, the isomorphic form is more like a collective plural, referring to an unindividuated group, usually in the context of hunting.

(7)   Over *1,000 elephant*, together with several species of *buck*, *zebra*, and *crocodile*, are to be herded onto private game ranches ...

Turning now to syntax, the prototypical syntactic function of nouns is to head noun phrases (NPs). We will have a lot more to say about noun phrases in Chapter 7. For now you can think of a phrase as simply a group of one or more words that "clump together" syntactically. In Section 7.2, the notion of semantic headship is defined using nouns and noun phrases as the prime example. As a precursor to that discussion, we can define the (semantic) Head of a noun phrase as the one word within the phrase that refers to the same discourse stage participant that the whole phrase refers to. In a noun phrase like *corner table*, the whole phrase refers to a table, not to a corner; therefore *table* is the Head of this phrase. Another way of saying this is that the semantic Head PROJECTS its semantic properties onto the whole clump of which it is a part.

Within noun phrases, nouns can be MODIFIED. Modification is a very general syntactic function that can be filled by several different syntactic categories, including adjectives, nouns, adverbs, prepositional phrases, and even whole clauses. The Modification function is discussed in detail in Chapter 10. Since Modifiers are always "optional," a noun by itself can function as a noun phrase in clause structure:

(8) | **Noun/noun phrase** | **Modified noun phrase** |
|---|---|
| fox | old red fox |
| slide | trombone slide |
| bear | bear with very little brain |
| tree | tree that loses its leaves in autumn |

Modifiers that occur within noun phrases are sometimes said to be functioning ATTRIBUTIVELY or ADNOMINALLY. So the words *old* and *red* in the phrase *old red fox* attribute the properties of oldness and redness to the bare schematic image evoked by the word *fox*. The syntax of noun phrases is discussed in more detail in Chapters 7 and 10. For now the important concept to remember is that nouns have the following syntactic properties:

- They can be Heads of noun phrases.
- They can be Modified by attributive Modifiers.

Discourse pragmatic properties of prototypical nouns (use)

We have just discussed the semantic (meaning) and morphosyntactic (structural) properties of nouns. In this section we will discuss one respect in which these properties affect and are affected by how nouns are used in communication.

Prototypical nouns refer to DISCOURSE MANIPULABLE participants on the discourse stage (Hopper and Thompson 1984). Consider the following examples:

(9) a. Early in the chase the hounds started up *an old red fox*, and we hunted him all morning.
     b. We went *fox* hunting in the Berkshires.

In (9a), *fox* is a prototypical noun. It has all the morphosyntactic properties of nouns, e.g., it may be inflected for plural, it may take a possessor or other determiners, and it may occur with a full range of Modifiers.

(10) Early in the chase the hounds started up *the old red fox.*
                                                 the king's old red fox.
                                                 twenty-seven lovely old red foxes.

In (9b), on the other hand, the same concept, *fox*, is expressed by a form that has *none* of the morphosyntactic properties of nouns. It may not take plural marking, Determiners, or Modifiers:

(11) *We went *the fox* hunting in the Berkshires.
      *   *foxes*
      *   *an old red fox*

The question that Hopper and Thompson (1984) ask is "Why does a noun, such as *fox*, lose its morphosyntactic properties when it is incorporated into a verb?" Their answer is that in (9a) *fox* is presented as a discourse-manipulable participant, whereas in (9b) it is not. Imagine (9a) as a description of a scene in a play. In that case the fox would be an actual participant in the drama. A particular fox would be set up (or ACTIVATED) on the discourse stage. On the other hand, if (9b) described a scene in a play, there would not necessarily be any fox on stage. People who are *fox hunting* are not necessarily interacting with any foxes at all! Thus prototypical nouns have the discourse pragmatic property of referring to discourse-manipulable participants – participants that can be referred back to over and over again in subsequent discourse. For example, the following invented sequence is reasonable:

(12) Early in the chase, the hounds started up an old red fox.
      It jumped over a log and 0 dashed into the woods.

In this example the referring expressions *it* and *0* (zero – a conspicuous gap) both refer back to the *old red fox* introduced in the previous clause.

When nouns refer to non-manipulable, or non-activated, participants they may lose some of the morphosyntactic trappings typical of the category noun:

(13) We went fox hunting in the Berkshires.
      ??It jumped over a log and 0 dashed into the woods.

In this case, *it* and *0* cannot refer back to *fox* in the previous sentence because there is no *fox* on stage to refer back to; it is not discourse manipulable. So we see that discourse pragmatic use, as well as meaning, also affects morphosyntactic form.

5.2   Subclasses of nouns

Because the world of discourse is complex and multifaceted, the possible referents for nouns include an extremely diverse collection of people, places, things, and ideas. So in describing "semantic properties of nouns" we can only talk in very general terms; concepts like "time-stable," "individuated," and "bounded" are somewhat vague and are all a matter of degree. The world as depicted in human discourse consists of humans and non-humans, animate beings and inanimate objects, things with different kinds of parts, things that consist of collections of identical parts, things you can touch, things you can't touch, *ad infinitum*. Anyone who tries to categorize exhaustively all the possible referents in the world of discourse on the basis of semantic properties has a never-ending task!

Although the potential number of semantically based subclasses of nouns is infinite, the human mind is finite (though stunningly complex). Therefore, there is a very strong tendency for human categorization systems, like vocabularies of languages, to DISCRETIZE, i.e., make into distinct structural categories, particular "areas" of semantic space that are similar enough to count as the same. Such is the case with subclasses of nouns. In this section we will discuss some of the usage- and meaning-based subclasses of nouns that are treated as distinct by the grammar of English. It is important to remember that these are *grammatically* distinct classes – they are defined by grammatical properties – but they are usage- and meaning-based. Meaning and use motivate these categories, but do not directly define them.

Proper names vs. common nouns

Proper names constitute a usage-based subclass of nouns that has specific grammatical consequences. Proper names are special nouns that are used to address and identify particular beings, things or places that are familiar and uniquely IDENTIFIABLE to speaker and audience in a particular context. Since proper names prototypically refer to specific entities both speaker and audience can identify, their referents do not usually need to be further determined or restricted with ARTICLES, restrictive modifiers, possessors, restrictive RELATIVE CLAUSES, or other elements that make nouns more specific, although they may. It is quite possible to convert proper names into non-unique common nouns, in which case they may exhibit the properties of ordinary common nouns:

(14)	Genitive pronoun:	That's *my Canada.*
	Definite article:	It's not *the Canada* I used to know.
	Quantifier:	There are really *two Canadas.*
	Indefinite article:	*A Mr. Gregory* was injured when a lorry driven by *a Mr. Hill* knocked him off his motorbike.
	Attributive Modifier:	For better conditions, less crime, *a better Britain* and the way ahead …

All of the examples in (14) may be considered instances of "class shifting" in which forms that are basically proper names are construed as common nouns for particular communicative purposes.

Countable vs. non-countable nouns

Many languages, including English, treat nouns that refer to things that are bounded and individuated enough to be counted, such as *fox, tree,* and *mausoleum,* as grammatically distinct from those that can't easily be counted, like *air, sincerity,* and *laughter.* The former are called COUNTABLE NOUNS or COUNT NOUNS, while the latter are variously called NON-COUNTABLE NOUNS, NON-COUNT NOUNS, or MASS NOUNS. The term "mass noun" is a bit of a misnomer because only some non-countable nouns refer to "masses," like *water, sand, air, wood.* However, there are several other semantic categories of nouns that also fall into the non-countable subclass (see Table 5.1 below).

It is important to recognize that, like word class membership in general, countability is a property of words in context. Very few words are inherently and absolutely categorized as countable vs. non-countable in the lexicon, though some may be. Rather, concepts are *presented as* countable or non-countable in particular contexts. The morphosyntactic properties described here interact with the semantic

Table 5.1 **Some groups of nouns normally used in a non-countable sense**

Concrete "masses"	Concrete "collections"	Abstract nouns	Action nominalizations
sand	jewelry	music	dancing
water	furniture	sincerity	running
air	food	love	playing
DNA	lingerie	volleyball (game)	destruction
compost	architecture (the product)	architecture (the discipline)	robbery
cheese	baggage	linguistics	revival
beer	lumber	chess	imitation
grass	footwear	silence	laughter
chocolate	hardware	happiness	evacuation
etc.			

properties of individual words to allow speakers to express particular intended meanings, some of which are countable and some not.

Some examples of nouns that are often used in a non-countable way are listed in Table 5.1. These words are sorted into columns that reflect some of the semantic categories that affect the meaning and use of non-countable nouns.

What all the nouns in Table 5.1 have in common grammatically is that when they occur in the plural form, they express a different, countable, sense. Also, the range of quantifiers that may occur with non-countable nouns is different from those that can be used with countable nouns:

(15)   Nouns used in a non-countable sense:

*many sands	*one sand	much sand	a lot of sand
*many jewelries	*one jewelry	much jewelry	a lot of jewelry
*many musics	*one music	much music	a lot of music
*many runnings	*one running	much running	a lot of running

Nouns used in a countable sense:

| many trees | one tree | *much trees | a lot of trees |
| many foxes | one fox | *much foxes | a lot of foxes |

Because of what these nouns refer to (i.e., their semantic properties), they are more or less likely to be used in a countable sense.

The semantic effects of plural marking on basically non-countable nouns are slightly different, depending on the subclass of the noun, as represented in the four columns of Table 5.1. For example, concrete "mass" nouns (column 1) when pluralized usually refer to a particular quantity of the substance. Often that quantity can be specified with a QUANTITY or PARTITIVE NOUN (see below), but if the quantity is the "default" or expected amount for a given context, the quantity noun may be omitted:

(16)   We'll have three *waters* please.

In the context of diners ordering food in a restaurant, example (16) will be understood to mean three *glasses* of water, and not, say, three *gallons* of water. In another context, e.g., where water was being sold in gallon jugs, alongside gallon jugs of lemonade, example (16) may be understood to refer to three gallon jugs of water.

Mass nouns in the plural can also refer to several different *types* of the mass item, as these examples from the BNC show:

(17)   a.   Bring me the finest *meats* and *cheeses* for a clubhouse feast!
        b.   *Manures* make a greater contribution to soil aggregation than *composts*, ...
        c.   Fragile *DNAs* were replaced with better genetic machinery.

In fact, example (17c) is ambiguous, at least to someone not familiar with genetic biology. Does *DNAs* in this example refer to default bounded quantities, e.g., *strands* of DNA, or to different *types* of DNA? Grammatically speaking, it could be either one, and only English speakers who are familiar with this particular context would be able to interpret this utterance in the way intended by the writer.

Nouns that refer to concrete "collections" of potentially distinct items, like *jewelry* and *furniture*, are not understood as bounded quantities when used in the plural. Rather they are only understood as different types of the collection. Again, this can be understood as a consequence of the semantic properties of these nouns:

(18)   Everybody milled around, eating from trays of finger *foods.*
       These imported *lumbers* have been sustainably harvested.
       You shop for *linens* to *hardwares* to baby *clothes* to – I don't know …

Turning now to the third column of Table 5.1, some abstract nouns in the plural can only be understood in the type sense:

(19)   Multicultural *musics* offer a wealth of rich musical works for students to explore.

It is extremely difficult to imagine this example referring to default quantities of music, e.g., performances, or pieces of music:

(20)   ??We listened to four musics this afternoon. (0 examples of this sense in the corpora)

Example (20) is an invented example, but if it were to occur in conversation, it could only coherently mean four *types* of music, rather than four musical pieces, or four performances.

Other abstract nouns are understood as referring to *instances* of the abstract idea, and not types or bounded amounts of it:

(21)   As a boy he was reckless and fun-loving, yet given to long *silences.*
       his dubious *sincerities.*
       human *hopes* and *fears, desires* and *happinesses.*
       There was movement and low voices, then a pair of *laughters.*

The last column of Table 5.1 illustrates ACTION NOMINALIZATIONS. These are nouns derived from verbs, and include present participles such as *dancing* and *running*. It is very difficult to think of a word like *dancing* as expressing a bounded, individuated concept since it inherently involves motion and change. However, let us look at the morphosyntactic properties of this form to determine just how "nouny" (or "Thingish" in Winnie the Pooh's terms) it is. Prototypical nouns can function as

Heads of noun phrases. Noun phrases, in turn, can be Subjects or Objects of clauses. Can *dancing* be the Subject or Object of a clause? The following examples show that *dancing* passes this syntactic "test" for nounhood:

(22) Subject: *Dancing*, mime and movement are often now absorbed in Cultural Activities and Music syllabuses.
Object: For my good lady loved singing and *dancing*.

Other structural properties of prototypical nouns include the possibility of occurring with attributive Modifiers, genitive case pronouns, and quantifiers. Again, the word *dancing* has these properties:

(23) Descriptive Modifiers: Irene did say she wasn't very keen on this *modern dancing*.
Genitive case pronouns: The fact is she's she's dedicated to *her dancing*.
Quantifiers: And I think there was *a bit of dancing* was there?

In spite of the fact that present participles, such as *dancing*, pass most of the tests for prototypical nounhood (or "Thingishness"), they are clearly non-countable, since they don't normally occur in the plural, and don't take numeric quantifiers.

(24) ??many dancings
??three dancings

Other action nominalizations, such as *destruction* and *laughter*, also exhibit similar, though not identical, clusters of noun-like properties.

Nouns that refer to certain foods provide a nice illustration of the fact that countability is a semantic feature of words in context, and not an inherent feature of words in the lexicon. Many food items are countable before they are prepared for eating, but become non-countable by the time they reach the table. So, my neighbor raises *chickens* (countable), but we had *chicken* for dinner (non-countable). I bought *a melon* (countable) at the store, but we are having *melon* (non-countable) for dessert. It seems that when something is prepared for eating, it loses its individuality and its parts become less individuated and bounded. Wierzbicka (1988:499–554) provides an engaging and informative discussion of the question of countability from a linguistic perspective.

Besides the non-countable nouns illustrated in Table 5.1, there is an additional group of non-countable nouns that seem to appear only in the plural. These are sometimes called PLURALIA TANTUM nouns. Some of these are listed in Table 5.2.

The terms illustrated in Table 5.2 are a very diverse group, and may not really have much in common as a class at all, other than the fact that they all end with *-s*

Table 5.2 *Pluralia tantum* nouns (conventional quantity nouns are given in parentheses)

Games (a game of …)	Diseases (a case of …)	Disciplines (no conventional quantity)	Bifurcated objects (a pair of …)	Others (no conventional quantity)
checkers	measles	gymnastics	scissors	news
dominos	mumps	linguistics	glasses	olympics
darts	shingles	semantics	trousers	groceries
cards	the blues	genetics	pliers	
Pooh sticks	herpes	mathematics	binoculars	
craps	chicken pox (?)		tweezers	
etc.				

and hence seem to be morphologically plural. Some of them occur with conventionalized quantity nouns, and some do not:

(25)   a game of checkers
       a case of measles
       a pair of scissors
       a ?bit/*story of news
       an ?event/a *meet of gymnastics

For some of the nouns in Table 5.2, the apparent plural ending is sometimes lost when the noun functions as a Modifier, and sometimes not. With a few nouns ending in -*ics*, the derivational ending -*al* is needed to shift the noun into the class of adjectives:

(26)   *s*-less Modifier | *s*-full Modifier | -*al* Modifier
       a linguistic generalization | a linguistics textbook | *a linguistical joke
       *a mathematic generalization | a mathematics class | a mathematical proof
       an olympic team | an olympics committee | *an olympical sport
       a checkerboard | a checkers player |
       a card game | a cards fanatic |
       a crap shooter | a craps game |

With many of these nouns speakers seem to have a hard time deciding whether they are grammatically singular or plural. The game of *checkers* almost universally triggers singular agreement when functioning as the Subject of a verb (0 examples of plural agreement in the major corpora), while *cards* can go either way:

(27)   a.   *Checkers is /*are* a great game.
       b.   I realize that *cards are* a dreadful waste of your youthful hours,
       c.   *Cards is* a fantastic way for our family to spend the evening.

Perhaps this is because games of *cards* are played with items called *cards* that are easily counted and individuated. The game of *checkers*, on the other hand, is not played with individual things called *checkers*. What is *a checker* in a game of checkers anyway? But consider the disease *herpes*. My dictionary (American Heritage 2006) lists *herpes* as a singular non-countable noun, exactly like the game of *checkers*; there is no word *herpe* in that dictionary. Nevertheless, *herpes* is often treated as plural:

(28)   Herpes *are* caused by the herpes simplex virus (HSV). (COCA)
        Are genital herpes curable?
        (wiki.answers.com/Q/Are_genital_herpes_curable)

At this point we are pretty much talking about lexical features of individual words in the minds of individual speakers. While there is some grammatical reality to the general classes of countable and non-countable nouns, at the level of individual lexical items there tends to be quite a bit of variation.

Countability is but one example of how a semantic property of a noun affects its morphosyntactic properties. The less prototypical a noun is in terms of its meaning or its function in discourse, the less "nouny" it seems in terms of its morphosyntax.

Collective nouns and collective plurals

The last set of subclasses of nouns I'd like to discuss are collective nouns and collective plurals. These subtypes of nouns are different from each other, and both are different from non-countable nouns that describe "collections," like *furniture*, *jewelry*, etc. (see Section 5.2). Collective plurals are "special" plural forms of nouns that exist alongside regular plurals. This is a very small class of words that seems to consist of only six members, *people, cattle, swine, fowl, vermin,* and *kine*.[2] I've ordered these roughly according to my impression of how viable they are as plurals in Modern English (high to low). There is no doubt that others will disagree with my impressions and will perhaps even come up with additional examples, but there can also be no doubt that this group forms a class that is distinct from other subclasses of nouns in grammatically significant ways.

The first property of collective plurals that distinguishes them from collective nouns is that collective plurals are consistently plural. This is shown by the fact that they always trigger plural verb agreement when functioning as the subject of a clause:

(29)   the people are /*is overemployed
        Cattle have/*has very sensitive muzzles.
        swine forage/*forages for roots, berries, and nuts ...

other fowl have/*has become less resistant to disease
the vermin were/*was numerous and hungry

Secondly, collective plurals exist alongside regular plurals such as *persons, cows*, and *pigs. People* is currently the most well-installed collective plural in the English language. It is the ordinary way of referring to more than one person. The morphologically regular plural, *persons*, is the marked, unusual form. For other collective plurals, the corresponding regular plural usually emphasizes the individuality of the members, rather than an undifferentiated group. For example, it is more common to use the regular plurals when counting: *two cows* (23 examples in the COCA) is more likely than *?two cattle* (2 examples). However, when talking about larger numbers of animals, *cattle* is more likely (20 examples of *million cattle* in the COCA, and 3 examples of *million cows*).

In summary, collective plurals constitute a small, special subclass of nouns that are grammatically and semantically plural. They exist alongside regular plurals, and contrast with the regular plurals in that they emphasize a collection as a whole, rather than individual members.

Collective nouns, on the other hand, constitute a much larger subclass of nouns that refer to conventionally recognized groups of things. Examples include *army, audience, band, class, committee, crowd, family, flock, government, group, heap, herd, jury, public, staff, team*, and dozens more. Collective nouns are not plurals. This is evidenced by the fact that they can be pluralized themselves: *armies, audiences, bands*, etc. Also, if collective nouns were plurals, what would the singulars be? Is *bureaucrat* the singular form of *government*? Maybe. Finally, collective nouns may trigger singular or plural verb agreement:

(30) **Collective nouns triggering singular agreement (normally when the collection acts as one)**
The committee *has* not met yet.
However, the Government *has* no intention to privatise health care.
The crowd *is* segregated from the away supporters now.

(31) **Collective nouns triggering plural agreement (normally when the individual members of the collection act separately)**
The executive committee *have* agreed to changes.
I'm ashamed of some of the things the present government *have* done.
The vast crowd *are* allowed to walk freely in this area.

Certain collective nouns are conventionally associated with particular groups of things, usually animals that tend to congregate in groups. The following are some that most English speakers are aware of:

(32) a *crowd* of people
a *herd* of cattle/cows/elephants

a *flock* of birds/sheep/chickens
a *pack* of wolves/dogs/hyenas
a *school* of fish
a *swarm* of bees/hornets/wasps
etc.

5.3   Pronouns

PRONOUNS are referring expressions that can be thought of as abbreviated versions of determined noun phrases. In particular, every position in syntactic structure where a determined noun phrase (DP) may occur, some type of pronoun may appear instead. There are some places in clause structure where pronouns may occur that full DPs may not appear, and we'll see examples of this below, but the reverse is not the case.

Sometimes it is said that pronouns substitute for nouns, but this is a misconception, as is easily proven: The word *girl* is a noun; if pronouns substituted for nouns, we should be able to say **the she*, **a tall she*, etc. But we don't. This is because pronouns, like *she*, have the syntactic properties of whole phrases, not individual nouns.

(33)   a.   *The girl who was supposed to wrap it* had broken up with her boyfriend.
       b.   *She* had broken up with her boyfriend.

Often, of course, a phrase consists of only one word, e.g.:

(34)   a.   Daisy was rehearsing.
       b.   I love children, don't you?

The nouns *Daisy* and *children* in these examples are DPs that happen to consist of only a noun, so it is possible to replace these words with the pronouns *she* and *them* respectively. However, such pronouns replace the determined noun *phrases*, not the nouns alone, as indicated by the ungrammaticality of the following:

(35)   a.   *The she with the light brown hair was reheasing.
       b.   *I love my them.   (cf. I love my children.)

Of course, by now you are used to the fact that very few generalizations in linguistics are *always* true. There are situations when some pronouns can substitute for nouns or noun phrases (NPs), rather than DPs. The primary example is the interrogative pronoun *what* used in ECHO QUESTIONS (example from Huddleston and Pullum 2002:429):

(36)   I just bought a new car.   You bought a new *what*?!
                                  You bought a *what*?!
                                  You bought *what*?!

Since in this context *what* can take a determiner, it is reasonable to assert that *what* may substitute for the noun *car*, the NP *new car*, or the whole DP, *a new car*. However, this only seems to occur for *what*, and *one*, e.g., *a big one*, though it is arguable whether *one* is really a pronoun here (see below). There are also situations where pronouns are simply treated as nouns in their own right rather than as replacements for some other noun or noun phrase, as in:

(37)   I can't tell if it's a *he* or a *she*.

This kind of example is an illustration of the "shiftiness" of word classes, sort of like the use of conjunctions as nouns in *no ifs, ands, or buts about it* discussed in Chapter 3. This is not one of the ordinary functions of pronouns.

Another reason for not saying that pronouns are "substitutes" for nouns is that some pronouns, namely those that express first and second persons, do not substitute or "stand for" anything – they simply refer directly to speaker and hearer. One would have to take a very abstract view of the meaning of first and second person pronouns, one in which *I* always "stands for" an abstract DP like *the person who is speaking*, and *you* always "stands for" *the person I am speaking to*, in order to maintain a consistent definition of pronouns as substitutes for something else.

There are several subclasses of pronouns in English, principally PERSONAL PRONOUNS, INTERROGATIVE (WH-) PRONOUNS, DEMONSTRATIVE PRONOUNS, INDEFINITE PRONOUNS, and QUANTIFIED PRONOUNS. In the following paragraphs, each of these types of pronouns is presented and discussed in turn. The specific uses of pronouns in particular constructions (e.g., questions and relative clauses) are discussed in subsequent chapters.

Personal pronouns

PERSONAL PRONOUNS are words that are used to refer to participants that are judged by a speaker to be already present or ACTIVE in the mind of the audience. Something that is judged to be already "on stage" and uniquely identifiable may be referred to with a personal pronoun. In this sense personal pronouns have the same syntactic properties (or the same DISTRIBUTION) as definite DPs, like *the girl, my mother*, etc. The personal pronouns are those we probably first think of when we think of "pronouns." Table 5.3 represents the personal pronouns of Contemporary Standard English, plus several older forms that survive in literature and in a few linguistically conservative communities today. These older forms are given in parentheses in Table 5.3.

The demise of the older personal pronouns in parentheses in Table 5.3 has caused a big problem for Modern English speakers. Notice that all the Modern English pronouns in the dark box in the middle of Table 5.3 are the same. This means that the one form *you* can refer to one person or many people, to actors

Table 5.3 **Personal pronouns of Contemporary Standard English (archaic forms are given in parentheses)**

Person	Number/ Gender	Nominative	Accusative	Independent genitive	Dependent genitive	Reflexive
First person (the speaker)	Singular	I	me	mine	my	myself
	Plural	we	us	ours	our	ourselves
Second person (the addressee, or audience)	Singular	you (thou)	you (thee)	yours (thine)	your (thy)	yourself (thyself)
	Plural	you (ye)	you	yours	your	yourselves
Third person	Singular Feminine	she	her	hers	her	herself
	Singular Masculine	he	him	his	his	himself
	Singular Neutral	it	it	its[3]	its	itself
	Plural	they	them	theirs	their	themselves

(NOMINATIVE CASE) or non-actors (ACCUSATIVE CASE). This can lead to serious communication problems.

The reason this ambiguity exists is that at some point in the twelfth century or so, people started thinking of the plural accusative form, *you*, as being more polite than the other forms, and started to use it for all 2nd person categories in formal situations. So for several centuries, probably under the influence of French and other European languages, *thou*, *thee*, and *ye* were "familiar" forms and *you* was the only polite form. Then the familiar forms eventually dropped out, leaving a big "hole" in the pronoun chart – there was no way to refer to second person plural as distinct from second person singular! This kind of ambiguity is intolerable in most languages of the world, and in fact there have been many attempts to reinstitute a second person plural pronoun in English. Most of us are familiar with the form *y'all*. This is completely standard in spoken English in many parts of the USA, and has made it into most good dictionaries. However, it remains non-standard for written CSE. In other parts of the English-speaking world, several other innovative second person plural forms have arisen. These include:

(38) youse/yous   Scotland, South Africa, Australia, New Zealand, Urban
                       Eastern USA and Canada.
    yez   Ireland
    yinz/yins   Western Pennsylvania, Scotland
    you'uns   Southern USA
    you lot   UK
    you mob   Australia
    you guys   Generalized USA

The very common form *youse* (or *yous*) is clearly a result of the regular plural noun suffix *-s* extended to the pronoun system. This is an instance of PARADIGM LEVEL-LING, a common process of language change in which DEFECTIVE paradigms (sets of forms that are missing logically possible members) are made more regular by extending patterns from other paradigms. Likewise, *you'uns* or *yinz* (chiefly western Pennsylvania) are extensions from a derivational plural marker *'uns* (from *ones*) used to form nouns from adjectives in some varieties, e.g., *young'uns*, *those'uns*, *big'uns*, etc. *You lot* and *y'all* are associated with particular regions in England and Ireland respectively, and have been taken up by Americans in various parts of the USA (Hogg 2001:149ff.).

The fact that CSE has resisted the institution of a new second person plural pronoun is a good illustration of why we say that pronouns constitute a "closed" word class (see Section 3.4). It is very difficult to innovate or borrow a new pronoun, even when faced with an obvious and insidious functional gap in the pronoun system. Compare this to the class of verbs, for example. Every new edition of a dictionary includes many new verbs that seem to be established effortlessly and without limit in order to meet the constantly changing communication needs of English speakers.

Interrogative (WH-) pronouns

There is a set of pronouns that have special functions in CONTENT QUESTIONS of various sorts (see Chapter 14) and in several kinds of dependent clauses. We will call these WH-PRONOUNS, because they all contain a *w* and an *h*. In fact, they all start with *wh-*, except for *how*. You may think of *how* as being a kind of "honorary" WH-pronoun – it just hasn't gotten its *w* and *h* in quite the right places!

The function of WH-pronouns in questions is discussed in Section 15.4. The function of WH-pronouns to introduce dependent clauses, such as relative clauses, is discussed in Chapter 14. In this section we will simply consider the various forms and comment briefly on their usages.

It is appropriate to consider the forms in Table 5.4 as pronouns because they are anaphoric devices. The way we know this is that these forms vary according to semantic features of the message-world participant they refer to, e.g., humanness and semantic role. For example, *whom* is the somewhat archaic "accusative" form for human participants, and in some communities it is still used in that way. The following questions from the BNC illustrate *whom* used in an accusative role:

(39) *Whom* is Stephen Baldwin supporting? WHOM = Direct Object of *supporting*

    Whom is that terror affecting? WHOM = Direct Object of *affecting*

Table 5.4 **Interrogative pronouns of CSE**

		Human/animate	Non-human/inanimate
Nominative		who	what
Accusative		who/whom	
Nom/Acc alternative		which	which
Genitive		whose/who's	whose/who's
Oblique	Location		where
	Source		whence
	Destination		whither
	Time		when
	Manner, means, extent		how
	Reason		why/wherefore

> *Whom* will he send the news to?   WHOM = Complement of *to*
> So, for *whom* do you produce these avant-garde designs of yours?
>   WHOM = Complement of *for*

Though *whom* is the standard and historical accusative form, *who* is more common both for nominative (40a) and accusative (40b) functions. This is true both for the BNC and the COCA:

(40)   a.   *Who* is Madonna?   WHO = Subject of *is*
           Who hates who and *who* likes who?   WHO = Subject of *hates* and *likes*
           Who would like to answer that one?   WHO = Subject of *would like*
       b.   *Who* do you blame for not having gotten that?
                               WHO = Direct Object of *blame*
           Who hates *who* and who likes *who*?   WHO = Direct Object of *hates* and
                                                 likes
           Who are we going to be a superpower against?
                               WHO = Complement of *against*

The form *what* is the generic non-human WH-pronoun:

(41)   *What* about my suffering?
       What kind of stories do they seem to prefer?
       What just bit me?

The form *which* functions mostly to select one referent among a set of possibilities, regardless of whether the referent is human or not:

(42)   *Which* local group had a hit with this one?
       Which part of the church are we in now?
       I don't know *which* one to choose.

Whose is the standard spelling for the genitive case WH-pronoun, though *who's* is also common:

(43)   *Whose* birthday is it tomorrow Christopher?
       Whose turn was it this time?
       Who's feet are biggest?
       Who's class is he in?

The spelling *whose* is standard, probably because this spelling distinguishes it from the homophonous (same sound) contraction of *who is*, as in *Who's coming to dinner?*

The forms *whence* and *whither* sound rather archaic to many modern English speakers, though they are recognized and do occur in written material and in planned oral speech. They hardly ever appear in spontaneous conversation in either the BNC or the COCA:

(44)   You do not know *whence* it comes or *whither* it goes. Sermon
       Whence it came it will return.   Classroom lecture
       Whither Bill Clinton?   News interview
       You can't just ignore from *whence* you came.   News interview
       but *whence* would we get sufficient water?   Novel
       Say from *whence* you owe this strange intelligence?   Non-fiction prose

When, of course, refers to clause elements that specify the semantic role of TIME:

(45)   *When* can you bring it in?
       So *when's* your next starring role?

How questions or replaces clause elements that have the semantic roles of MANNER, MEANS, and EXTENT:

(46)   *How* will firms react to it?   MANNER
       I don't know *how* to do that.   MEANS
       By *how* much should we increase them? EXTENT
       How good are its on-line facilities?   EXTENT

Why questions elements that express REASONS:

(47)   *Why* do we need two mathematicians?
       Why might protectionism lead to volatility?

Demonstrative pronouns

There are four demonstrative pronouns, listed in Table 5.5. These forms also function as demonstrative determiners (not adjectives, see Chapter 10). What

Table 5.5 **Demonstrative pronouns**

	Singular	Plural
Near	this	these
Far	that	those

makes them pronouns is that they can alone constitute a reference to a participant. This is not a normal function for adjectives:

(48)   I've got *this* organized now.
        I wondered where *that* had gone!
        These follow a rather different pattern and generally exclude part-timers.
        Did *those* used to be big things?

Demonstrative pronouns imply actual or figurative "pointing." That is, the referent of a demonstrative pronoun is identified from the context, either the physical environment in which the conversation takes place, or the surrounding text in the discourse. This latter usage is very common in written English. In fact, *this* and *that* as demonstrative pronouns *usually* refer to some idea in the surrounding text. *This* occurs far more often in this DISCOURSE DEIXIS usage than in its "ordinary" usage to refer to some physical object. Here are a few examples:

(49)   ... there are few other assessments of instruction in community college occupational programs. *This* may be due to several factors.
        Why is he apologizing? I think *this* makes him look weak.
        If it turns out it's untrue, they'll be placed back in their home. *This* happens every day.

The pronoun *this* in each of these excerpts refers back to an idea expressed in the previous clause. *That* is also used in this way, but not as commonly as *this*. *These* and *those* are apparently not used in this discourse deixis function.

Impersonal pronouns

The forms *one*, *they*, *them*, and *you* can be used as pronouns to refer to an impersonal, unidentified participant. For example:

(50)   a.   I think *one* may with pleasure celebrate an anniversary of *one*'s nuptials,
             One acts on assumptions.
        b.   *They*'re building a new overpass on Chambers.
             They shoot horses, don't *they*?
        c.   *You* have to be over 18 to vote.
             You never know what he'll come up with next.

In all of the contexts from which these examples were taken, the italicized pronouns do not refer to any particular person or group of people.

In a related usage, sometimes impersonal second person pronouns, *you* or *your*, can include reference to the speaker. This usage seems especially to occur in descriptions of harrowing experiences, such as the following:

(51) *Your* heart's beating and *you* really don't know what to expect, whether they're going to come after *you* next or what.

This is from an interview with a witness to a terrorist attack. From the context it is clear that the speaker is referring to her own experience, but she couches it in the second person. This has the effect of "distancing" the speaker from the event itself, as though she were watching it from the outside, rather than experiencing it herself.

Indefinite and quantified pronouns

There is a set of forms in English which I would like to call "pronouns," but which are often treated as special kinds of determined noun phrases (see, e.g., Huddleston and Pullum 2002:423). These are the following.

(52)

Indefinite, referential pronouns	Indefinite, non-referential pronouns	Quantified pronouns	
somebody	anybody	everybody	nobody
someone	anyone	everyone	no one
something	anything	everything	nothing
somewhere/ someplace	anywhere	everywhere	nowhere
sometimes/ someday	anytime/ anyday	everytime/ always	never
some how	anyway/ anyhow	every way	no way/ no how

It is true that this set of forms seems to "fade into" indefinite and quantified determined noun phrases, e.g., if *everytime* and *someday* are members of the set, why aren't *everyday*, *every week*, and *some year*? If these latter examples are members of the set, why aren't *every desk*, *every mausoleum*, and *any birthday*? Like most of the classes and subclasses we've looked at, this set of forms has "fuzzy" boundaries. There are very good examples of the set (*somebody, anybody, everyone* . . .), and examples that clearly are not in the set (*every mausoleum, any birthday* . . .). Then there may be others that have some properties of the set, but not all of them (*everytime, anyday*). In general, the ones in the higher rows of (52) are the more central members of this set.

INDEFINITE PRONOUNS have the same syntactic properties as indefinite determined noun phrases. Therefore, we might say that they "substitute for" indefinite DPs. An interesting feature of indefinite pronouns, though, is that they exhibit a distinction not grammaticalized in full indefinite DPs – the distinction between referential and non-referential referring expressions. The pragmatic statuses of referential and non-referential referring expressions are discussed in more detail in Section 15.1. For now, we can think of referential expressions as referring to participants that are present on the discourse stage. Non-referential expressions do not refer to participants on the discourse stage, but only to potential, possible, or hypothetical participants. To understand the difference between referential and non-referential referring expressions, consider example (53). This invented clause may be ambiguous, depending on the context:

(53)   I'm looking for a good book.

In (53), *a good book* is treated as indefinite, meaning the speaker does not assume that the hearer can identify the particular *good book* the speaker has in mind at the moment the clause is uttered. However, *a good book* could be referential or non-referential (see Chapter 15). If the speaker is setting a particular participant up to be mentioned in subsequent text, then it is referential. In this case the next utterance might be *It is dark blue and has a hard cover.* On the other hand, if the speaker is looking for *any* book that happens to be good, then *a good book* in (53) is non-referential; in which case the next utterance might be *Can you recommend one?*

This distinction between referential and non-referential expressions underlies the difference between the indefinite pronouns that begin with *some-* and those that begin with *any-*. Consider the following two clauses:

(54)   a.   I'm looking for something.
      b.   I'm looking for anything.

In (54a), the speaker probably has some particular thing in mind, while in (54b), the speaker probably doesn't have any particular thing in mind – the Object is non-referential. Because of this contrast, indefinite non-referential pronouns are much more likely in negative clauses than are indefinite referential pronouns:

(55)   a.   I don't have anything.   I'm not seeing anyone.   They didn't stay anywhere.
      b.   ?I don't have something.   ?I'm not seeing someone.   ?They didn't stay somewhere.

QUANTIFIED PRONOUNS refer to an identifiable set of potential referents. The forms beginning with *every-* refer to all members of the set, while the one ones beginning with *n-* negatively refer to none of the members of the set:

(56) a. I think *everybody* / *nobody* was taken by surprised.
      b. Obviously, he believes *everyone* / *no one* he meets is a doctor.
      c. I am poor indeed in *everything* / *nothing* compared to you,
      d. *Everywhere* has a town council doesn't it?   She's getting *nowhere*.
      e. My money goes on the spouse, *everytime*. My money *always* goes on the spouse. My money *never* goes on the spouse.

In each of these examples, the context makes it clear what identifiable set the quantified pronoun refers to. In (56a), *everybody* or *nobody* refers to the set of people in the room where the scene takes place. In (56b), *everyone* or *no one* refers to the set of people specified in the following relative clause, *he meets*. And so on.

Either, neither, and certain quantifiers

The words *either* and *neither* are difficult to assign to a word class. They are usually classified as adverbs, since it is clear that they do often function as adverbial Modifiers. However, it is also clear that they both may be used as pronouns. The following is an example of the pronoun usage of *either* from the BNC:

(57) A solid modeller may employ *either* in an attempt to construct a general model definition.

Here *either* has an indefinite, referential meaning because it refers to one of two methods described earlier in the text, but the specific method is not identified.

The following is an example of the pronoun usage of *neither* taken from a newspaper tabloid. *Neither* occurs toward the end of this extended passage:

(58) "What a pathetic pair of posers," he says. "Hit Man's hair is so greasy you could cause a major oil glut just by draining his head. And as for the Bulldog, I hear that his wife takes him for walks at night to stop him making a mess." *Neither* is worthy of a WWF title, but Bulldog has the clear advantage.

Here two wrestlers are being contrasted, and the conclusion of the writer is that *neither* one of them is worthy of a World Wrestling Federation title. This is equivalent to saying *both* of them are *not* worthy of the title.

Some quantifiers, such as *both, all, half, some, each,* and the numerals, may functions as pronouns:

(59) *Both* are very manpower dependent.
      We do a selection of facials, *all* are very nice.
      Nearly *half* had been given the wrong advice ...
      Eight firebombs were planted but only *three* went off.

Summary

In this chapter we have looked at the functional domain of participant reference. Nouns and related elements serve the important communicational function of referring to or mentioning participants on the discourse stage.

First, nouns were described in terms of three interrelated sets of properties:

- Semantic properties
- Morphosyntactic properties
- Discourse-pragmatic properties

Then, several grammatically distinct, but semantically motivated, subclasses of nouns were compared and contrasted. These include:

- Proper names vs. common nouns
- Countable vs. non-countable nouns
- Collective nouns
- Collective plurals

Non-countable nouns include abstract nouns and action nominalizations.

Finally, the functions of pronouns were introduced. Pronouns are not "substitutes" for nouns. Pronouns are referential expressions that have similar distributional properties to determined noun phrases. There are some types of pronouns that distribute differently than determined noun phrases, but there are no syntactic positions where determined noun phrases can be used where pronouns cannot be used. Several types of pronouns were discussed, including:

- Personal pronouns
- WH-pronouns
- Demonstrative pronouns
- Impersonal pronouns
- Indefinite and quantified pronouns

In addition, a few quantifiers and the forms *either* and *neither* also have uses as pronouns. These were discussed in the final section of this chapter.

FURTHER READING

Katz (1990) and Lakoff and Johnson (1999) are outstanding treatments of the nature of meaning and reference from a linguistic philosophical perspective. Keizer (2007) gives a detailed linguistic treatment of the meanings and uses of nouns and noun phrases in English based on naturally occurring data. Mahlberg (2005) treats the use of nouns and noun phrases in English using natural discourse data.

Exercises

1. For each of the following nouns, indicate its subclass, giving evidence for your claims. If any of these can be used in more than one sense, describe at least two of the senses. You may want to look some of these up in a good dictionary.

   Example: Michelle   This is a proper name because it probably refers to a unique individual. It does not require a determiner in order to function as a Determined NP: "Michelle loves children."

   a. art
   b. leaf
   c. groceries
   d. chirping
   e. AIDS

   f. pottery
   g. intelligentsia
   h. squad
   i. baggage
   j. science

2. Provide a reasonable quantity or partitive noun in each of the following sentences:
   a. A gentle _____ of wind sent the letters flying.
   b. Let's have a _____ of applause for Jessica Parker.
   c. We had at least three _____ of drinks.
   d. Her smile was a _____ of light in my gloomy space.
   e. She came upon a _____ of parrot fish on her first dive.
   f. I felt a _____ of guilt over the ruined manuscript.
   g. Let me give you a _____ of advice.
   h. He left without one _____ of thanks.
   i. The police couldn't find a _____ of evidence.
   j. The amnesty will be a grand _____ of magnanimity.

6 Actions, states, and processes

They've a temper, some of them – particularly verbs: they're the proudest – adjectives you can do anything with, but not verbs – however, I can manage the whole lot of them!

Lewis Carroll (1872)

In Chapter 5 we looked at the various ways that speakers of English refer to or mention participants that are "on stage" in the metaphorical play that constitutes any communicative act. In addition to mentioning participants, speakers also need to say what those participants do, what conditions they are in, and what happens to them. These communicative functions are usually associated with verbs, although, as we will see in this chapter, the FRAMES or CONSTRUCTIONS within which verbs, nouns, and other elements are arranged also deeply affect the meanings expressed by particular verbs. Certainly verbs are crucial to expressing actions, states, and processes but, like all form–function composites, their functions are significantly affected by their contexts. Verbs are not strait jackets that dictate exactly what kind of scene a speaker may express. Rather, they are tools that speakers may use in any number of ways to create rich and nuanced discourse scenes.

6.1 Semantic roles

In order to understand how the verbs of any language work it is very helpful to understand the notion of SEMANTIC ROLES. Semantic roles are conceptual roles and relationships on the discourse stage. In any play, there are various actors with particular roles to play. If a scene involves, for example, an event of eating, there must be two participants on stage, each with a very particular role – there must be someone or something that initiates and controls the action (the "eater"), and something that is affected by the action (the "eaten thing"). If there is no controller, or no affected participant, it is hard to imagine a scene being described as "eating." We might say that these roles help define the very notion of EAT (remember that capital letters represent semantic concepts, rather than words of English).

Like all semantic concepts, semantic roles are not absolutely rigid categories, with clear boundaries. Rather, they are defined in terms of PROTOTYPES, with some examples being very easy to identify, and others being rather elusive. This is the nature of semantic categorization in general, and is a major theme in much recent linguistic literature, as well as throughout this book. Meaning can be thought of as an infinitely varied "space" with no inherent categorization scheme. The human mind, however, is finite, and therefore must make clear categories when referring to semantic space. For this reason, linguistic categories (like noun, verb, Subject, Object, etc.) tend to be much more rigid and fewer in number than possible semantic notions – though even linguistic categories are themselves quite variable. We have already seen, and will see again in the following pages, many examples of how linguistic structure "discretizes" (makes into discrete categories) continuously variable semantic space.

Though semantic roles influence the grammar profoundly, they are not primarily grammatical categories. Ideally, semantic roles are the roles that participants play in discourse-world situations, quite apart from linguistic expression of those situations. So, for example, if in some imagined world (which may or may not correspond to objective reality), someone named Waldo paints a barn, then Waldo is acting as the AGENT (the initiator and controller) and the barn is the PATIENT (the affected participant) of the painting event, regardless of whether any observer ever utters a clause like *Waldo painted the barn* to describe that event. Many potential linguistic utterances, such as all of those in (1), may be used to describe the same situation, but the roles of AGENT and PATIENT and the identities of the participants that fill these roles cannot change from one utterance to the other without changing the scene being described:

(1)   Waldo painted the barn.
      The barn was painted by Waldo.
      Waldo seems to have painted the barn.
      The barn got painted.
      Waldo might have painted the barn.
      Waldo just got done painting.
      Who painted that barn?
      It was the barn that Waldo painted.
      Waldo was the one who painted the barn.
      Waldo used this paintbrush to paint the barn.
      Paint the barn, Waldo!
      Waldo painted the barn for his mother.

Some of these expressions describe scenes that are more detailed than others, as speakers may choose to enrich a scene by adding additional participants, or leave it a little vague by failing to mention one or more of the participants. But in all these examples the scene itself does not necessarily change. If a speaker changes the description so much that someone else is presented as the AGENT, or something else as the PATIENT, then a different scene is being expressed.

(2) The barn painted Waldo.
Waldo and the barn got painted.
Osmond painted the barn.
Waldo painted the garage.

The utterances in (2) describe different scenes than those represented in (1): therefore their TRUTH VALUES may be different. In other words, if *Osmond painted the barn* is true, *Waldo painted the barn* may or may not also be true. If any of these utterances is meant to represent some objective reality in which Waldo IS the AGENT and the barn IS the PATIENT, then we might say the speaker is lying, or has misunderstood the situation.

There is a large literature on the notion of truth values, and the relationships among utterances as functions of their relative truth values (see, e.g., Partee *et al.* 1990). In Chapter 14 on clause combining, we will employ some of the notions from this literature in discussing the structure of English complex clause constructions. For now, the important point to remember is that semantic roles relate to scenes in the discourse world. When it comes to grammar, the choice of different verbs and constructions strongly depends on the semantic roles in the scenes speakers are attempting to express. Therefore, understanding semantic roles goes a long way in helping an English language professional understand English grammar.

Certain semantic roles are very influential in determining verb choice, while others are more likely to affect the choice of prepositions or adverbial elements. The semantic roles that influence verb choice the most are those that are typically expressed via the CORE GRAMMATICAL RELATIONS of Subject, Object, and perhaps Indirect Object in English (see Section 7.2 for a more detailed discussion of grammatical relations). These semantic roles are AGENT, THEME, FORCE, INSTRUMENT, EXPERIENCER, PATIENT, RECIPIENT, and GOAL. Others, e.g., various subtypes of LOCATION, DIRECTION, SETTING, PURPOSE, TIME, MANNER, and many more, are more likely to be expressed as OBLIQUE phrases (usually Complements of prepositions).

In considering the following definitions, it must be remembered that semantic roles are defined in terms of prototypes. There are very good examples and some marginal examples of each of these semantic roles. In the process of communication speakers constantly and unconsciously evaluate how best to express their ideas in terms of particular roles in particular situations. The roles mentioned here have proven useful in describing and understanding many facts about English. They are not to be taken, however, as absolute, invariable, objective categories.

An AGENT can be described as "the typically animate perceived instigator of the action" (Fillmore 1968).[1] In scenes likely to be described by the following invented clauses, *Waldo* would refer to the AGENT:

(3) a.   Waldo ate beans.
     b.   That barn was painted by Waldo.
     c.   Waldo ran around the block.
     d.   Whom did Waldo kiss?
     e.   It was Waldo who deceived the President.

In some of these sentences Waldo is a "better" or more prototypical AGENT than others. A prototypical AGENT is conscious, acts with VOLITION (on purpose), and performs an action that has a physical, visible effect in the discourse world. An AGENT is a powerful controller of an event. According to this characterization, *Waldo* in (3a) and (3b) refers to a near prototypical AGENT. In (3c), although Waldo is conscious and presumably acts with volition, there is no obvious, visible change in the discourse world that results from Waldo's running around the block. The same sort of observation can be made for (3d) and (3e). Therefore, Waldo is a less-than-prototypical AGENT in (3c), (3d), and (3e). Nevertheless, he is still presented as the instigator and controller of the event, so his semantic role is still AGENT.

A FORCE is an entity that instigates an action, but not consciously or voluntarily. For example, *wind* is a FORCE in the following clauses:

(4) a.   It was wind that formed those rocks.
     b.   What did the wind knock over?
     c.   The wind is carrying us to freedom.
     d.   Our sails were filled by a strong east wind.

Again, these examples are ordered according to a rough "degree of prototypicality," with *the wind* in (4a) being the most prototypical and in (4d) the least prototypical example of a FORCE.

A prototypical PATIENT undergoes a visible, physical change in state. In the following clauses, *Waldo* is the PATIENT:

(5) a.   Waldo was eaten by the T-Rex.
     b.   Montezuma punched Waldo.
     c.   Waldo fell from the third floor.
     d.   Who washed Waldo?

The notion of CHANGE OF STATE is central to the semantic role of PATIENT. The most prototypical change in state is a visible, physical, "whole body" change, such as in (5a). In the other examples in (5), Waldo is a less prototypical PATIENT.

A THEME is a participant that moves, or is the locus of an action or property that does not undergo a change. For example, *Waldo* is the THEME in the following clauses:

(6) a. Waldo fell into the well.
     b. I'm Waldo.
     c. We love Waldo.
     d. Scooby forgot Waldo.
     e. Waldo seemed standoffish.

Another important point about semantic roles is that one participant on the discourse stage may have more than one semantic role. For example, in the case of (6a), Waldo is a THEME because he is a participant that moves; however, he is also affected by the action – certainly falling into a well affects someone! So Waldo is also somewhat of a PATIENT in this sentence as well. Going back to example (5c), the same verb is used, but in that case (falling from the third floor) Waldo is probably more affected by the event, and so may be even more PATIENT-like. But this is a subjective impression of what might be happening in the discourse world, and the grammar of English makes no overt distinction – *Waldo* is the Subject of the verb *fall* in both examples.

An INSTRUMENT is something that causes an action indirectly. Normally an AGENT acts upon an INSTRUMENT and the INSTRUMENT accomplishes the action. For example, in the following clauses *a hammer* is an INSTRUMENT:

(7) a. I'll smash it with a hammer!
     b. That box was smashed by a hammer.
     c. A hammer smashed the box.
     d. What did Uzma smash with a hammer?
     e. It was a hammer that Uzma smashed it with.

Notice that there is no absolute correlation between the semantic role of INSTRU-MENT and any particular grammatical expression. So in (7a, d, and e), the hammer is the Complement of the preposition *with*, while in (7b) the hammer is the complement of the preposition *by*, and in (7c) it is the Subject of the sentence.

An EXPERIENCER neither controls nor is visibly affected by an action. Proto-typically an EXPERIENCER is an entity that receives a sensory impression. For example, in the following clauses, *Waldo* is an EXPERIENCER:

(8) a. Waldo saw the bicycle.
     b. The explosion was heard by Waldo.
     c. What did Waldo feel?
     d. It was Waldo who smelled smoke first.
     e. Waldo broke out in a cold sweat.

A RECIPIENT is the typically animate destination of some moving object. A GOAL is simply the endpoint of a trajectory of motion. The difference between RECIPIENT and GOAL is similar to the difference between AGENT and FORCE. Because RECIPIENT and GOAL are so similar, the forms used to express these roles tend to be similar. For example, English may use the preposition *to* to mark both RECIPIENT and GOAL:

(9) a. I sent the book to Lucretia.   (Lucretia = RECIPIENT)
      b. I sent the book to France.   (France = GOAL)

In summary, semantic roles are roles that participants may play in discourse world events. We have just discussed eight semantic roles that are often referred to in the linguistics literature – AGENT, FORCE, PATIENT, THEME, INSTRUMENT, EXPERIENCER, RECIPIENT, and GOAL. These terms describe areas within the potentially infinite range of semantic roles in conceptual space. They are the kinds of roles that are most often expressed by the core grammatical relations of Subject, Object, and Indirect Object in English. There are several other semantic roles that will be referred to in the following discussion, and in the rest of this book. Indeed, there is no logical end to the number of semantic roles speakers may need to express, though there must be a finite number of linguistic categories. Language imposes discrete structure on infinite semantic space.

6.2   Verb subclasses

Verbs, like all words, are just gestures (often made with the vocal apparatus) associated with particular meanings. The meanings of verbs can be thought of metaphorically as idealized "scenes" that the verbs evoke in the minds of users of the language (Fillmore 1976, 1977). Semantic features of such idealized scenes profoundly affect the *grammatical* features of individual verbs that evoke them. For example, scenes that inherently involve only one major participant tend to be expressed grammatically by clauses with only one core ARGUMENT,[2] usually thought of as the SUBJECT of the clause (see Section 7.2 for a discussion of Subjects, Objects, and other GRAMMATICAL RELATIONS).

Any particular arrangement of semantic roles and grammatical relations is sometimes called a CASE FRAME, or an ARGUMENT STRUCTURE. For example, the verb *grow* in English can evoke a scene that requires only one participant – a person or thing that grows. For this reason, clauses based on the verb *grow* only require one related noun phrase,[3] the Subject. The argument structure (or case frame) of this kind of clause can be represented schematically as follows:

(10)   Scene: PATIENT   GROW

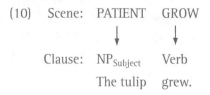

Clause: NP_{Subject}   Verb
The tulip   grew.

In the case of *grow*, the only required participant is a semantic PATIENT – namely the person or thing that undergoes the change of state expressed by the verb. Many other noun phrases and other elements *may* occur, and usually do, in a clause constructed around the verb *grow*, but in order to qualify as an event of *growing*, only one participant is absolutely necessary. Verbs whose core meanings evoke scenes that only require one participant are sometimes referred to as INTRANSITIVE VERBS, and clauses whose argument structure requires only one noun phrase are sometimes referred to as INTRANSITIVE CLAUSES.

We have seen that the verb *grow* involves a PATIENT that may be expressed as a Subject. Other intransitive verbs occur in argument structures in which the Subject is an AGENT (11), a THEME (12), an EXPERIENCER (13), or any number of other possible semantic roles:

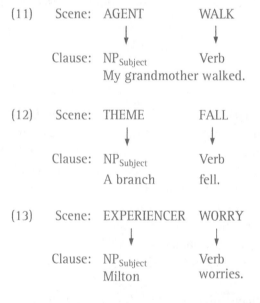

(11)   Scene: AGENT   WALK

Clause: NP_{Subject}   Verb
My grandmother walked.

(12)   Scene: THEME   FALL

Clause: NP_{Subject}   Verb
A branch   fell.

(13)   Scene: EXPERIENCER   WORRY

Clause: NP_{Subject}   Verb
Milton   worries.

It is hard to find syntactic properties that distinguish these classes of verbs in English, though there are some. For example, the past participle of patientive (Subject = PATIENT) intransitive verbs, like *grow*, can often be made into adjectives that modify the Subject, whereas the past participles of agentive (Subject = AGENT) intransitive verbs generally cannot:

(14)   Past Participles used as adjectives

Patientive intransitive verbs	Agentive intransitive verbs
a grown child (a child that grew)	?a/my *walked* grandmother (a grandmother that walked)
some *melted* ice cream (ice cream that melted)	?a *talked* child (a child that talked)
a changed man (a man that changed)	?a *jumped* athlete (an athlete that jumped)
	?a *breathed* baby (a baby that breathed)

The (very small) class of intransitive experiential (Subject = EXPERIENCER) verbs seem to pattern with the patientive class in this respect:

(15)   Past participles of experiential intransitive verbs used as adjectives
   A worried gentleman (a gentleman that worries)
   An *agonized* face (a face displaying an EXPERIENCER's agony)[4]

In addition to intransitive verbs, there are verbs that evoke scenes that require more than one participant. This is the case of the verb *eat* mentioned earlier. One major way that semantic roles are expressed for this verb consists of an argument structure in which the AGENT is the Subject and the PATIENT is the Object. This structure, and a possible clause that instantiates it, is illustrated in (16):

(16)   Scene: AGENT   EAT   PATIENT
             ↓   ↓   ↓
    Clause: NP$_{Subject}$ Verb   NP$_{Object}$
             Waldo   ate   ice cream

To a certain extent, argument structures are independent of individual verbs. For example, the verb *eat* perhaps normally occurs in an argument structure such as (16), but may in conversation occur in any number of other argument structures, depending on the communicative needs and creativity of the speaker. Here are some suggestive examples:

(17)   a.   She ate her way through her first year of college.
       b.   I fished, I ate, I slept.
       c.   This soup eats like a meal.
       d.   The battery acid ate a hole in my jeans.

In (17a), no PATIENT is expressed, but an AGENT and a PATH are mentioned, as though the AGENT traveled along the PATH by means of eating. In (17b), again no

PATIENT is expressed. Nevertheless it is understood that the AGENT ate something. In (17c) there is no AGENT expressed – only the "eaten thing," the soup, as though the soup itself is responsible for the action! Finally, in (17d), technically no AGENT is expressed at all. Since battery acid does not act with volition, it is technically a FORCE rather than an AGENT. Furthermore, in this example *a hole* is not an "eaten thing" (PATIENT). Rather it is a PRODUCT – something that comes into existence as a result of the "eating" event. Some grammarians would say that this is a distinct sense of the verb *eat* – one that doesn't require an AGENT and PATIENT, but that different sense is only understood because of the argument structure "frame" in which the verb *eat* occurs. These examples show that a good portion of the meanings of clauses depends on the frame in which a verb is presented.

Good dictionaries will exemplify the major argument structures that each verb typically occurs in (sometimes as different "senses" of the verb), but cannot possibly list all conceivable frames within which a verb might be used by speakers using their language creatively to express novel and complex ideas. On the other hand, the core meaning of a verb does seem to limit the possible argument structures in which it may occur – verbs don't just randomly occur in any argument structure imaginable. Here is a comparison of some argument structures for the verbs *pound* and *eat*. From now on we will be presenting argument structures (the alignment between semantic roles and grammatical relations) horizontally, just to save space:

(18)   a.   AGENT→Subject, PATIENT→Object, INSTRUMENT→Oblique:
            She pounded the table with a hammer.
            She ate the ice cream with a spoon.
       b.   AGENT→Subject, THEME→Object, PATIENT→Oblique:
            She pounded the hammer on the table.
            *She ate the spoon on the ice cream.

There is something about the *meanings* of these verbs that makes argument structure (18a) work for both, while (18b) works for *pound* and not *eat*. So we see that possible argument structures are part of what every speaker of a language must know in order to use verbs understandably in conversations.

As we've seen, the meaning of a verb has a lot to do with the argument structures it can plausibly participate in. In particular, many verbs can occur in both transitive and intransitive argument structures (or frames), though they vary in how the transitive and intransitive frames relate to one another. For example, the verbs illustrated by *grow* in (10) take a PATIENT as Subject. These verbs can, for the most part, also occur in a transitive frame in which an AGENT is the Subject and the PATIENT is the Object:

(19) a. PATIENT→Subject   b. AGENT→Subject,
                                       PATIENT→Object

melt	The ice melted.	Milton melted the ice.
grow	The tomatoes grew.	Milton grew the tomatoes.
change	The city changed.	The mayor changed the city.
break	The stick broke.	Waldo broke the stick.
burn	Dinner burned.	Mable burned dinner.

Other verbs that occur in argument structure (19b) have AGENTS as Subject when used intransitively:

(20) a. AGENT→Subject   b. AGENT→Subject,
                                     PATIENT→Object

jump	Milton jumped.	Milton jumped the burglar.
run	Mabel runs (to school).	Mable runs the program.

In order to express the PATIENT as the Subject of these verbs, a PASSIVE construction is required (see Chapter 13 on voice and valence):

(21) The burglar was jumped (by Milton).
       The program is run (by Mabel).

Yet other verbs that have an AGENT as their Subject in an intransitive frame have a THEME as the Object in a transitive frame:

(22) a. AGENT→Subject   b. AGENT→Subject,
                                THEME→Object

nod	Frank nodded.	Frank nodded his head.
swim	Maynard swam.	Maynard swam the Strait of Gibraltar.
play	Mabel played.	Mabel played the Moonlight Sonata.

Still other verbs take EXPERIENCER Subjects when occurring in an intransitive argument structure. It is often awkward to place such verbs in any kind of a transitive frame:

(23) EXPERIENCER→Subject   TRANSITIVE FRAME?

sneeze	Jane sneezed.	Jane sneezed the kleenex off the table.
cry	The baby cried.	The baby cried herself to sleep.
sweat	The athlete sweated.	Orual sweated the final exam.
blush	Martin blushed.	?Everett blushed his cheeks.
doze	Alfred dozed.	Ilongo dozed the night away.

In addition to verb subclasses distinguished by their plausible argument structures, verbs are subclassified according to other features of the idealized scenes that they evoke in the discourse world. For example, scenes that involve weather phenomena (*to rain, to snow, to hail*) do not have any specific participants. Therefore, verbs that evoke such scenes often have a "dummy" argument that doesn't refer to any entity at all:

(24) ???→**Subject**
It rained last night.

What rained? The weather? The sky? The pronoun *it* in this clause really doesn't refer to anything. *It* is just there because English clauses have to have Subjects! Sometimes *it* in such cases is called a DUMMY PRONOUN.

The following list describes some situation types that motivate (provide a plausible explanation for) certain grammatical classes of English verbs. The categorization presented here is based largely on Chafe (1970), Jackendoff (1986), and Talmy (2007), though there are several different semantic categorization frameworks that may be useful in analyzing the structures of English. Verbs that express similar situation types tend to have similar grammatical properties, including allowing similar collections of argument structures. Therefore, in order to understand the grammatical behavior of particular verbs, it is useful to consider them in terms of the scenes that they characteristically evoke.

States

States are situations in the discourse world in which there is no change, and no action:

(25) Tyrion *is tall*, proud, and fair.
Little Issi *knows* nothing of the complex politics behind his hunger.
I first *saw* Mr. Belville at the masquerade.
But she *had* money …

The prototypical scenes evoked by the predicates *be tall, know, see,* and *have* do not involve any movement or change. Consequently, these predicates tend not to occur in constructions that imply progression or dynamic actions. For example, the PROGRESSIVE CONSTRUCTION in English is the construction that involves the auxiliary verb *be* plus another verb with the suffix -*ing* (see Chapter 12). The progressive is DYNAMIC in that it expresses events in progress, i.e., situations that inherently involve activity and change. Since states inherently *don't* involve activity or change, verbs that express states tend to sound a bit awkward in the progressive construction:

(26) a. ?Fezzik is being tall.   c. ?They are knowing the answer.
b. ?She is seeing the airplane. d. Sudha is having a cow/a bad day.

All of these constructions can be used in the right context, but notice that the effect is to change a state into a dynamic event. If Fezzik is *being tall* it seems to imply that he is doing something on purpose to make himself tall. This is quite different from the state described by a clause like *he is tall.* In some varieties of English *to have a cow* (26d) is an idiom meaning something like "to react in an extremely emotional manner." This is an extension of the expression *to have a baby* meaning "to give birth." Notice that giving birth is a dynamic event – something that involves movement and change – rather than a state. This is very different from the state implied by the scene evoked by a clause like *Sudha owns a cow.* Similarly, in the construction *Sudha is having a bad day,* quite a different sense of *have* is expressed. Rather than *owning* a bad day, Sudha is being presented as *experiencing* a bad day. Though experiencing something is obviously not as active as giving birth to something, still it is more active than the simple state of ownership.

Stative clauses tend to require only one participant, since there is no action to transfer from one participant to another, though there may be a second, non-affected participant, e.g., the word *answer* in a stative situation like *she knew the answer, mountain* in *she saw the mountain,* or money in *she has money.*

Other stative concepts are often expressed via *be* plus adjectival, nominal, or locational Complements.

(27)   Those roses are complimentary.
         She is a math teacher.
         Waldo was in the kitchen.

Complementation as a syntactic function will be discussed in more detail in Chapter 9.

Processes

A process is a situation that involves change over time. Processes can be either involuntary or voluntary. In an involuntary process, there is only one participant, and that participant:

- undergoes a change in state,
- does not act with volition,
- does not necessarily move through space, and
- is not the source of some moving object.

For example, the intransitive senses of *grow, die, melt, wilt, dry up, explode, rot, tighten,* and *break* belong to this class.[5] These verbs occur in answer to the question "What happened to X?," but less easily "What did X do?":

(28)   What happened to Sylvan?   He died.
         What did Sylvan do?   ?He died.
         What happened to the mustard?   It dried up.
         What did the mustard do?   ?It dried up.

Motion

All expressions of motion involve a THEME (a thing that moves), and an expressed or implied PATH along which the THEME moves. The path may be specified in terms of the starting point, the ending point, both starting and ending points, or neither. It may simply be implied. Motion can also involve a MANNER in which the motion is accomplished. In English, the most semantically neutral verbs of motion are *come* and *go*. These verbs are anchored to a point called the DEICTIC CENTER. For *come* and *go*, the deictic center is usually the place where the clause is uttered, or some other salient location like "home." *Come* means the THEME follows a PATH toward the deictic center while *go* means the THEME follows a PATH away from the deictic center; other people will *come* to where I am, but I will *go* to where they are. Sometimes the deictic center can be shifted. For example, if I am talking to someone on the telephone and I say *I'll come to your house tomorrow* I'm shifting the deictic center to the place where my audience is located. Telephone conversations are tricky when it comes to deixis. Since the location of the speaker and the location of the hearer are different, sometimes it is difficult to determine exactly where the deictic center should be.

For other motion verbs, the PATH or the MANNER of motion are more salient than the deictic center (see Section 2.3). MOTION+MANNER verbs seem to be more common and more productive in English, though there are quite a few MOTION+PATH verbs:

(29)

SIMPLE MOTION	MOTION+PATH	MOTION+MANNER
come	enter	run
go	exit	walk
	circle	drive
	arrive	fly
	leave	swim
	depart	sail
	ascend	float
	descend	motor
	fall	limp
	rise	slide
	pass	sidle

Some motion constructions describe TRANSLATIONAL MOTION – motion from one place to another. These constructions are grammatically distinct from other expressions of motion. For example, the past participles of MOTION+PATH verbs like *escape*, which inherently means "move from a place of captivity to freedom," can be used adjectivally (30a, b, c), whereas the past participles of non-translational motion verbs cannot (30d, e, f). This is in spite of the fact that the semantic role of the Subjects of all of these verbs is the same – an AGENT/ THEME:

(30) **Inherently translational motion verbs** **Other motion verbs**

    a. an escaped prisoner   d. *a gone student

    b. the deplaned passengers   e. *a flown bird

    c. a departed loved one   f. *a swum child

Translational motion verbs, then, pattern with the patientive (Subject = PATIENT) intransitive verbs exemplified in (14), even though the semantic role of the Subject of these verbs is better described as a THEME than a PATIENT. It is as though the transition from one place to another is considered analogous to the transition from one physical state to another for patientive verbs like *grow*, *change*, and *melt*.

Position

Verbs that describe the static position of an object, e.g., *stand, sit, crouch, kneel, lie*, and *hang*, tend to have morphosyntactic properties similar to verbs of motion. For example, verbs of position and motion can both appear in PRESENTATIONAL constructions (see Section 9.5). Other kinds of verbs cannot as easily be used in such constructions:

(31) MOTION   Here comes my bus.

                    Under the bed scurried the cat.

      POSITION   There sits my bus.

                    Under the bed crouched the cat.

                    On the wall hung a portrait of Mao.

      OTHER   ?There burns my bus.

                    ?Under the bed died the cat.

                    ?On the wall smiled a portrait of Mao.

Actions

Actions are situations that are initiated by some conscious or unconscious force, but do not necessarily involve an affected participant, e.g., *dance, sing, speak, sleep/rest, look (at), read, deceive, care for*. Note that actions can be either DYNAMIC, i.e., they involve change (*dance, sing, speak*), non-dynamic (*rest, look at*), or somewhere in between. These verbs may occur in answer to the question "What did X do?" but less easily "What happened to X?" unless a slightly ironic, sarcastic, or extended meaning is desired:

(32) What did Reginald do?   He danced the tango.

      What happened to Reginald?   ?He danced the tango.

      What happened to the tango? ?Reginald danced it.

(33) What did Inigo do? He read *War and Peace.*
      What happened to Inigo? ?He read *War and Peace.*
      What happened to the book? ?Inigo read it.

(34) What did Carol do? She cared for her son.
      What happened to Carol? ?She cared for her son.
      What happened to Carol's son? ?Carol cared for him.

Action-processes

Action-processes are situations initiated by some conscious or unconscious force, and which affect a distinct PATIENT, e.g., *kill, hit, stab, shoot, spear* (and other violent events), plus the transitive senses of *break, melt, crash, change,* and others. Verbs that express action-processes may occur in answer to both the questions "What did X do?" and "What happened to Y?":

(35) What did Michael do? He melted the ice.
      What happened to the ice? Michael melted it.
      What did Waldo do? He broke Trevor's nose.
      What happened to Trevor's nose? Waldo broke it.

Production verbs

Production verbs are those that describe the coming into existence of some entity, e.g., *build, ignite, form, create, make, gather* as in "a crowd gathered," and others. The semantic role of the entity that comes into existence is sometimes referred to as the PRODUCT, and sometimes as the THEME.

(36)

	AGENT		PRODUCT		PRODUCT	
	↓		↓		↓	
	NP_Subject	Verb	NP_Object		NP_Subject	Verb
a.	Martin	built	three houses.	b.	A crowd	gathered.

Cognition

Verbs of cognition express such concepts as *know, think, understand, learn, believe, regret, worry about, remember,* and *forget.* For most of these concepts the participant that "cognizes" does so at least somewhat volitionally. Therefore, we can say the main participant is "somewhat agentive," though not a prototypical AGENT since there is no visible movement or change involved with a cognition concept. For now let's refer to the main participant of a cognition verb as the

COGNIZER. We can think of this as a kind of combination of EXPERIENCER and AGENT. Most of these concepts may also include a SOURCE of the experience.

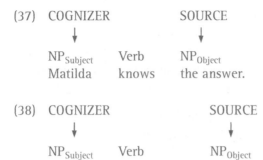

(37) COGNIZER   SOURCE

     ↓   ↓

    NP$_{Subject}$ Verb   NP$_{Object}$
    Matilda   knows   the answer.

(38) COGNIZER   SOURCE

     ↓   ↓

    NP$_{Subject}$ Verb   NP$_{Object}$
    Chris   worries about   money.

Sensation

Sensation (or sensory impression) verbs express concepts involving the senses, e.g., *see, hear, feel, taste, sense, observe, smell, perceive*, etc. As with concepts of cognition, there are two potential participants in a scene involving a sensory impression. One is the EXPERIENCER, and the other is the SOURCE of the sensation:

(39) EXPERIENCER   SOURCE

     ↓   ↓

    NP$_{Subject}$ Verb   NP$_{Object}$
    We   saw   you   at The Bronze.

Emotion

As with cognition concepts, concepts that refer to emotions, such as *fear, like/love/ please, be angry/sad/mournful, be happy/joyful/pleased, grieve/mourn* require an EXPERIENCER that may or may not be a little bit agentive:

(40) Tories now *fear*, however, that the whole sorry episode has damaged the Prime Minister.
He *feared* he would get tagged as a soap star.
they continue to *grieve for* their youngest child.

The verb *please,* in the sense of *be pleasant to*, is an interesting emotion verb in that the SOURCE of the emotion is expressed as the Subject, and the EXPERIENCER as the Object. Often in the corpora the EXPERIENCER is a sense, such as *touch* or *smell*, as in (41b):

(41) a. It certainly *pleases* me.
     b. Like their odour *pleases* the sense of smell.

Utterance

Utterance verbs, such as *speak, talk, say, tell, ask, answer, shout, yell, whisper, call, assert, imply, state, affirm, declare, murmur, boom, blurt, babble, sputter, converse, chat, discuss,* and *sing* only require an AGENT, but may also involve a THEME referring to the content of the utterance. These verbs often exhibit irregular phonological, morphological, and/or syntactic properties. For example, utterance verbs allow unusual word orders:

(42)   a.   "I'll be there in a minute," said John.
       b.   "Where are we going?" asked Marilyn.
       c.   "Crash!" went the toy.

In these clauses the grammatical Subject follows the verb, even though with most other verb classes this is not allowed in English. Example (42c) is particularly interesting in that we see the verb *go*, which prototypically expresses motion, being used as a verb of "utterance" (the toy "says 'crash'"). As such it follows the grammatical pattern of verbs of utterance by allowing the unusual Verb+Subject word order.

Manipulation

Manipulation verbs prototypically express concepts that involve physical or rhetorical force to get someone to do something. Examples include *force, oblige, compel, urge, make, cause, let, allow,* and *permit. Forbid, prohibit, impede, and others* are manipulation verbs that imply the use of force to *prevent* someone from doing something (see Chapter 13 on causative constructions). While it is natural to think of manipulation events as being initiated by an AGENT, in fact in actual usage most of these concepts are either expressed in the passive voice (see Chapter 13), or the initiator is an inanimate FORCE, such as circumstances, policies, or internal motivation of the participant manipulated. Here are a few examples from the BNC:

(43)   the call of other duties *compel* me to step down.
       What must it take to *compel* me into it?
       house prices *compelled* people to take on huge mortgages
       ... when one is *compelled* to stop driving a motor car.
       I do not feel *compelled* by courtesy to keep my eyes on her lipstick.

(44)   Prince has been *forced* to release TWO versions of his forthcoming album.
       the freewheeling winding current may be *forced* to reverse direction.
       Flooding in London *forced* a quick change of travel plans.
       an outraged public *forced* them to return to the original.

Some verbs of utterance, such as *ask* and *tell*, can also express manipulation:

(45) He *asked* hospital staff to keep the accident details secret.
      No don't *tell* me to have my dress cleaned.
      I told her to stay in there as well.

This concludes our discussion of semantic roles, and how the semantics of particular verbs interact with semantic role "frames" to create very specific scenes to be communicated in discourse. As linguists, we are interested in semantic categorization that has structural consequences for the language, being careful not to impose a categorization scheme that may seem reasonable, but for which there is no concrete grammatical evidence. It is also important to keep in mind that there are many more semantic roles and semantically based subclasses of verbs that cohere grammatically in various ways. Dixon (2005) and Levin (1993) are particularly good resources for further detail in this area.

6.3 The forms of English verbs

Having described a major portion of the kinds of concepts and semantic frames that affect the grammatical behavior of verbs, we will discuss briefly the five inflectional forms of English verbs.

All lexical verbs of English have five forms. *Be* is the only "verb-like" lexeme that has more forms than this, but, as discussed in Chapter 11, *be* is unusual in a number of ways (e.g., syntactically it patterns more with auxiliaries than with lexical verbs). The five forms of English verbs are the following, with a representative set of example verbs:

(46) The bare form: *walk*   *go*   *give*   *sing*
      The -s form: *walks*   *goes*   *gives*   *sings*
      The past tense: *walked*   *went*   *gave*   *sang*
      The past participle: *walked*   *gone*   *given*   *sung*
      The present participle: *walking* *going*   *giving*   *singing*

The labels for these forms (mostly from Greenbaum and Quirk 2004) are convenient names that represent a mixture of formal ("bare form," "-s form") and functional ("past...," "present...") notions. To be consistently structural, the last three should be designated "the -d form," "the -en form," and the "-ing form" respectively.[6] However, these three forms are closely enough associated with the functions of past tense, past participle, and present participle that these labels are not hopelessly misleading. It *must* be kept in mind, however, that form and function are *different*! The "past tense" form doesn't always refer to "past time" (see Chapter 12), and the participles have a number of quite distinct functions that usually have little to do with "present" and "past." These five forms are *forms*, even though some of the labels sound a bit functional.

6.4 "Phrasal verbs" – on the cutting edge of the lexicon

There is a large class of verbs in English sometimes known as "phrasal verbs." These are verb-like constructions involving a root word and one or two preposition-like "particles." For example:

(47) Root word + particle (+ preposition)

come	across	
crop	up	
bring	about	
egg	on	
follow	up	
follow	up	on
follow	through	with
rely	on	
confess	to	
think	through	

Phrasal verbs have all the properties of verbs in general, as described earlier in this chapter – they occur in various argument structures, they express different semantic classes of situations, such as states, actions, processes, and action-processes, and they occur in all five of the inflectional forms common to all English verbs. The only difference between ordinary verbs and phrasal verbs is that phrasal verbs consist of two (or three) parts: the verb and a preposition-like particle or two. The particles are drawn from a set of forms that can function either as prepositions or directional adverbs, such as *on*, *in*, *up*, *down*, and *across*.

Phrasal verbs and related constructions present particular problems for second language learners of English for a number of reasons:

- Syntactic properties vary considerably from one phrasal verb to another (see below).
- They are ubiquitous (in other words they "crop up" a lot) in conversation, though they are less common in formal, written discourse. This means that traditional and pedagogical grammars, which are often biased toward the written language, usually give them short shrift.
- Their meanings are often figurative rather than literal. In this sense they are like compound words in that the meaning of the whole cannot always be inferred from the meanings of the parts.
- There are usually single-word paraphrases that show up first in bilingual dictionaries, though the paraphrase often has a different connotation than the phrasal verb.

In spite of these difficulties, phrasal verb constructions are very useful, and new phrasal verbs are constantly entering the mainstream of the world's Englishes. Therefore to describe, teach, or learn phrasal verbs is important, yet doing so is like trying to hit a moving target.

In the following paragraphs we will see and discuss the grammatical properties of a portion of the thousands of phrasal verbs in common use in the USA and UK in the early twenty-first century. Many additional phrasal verbs exist in various Englishes spoken and written around the world. There are many Internet sites that classify and list phrasal verbs. The sample below will give us enough data to understand the major classifications of phrasal verbs and to develop a sense of the "spirit" of phrasal verbs – what gives rise to them and how they serve the needs of English-speaking communities.

The following are some examples from the BNC and COCA illustrating phrasal verbs in intransitive and transitive frames:

(48)   **Intransitive**   **Transitive**
       The traffic had *jammed up*.   there's loads of cars *jamming* it *up*.
       I just had to *give up*.   I advise you to *give* it *up*.
       all those sort of things *add up*.   Yes, I've *added* mine *up*.
                                              this is how we have to *add up* fractions.

Transitive phrasal verbs can be "separable" or "inseparable." This terminology is a little misleading, since probably all phrasal and prepositional verbs allow certain adverbs to separate the verb from the particle:

(49)   The traffic jammed right up.
       They had to back right down.

However, only certain phrasal verbs allow the *Object* of the multipart verb to separate the verb from the particle. These are called separable phrasal verbs, or simply "phrasal verbs." Those that don't allow the Object to occur between the particle and the verb are called inseparable phrasal verbs, or "prepositional verbs" for those grammarians who use this term (e.g., Greenbaum and Quirk 2004):

(50)   **Inseparable phrasal verbs (or prepositional verbs)**
       a.   I may *call on* Doctor Manchago to second the motion.
            *I may *call* Doctor Manchago *on* to second the motion.
       b.   She was sort of *getting over* the disappointment.
            *She was sort of *getting* the disappointment *over*.
       c.   But I mean we've been *going over* and *over* that proposal.
            *But I mean we've been *going* that proposal *over* (and *over*).
       d.   That *goes for* the rest of the team.   *That *goes* the rest of the team *for*.

    e. The Board are trying to *look after* our interests in that respect.
        *The Board are trying to *look* our interests *after* in that respect.

    f. they just happen to *run across* Wee Mac,
        *they just happen to *run* Wee Mac *across*,

    g. they *ran into* difficulties.   *they *ran* difficulties *into*.

    h. I *take after* my mum.   *I *take* my mum *after*.

It should be noted that not every example of a verb plus preposition is a phrasal verb. In particular, most occurrences of *go over* and *run across* in the BNC are not phrasal verbs (or prepositional verbs) at all, but simply lexical verbs that happen to be followed by prepositional phrases:

(51)   they've all *gone over* to Luton.
       make up *goes over* your moisturizer.
       Yeah a pheasant *ran across* the road.
       there was a brook *running across* King George's playing fields.

The examples in (51) illustrate the literal meanings of "going over" and "running across." In order to be a phrasal verb, a construction must exhibit some semantic and/or structural shift. As a phrasal verb, to *go over* X means "inspect X" and *run across* X means "accidentally find X." These meanings are so different from the prototypical meanings of these verbs that it is reasonable to assert that they represent distinct lexical entries.

   Separable phrasal verbs are even further along on the continuum of lexicalization than inseparable phrasal verbs (see below for a discussion of how phrasal verbs arise). Here are a few examples. The first example of each of the following pairs actually occurs in the corpora. The second example is also fully grammatical and equivalent in its basic meaning:

(52) a. it's like *blowing up* a balloon.
         it's like *blowing* a balloon *up*.

      b. And is that the only thing which would influence you to *call off* this strike?
         And is that the only thing which would influence you to *call* this strike *off*?

      c. I haven't *filled out* a form.
         I haven't *filled* a form *out*.

      d. they used to have to *fill up* little sacks.
         they used to have to *fill* little sacks *up*.

      e. Doc Threadneedle had *fixed* her body *up* so she healed quick.
         Doc Threadneedle had *fixed up* her body so she healed quick.

      f. You're actually *giving away* nothing.
         You're actually *giving* nothing *away*.

    g.   you have to *give back* what you don't use.
          you have to *give* what you don't use *back*.
    h.   *Hang* your coat *up*.
          Hang up your coat.

Some separable phrasal verbs are almost obligatorily separated from the particle:

(53) a.   Genie had to *do* his homework *over* again.
         ?Genie had to *do over* his homework again.
     b.   They *shut* the records *up* in the garage.
         ??They *shut up* the records in the garage.
     c.   She *asked* her boyfriend *out* on Friday.
         ?She *asked out* her boyfriend on Friday.

One important property of all separable phrasal verbs is that when the Object is a pronoun, it must separate the verb and the particle:

(54) a.   Did you *use up* your seventy thousand?
         Did you *use* it *up*?
         *Did you *use up* it?
     b.   She was a eye witness and she *picked out* the suspect.
         She was a eye witness and she *picked* him *out*.
         *She was a eye witness and she *picked out* him.
     c.   But then Salford *turned on* the heat.
         But then Salford *turned* it *on*.
         *But then Salford *turned on* it.

There are at least two distinct meanings for the phrasal verb *turn on*. First, there is the separable phrasal verb illustrated in (54c). The meaning of this one is roughly "start X" where X is some device. This meaning can also be extended to animate beings, in which case it means "arouse." When this meaning is intended, both verb and particle receive word stress. Then there is the inseparable prepositional verb which means "to attack." In this usage, only the verb receives word stress. The preposition is unstressed, as is normally the case for ordinary prepositions that head prepositional phrases:

(55) He *turns on* him suddenly.
     Then she *turned on* the crowd and accused them of being cowards.

This interpretation is eliminated if the particle is separated from the verb – so *She turned the crowd on* can only mean "she aroused the crowd." This meaning is also likely even if *on* precedes the Object, as long as it receives word stress – *She túrned ón the crowd* would probably also mean "she aroused the crowd." Finally, there's also the simple verb *turn* plus a prepositional phrase that happens to start with *on*:

(56)   They *turned* on 32nd street.
       We *turned* the compost on Friday.

Thus, these distinct expressions illustrate all the stages in the continuum from verb+prepositional phrase to separable phrasal verb.

A third type of phrasal verb may be called ditransitive in that the verb itself takes a Direct Object, in addition to the Complement of the preposition. All phrasal verbs of this type are "inseparable" in that the Complement of the preposition may not precede the preposition. Examples of this type include the following (the verb and preposition are italicized and the X and Y elements are underlined in these examples):

(57)   *deprive X of Y*   Parliament has *deprived* the courts *of* any power of
                            detention.
       ply X with Y   She *plied* him *with* questions.
       provide X with Y   Federal government shall *provide* the deprived areas
                            with three new hospitals

Phrasal verbs actually have a very old and respectable pedigree in the Germanic languages of Northwestern Europe. For example, Modern Dutch and Modern German have many verbs with separable particles that also function as prepositions. The following examples are from Modern German (Fernando Zuñiga, p.c.):

(58)   Ich   wache   morgens   auf.   'I wake up in the morning.'
       I   wake   morning-GEN   up
       Ich   lache   Sie   aus.   'I laugh at you.'
       I   laugh   you   at

Old English also had these kinds of verbs, so there has been a pattern of preposition-like post-verbal particles available for use in English conversations for at least 1500 years. However, in the last 700 years or so, English has taken this pattern and gone wild with it. Hiltunen (1999) counted 5,744 examples of phrasal verbs in the writings of Shakespeare.

The way phrasal verbs develop is something like the following: as particularly useful assemblies consisting of a verb followed by a prepositional phrase become very frequent, speakers start to think of them as instances of the already existing verb plus particle construction, with the Complement of the preposition becoming the Direct Object of the new two-part transitive verb. As such REANALYZED structures become entrenched as fixed expressions, the familiar process of lexicalization kicks in and the assemblies begin to evolve in meaning and form, such that they almost become unified lexical items. Once the pattern of expressing nuances of meaning by such COLEXICALIZING of prepositions and verbs is established, that pattern becomes a template for creation of new collocations with metaphorically related meanings. Perhaps another way of looking at this is to say the all-powerful lexicon of English has a tendency to "suck up" (absorb) functions originally accomplished by verbs plus prepositional phrases. The following is a schematic diagram of this process:

(59)   *Stage 1:* Verb + [Preposition + Object] The farmer looked [over the hill].
       Stage 2: [Verb + Particle] + Object The lawyer [looked over] the documents.
       Stage 3: Phrasal Verb [+ Object] The lawer looked [the documents] over.

By stage 3, the fact that the erstwhile preposition, *over* in example (59), can follow the Object is concrete evidence that its reanalysis as a particle is now complete.

The category of phrasal verbs is now so useful that some members of the category don't even require Objects anymore. While *over* (and several other words, including *up*, *down*, *in*, *on*, and *to*) began life (at least as far back as historical records can take us) as prepositions, they have proven to be so useful as post-verbal particles that they even occur in intransitive expressions:

(60)   Our dog just learned to *roll over*.
       Waldo decided to *give up*.
       Our company is having to *scale down*.
       I'll *drop in* as soon as I have a chance.
       Come on! Let's go.
       Mary was unconscious for two hours before she *came to*.

As more and more of these Verb+Particle constructions began to arise in English, the pattern itself became entrenched as a means of creating new and useful lexical items. In Modern English it is extremely common and easy to invent novel Verb+Particle constructions. Those that become established as ordinary lexical items can be termed "Phrasal Verbs."

Summary

In this chapter we have looked at the important functional domain of expressing actions, states, and processes. The primary means that any language employs for accomplishing this range and functions are verbs and verb-like constructions. In order to understand the morphosyntactic and discourse-pragmatic properties of verbs, it is important to understand semantic roles, and the ways that semantic roles are aligned with the core grammatical relations of Subject, Object, and Indirect Object. Semantic roles are roles that participants play in events, while grammatical relations are relations between nouns and verbs in sentences.

The verbs of English can be grouped into several semantic subclasses. Each of these categories is characterized by its own morphosyntactic properties. The subclasses discussed in this chapter are:

- States
- Processes
- Motion
- Position
- Actions
- Action-processes
- Production
- Cognition
- Sensation
- Emotion
- Utterance
- Manipulation

After discussing the characteristic morphosyntactic properties of verbs that express these situation types, a brief description of the five morphological forms of English verbs is provided.

Finally, a section on "phrasal verbs" discusses a growing "family" of construction types in modern English that is both very useful, and quite problematic for English language professionals. These constructions are on "the cutting edge of the lexicon" in that they clearly have idiosyncratic semantic and morphosyntactic features of the sort one expects to find in lexical items, yet transparently derive from syntactic assemblies, principally verbs plus prepositional phrases.

FURTHER READING

Vendler (1967) and Chafe (1970) are foundational works on event types. Levin (1993) is an excellent compendium of argument structures, event types, and collocational possibilities for English verbs. The FrameNet database (http://framenet.icsi.berkeley.edu/) is also very useful in this regard. Dixon (2005) is a thoroughly semantically based approach to English grammar.

Exercises

1. Argument structures of English verbs.
    A. Give examples of three English verbs that can fit into each of the following frames (provide nine different verbs altogether):
       a. Bilbo _____ his way up the mountain.
       b.   _____
       c.   _____

    d. Sydney _____ the criminal out the window.

    e.   _____

    f.   _____

    g. This Rembaldi manuscript _____ easily.

    h.   _____

    i.   _____

  B. For examples, a, d, and g above give the semantic role of *Bilbo, Sydney, the criminal,* and *this Rembaldi manuscript.*

  C. Now, for each of the nine verbs you have provided above, give one sentence that uses the verb in a *different argument structure.* In other words, use each verb with a different arrangement of semantic roles and grammatical relations than those used in the first nine examples. Indicate the semantic role of the Subject and Object arguments for each of your new examples.

2. The following examples from second language learners of English illustrate non-standard argument structures for English verbs.

  A. For each example, give the *same verb* in a more standard argument structure, and give the full argument structure diagram (your answers do not need to express the same meanings as the non-standard examples).

  B. Try to express the ideas intended in each of these examples using a *different verb.*

    a. He said me the answer. A: He said the word. AGENT (*he*) → Subject,

                                   THEME (*the word*) → Object

                B: He told me the answer.

    b. Please borrow me a can opener.

    c. My mother went the doctor this morning.

    d. Our company makes business in seven different countries.

    e. I must clean on my shoes before we leave.

    f. They gave for me a prize.

    g. It does kind of hurt to me.

    h. This music communicates listeners a sense of serenity.

    i. Yatsuko grew in Tokyo, but now lives in California.

    j. I am considering on a new apartment.

7 Basic concepts in English syntax

Linguistics is shear servitude and drudgery until we have the joy of seeing order emerge from chaos.

Robert Longacre (p.c.)

To this point we have been talking mostly about the functional and structural properties of words and parts of words (the lexicon and morphology). In this chapter we will begin to talk more specifically about syntax – how words combine into larger structures such as phrases and clauses. Along with the lexicon and morphology, the syntax of any language provides speakers with an important structural dimension that allows them to communicate meaning. In this chapter, we will discuss some universal features of syntactic structure that all methods of syntactic analysis must be able to represent. Then we will discuss the differences between syntactic categories and syntactic functions. Finally, we will outline a few analytical methods for understanding English syntax, and will propose a couple of different ways of displaying syntactic structures. In Chapter 8, the concepts and methods described in the present chapter will be applied to a few advanced topics in English clause structure.

7.1 Universal features of syntactic structure

LINEAR ORDER, CONSTITUENCY (also referred to as SYNTACTIC MERGER, "grouping," or "clumping"), and HIERARCHICAL STRUCTURE (also referred to as "nesting") are major features of the syntax of all human languages. All these features provide important clues to a speaker's intended meaning.

Linear order

Because words are pronounced one after another in time, differences in the order of words can be exploited to express differences in meaning. For example, in the following clauses, linear order is the only signal of the difference in meaning:

(1)   a.   Waldo saw the duke.
      b.   The duke saw Waldo.

The observation that the order of words can be adjusted to express this kind of difference in meaning may seem obvious to most people; but as we have seen in Chapter 2, not every language uses linear order in exactly the way English does, so it is an important variable for English language professionals to make note of.

Constituency

If linear order were the only respect in which units in the linguistic stream could be related to one another, language would be very simple indeed. Utterances would be short, and the ideas expressed would be quite limited. In fact, this kind of language would be very similar to several animal communication systems that have been studied by zoologists. One characteristic that seems to distinguish human languages from other natural communication systems is that human language exhibits constituency and hierarchical structure. Constituency means that linguistic units "clump together" or "merge" (Chomsky 1995) in discourse. This is a fact that all language users unconsciously know about their language. For example, the following two phrases have exactly the same words in identical linear order. Nevertheless, the meaning can vary depending on how the hearer clumps the words.
     In these examples, constituents (clumps) are indicated in boxes:

(2)   a. | Good girls | and boys

      b.   Good | girls and boys |

In (2a) *good girls* is treated as a constituent which is then combined with *boys* to form a complex phrase that refers to a set of good girls plus boys that may be good, bad, or neither. In (2b), *girls and boys* form a constituent that is modified by the adjective *good* to yield a complex phrase that refers to a set of good girls and good boys only.
     Of course, in actual conversation, intonation and many other factors help a hearer infer the precise constituent structure intended by the speaker in a particular context. This example simply illustrates that constituency, or how linguistic units are clumped, is a significant factor in how any language, English in particular, expresses meaning.

Hierarchical structure

Hierarchical structure refers to the fact that linguistic units and clumps tend to "nest" within one another. Hierarchical structure is good, because it makes life easier. Psychological experiments (as well as common sense) have shown that the human mind can only deal with a small number of things at a time – from four to six at most. Have you ever been given an important phone number when you had no pen or paper to write it down with? What did you do? First you probably tried to repeat it several times to get it "ingrained" in your mind (this is sometimes called "overlearning"). Then you probably unconsciously "clumped" it into two or more parts: 928, 4056, or maybe 92, 84, 056. When you memorize clumps in a series like this, you effectively convert the clumps into units (undivided pieces) in your memory. Once they are units, you can clump them again at a higher level to form even larger units. Once you have memorized a clump, you no longer have to think about its internal complexity – you can just deal with it "from the outside," as a unit equivalent to other units of the same type.

Telecommunications companies are very aware of this cognitive fact, and so they usually present phone numbers in clumps. Country codes, city codes, or area codes are clumps that enter into the hierarchical structure of more complex phone numbers. Imagine how difficult it would be to remember phone numbers if they were all 12 to 15 random digits in length, with no structure as to which digits represented the country, the area, or the city code! Hierarchical structure in language is another example of this human tendency to nest symbolic units within other units. A NOUN PHRASE, for example, is a unit that can have very simple or very complicated internal structure:

(3) a. Simple noun phrase: the dog
     b. Complicated noun phrase: the big black dog that always barks at me as
         I try vainly to sneak past the junkyard on my way home from my piano lesson

The phrase in (3b) has quite a bit of internal complexity, and therefore requires a lot of mental processing. However, once it is processed, it can enter into larger structures as easily (well, almost as easily) as simple structures such as (3a). They are both just noun phrases as far as the structure of the larger clause is concerned:

(4) a. ⎡The dog⎤ attacked the postman.

     b. ⎡The big black dog that always barks at
         me as I try vainly to sneak past the junkyard⎤ attacked the postman.
         on my way home from my piano lesson

The boxed clump in (4b) itself contains several clumps, including a complete clause (*I try vainly to sneak past the junkyard...*). But once you have treated the entire clumped portion as a noun phrase, you do not have to be concerned with its internal structure. It is just a unit, like any number of others, that is available for deployment in larger structures.

The fact that hierarchical structure is important for expressing meaning is apparent in many examples involving STRUCTURAL AMBIGUITY. The following is an actual headline I once observed in our local newspaper:

(5)   Police kill mentally deranged man with knife

What is "odd" about this headline? There are two possible interpretations – either the deranged man had a knife, or the police used a knife to kill the deranged man! This last interpretation is probably not what the reporter had intended, but of course as linguists we notice these kinds of ambiguities more readily than normal people do. So, what is the source of the ambiguity? Well, part of it has to do with the meaning of the preposition *with*. This preposition exhibits LEXICAL AMBIGUITY – it can mean that its Complement is a semantic INSTRUMENT (see Chapter 6 on semantic roles), or it can express ACCOMPANIMENT, i.e., the idea that the knife accompanied ("was with") someone. This distinction is apparent in the following examples:

(6) a.   I ate the ice cream with a spoon.   with = INSTRUMENT
     b.   I ate the ice cream with my mother.   with = ACCOMPANIMENT

But going back to example (5), both the ACCOMPANIMENT and the INSTRUMENT interpretations are possible given the context. What makes the difference? The difference is hierarchical structure. In one interpretation the prepositional phrase *with knife* is nested within the Predicate Phrase headed by *kill*. In the other interpretation, the prepositional phrase is inside the noun phrase headed by *man*. These two structures are diagrammed using boxes below:

(7) a.   Police | kill | mentally deranged man | with knife |

     b.   Police | kill | mentally deranged man | with knife |

In (7a), *mentally deranged man* is the Object of kill, and *with knife* is a separate constituent of the clump containing *kill*. A paraphrase might be *Police kill with knife mentally deranged man*. In (7b), on the other hand, the prepositional phrase modifies man – "man with knife." As you can see, hierarchical structure *is* important for expressing meaning!

7.2   Syntactic categories and syntactic functions

Consistent with the approach taken throughout this book, and in much recent theoretical work in functional (or communicative) linguistics, we will be looking at syntactic elements in terms of their functions as well as their forms. To recall a metaphor introduced in the Introduction, just as employees have jobs within a corporation, so syntactic elements have jobs within syntactic structures. A particular employee may be trained, for example, to be a communications specialist, but her function within the structure of the communications department might be as a "manager," "assistant manager," "copy editor," or any number of other specific jobs. The communications department itself, then, has a function within the larger corporate structure. Syntax is kind of like that. What I am calling "syntactic elements" can be individual words, or they may be clumps of words that work together to accomplish some function at a higher level. What all syntactic elements have in common is that they all have a basic structural identity – what they *are*, and they all have a function within a larger structure – what people *do* with them.

Let's look at some preliminary examples. Consider the following simple English noun phrases:

(8)   a.   little lamb
      b.   garbage truck

In (8a), the whole phrase refers to a lamb, so we can say the word *lamb* is the semantic Head of this phrase (see the next section on the notion of semantic and syntactic headship). *Little* is a word whose identity is best described as an adjective. We have already discussed the word class of adjectives in Chapter 3. The word *little* is a near prototypical example of an adjective. In this case it is functioning to Modify the Head noun *lamb*. So its syntactic category is adjective and its syntactic function is to Modify a noun.

In (8b) we have two words that are best identified as nouns. Both *garbage* and *truck* have most of the properties of prototypical nouns discussed in Chapters 3 and 5. In this case, however, the whole phrase refers to a truck, and not to garbage. Therefore *truck* is functioning as the Head of the phrase, and *garbage* is doing the same thing as *little* is doing in (8a) – Modifying the Head. So the syntactic category of *garbage* is noun, but its syntactic function in this particular phrase is to Modify another noun. In this book, when we indicate syntactic category and syntactic function of units, we will write the category below the unit and the function above it, as in the following diagrams:

(9)   Syn. function:

MOD H		MOD	H
little lamb		garbage	truck

Syn. category: ADJ N   N   N

The first of these diagrams could be read as "a clump consisting of an adjective functioning as a Modifier, and a noun functioning as the Head." The second would be "a clump consisting of a noun functioning as a Modifier and another noun functioning as the Head."

Syntactic categories

The basic building blocks of syntactic structure are called SYNTACTIC CATEGORIES. There are two subtypes of syntactic categories: LEXICAL CATEGORIES and PHRASAL CATEGORIES. Lexical categories are pretty similar to the word classes we have been

Table 7.1 **Syntactic categories used in this book**

Lexical categories (abbrev.)	Phrasal categories (abbrev.)
Noun (N)	Noun phrase (NP)
Pronoun (PRO)	
Verb (V)	Verb phrase (VP)
Adjective (ADJ)	Adjective phrase (AdjP)
Article (ART)	Determined noun phrase (DP)[1]
Adverb (ADV)	Adverb phrase (AdvP)
Preposition (P)	Prepositional phrase (PP)
Auxiliary (AUX)	Inflected verb phrase (IP)
Empty inflectional element (INFL)	
Complementizer (COMP)	Complement phrase (CP)
Genitive clitic (G)	Genitive noun phrase (GP)
Special category (abbrev.)	
Clause (S)	

discussing to this point, but they are different. "Lexical category" is just a phrase commonly used in the linguistics literature to refer to positions in syntactic structures; therefore, when we are talking about syntactic structures, we will use the term lexical category rather than word class.

Lexical categories consist of units that do not have internal syntactic structure themselves. For example, a noun may have morphological structure (prefixes, suffixes, etc.) but is not made up of syntactically distinct units. Phrasal categories, on the other hand, may have internal syntactic structure. For example, a noun phrase must contain a noun, but may also contain adjectives and many other units that "clump together" with the noun. Note that a phrasal category may consist of only one unit. For example, a noun like *Lucretia* may also be a noun phrase. *Lucretia* just happens to be a simple noun phrase with no Modifiers or other syntactic elements cluttering it up. Table 7.1 lists all of the syntactic categories we will be dealing with in this book, along with their common abbreviations.

The highest level category usually recognized in phrase structure is the special category symbolized by the letter S. In earlier versions of Generative Grammar this was a mnemonic for "Sentence"; however we will refer to it as "clause," or "the clause level." It is generally assumed in Generative Grammar that linguistic structure above the S level is not amenable to phrase structure analysis, though some theoreticians, notably van Dijk (1972), pointedly disagree with this assertion. Later in this chapter we will see some hints as to how phrase structure analysis higher than the sentence level may be approached. More recent versions of Generative Grammar (in particular, MINIMALISM) have eliminated the need for this special category altogether, having subsumed it under the phrasal category labels. However, for now it will be convenient to continue to use the S label.

We can consider a clause to be the grammatical expression of a PROPOSITION. A proposition is a semantic notion, whereas a clause is a grammatical notion. In other words, a proposition has to do with entities in the message world and semantic relations among them, whereas a clause has to do with elements in syntactic structure and the syntactic relations among them. We can informally think of a proposition as a "complete thought." It consists of one or more entities and a property or relation. For example, the semantic notion (or "thought") *CAROLYN LOVES HER CAT* consists of two participants described as *CAROLYN* and *HER CAT*, and a relationship described as *LOVES* that relates them. This proposition may be expressed in any number of grammatical clauses, e.g.:

(10) a. Carolyn loves her cat.
      b. Carolyn loved her cat.
      c. Her cat is what Carolyn loves.
      d. It's her cat that Carolyn loves.
      e. Carolyn might love her cat.

It is fairly clear that a good portion of human thought and communication is propositional in the sense that it consists of such entities and relations. However, recent research (see, e.g., Lakoff and Johnson 1999) is beginning to show that *images*, rather than simply propositions, may be more relevant to human thought and communication than had previously been thought. Nevertheless, most linguistic theories, in particular generative grammar, are primarily concerned with the propositional component of linguistic communication.

Syntactic functions

The following paragraphs list and describe the major syntactic functions we will be concerned with in this book. These are the jobs that syntactic categories perform in the "corporate organizational chart" of a phrase, clause, or discourse.

Syntactic and semantic Head

There are at least two senses in which linguists use the term HEAD of a phrase. In all syntactic clumps there is one element that determines the distributional, or syntactic, properties of the clump, and one element that expresses the main meaning of the clump. The element that determines the syntactic properties of the clump is sometimes referred to as the syntactic Head, whereas the element that expresses the main meaning of the clump is referred to as the semantic Head.

Often the same element is both the syntactic and semantic Head of a phrase. This is almost always true of noun phrases (sometimes abbreviated as NPs). For example, in a noun phrase like *old man* there is no question that *man* is both the syntactic and semantic Head. It is the syntactic Head because, for example, if you remove *old*, the part that is left still has the same syntactic properties as the original clump. In examples (11b) and (11e) we see that *man* can occur in the same syntactic slot as *old man*. However, if you remove *man*, what is left cannot be used in the same way as the original clump (11c and f):

(11) a. The old man of the sea ...   d. He told a story about this old man.
      b. The man of the sea ...   e. He told a story about this man.
      c. *The old of the sea ...   f. *He told a story about this old.

So it appears that the phrase *old man* and the noun *man* have the same distributional properties, but *old* by itself has different properties; therefore *man* is the syntactic Head of this phrase. Another way of saying this is that a noun phrase is a PROJECTION of its syntactic Head. That is, the syntactic Head noun "projects" its nouniness onto the whole phrase. The word *man* is also the semantic Head of the phrase *old man* because the whole phrase refers to a man, and not to "oldness."

While it is almost always the case that for noun phrases the syntactic Head and the semantic Head are the same word, this is not always true for other kinds of phrases. We will see examples of a "mismatch" between types of Heads in the following paragraphs. The important point to remember about syntactic headship is that the syntactic Head of a phrase is that element of the phrase that determines the syntactic properties of the whole phrase. Every phrase must have a Syntactic Head. The main point about semantic Heads is that the semantic Head of a phrase is the element of the phrase that expresses the main meaning of the whole phrase. Throughout this book, when we label the syntactic functions of elements in phrase structure, the Head (H) will always indicate the *syntactic* Head of the phrase. This often happens to be the semantic Head as well, but in *syntactic* structures, *syntactic* Headship is the most relevant.

The Determining function

As used in many linguistic theories, the term DETERMINER describes a syntactic function, rather than a word class. Syntactic elements that accomplish the Determining function specify, identify, or quantify the following noun phrase, and can belong to any number of syntactic categories. Here are a few examples:

(12) **Example**   **Syntactic category serving as Determiner:**

      a. *a* system error; *the* system error,   Articles, *a/an*, *the*

b.	Ø systematic errors; Ø clean air; Ø Zimbabwe.	Zero (or "null") article for non-identifiable plural noun phrases, non-countable nouns, and proper names
c.	*this* ridiculous textbook	Demonstratives: *this, that, these, those*
d.	*each* student; *no* father	Quantifiers: *each, every, many, any, much, some, few, thirty-seven, every other, no* etc.
e.	in *either* case; *neither* end	either, neither
f.	*What* fingerprints?	Some WH-words
g.	*My* fingerprints; *Oberon's* fingerprints; *The Queen of England's* fingerprints	Genitive pronouns and phrases
h.	*You* linguists; *we* intellectuals	Some personal pronouns

Like auxiliaries and prepositions, elements that serve a Determining function are arguably the syntactic Heads of their phrases. The reason for this is that determined noun phrases (noun phrases with Determiners) have different syntactic properties than "undetermined" noun phrases, as we will see in Section 8.1.

Complementation

A Complement (not "compliment"!) is something that "completes" something else. Any element of a phrase that is not the Head of the phrase, yet is required in order to complete the phrase, can be called a Complement.[2] For example, a preposition is the Head of a prepositional phrase because the syntactic properties of the whole phrase are determined by the preposition – what makes it a prepositional phrase is the presence of the preposition. However, a preposition alone is not a prepositional phrase in the same way, for example, a verb alone may be a verb phrase. Therefore a prepositional phrase needs a Complement. The DP that follows a preposition in a prepositional phrase can be said to have the syntactic function of Complement of the phrase. Here is how a prepositional phrase would be diagrammed using our "labeled box" notation:

(13)

H	C
over	the river
P	DP
PP	

In this diagram we have labeled the whole clump with its category label, PP, at the bottom. If this PP were functioning in a larger structure, then its syntactic function would be indicated above the large box. Inside the PP, there are two elements – a P functioning as the Head (H) of the phrase, and a DP functioning as the Complement (C) of the Head.

Inside the DP in example (13) there are also two elements. These are not labeled in (13), because the internal structure of the DP is not in focus. However, DPs also have Heads and Complements, so let's illustrate the function of Complement using a DP:

(14)

$$\begin{array}{cc} \text{H} & \text{C} \\ \text{the} & \boxed{\text{river}} \\ \text{ART} & \text{NP} \\ & \text{DP} \end{array}$$

In (14) the large box represents the whole DP. Since this example is not given in the context of a larger syntactic structure, we can't label its syntactic function. It could be a Subject, Object, Complement of a preposition, or something else. The DP contains two elements – an article functioning as the syntactic Head (H), and a NP functioning as the Complement (C). Inside the NP there is only one element, which happens to be a noun functioning as the Head of the NP. However, since the internal structure of the NP is not in focus, we have not labeled its content, though we could have done so. It is important to note that the Complement of a Determiner is a noun *phrase*, even if it happens to consist of just a noun.

Grammatical relations (relational functions)

Grammatical relations (GRs) are syntactic functions of nominal elements in clauses. In this book, we will consider six grammatical relations in English, SUBJECT, DIRECT OBJECT, INDIRECT OBJECT, OBLIQUE, SUBJECT COMPLEMENT, and OBJECT COMPLEMENT. Examples of DPs filling each of these syntactic functions are given in (15) below:

(15) **Example**   **Grammatical relation of DP**
   a. *A little lamb* followed Mary.   Subject
   b. Mary saw *a little lamb*.   Direct Object
   c. Mary showed her pictures to *a little lamb*.   Indirect Object
   d. The children laughed at *a little lamb*.   Oblique
   e. It was *a little lamb*.   Subject Complement
   f. They consider it *a little lamb*.   Object Complement

Direct Object, Indirect Object, Oblique, Subject Complement, and Object Complement functions are all subtypes of the Complement function described above.

Direct and Indirect Objects are Complements of particular predicate types (e.g., transitive and bitransitive predicates), Obliques are Complements of prepositions, and Subject and Object Complements are Complements of certain other predicates. Complementation will be discussed in more detail in Chapter 9.

Sometimes the Oblique function is considered to be the *absence* of a grammatical relation. In this book we will consider the DP that follows a preposition to be a Complement of the preposition but to have an Oblique function within the larger predication. This will help in our discussion of voice and valence in Chapter 13, and is consistent with the way most linguists use the term "Oblique." Similarly, the DP that follows the preposition *to* in a three-argument construction is a Complement of the preposition, but has the Indirect Object function within the larger predication. The reason an Indirect Object is considered a Complement rather than just another Oblique is that it is required to "complete" a three-argument construction. For example, consider the following:

(16)   Mary gave the money.

The scene evoked by the verb *give* necessarily involves three participants – an AGENT (*Mary*), a THEME (*the money*), and a RECIPIENT (the person or people who receive the money). In (16), the RECIPIENT is not mentioned; however, it is still understood that someone must receive the money. It just doesn't matter who that is in this particular case.[3] Since a RECIPIENT is necessary to complete the idea of giving, any expression of the RECIPIENT in a clause that describes an act of giving must have the syntactic function of Complement.

Sometimes the term ARGUMENT is used to refer to any nominal that has a grammatical relation to a predicate. This sense of the term "argument" is borrowed from mathematical logic, where an argument is an independent variable in a predicate function; in other words, a thing that has a property, or is related to some other thing. A nominal that doesn't have a specific grammatical relation to some other word is called either a "non-argument" or an Oblique. Sometimes we will make a distinction between core arguments (Subject and Object) and non-core arguments (the other four).

Like other syntactic functions, GRs are *defined* independently of semantic or pragmatic function (such as topicality). Nevertheless, it is important to recognize that GRs play a significant role in expressing meaningful distinctions, such as who is acting upon whom, what is topical in a conversation, and so on. The three main structural features that reflect grammatical relations in a clause are the following:

- pronoun case
- verb agreement
- constituent order

The simplest illustration of a grammatical relation is probably the Subject relation that may hold between a DP and an IP. For example, in all of the following English clauses, the pronoun *I* is the Subject:

(17)   a.   I exercise every evening.
        b.   I can see the Statue of Liberty already!
        c.   I carry nothing.
        d.   I was smeared by the *New York Times*.

The semantic role of the referent of the pronoun *I* and the rest of the clause in each of these examples is quite different. In (17a), *I* refers to an AGENT – someone who controls the action described by the verb and does it on purpose (see Chapter 6 for discussion of semantic roles). In (17b), *I* refers to an EXPERIENCER – someone who receives a sensory impression, but does not control the event or perform it on purpose. In (17c), *I* refers to someone who does not do anything with respect to the following verb. Finally, in (17d) *I* refers to something like a PATIENT.

In spite of these very different semantic roles, in each case the grammatical relation of *I* to the rest of the clause is the same. How do we know this? We look at the grammatical properties that commonly distinguish grammatical relations. In English, the Subject relation is expressed partially by the nominative case of personal pronouns. The pronoun *I* specifically refers to first person, singular *Subjects* only. If a first person singular participant is not a Subject, another form of the pronoun is used, either *me* or *my*:

(18)   Mr. Frodo's not going anywhere without *me*.
        American girls would seriously dig *me* …
        … with *my* cute British accent.
        Do you mean you wish to surrender to *me*?

What about participant reference marking on verbs (agreement)? English does have a system of verb agreement, though it is rather impoverished compared to agreement systems of many other languages, even within the Indo-European family. In the present tense of English major class verbs, there is a suffix spelled *s* (without the apostrophe) that appears when the Subject is third person singular: *He hates pills*.

When the Subject is a different person, or a different number, this *-s* goes away (at least in standard Englishes):

(19)   They hate pills.   *They hates pills.
        We hate pills.   *We hates pills.

Therefore, this *-s* is an expression of verb agreement with the Subject, and is another grammatical property of the relational notion of *Subject* in English.

Finally, what about constituent order? Constituent order does help us distinguish the Subject from other nouns in a clause, but we need to be careful how we state the pattern. We may be tempted to say something like "the Subject is the first NP in the clause." This usually is true, but not always. Consider the following:

(20) a. The King's stinking son fired me.
      b. Fezzik, are there rocks ahead?
      c. On the horizon appeared a ship.
      d. "A giant!" yelled Frodo.
      e. What house do you live in?

The first noun phrase in each of these examples is *the king*, *Fezzik*, *the horizon*, *a giant*, and *what house*. None of these have the other grammatical properties of Subjects, and none of them would be considered the Subject according to any respectable linguistic theory. Therefore, we need to qualify our statement concerning the position of Subjects in English somehow.

How about "the Subject is the noun phrase that appears right before the main verb or auxiliary"? We can see from the examples in (20) that this generalization isn't always true either. In (20b) a non-subject, *Fezzik*, appears right before the auxiliary, *are*. In (20c, d, and e) the noun phrase that comes right before the verb or auxiliary is also not a Subject.

In spite of these problems in determining the position of the Subject in the clause, we still have this commonsense idea that the "Subject comes first." Why is that? The reason is that it very frequently *does* come early in the clause, normally right before the verb or auxiliary. This is a well-oiled habit pattern of English. This pattern can be varied for special purposes, such as questions (20b and e), presentationals (20c), and QUOTATIVES (20d). These are all PRAGMATICALLY MARKED constructions, in the sense that they are used in special contexts, e.g., when information is being requested, when new participants are being introduced into the discourse, etc. Clauses in which the Subject comes right before the verb or auxiliary are pragmatically neutral (see Chapter 15). So, to describe the position of the Subject in English, we need to clarify that we are only talking about pragmatically neutral clauses.

(21) The Subject is the noun phrase or pronoun that immediately precedes the verb or auxiliary in pragmatically neutral clauses.

While you may be able to think of apparent counterexamples to this statement, it is a reasonably good generalization regarding Subject position in English.

Predication

The main syntactic functions in a clause are a Subject and a Predicate. This is because the main semantic functions in a proposition are an entity and some characteristic or relationship regarding that entity. Recall that a clause is the linguistic expression of a proposition. We have earlier described a proposition as a "complete thought." The idea is that an entity by itself is not news. When an entity is simply mentioned, there is no thought communicated unless something is said or implied *about* that entity. Even one word answers to questions still imply whole propositions.

(22) a.   Q: Where are you going?   A: Cambridge.
      b.   Q: Is this information available?   A: Yes.

The meaning of the answer to (22a) can be expanded in the context to a complete thought, something like I AM GOING TO CAMBRIDGE.[4] Similarly the answer to (22b) consists of the proposition THIS INFORMATION IS AVAILABLE. The idea is that any utterance (indeed, any gesture at all) that is intended to be communicative must express a proposition. Some have even attempted to make propositional communication out of exclamations such as the following (see Sperber and Wilson 1995):

(23) **Exclamation**   **Proposition expressed**
      Mommy!   I WANT MOMMY TO ATTEND TO ME
      Ouch!   I HAVE JUST BEEN HURT
      Ohmigosh!   SOMETHING IS STARTLING/SURPRISING TO ME

"Predicate" is a term from logic that refers to a characteristic asserted of a single entity or a relation asserted to hold between entities. In this book, we will borrow this term from predicate logic to refer to a syntactic function prototypically filled by the syntactic categories of inflected verb phrase (IP) and uninflected verb phrase (VP). In the following examples, the boxed portions are the syntactic categories that fill the Predicate function:

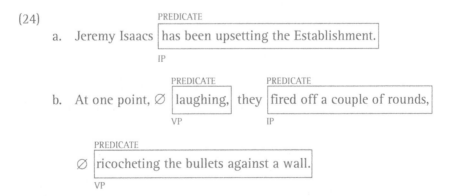

In these examples we see IPs and VPs both filling predicating functions. In (24b), three complete thoughts are expressed.

(25)   THEY LAUGHED
       THEY FIRED OFF A COUPLE OF ROUNDS
       THEY RICOCHETED THE BULLETS AGAINST A WALL

Only one of these three, the second, is expressed by a clause that is inflected for tense. The clauses that express the other two propositions do not carry their own tense, but their time reference is established by extension from the tense of the inflected clause. We say that the other two clauses are uninflected. In Chapter 8 we will see why it is important to distinguish VPs from IPs. The point here is that both VPs and IPs can fill the Predicate function. Other phrasal categories, such as determined noun phrases (DPs), prepositional phrases (PPs), and adjective phrases (AdjPs) also may serve as Predicates (see Chapter 9). Therefore, although VP and IP are very good ways of accomplishing the function of Predication, the function itself is logically distinct from the syntactic categories that might fill it.

Modification

The terms "modification" and "modifier" are used in a number of ways in traditional and theoretical discussions of grammar. In this book we will be using this term to refer to an "optional" syntactic function accomplished within phrases and clauses. If an element is not required in order to complete the thought expressed by a phrase or clause, it is probably a Modifier. You might think of Modification as a "macro-function" in that it covers a very wide range of possible semantic notions, from various kinds of adverbial functions to nominal Modification (size, shape, color, value, etc.), for example:

(26)   **Syntactic category serving**
                                                  a Modifying function

       a *little* lamb   Adjective
       Mary loved her lamb *a little bit.*   DP
       The children laughed *heartily.*   Adverb
       The children laughed and played
       to see a lamb at school.   VP
       a little lamb who *followed Mary to school*   Clause

The syntactic function of Modification, including syntactic structures that commonly fill this important function, will be discussed in more detail in Chapter 10.

7.3   Tests for constituent structure

Like all sciences, linguistics has its ways of "probing and poking" its subject matter in order to understand it better. Even as chemists use various techniques for analyzing chemical compounds, so linguists use various techniques for analyzing clause structure. Usually the techniques employed by linguists involve changing the order of pieces, adding pieces, or taking pieces out of a linguistic structure, and then seeing how native speakers react to the resulting structures. Some techniques are better for analyzing certain kinds of structures, or for elucidating certain kinds of properties than others. For example, the tests for syntactic headship illustrated in the examples in (11) above will not necessarily work for all purposes. In other situations, other tests may be more appropriate. This is similar to the problem a chemist faces when analyzing, for example, a piece of rock versus an unknown liquid – the goal may be the same (come up with a chemical analysis), and there will probably be a good deal of methodological overlap, but the exact techniques and procedures will not be identical.

Of course, some features of syntactic structure are very easily observed, and need no special "tests" to reveal them. For example, linear order is not a problem. Even if you are listening to (or reading) a language you have no knowledge of, you can tell fairly easily what order the noises are arranged in. There are no special tests needed to determine this property of syntactic structure.

The other two properties, constituency and hierarchical structure, as well as syntactic category and syntactic function, are more difficult to determine just by looking at, or listening to, the language. As illustrated earlier, a sequence like *good girls and boys* can have more than one constituent structure. Also, native intuition, while helpful, is not reliable in determining the constituent structure of longish strings, such as (4b) above. Therefore, we need ways of "probing and poking" syntactic structures in order to determine how units clump together, where the boundaries between units and clumps are, and how clumps nest within one another.

Let's look at a simple example. A pair of words like *the dog* can be a clump, but if we have a longer string like (27), how do we know whether *the dog* is a constituent, as opposed to, maybe, *dog watched*, *watched a fluffy*, or some other random portion of this string of words?

(27)   The dog watched a fluffy cat.

There are two major tests and three secondary tests that can be used to reveal the constituent structure of a string such as this. The two major tests are:

- movement
- substitution

The three secondary tests are:

- interposition
- coordination
- omissibility

We will briefly discuss each of these tests in the following paragraphs. Then we will attempt a constituent structure analysis of some simple English data.

Movement

Every language allows some constituents to appear in various positions in a syntactic structure. Such variable positioning is often metaphorically referred to as "movement." For example, in English, DPs can be placed in unusual positions for purposes of asking questions, or making statements with some kind of special focus:

(28) a. Beans I like.   (Object, *beans*, placed before the Subject.)
      b. What does Frieda want?   (Object, *what*, placed before the auxiliary.)
      c. Here comes my bus.   (Subject, *my bus*, placed after the verb.)

A good test for whether an element is part of a phrase or not, then, is if it moves with the Head when the Head moves. So, in example (27), if *the dog* is a constituent, we should be able to move it around, contrast it, etc. without affecting the grammaticality of the clause. The sequence *the dog* does pass this test for constituency:

(29) *The dog* is what watched a fluffy cat.
      What watched a fluffy cat is *the dog.*

Since these are both grammatical strings of English, this is evidence that *the dog* is a constituent.

However, what about *watched a* in example (27)? Is it possible to treat this as a constituent for purposes of movement? Let's try:

(30) **Watched a* is the dog what fluffy cat.
      **The dog what fluffy cat is *watched a.*

Clearly *watched a* fails this test for constituency.

Now let's try one that is a little trickier. What about *watched a fluffy cat*? Is there any clumping or nesting structure in this sequence of words? Consider the following examples:

(31) a. *Watched a fluffy cat* is what the dog did.
      b. **Watched* is what the dog did a fluffy cat.

Example (31a) is evidence that *watched a fluffy cat* can move to the front of the clause as a unit, and therefore is a constituent. This constituent we will call an INFLECTED VERB PHRASE, or IP. (31b) shows that the verb *watched* cannot be moved out of this constituent. Of course, it is possible for an IP to consist only of a verb (32a), in which case the verb alone can be moved (32b):

(32) a. Finkelstein *sweated.*
      b. *Sweated* is what Finkelstein did.

But if there are other elements in the IP, they all must be fronted together with the verb.

Now consider the following:

(33)   *A fluffy cat* is what the dog watched.
        What the dog watched is *a fluffy cat*.

The examples in (33) prove that *a fluffy cat* is a constituent. But we just saw that *watched a fluffy cat* is also a constituent. How can this be? The answer, of course, is hierarchical structure! Constituents may "nest" within other constituents. These kinds of examples show that the DP that follows the verb is a constituent that is nested within the inflected verb phrase. In other words, the correct phrase structure for the IP in (27) is as given in (34a) rather than (34b):

(34)   a. Correct syntactic analysis: watched [a fluffy cat]

        b. Incorrect syntactic analysis: watched [a fluffy cat]

Now consider the following:

(35)   a. Finkelstein swated the final exam.
        b. Sweated the final exam is what Finkelstein did.
        c. The final exam is what Finkelstein sweated.
        d. *Sweated is what Finkelstein did the final exam.
        e. *Final is what Finkelstein sweated the exam.
        f. *Exam is what Finkelstein sweated the final.
        g. *The is what Finkelstein sweated final exam.
        h. *The final is what Finkelstein sweated exam.

These examples show that *the final exam* or *sweated the final exam* are the only parts of the inflected verb phrase that can be moved out (or EXTRACTED). It is not possible to move *sweated, the, final, exam*, or any subgroup of these out of this structure. So it seems that *sweated the final exam* is a constituent, and *the final exam* is another constituent embedded within it. The inflected verb phrase is, in turn, embedded within the whole clause *Finkelstein sweated the final exam*. Another way of expressing embedding relationships that is a little simpler to type than boxes is multiple bracketing, as in (36):

(36)   [Finklestein [sweated [the final exam]]]

Notice that there are just as many left-hand brackets as there are right-hand brackets. Sometimes each bracket can be labeled (usually with small subscripts) to make it clear which left-hand bracket goes with which right-hand bracket:

(37)   [$_1$ Finklestein [$_2$ sweated [$_3$ the final exam]$_3$]$_2$]$_1$

The labeling makes it clear that clump 1 is the "largest" clump in this structure. The others are contained within it. The clump labeled 3 is the smallest clump in this structure. It is contained within clump 2 and clump 1.

Finally, the brackets are often given meaningful labels, corresponding to the syntactic category of the clump they represent. Example (38) shows how this labeling may work:

(38)   [$_s$ Finklestein [$_{ip}$ sweated [$_{dp}$ the final exam]$_{dp}$]$_{ip}$]$_s$

Substitution

The second major test for constituency is SUBSTITUTION. This refers to the fact that a constituent may be replaced by a substitute word, whereas other random strings of units may not. The substitute words are sometimes called PRO-FORMS, of which pronouns and the PRO-VERB *(so) do* in English are subtypes. For example, *so do* can substitute for the verb *escape* in the following:

(39)   The Duke escaped and *so did* Aileron.

This means that Aileron also escaped. Therefore *escape* is a constituent all on its own. Well, what happens when a phrase like *a fluffy cat* follows a verb? Does *so do* substitute for just the verb, or the verb plus the noun phrase that follows?:

(40)   a.   The dog watched a fluffy cat and *so did* the elephant.
       b.   *The dog watched a fluffy cat and *so did* the elephant a scruffy mouse.

These examples show that *so do* substitutes for the whole string *watched a fluffy cat*, rather than just the verb *watched*. This is yet more evidence that *watched a fluffy cat* is a constituent, and that the clump *a fluffy cat* must be a part of the phrase that contains *watched*.

Movement and substitution are the main tests for constituency. The other three tests, interposition, coordination, and omissibility, can be used to confirm or refine hypotheses made on the basis of movement and substitution.

Interposition

INTERPOSITION is based on the fact that elements that affect a whole phrasal category can more easily be inserted between constituents of that category than inside of its constituents. For example, the adverb *surreptitiously* can only be inserted in certain places in a clause:

(41)   a.   Surreptitiously the dog watched the fluffy cat.
       b.   *The surreptitiously dog watched the fluffy cat.
       c.   The dog surreptitiously watched the fluffy cat.

d. ?The dog watched surreptitiously the fluffy cat.
e. *The dog watched the surreptitiously fluffy cat.
f. *The dog watched the fluffy surreptitiously cat.
g. The dog watched the fluffy cat surreptitiously.

It turns out that the only places an adverb can naturally be placed in a clause are at the beginning (41a), at the end (41g), and at the major constituent boundary between the Subject and the Predicate (41c). It can possibly occur between the verb and its Object, but this is highly unnatural (indicated by the question mark at the beginning of (41d)).

Coordination

The next secondary test for constituency is COORDINATION. This test is based on the universal linguistic principle that only units that are of the same category can be linked together by the syntactic construction known as coordination – often expressed with the word *and* in English. For example, the following are acceptable coordinate structures:

(42) a. A boy and a girl
      b. The boys and girls
      c. The scruffy dog and fluffy cat
      d. over the river and through the woods
      e. ... saw a fluffy cat and cried
      f. Oberon cleaned the house and Slumbat watched television.

The fact that we can comfortably coordinate two clumps is evidence that the clumps belong to the same syntactic category. If we were to try to coordinate two distinct syntactic categories, for example a DP and a PP, a DP and a VP, or a VP and a Clause, an ungrammatical sequence would result:

(43) *the boys and over the river
      *a scruffy dog and saw a fluffy cat
      *humming an Italian aria and Slumbat watched television

The sequences in (43) cannot be grammatical *constituents* in English, though they may occur as random, non-clumped sequences, for example:

(44) I shouted at the boys and over the river they flew.
      She heard a scruffy dog and saw a fluffy cat
      Oberon cooked dinner humming an Italian aria and Slumbat watched television.

However, movement and substitution will clearly reveal that the sequences in (43) cannot be clumps:

(45)   *the boys and over the river is what I shouted at they flew
       *a scruffy dog and saw a fluffy cat is what she heard
       *humming an Italian aria and Slumbat watched television is what Aileron cooked dinner.

Therefore, coordination can be a way of confirming what phrasal category a clump belongs to, or whether it is a clump at all. However, it can't be the major way of determining constituent structure.

Omissibility

Every language allows ELLIPSIS – the omission of certain words or phrases when it is obvious from the context what those words or phrases would be. This is most easily illustrated in answers to questions. For example, the following yes/no question may elicit any number of affirmative responses:

(46)   Q: Do you always begin conversations this way?
       Response A: Yes, I always begin conversations this way.
       Response B: Yes, I always do begin conversations this way.
       Response C: Yes, I always begin conversations this way.

Response A does not leave anything out of the original question. Response B leaves out the phrase *begin conversations this way*, and response C leaves out the whole clause *I always begin conversations this way*. This is evidence that the omitted portions are constituents. There are certain other sequences that are not comfortably omitted in such a response:

(47)   Q: Do you always begin conversations this way?
       Response D: ☺Yes, I always begin conversations this way.
       Response E: *Yes, I always do begin conversations this way.
       Response F: *Yes, I always begin conversations this way.
       etc.

Response D is not ungrammatical, in the sense described above. It is an utterance that is sanctioned by the grammatical patterns of English. However, it is just not an appropriate response to the question. It does not constitute a reduced form of the full response *Yes, I always begin conversations this way*. Responses E and F are more clearly ungrammatical, as well as being inappropriate answers to the question. These examples are evidence that the omitted portions of the responses are not syntactic constituents.

Omissibility needs to be used with caution for a couple of reasons. First of all, in practice just about anything can be omitted from a clause if the speaker believes the omitted portion can be recovered by the hearer in the context. Consider the following:

(48)   a.   Been there, done that.
       b.   How many on board, Mr. Murdoch?

In example (48a), the sequence *I have* has been omitted twice. Yet the major tests for constituency show that *I have* is not a constituent. Similarly, (48b) can be considered a reduction of *How many people are on board, Mr. Murdoch?* Again, the omitted portion, *people are*, clearly is not a constituent:

(49)   *People are how many on board, Mr. Murdoch?
       (*People are* moved to beginning of clause)
       *How many *people are* on board, and so/such/do on shore, Mr. Murdoch?
       (Various possible pro-forms substituted for *people are*)

The second reason why omissibility should be used with caution is that it is only reliable in distinguishing certain constituent boundaries, and not others. For example, we have seen that there are major constituent boundaries between the Subject and the Predicate of a clause. Also, there is definitely a syntactic boundary between a verb and its Object. Finally, we will also see below that there is a "small" constituent boundary between a Determiner and the remainder of a DP. None of these boundaries is testable using the omissibility criterion:

(50)   Q: Did you see the gnarly tree?
       Response A: *Yes, I ~~saw the gnarly tree~~.
       Response B: ☹ Yes, I saw ~~the gnarly tree~~.
       Response C: *Yes, I saw the ~~gnarly tree~~.

The fact that A, B, and C are not comfortable responses to the question seems to indicate that the omitted portions are not constituents. However, the major tests for constituency show that, at some level, these all must be considered constituents. Therefore, omissibility, along with the other secondary tests for constituency, must be used with caution. The secondary tests are ways of "poking" a syntactic string in order to derive clues as to its internal structure, but they are not necessarily applicable in every situation.

7.4   Constituent structure trees

Up to this point we have been using labeled brackets and box diagrams to represent phrase structure. Labeled brackets have the advantage of being relatively easy to type, and they don't take up much space. However, when dealing with complex phrase structures, labeled bracketing soon becomes unwieldy. Box diagrams have the advantage of being very explicit, and allowing a consistent way of indicating the syntactic functions as well as the syntactic categories of elements in phrase structure. They can also be a useful way of illustrating syntactic structures in ESL/EFL classes. However, box diagrams are difficult to type, and take up a lot of space, especially when representing very complex structures.

We will continue to use bracketing and box diagrams as they prove useful in the remainder of this book. At this point, however, we will introduce another method of representing phrase structure that is used extensively in the linguistics and applied linguistics literature – CONSTITUENT STRUCTURE TREES. Constituent structure trees (also called "phrase markers" or "tree diagrams") have the advantages of taking up less space than box diagrams or long strings of labeled brackets. They are also used extensively in the literature, so English language professionals will profit from understanding them. However, like box diagrams, trees are rather difficult to draw in a word processing document. More importantly, tree diagrams do not allow easy representation of syntactic or semantic functions. The nodes on the constituent structure trees in these pages consist of syntactic category labels only. This is a very important point to remember. Syntactic categories and syntactic functions are *different*, and constituent structure trees do not normally indicate syntactic functions.

Here is an example of how constituent structure trees work. A clump like *the dog* consists of an article plus a noun. We have already used labeled brackets to represent this structure. Let's just call it a DP for now:

(51)   [$_{dp}$the dog]$_{dp}$

The brackets indicate that the article and noun constitute a constituent, or "clump," and the small lowered labels indicate the phrasal category of the clump. The "tree" corresponding to this structure is the following:

(52)

```
        DP
       /  \
    ART    N
     |     |
    The   dog
```

In this tree, the phrasal category is written at the top (DP), while the parts are written underneath. They are linked to the phrasal category label by lines, called BRANCHES. Each labeled point is called a NODE. PHRASAL NODES designate phrasal categories (DP in this example), and TERMINAL NODES designate lexical categories at the ends of the branches (ART and N in this example).

You will probably notice that this does not look much like a tree at all. Linguistic trees are really more like upside down trees, or the root systems of biological trees. In fact, constituent structure trees are sometimes written the other way – with the phrasal category label at the bottom and the branches extending upwards to the lexical category labels as "leaves." However, this rather odd, upside down way of displaying syntactic trees is more common. In Chapter 8, we will use tree diagrams as a way of illustrating the arguments for three somewhat controversial phrasal categories of English syntax – DP, IP, and GP.

Summary

In this chapter we have begun to approach the syntax of English from a linguistic perspective. The universal features of syntactic structure that any syntactic theory must be able to represent are:

- linear order
- constituency (clumping)
- hierarchical structure (nesting)

Three methods for representing or "modeling" syntactic structures were proposed:

- labeled brackets
- box diagrams
- constituent structure trees

The difference between syntactic categories and syntactic functions was discussed. It is important to define syntactic categories and syntactic functions independently of one another, since one function may be served by various categories, and one category may serve more than one function. A way of remembering the difference is that syntactic category labels describe what an element *is*, while syntactic functions describe what an element *does*. Five syntactic functions were then defined, discussed, and exemplified:

- syntactic Head
- the Determining function
- Complementation
- grammatical relations
- Predication

Every science has its ways of "probing and poking" its subject matter in order to understand it better. Linguistics has various "tests for constituency" that help linguists understand phrase structure. Two major tests and three secondary tests for constituency are outlined:

Major tests:

- movement
- substitution

Secondary tests:

- interposition
- coordination
- omissibility

FURTHER READING

Radford (1997) is probably still the best introduction regarding basic principles of syntactic structure, including the tests for constituency. Radford (2004) addresses some of these same principles applied exclusively to English.

Exercises

1. For each of the underlined constituents in the following excerpt, indicate its semantic role(s) and its grammatical relation(s) (passage from "Rain," by W. S. Maugham):

   "I'll just go down and see how she is now," said Dr. Macphail.

   When he knocked at her door it was opened for him by Horn. Miss Thompson was in a rocking chair, sobbing quietly.

   "What are you doing there?" exclaimed MacPhail. "I told you to lie down."

   "I can't lie down. I want to see Mr. Davidson."

   "My poor child, what do you think is the good of it? You'll never move him."

   "He said he'd come if I sent for him."

   MacPhail motioned to the trader. "Go and fetch him."

2. Each of the following sentences is structurally ambiguous. Some may be lexically ambiguous as well, but the focus of this exercise is structural ambiguity. Most of these are actual newspaper headlines, though some are constructed for this exercise.

   A. For each example, explain the two (or more) meanings that arise because of the structural ambiguity.

   B. Draw two phrase structure trees, each corresponding to one of the possible meanings.
      a. I saw a man with a telescope.
      b. Fruit flies like rotten bananas.
      c. British left waffles on Falkland Islands.
      d. Raila takes over green party leadership.
      e. Marilyn wrote an article on a train.
      f. Well-trained pets and owners compete for grand prize.

3. Using the tests for constituency described in Chapter 7, determine whether the underlined sequences are constituents or not. (Not all tests will work in each case, nor will any one test necessarily be conclusive.)
   a. The driver put the valuables in the back seat.
   b. The driver forgot the valuables in the back seat.

c. We saw <u>elephants, zebras and a rhino</u> in the <u>game park</u>.
d. I've been worrying about <u>the water pressure</u> for weeks.
e. I've been worrying about <u>the water pressure</u> in the kitchen.
f. It <u>will have been being</u> played for ten minutes.
g. It will <u>have been being played</u> for ten minutes.

Advanced concepts in English syntax

Language exerts hidden power, like the moon on the tides.

Rita Mae Brown

In this chapter we will consider three hypotheses regarding the clause structure of English using the analytical methods and modeling techniques described in Chapter 7. Two of these hypotheses – the DP and IP hypotheses – represent recent proposals within the "Minimalist" tradition of Generative Grammar (Chomsky 1995, Radford 1997). These hypotheses provide helpful insights for the English language professional in that they highlight the importance of Determiners in the nominal system and Inflection in the verbal system. Determiners "anchor" noun phrases in pragmatic space while Inflection "anchors" verb phrases in time and reality (see Chapter 15). The third hypothesis – the GP hypothesis – while not central to an understanding of the overall syntactic character of English, is a logical consequence of the theoretical principles introduced in Chapter 7, and is helpful in understanding the meaning and use of genitive noun phrases.

8.1 The DP hypothesis

To this point we have been using the terms NP and DP without giving much evidence for why it is necessary to posit these two distinct phrasal categories, or how to tell one from the other. In this section I would like to provide evidence, using the tests for constituency described in Chapter 7, to show that DP is in fact an important phrasal category in English grammar. These facts are important to English language professionals for a couple of reasons. First, not every language requires a syntactic category corresponding to DP – the grammar of many languages can be adequately described and understood by positing NP as the only phrasal category functioning in the domain of participant reference. Learners who try to "translate" DPs in English on the model of NPs in their first language will have a very difficult time using the participant reference system of English with accuracy and fluency. Second, the use of articles and other categories that function as Determiners will only be mastered by second language learners of English if the difference between DPs and NPs is well established in the unconscious grammar of the interlanguage. Understanding DPs isn't the *only* thing one needs to know in order to use English articles properly, but without having an intuitive sense of what DPs are, the task is utterly hopeless!

Let's start with some simple examples and work our way up to some more realistic and interesting utterances. In Chapter 7 we have seen that a clump of three or more words may have more than one constituent structure. Tests for constituency help us decide on the correct structure for a particular clump. Consider the following:

(1) The gnarly tree

This is clearly a clump, because, for one thing, a pronoun can substitute for the whole string (major test for constituency #2):

(2) a. The gnarly tree fell down.
     b. It fell down.

However, what about internal constituency? Is there any reason to argue for or against any of the following possible internal structures of this simple phrase?

(3) a. [the gnarly tree]   (All one clump – no internal constituency)
     b. [the [gnarly tree]]
     c. [[the gnarly] tree]

These three possible constituent structures can be represented with three different trees (we'll add labels to all the nodes in a minute):

(4) a.

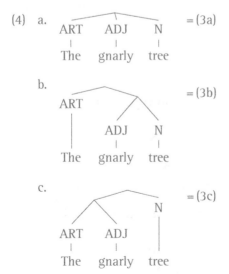

How can we "probe and poke" this structure to see which of these analyses is best? We can apply the tests for constituency to see if *the gnarly* or *gnarly tree* is a constituent. If neither one is a constituent then analysis (4a) must be correct.

What about movement? Well, the examples below show that movement doesn't tell us anything:

(5)   a.   *The gnarly* is what tree fell down.
      b.   *Gnarly tree* is what the fell down.

What about substitution? Consider the following:

(6)   You like this gnarly tree and I like that *one*.

The word *one* in this example is used as a non-specific pronoun. What does it substitute for? I think most English speakers agree that it stands for *gnarly tree*, and not simply *tree* – the second tree must also be a *gnarly tree*, and not just an ordinary tree. This is one small piece of evidence that *gnarly tree* is a clump.

Here is some more poking and probing that involves substitution:

(7)   a.   *The gnarly tree* that it is, I still love it.
      b.   *The gnarly* that it is, I still love it.
      c.   Gnarly tree that it is, I still love it.

What does this show? In (7a) the pronoun *it* (both instances) is substituting for the whole phrase, *the gnarly tree*. In (7b), the pronoun is substituting for *the gnarly* alone. These are both totally ungrammatical. Finally, example (7c) shows that *it* can easily substitute for *gnarly tree*, thus providing additional evidence for analysis (3b) above.

What about interposition? Well, I think you can place adjectives on either side of *gnarly* in this phrase, so I don't think interposition helps.

(8)   a.   The old gnarly tree.
      b.   The gnarly old tree.

How about coordination? Consider the following expressions:

(9)   a.   The gnarly and rotten tree
      b.   The gnarly tree and rotten log
      c.   The gnarly tree and the rotten log
      d.   ??The gnarly and the rotten tree.

Example (9a) shows that *gnarly and rotten* can form a clump, but this is not surprising, since they are both fairly clearly adjectives. Remember that coordination shows that coordinated elements are of the same syntactic category, so it makes sense that two adjectives can be coordinated. What does (9b) show?

This shows that *gnarly tree* and *rotten log* can be coordinated. In other words, it shows that something like the following tree is the appropriate analysis for (9b):

(10)

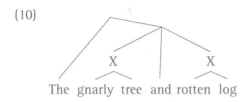

The gnarly tree and rotten log

In this example, the X symbols just indicate that the two clumps, *gnarly tree* and *rotten log*, must belong to the same category. If they didn't, you wouldn't be able to coordinate them like this. This is some more evidence that an adjective and a noun can clump together, separately from the Determiner within a phrase.

Example (9c) shows that *the gnarly tree* and *the rotten log* belong to the same category, and therefore can be coordinated. This, again, is not surprising at all, since we have already determined that such strings are clumps.

Example (9d) is a little problematic. It seems as though it is trying to coordinate *the gnarly* and *the rotten*, leaving *tree* out. This would show that the following is a conceivable tree structure for this phrase:

(11)

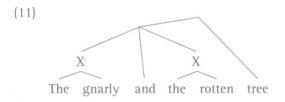

The gnarly and the rotten tree

However, the fact that many native speakers reject this phrase indicates that maybe it's not all that grammatical (grammaticality is, after all, an intuitive notion, and speakers often disagree). Even those English speakers who accept this phrase as grammatical will agree that (9b) sounds "better" somehow. Actually, if we think a little more about this phrase, we find that it sounds a little better if the noun is plural:

(12)   The gnarly and the rotten trees

What does this tell us? It seems to make more sense if we are talking about a grove of trees, some of which are rotten and some of which are gnarly. If they were all gnarly and rotten, we would be more likely to say *the gnarly and rotten trees*. Example (9d) would be a reduction from something like *the gnarly trees and the rotten trees*, with the first instance of *trees* just omitted because it is coreferential with the Head of the following clump. Therefore, it can be seen as another example of the kind of structure illustrated in (9c), but with one of the nouns eliminated, because it is the same as another noun in the same phrase:

(13)

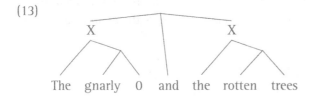

The gnarly 0 and the rotten trees

All of this poking and probing has given us some evidence that within the simple three-word phrase *the gnarly tree*, there is clumping – first between *gnarly* and *tree*, and then between this clump and the article *the*. In other words, the tree in (4c) above is more consistent with the syntactic facts of English than the tree in (4b).

Now let's consider how to label the tree in (4c). When we look at the whole grammar of English, we notice that determined noun phrases, i.e., noun phrases that begin with one of the many possible elements that can function as Determiners,[1] have different distributional properties than "undetermined" noun phrases. We've already seen some examples of this above. Other examples include the fact that Subjects of verbs must be determined:

(14) a. The tree fell down.
      b. That tree fell down.
      c. Farmer John's tree fell down.
      d. *Tree fell down.
      e. *Gnarly tree fell down.

Note that *gnarly tree*, without the Determiner, can appear in examples like (7c), but the same phrase cannot occur in examples like (14e). Therefore, it is clear that NPs with a Determiner and those without one have different syntactic properties. Since the presence of a Determiner governs the syntactic properties of the whole phrase, it makes sense to think of the Determiner as being the syntactic Head of the phrase. By the projection principle (syntactic Heads project syntactic properties onto their phrasal categories), it is reasonable to consider the whole determined noun phrase a DETERMINER PHRASE, or DP. A noun phrase, then, would be the part that doesn't include the Determiner. Under this analysis, the complete structure of our famous phrase would be the following. I've given both the tree diagram and the labeled box diagram, just for comparison:

(15)

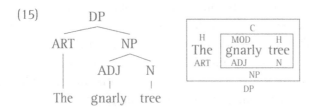

In this structure, there are two phrases – a determiner phrase with a noun phrase nested within it. The terminal nodes, ART and N, represent the syntactic Heads of these two phrases respectively. The adjective *gnarly* is an optional Modifier within the NP. The NP is functioning as the obligatory Complement of the Head of the DP. The two methods for representing this structure are equivalent, except that the box diagram represents syntactic functions as well as syntactic categories. Even as prepositions have the syntactic function of Head of a prepositional phrase, so the Determiner has the syntactic function of Head of a determiner phrase.

8.2   The functions of DPs vs. NPs – why distinguish the two?

I have just given standard arguments that DP and NP are distinct phrasal categories in English grammar. This observation immediately raises the question as to why a language should make this structural distinction. What good is the difference between DP and NP in the task of communication? This section is a brief and preliminary attempt at such an explanation.

Determined noun phrases "anchor" discourse world referents in "pragmatic space," while undetermined noun phrases do not. For example, an undetermined NP like *coffee table* can describe some potential entity, but it doesn't indicate whether that entity is a specific object that has already been referred to in the conversation, something new the speaker is going to continue talking about, or all coffee tables in general (see Chapter 15 for a discussion of pragmatic statuses). Similar to the way Inflection in a verb phrase "anchors" a situation in time and reality, so Determiners help "anchor" noun phrases in pragmatic space. As discussed below in Section 8.3, without Inflection a verb phrase may describe a semantically coherent situation, but it is not anchored or "located" in some time/ reality frame – it doesn't assert any specific discourse world situation:

(16)   a.   Morton *jumped off the coffee table.*
       b.   Mildred dared Morton *to jump off the table.*

The italicized portion of example (16a) is an inflected verb phrase. If this scene were enacted in a play, you would see someone named Morton actually jump off a coffee table. On the other hand if (16b) were a scene in a play, you would see Mildred daring Morton to jump off a table, but you wouldn't actually see Morton jump. The uninflected verb phrase *to jump off a table* is not anchored to any actual event in the discourse world.

The difference between determined and undetermined noun phrases is something like this, but in the domain of participant reference. An undetermined NP is kind of like an uninflected VP in that it doesn't tie the referring expression to any particular pragmatic status. Consider the following:

(17)　Morton was thumbing through a *coffee table* art book.

The italicized part of example (17) is an undetermined noun phrase functioning as a Modifier of the NP headed by *book*. In the scene evoked by this clause, one sees a book on stage, but not necessarily any particular coffee table. This is the sense in which pragmatic status of noun phrases is analogous to time and reality of verb phrases. English seems to need to anchor referring expressions in pragmatic space just as it needs to anchor situations in time and reality. Determined noun phrases are the syntactic category within which referents are pragmatically anchored.

8.3　The GP hypothesis

In Section 8.1, I argued on the basis of syntactic tests that it is necessary to posit DP as a phrasal category distinct from NP. There is one other syntactically distinct "type of NP" that needs to be argued for, albeit briefly, at this point. This is the GENITIVE NOUN PHRASE, or GENITIVE PHRASE (GP). In Chapter 4 we discussed the genitive morpheme, usually spelled - *'s*, as an enclitic that attaches to noun phrases. Although this enclitic can in no wise be considered a word separate from the host to which it attaches, it does have a very important function at the phrase level; it is not just a suffix that relates to a noun, but rather an element that affects the whole phrase it attaches to. DPs that are immediately followed by the genitive enclitic have different syntactic properties than other DPs; therefore, they are a different phrasal category from DPs, one which is naturally called GP, or genitive phrase.

The central property of GPs that distinguishes them from other phrasal categories is that they may function as Determiners. Since other phrasal categories, in particular NP and DP, do not function in this role, GP must be considered a distinct category. Consider the following:

(18)　a.　the teacher
　　　b.　we teachers
　　　c.　some teachers
　　　d.　any teachers
　　　e.　her teacher
　　　f.　Mary's teacher
　　　g.　the woman behind the counter's teacher

All of the phrases in (18) are DPs, and they all may function as Subjects, Objects, and all other syntactic functions served by DPs. In each case, the element preceding the word *teacher(s)* is the Determiner element, functioning as the Head of each DP, as argued in the previous section. In Chapter 7 (example (12)) a list and examples of elements that can function as Determiners is given. In examples (18e), (18f), and

(18g), genitive elements function as Determiners. We know that these must themselves be Determiners because (a) the phrases that they Head function exactly like determined noun phrases, and (b) they exclude the possibility of another Determiner:

(19) *the her teacher
      *a Mary's teacher
      *her the woman behind the counter's teacher

So genitive phrases, such as *Mary's* or *the woman behind the counter's* can function as Determiners. Notice, however, that this is a function that neither ordinary DPs nor NPs can serve:

(20) *Mary teacher
      *the man teacher
      *three dogs teacher
      *fast car teacher

While these examples may have interpretations in some context, they are uninterpretable as DPs in which *teacher* is the semantic Head and *Mary*, *the man*, *three dogs*, and *fast car* are Determiners respectively.

Since genitive phrases, or GPs, can function as Determiners, and DPs and NPs cannot, then GP must be a different phrasal category from DP or NP. Furthermore, the presence of the genitive enclitic -*'s* determines the syntactic properties of this phrasal category therefore it is reasonable to propose that the enclitic is the syntactic Head of the GP. Thus the relevant syntactic analysis of the phrase *the boy's teacher* would be the following:

(21)

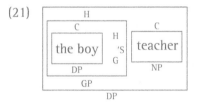

This structure is a DP in which the element serving the Determining function is a GP, and its Complement is a simple NP containing only the Head noun *teacher*. The GP Head of the phrase consists of a DP Complementing the genitive enclitic G. It makes sense to treat G as the syntactic Head of the GP because the presence of G makes it possible for the preceding DP to function as a Determiner. This is parallel to the arguments that Determiners are syntactic Heads of DPs and prepositions are syntactic Heads of PPs. The syntactic Head of a phrase is the element of the phrase that determines, or "projects," the syntactic properties of the whole phrase.

One interesting fact about GPs is that they can function in some roles prototypically served by DPs, though the inverse is not true:

(22)   GPs functioning as Subject of clauses:
    a.   My, *my mother's* was five-two-nine-seven and *mine* was seven-five-one-eight-one.
    b.   ... has tended to focus on women's health issues, while *men's* are seldom discussed publicly.

The italicized portions of (22a and b) are GPs that seem to be functioning as the Subjects of their respective clauses. However, these could be construed as elliptical DPs, in which the NP Complement has been omitted because it is obvious from the context. In other words, *my mother's* and *mine* in (22a) are truncated forms of *my mother's account number* and *my account number*, since account numbers are being discussed in the preceding context (not given here). Similarly, *men's* in (22b) can be considered a shortened version of *men's health issues*, as made clear from the context.

GPs can also function as attributive Modifiers within NPs, as in the following (adapted from Huddleston and Pullum 2002:469–70):

(23)   a.   He lives in an *old people's* home.
    b.   It was a glorious *summer's* day.
    c.   She graduated from Hanyang *Women's* University.

In these examples, the italicized portions do not serve as Determiners. We know this because each of the phrases is preceded by another determining element, *an*, *a*, and the null proper name Determiner in (23c). Also, the GPs in these constructions do not necessarily occur first in their phrases. For example, (23b) probably refers to a glorious day in summer, rather than a day in a glorious summer. Thus *summer's* in this phrase is the second in a string of two Modifiers that both modify *day*.

Finally, I would like to mention the distinction between dependent and independent genitive pronouns (Huddleston and Pullum 2002:470ff) in connection with the GP vs. DP distinction. As mentioned in Chapter 3, English has two types of genitive pronouns, those Huddleston and Pullum term dependent vs. independent genitive pronouns:

(24)   **Genitive pronouns**

	Dependent	Independent
1sg	my	mine
2sg	your	yours
3sg Fem	her	hers
3sg Masc	his	his
3sg Neut	its	(its)
1pl	our	ours
2pl	your	yours
3pl	their	theirs

Except for a slight complication created by the homophony between dependent and independent *his* and *its*, these two sets of pronouns have very different syntactic properties; the dependent pronouns function as Determiners, while the independent pronouns function as DPs:

(25)   a.   I would give *my life* for a farthing.
      b.   I would give *mine* for a farthing.
      c.   *I would give *mine life* for a farthing.
      d.   *I would give *my* for a farthing.

In (25a) the DP *my life* is functioning as the Object of the verb *give*. Within the DP *my life*, the dependent pronoun *my* is functioning as the Determiner, i.e., the syntactic Head of the phrase. In (25b), the independent genitive pronoun *mine* "stands for" (is functioning in the same role as) the whole DP in (25a). Examples (25c) and (25d) show that the roles of dependent and independent genitive pronouns are mutually exclusive – in Modern English *mine* cannot function to Determine a following NP (25c) and *my* cannot function in the role of DP (25d). The same pattern holds for all of the genitive pronouns (with the complication of homophony in the case of *his* and *its*).

The two sets of genitive pronouns provide supporting evidence for the GP hypothesis in that they lexicalize the distinction between GP and DP. There are situations where dependent genitive pronouns may not substitute for full GPs (such as the examples in (23) above). However, for the most part, dependent genitive pronouns serve GP functions, while independent genitive pronouns serve DP functions. Notice that neither of these pronoun types serve NP functions. For example, they do not take attributive Modifiers, and cannot themselves be determined. Thus these pronouns provide important, though secondary, support for the three-way distinction among NP, DP, and GP.

Another way of thinking about independent genitive pronouns is as "fused" Determiner+Semantic Head forms. Just like the other personal pronouns, they are syntactically DPs but contain no Determiner element that is separate from the semantic Head itself. This is the approach taken by Huddleston and Pullum (2002:470ff).

While a consistent linguistic perspective on English grammar requires us to posit a distinct syntactic category of GP, in practice English language professionals and second language learners need not worry too much about internalizing this category as distinct from the phrasal category of DP. The important points to note, from a practical perspective, are:

- The genitive ending usually spelled - *'s* is a phrase level morpheme – it is an enclitic.
- Phrases that end in - *'s*, like the dependent genitive pronouns, may function as Determiners.
- Independent genitive pronouns function as determined noun phrases, and *not* as Determiners.

I will emphasize again here that DP *is* an important syntactic category for English language professionals and learners to understand and master.

8.4   The IP hypothesis

Now let's take a look at another common phrasal category – the verb phrase. Consider the following clauses:

(26)   a.   My daughter is reading an Igbo dictionary.
       b.   Is my daughter reading an Igbo dictionary?

The major question here is "What is the syntactic status of the auxiliary element, *is*? Is it part of a clump that includes *reading an Igbo dictionary*, one that includes *my daughter*, or neither? In fact, there are at least five possible syntactic analyses of example (26a). These are given below in (27). In these trees, the triangles are simply abbreviations for structures that are not relevant to the current discussion:

(27) a.

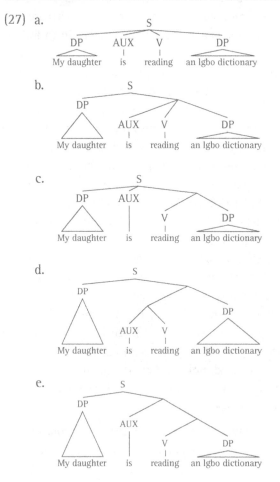

We have already dealt with noun phrases and determiner phrases, so we don't need to complicate our discussion by worrying about the internal structure of these elements anymore. Our focus now is on the external relationships of the DPs, as well as the syntactic functions of the AUX and the V. Also, we have left some nodes unlabeled, because these analyses are only possibilities at this point. We need to "probe and poke" the structure a bit to see which of these is most consistent with the facts of English. After we've done that, we'll worry about the category labels.

Analyses like (27a) are sometimes referred to as FLAT STRUCTURES. In a flat structure, there is no syntactic merger between any of the elements under the S node. This kind of structure would suggest that the order of these elements may be fairly "free" (though there still may be a "basic" or "normal" constituent order).

We will test this structure for English by applying the now familiar tests for constituency. Example (26b) shows that the AUX can move to the front by itself; therefore it is a constituent on its own at some level. This would seem to eliminate possibilities (27b) and (27d) immediately, since in these structures, the AUX is merged directly with other lexical categories. We would expect that if the AUX moved, its "sisters" would move too, but they don't:

(28)   Trying to move *is reading an Igbo dictionary* as a clump:

   Is reading an Igbo dictionary my daughter.

   Is reading an Igbo dictionary is what my daughter does.

   etc.

(29)   Trying to move *is reading* as a clump:

   Is reading my daughter an Igbo dictionary.

   Is reading is what my daughter an Igbo dictionary does.

   etc.

The other tests also show that *is reading an Igbo dictionary* (27b) and *is reading* (27d) cannot be constituents; therefore we can eliminate these two analyses and concentrate on (27a, c, and e).

Analysis (27a) suggests not only that *is* can be moved independently (and (26b) shows that it can) but also that *reading* should be able to so move also. This is not the case:

(30)   Trying to move *reading* independently:
       Reading my daughter is an Igbo dictionary.
       Reading is what my daughter is an Igbo dictionary does.
       etc.

Therefore we can pretty confidently conclude that analysis (27a) is out. So we are left with (27c) and (27e). These two structures, one with the AUX attached directly to the S node, and the other with the AUX connected at a lower level to the semantically main verb, are in fact the two most commonly proposed basic syntactic structures for English clauses. For many years (27c), with the AUX attached directly to the S node, was the favored analysis. In recent years, however, analyses more similar to (27e) have been preeminent. In the following discussion, we will "probe and poke" this structure a little more to see which analysis seems best, from the point of view of the tests for constituency provided above. The point of this discussion is simply to illustrate how constituent structure trees and the tests for constituency can be used to determine the hierarchical structure of linguistic units – not to argue conclusively for one particular analysis or another of English.

We have seen in example (28) that the sequence *is reading an Igbo dictionary* cannot move as a clump. This is one piece of evidence for analysis (27c). What about substitution? Consider the following:

(31) Trying to substitute (*so*) *do* for *is reading an Igbo dictionary*:
      *My daughter is reading an Igbo dictionary and *so does* my son.

Rather, it seems much easier to substitute *so* alone for the sequence *reading an Igbo dictionary*, leaving the AUX in place:

(32) Substituting *so* for *reading an Igbo dictionary*:
      My daughter is reading an Igbo dictionary and *so is* my son.

Furthermore, in answer to a question like "What is your daughter doing?" it is reasonable to expect an answer like (33a), but not (33b):

(33) a. Reading an Igbo dictionary
      b. *Is reading an Igbo dictionary

Interposition similarly seems to show that there is a major constituent boundary after *is*, but perhaps somewhat less major boundaries before *is* and after *reading*:

(34) a. My daughter is avidly reading an Igbo dictionary.
      b. ?My daughter avidly is reading an Igbo dictionary.
      c. ?My daughter is reading avidly an Igbo dictionary.

This seems to argue in favor of analysis (27c), in which the boundary between AUX and V is at the highest level.

Finally, coordination also provides evidence that *reading an Igbo dictionary* is a constituent, whereas *is reading an Igbo dictionary* is not:

(35) a. My daughter is reading an Igbo dictionary and chewing gum.
      b. ?My daughter is reading an Igbo dictionary and is chewing gum.

In summary, both of the major tests for constituency, and some of the minor tests as well, seem to point to the tree structure in (27c) as the most reasonable analysis for this English clause (and presumably for all other English clauses with auxiliaries, though more would need to be tested to make sure).

Now let us briefly consider why, in more recent theoretical work, analysis (27e) is considered more appropriate. The reasoning is that the AUX in a structure like (26a) is the syntactic Head of the rest of the clause. What is the evidence that AUX is a syntactic Head? First, the particular AUX chosen determines the form of the verb that follows. Consider the following:

(36)   a.   Frodo is leaving the Shire.
     b.   Frodo has left the Shire.
     c.   Frodo will leave the Shire.
     d.   Frodo ought to leave the Shire.

The examples in (36) illustrate four distinct auxiliaries, *be*, *have*, *will*, and *ought*, respectively (see Chapter 11 on auxiliaries). Each of these requires a distinct form of the verb that follows. Example (36a) shows that the auxiliary *be* takes an "*-ing* form" (traditionally called a PRESENT PARTICIPLE) of the following verb. Example (36b) shows that the auxiliary *have* takes a PAST PARTICIPLE form (*left*) of the following verb. Example (36c) shows that the auxiliary *will* is followed by the BARE FORM (*leave*) of the semantically main verb. Finally, example (36d) shows that the semi-auxiliary *ought* requires an INFINITIVE form (*to leave*) of the main verb. These facts are evidence that the AUX plus the verb have a close syntactic relation to one another. In particular, they provide one piece of evidence that the AUX is the syntactic Head of its phrase, since the grammatical properties (the particular verb form) of the semantically main verb depend on the AUX.

The second piece of evidence that the AUX is the Head of a phrase that includes the following verb is that the AUX takes the major inflectional information (tense and agreement) for the whole clause. For example, consider the following:

(37)   a.   Frodo is leaving the Shire.
     b.   Frodo was leaving the Shire.
     c.   Frodo and Bilbo are leaving the Shire.
     d.   Frodo and Bilbo were leaving the Shire.

In these examples, *leaving the Shire* is clearly the main action that is being described. Nevertheless, the auxiliary *be* (*is*, *was*, *are*, and *were*) is what varies for tense and for the number of the Subject. The semantically main verb, *leaving*, remains the same in all examples. This is a major defining property of auxiliaries in English – they express the inflectional information that is relevant to the semantically main verb that follows. Consider these additional auxiliaries:

(38)   a.   I have seen the lady.
     b.   I had seen the lady.
     c.   I can only eat organic food.
     d.   I could only eat organic food.

These examples show that the auxiliaries *have* and *can* also take the tense inflection for the whole clause, even though the verbs *see* and *eat* respectively express the main semantic content.

In summary, while the traditional tests for constituency seem to argue for a three-way branching under the S node in English (analysis (27c)), it is clearly the case that the AUX is more tightly related to the element to its right than it is to the DP to its left. Another way of looking at this is to say that the relationships among the three major constituents of the S (the first DP, the AUX, and the VP) are *asymmetrical*. That is to say, the AUX is syntactically "closer" to the verb than to the Subject of the sentence. The way this would be diagrammed in a tree structure would be the following:

(39)

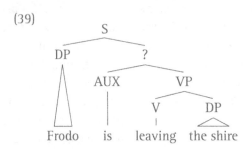

Since we have argued that the AUX is the syntactic Head of a constituent that includes the following verb, you might think that a reasonable label for the constituent labeled as "?" in example (39) would be Auxiliary Phrase, AP, or maybe AUXP (to help distinguish this phrasal category from Adjective Phrases and Adverb Phrases). This would be analogous to the way we sometimes use the term "determiner phrase" to refer to a phrase whose Head is a Determiner. Nevertheless, most recent accounts use the term INFLECTIONAL PHRASE (IP) to refer to the kind of structure that is headed by an auxiliary. There are good theoretical reasons for this that we will only touch on here. Briefly, not all constituents that have the syntactic properties of inflectional phrases have auxiliaries in them. Consider the following:

(40)   He roped himself a couple of sea turtles.

Since there is no auxiliary in this clause, we may want to diagram it as in (41):

(41)

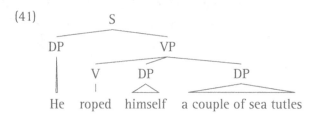

However, the "VP" in this structure has very different properties from a VP in a clause that has an auxiliary, such as (39). In particular, the verb *roped* is fully inflected. Its form is not governed by some other element, the way the form of the verb *leaving* in example (39) depends on the auxiliary *be*. It's just that the inflection in (41) is part of the verb, rather than being expressed in a separate auxiliary. What if we say there is an invisible "inflectional category" that migrates to the verb whenever there is no auxiliary to receive it? This analysis may be diagrammed as follows:

(42)

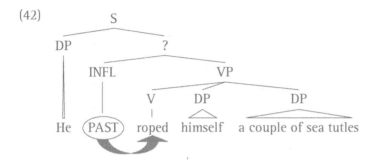

In this example, INFL stands for an "empty category" that has no overt realization, other than the inflection that shows up on the Head of the following VP.

If we are going to posit an abstract analysis such as this, it would be more convincing if it could do more for us than simply account for sentences in which main verbs carry the inflectional information. In this particular case, it would help us evaluate the empty category hypothesis if we could show that this analysis is needed to capture some other fact or facts of English syntax. Well, consider the pattern that is sometimes referred to as SUBJECT-AUX INVERSION.

Subject-AUX inversion happens in various kinds of questions in English. For example, if you want to ask someone a question, based on the statement *I can't have a normal boyfriend*, you may say:

(43)   Why can't I have a normal boyfriend?
        Can't I have a normal boyfriend?

Notice what happens to the auxiliary, *can't*, in these questions. In both examples, it precedes the Subject, *I*, rather than follows it, as in the statement. This inversion of Subject and auxiliary in questions is completely regular, for all auxiliaries in English.

Now, we may ask what happens to a clause like (40) when you apply Subject-AUX inversion. After all, it looks like there is no auxiliary in this clause, right? Well, check this out:

(44)   Why did he rope a couple of sea turtles?
        Did he rope a couple of sea turtles?

Voilà, the abstract inflectional element appears in the form of the auxiliary *do*, which then takes the tense inflection. Meanwhile, the semantically main verb, *rope*, goes back to its bare form. It's almost as though the auxiliary were there all along, lurking within the inflected verb. The inversion construction simply flushes it out into the open.

There are a couple of additional constructions that reveal the invisible inflectional element in an auxiliary-less verb phrase. Consider the standard negation construction. When there is an auxiliary in the affirmative, the negative particle, *not*, follows the auxiliary:

(45) **Negative**   **Affirmative**
      I am *not* being fired.   I am being fired.
      I can *not* see why you would be upset.   I can see why you would be upset.
      You would *not* believe how much I weigh.   You would believe how much I weigh.

In modern Englishes, it is not common for *not* to follow the verb:

(46) *I am being *not* fired.
      *I can see *not* why you would be upset.
      *You would believe *not* how much I weigh.

Well, what happens when you negate a clause that does not have an auxiliary?

(47) **Negative**   **Affirmative**
      I do *not* feel like parting with it.   I feel like parting with it.
      I do *not* even exercise.   I even exercise.
      I do *not* even have a picture of him.   I even have a picture of him.

Again, the auxiliary *do* automatically appears. One could say it appears *so that* the negative particle can follow it. This is yet another piece of evidence that something like the empty category analysis of inflected verb phrases in English is correct.

What these arguments show is that the "mystery constituent" (labeled "?") in examples (39) and (42) is really the same kind of constituent. In (39) the Head of this constituent is overtly expressed in an auxiliary, while in (42) the Head is "hidden" inside the main verb. The phrasal category that these constituents represent has recently been termed the IP, or inflectional phrase (see, e.g., Radford 1997:61–105). For our purposes, we may consider IP to stand for "inflected verb phrase."

Another advantage of the IP hypothesis is that it provides a nice way of accounting for AUXILIARY STACKING, which is a very notable fact of the syntax of English. Consider the following clauses:

(48) a. The winning side has paid you much better.
　　　b. The winning side would have paid you much better.
　　　c. The winning side would have been paying you much better.

Clauses can have up to four auxiliaries in English. It may take quite a while to imagine a context in which four auxiliaries naturally occur, but it is very possible:

(49) He *should have been being* paid by the winning side.

This is known as auxiliary stacking. Going back to the previous examples, notice that each auxiliary after the first one is "governed" by the auxiliary to the left. (48a) and (48b) *have* precedes the verb *pay*, and therefore the past participle form, *paid*, is required. In (48c), the auxiliary *have* precedes the auxiliary *be*; therefore, *be* occurs in the past participle form, *been*, while *pay* appears in the present participle form, *paying*. Why is this? Because in this example *pay* is governed by the auxiliary *be*, rather than the auxiliary *have*. What governs the form of *have* in example (48b)? The auxiliary *would* does. If it didn't, then the form of *have* would be the same as it is in (48a) – *has*.

　　Therefore, we see that there is evidence for a structure in which each AUX governs the element to its right. These facts of the grammatical knowledge of English speakers can be nicely captured in the following kind of tree diagram:

(50)

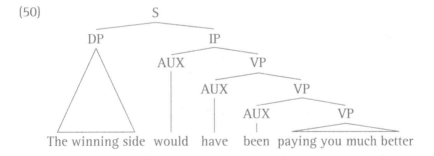

Notice that only the first constituent headed by an AUX is labeled IP. This is because this is the only "Verb Phrase" that is inflected (that's why we can call it an "inflected verb phrase"). In the others, each labeled VP, the form of the first element, *have*, *been*, and *paying*, is governed by the auxiliary to its left. None of them has its own inflection.

　　Of course, there are many more considerations and important theoretical principles that we are glossing over here, but this should provide a general idea of how the formalisms of early twenty-first-century linguistic theory (particularly theories in the tradition of Generative Grammar) work.

Summary

In this chapter we have treated three specific hypotheses related to the syntactic analysis of English. These hypotheses are:

- The DP hypothesis
- The GP hypothesis
- The IP hypothesis

Understanding DPs and IPs is very important for English language professionals who wish to understand the participant reference and verbal systems of English, and help their students and clients develop accuracy and fluency. The GP hypothesis is less central in this regard.

FURTHER READING

Chomsky (1995) and Radford (1997) are the best readings on the minimalist program of generative grammar in general. Radford (2004) applies minimalism specifically to English in an engaging introductory way. Bošković and Lasnik (2007) provide a selection of essential articles in minimalism by leading researchers in the field. Classic works on syntactic analysis beyond the clause are van Dijk (1972) and Longacre (1983). Hoey (2001) is a more recent introduction to this topic.

Exercises

1. Bracket the determined noun phrases and underline the inflected verb phrases in the following excerpt. Remember that there may be multiple embeddings, i.e., phrases within other phrases (excerpt from "The ice palace" by F. Scott Fitzgerald).

    The sunlight dripped over the house like golden paint over an art jar, and the freckling shadows here and there only intensified the rigour of the bath of light.

2. In the following excerpt, underline each determined noun phrase, inflected verb phrase, and genitive phrase. Then circle the syntactic Head of each of the phrases you have underlined. Remember that phrases can occur within other phrases (excerpt from Livio 2005:11).

    Indeed, what quality is shared by such different masterpieces as Jan Vermeer's *Girl with a Pearl Earring*, Pablo Picasso's *Guernica*, and Andy Warhol's *Marilyn Diptych*? ... This is not to say that all works of art evoke the same emotion. Quite the contrary: every work of art may evoke an entirely different emotion. The commonality is in the fact that all works of art do evoke some emotion.

9 Complementation

I like talking to Rabbit. He talks about sensible things. He doesn't use long,
difficult words, like Owl. He uses short, easy words, like "What about lunch?"

Winnie the Pooh (Milne 1956[2001]:222)

Now that we have introduced some basic and advanced concepts in syntactic
structure, we will begin to explore in more detail some of the syntactic functions
introduced in Chapter 7. In this chapter we will look at the syntactic function
known as Complementation. Any element that combines with the Head of a
phrasal category to "complete" a phrase is functioning as a Complement of
the Head. The following are simple examples of Complements within various
categories:

(1)			Head	Complement
	a.	Determiner phrase:	ART	NP
			the	*putty-nosed monkeys*
	b.	Inflected verb phrase:	AUX	VP
			have	*learned a small number of sounds*
	c.	Verb phrase:	V	DP
			learned	*a small number of sounds*
	d.	Prepositional phrase:	P	DP
			of	*sounds*

Complementation is distinct from Modification in that Modification is always
"optional" from a syntactic perspective (see Chapter 10). Modifying elements have
a much "looser" syntactic association with their Heads than Complements do.
Prototypical examples of Complements are tightly bound to their Heads and are
syntactically required within the phrasal category that contains them. For example,
a Determiner is not a determined noun phrase without a noun phrase Complement;
an AUX alone is not an IP without a VP, DP, AdjP, or PP Complement; and a
preposition alone is not a PP without a DP Complement. We will see examples in
this chapter in which particular Complements appear to be optional, but in such

cases there are independent reasons for considering such elements to be (non-prototypical) Complements rather than Modifiers.

It is important to remember that Complementation is a *syntactic function*. As such, it may be filled by different syntactic categories. For example, the Complement of an inflectional element in an IP may be a VP, a DP, an AdjP, or a PP. Similarly, the Complement of a verb in a VP can be a DP, a PP, or an adverbial element. We will see many examples of this in the following pages. In this chapter we will concentrate on PREDICATE COMPLEMENTS.

9.1   Predication and Complementation illustrated

As discussed in Chapter 7, Predication (or Predicate) is a syntactic function at the highest level of clause structure. The term "predicate" is borrowed from mathematical logic. In language, Subject and Predicate are the two syntactic functions that are needed to express a proposition, or a "complete thought." Example (2) illustrates a fully notated box diagram for a simple English clause that includes both Subject and Predicate functions, along with four instances of Complementation:

(2)

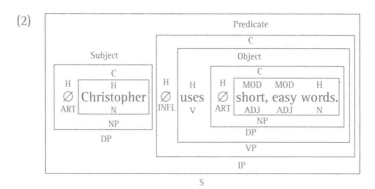

You won't find many complete box diagrams in this book, because, as you can see, they can be pretty complicated to draw and to read. However, they are very explicit in that they fully represent all syntactic categories and syntactic functions.[1] They are also iconic in a couple of ways. First, the boxes clearly illustrate the clumping and nesting relationships among syntactic elements. This kind of notation can be useful to English language professionals in conceptualizing and describing syntactic structures for their students and other clients. Second, the placement of category and function labels mirrors the form–function composite diagrams introduced in the Introduction. As always, syntactic category labels are written below each element, and syntactic function labels are written above each element.

The large box that surrounds the whole structure in (2) is labeled S, which is the mnemonic for "Sentence" or, as many prefer, "Clause." There is no syntactic function written above this large box because this utterance is taken out of context. We don't know how it may be functioning within a larger structure, so we can't give it a functional label. Syntactic functions always describe an element's job within the next larger structure. In this case, the whole clause may be background information, foreground information, a circumstance for some other assertion, or it may have any number of other functions in the discourse. Though it is possible to conceive of and actually attempt syntactic analysis beyond S, most linguists limit themselves to the S level, at least when they attempt to do detailed syntactic analysis as in (2).

The two largest boxes inside the S box of (2) represent the two highest level syntactic categories in the clause – a DP and an IP. These elements fill the syntactic functions of Subject and Predicate respectively. The DP that functions as Subject contains two constituents – a null article functioning as Head and an NP functioning as the Complement (C) of the article. The IP that functions as Predicate of this sentence also consists of two elements – an empty inflectional element (INFL) functioning as Head and a VP functioning as the Complement. The VP also consists of two elements – a verb functioning as Head and a DP functioning as Object. As mentioned in Chapter 7, we are considering the grammatical relations of Object and Indirect Object to be subtypes of the Complement function. Thus, the Direct Object of this clause, *short easy words*, is a kind of a Complement of the verb. This DP also has two elements – a null article functioning as Head and an NP functioning as a Complement of the article. Finally, the NP inside the Object DP consists of three elements – two adjectives functioning as Modifiers, and a noun functioning as the Head of the NP.

Example (3) below illustrates the same clause displayed as a constituent structure tree:

(3)

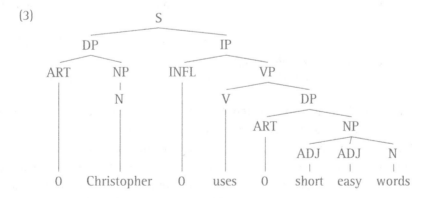

As you can see, a tree is a bit easier to read, but all the information about syntactic function is missing. It is possible to annotate each node on a tree for syntactic function, but that becomes just as complicated, if not more so, than fully notated box diagrams. It is important to remember that the labels on trees represent *syntactic categories*, and not *syntactic functions*. In many cases, syntactic functions can be deduced from the position of syntactic categories in a diagram such as (3), but that is a topic for a more advanced course in theoretical linguistics.

In the following sections, we will look at various elements that may fill the Complement function within the Predicating phrase (usually an IP).

9.2   Subject Complements

Subject Complement is a syntactic function within an IP. It is filled by a constituent that completes (or significantly enriches the semantic content of) the Predication but refers to or describes the Subject in some way. The examples in (4) below illustrate prototypical Subject Complements. As we will see, there is a continuum between prototypical Subject Complements, such as those illustrated in (4), and certain optional elements, called Obliques, or Oblique adjuncts. This continuum will be described later in this section, after several types of Subject Complements are introduced and discussed.

The italicized portions of the following examples are Subject Complements. The upper case labels to the right indicate the semantic relation between the Subject Complement and the Subject:

(4)   **Stative Subject Complements with *be***   Semantic relation
    a.   The venue for the meeting is *the Roxburghe Hotel*,   EQUATION
    b.   The estate car is *a Volvo*.   PROPER INCLUSION
    c.   You're *so young*.   ATTRIBUTION
    d.   Would you still love me if I were *old and saggy*?   ATTRIBUTION
    e.   that telly was *mine*   POSSESSION
    f.   Sometimes we're *on a collision course*,   LOCATION
    g.   the NHS was *for all of us*   BENEFACTEE
    h.   The five pound note was *for services rendered*.   IN EXCHANGE

The Inflection (marking for tense, aspect, mode, and agreement) in this type of construction is carried by *be*; therefore *be* is the syntactic Head of the Predicate. However, the Subject Complement is the element that expresses the main semantic content of the Predicate. In other words, the Complement is the semantic Head of the Predicate. Such constructions are sometimes identified by the syntactic category of the Complement, i.e., (4a), and (4b) can be called PREDICATE NOMINALS because the main predicator is a "nominal," in these cases determined noun phrases. (4c) and (4d) can be called PREDICATE ADJECTIVES because the Complements are adjective phrases. In the other examples, the type of construction is more likely to be identified by the semantic role expressed by the Complement. Example (4e) can be called a PREDICATE POSSESSIVE. Example (4f) indicates that the Subject is located at a metaphorical "place" called "a collision course." Such a clause can be called a LOCATIVE CLAUSE, or PREDICATE LOCATIVE.

Though examples (4a) and (4b) are both predicate nominals, they express quite different semantic relations between the Subject and the Complement. In (4a), the relation is EQUATION, meaning the Subject is identical to the Subject Complement; in this case *be* can be understood as an equals sign (=). Sometimes such clauses are called EQUATIVE CLAUSES. In (4b), the relation is PROPER INCLUSION, which means the Subject Complement specifies a set of things – all cars that can be designated as "a Volvo" – and predicates the idea that the Subject is completely, i.e., "properly," included within that set. In this case, *be* can be understood as a proper subset sign (⊂). When a Complement of *be* is an indefinite DP, the meaning is always proper inclusion. Examples (4c) and (4d) are ATTRIBUTIVE CLAUSES, because the Complements describe attributes *young, old and saggy*, of the Subject.

The following is a simplified box diagram for (4a), illustrating the syntactic functions of Predication and Subject Complementation:

(5)

It must be remembered that Subject Complement (along with Object Complement, Direct Object and Indirect Object) are subtypes of the general syntactic function of Complement – they all "complete" a Predication. In fact in the examples in (4), the Complement is the semantic head of the Predicate – *be* is just there to receive the inflection; it contributes little, if any, semantic content.[2] We may say that without the Subject Complement, example (5) would not express a complete thought – *the venue for the meeting is*. As we will see, however, in other examples the element that carries the inflection is a lexical verb that expresses significant semantic content itself, in which case the verb and the Subject Complement cooperate to express the total semantic content of the Predicate, e.g.,

(6)   She *turned red*.

In this case the verb *turned* and the Subject Complement *red* both contribute semantic content to the overall Predication.

A partial box diagram of (4h) is given in (7). This example, in comparison with example (5), illustrates how different syntactic categories, in this case DP and PP, can fill the syntactic function of Subject Complement:

(7)

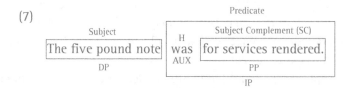

We will discuss a broad range of types of Complementation in the following sections. We will also have more to say about *be* as an auxiliary functioning as the Head of this type of construction in Chapter 11.

Another major semantic distinction in Subject Complements is between STATIVE and INCHOATIVE (or RESULTATIVE) Complements. This distinction is also relevant to Object Complements, as discussed further below. The examples in (4) are stative in that they simply assert various conditions (EQUATION, PROPER INCLUSION, ATTRIBUTION, etc.) that do not involve any kind of change. Inchoative Complements, on the other hand, assert that the Subject changes state, or "moves into" the state described in the Complement. Inchoative Complements are sometimes referred to as resultative, because the Complement describes a state that results from an action described by the verb. The following are examples of inchoative Subject Complements:

(8)   **Inchoative (or resultative) Subject Complements**
    a.   Javed Miandad's team have developed into *the most powerful combin-*
          ation on the international scene.   EQUATION
    b.   I've turned into *an English fruit.*   PROPER INCLUSION
    c.   After that, you became *a contract killer.*   PROPER INCLUSION
    d.   I became *obsessed with finding those responsible*   ATTRIBUTION
    e.   Things can only get *worse* then   ATTRIBUTION
    f.   Thou'rt got *into a fool's paradise.*   LOCATION

These examples are inchoative in that the relation indicated in capital letters is the end result of the situation described in the Predicate. In (8a), for example, the Predicate describes the team's entering into the state of equaling the most powerful combination on the international scene. (8b) describes the Subject's entering into the class of "English fruits," and so on.

Predicates headed by many sensory verbs may also contain Subject Complements. Subject Complements of sensory verbs are always stative. This is understandable, since *sensing* a situation does not cause that situation to come about:

(9)   **Stative Subject Complements with sensory verbs**
    a.   But you <u>seemed</u> *so sure.*
    b.   Their correct assembly <u>will appear</u> *identical to the original assembly drawing.*
    c.   It <u>looks</u> *like gravy.*
    d.   She <u>sounds</u> *like a very nice woman.*

    e. it <u>felt</u> *like heaven.*
    f. Your Mum <u>smells</u> *like prawns* as well.
    g. A freshly bought loaf, still warm from the oven, <u>smells</u> and <u>tastes</u>
        delicious.

The sensory verbs *smell, taste, feel,* and possibly others can also take Direct Objects as well as Subject Complements. Thus these verbs provide instructive illustrations of the contrast between Object and Subject Complements:

(10) a. they <u>smelled</u> *gas,*
      b. always <u>taste</u> *the pasta* yourself
      c. We touched the walls and <u>felt</u> *the waters* on them,
      d. He <u>felt</u> *the runway slip away from under the wheels.*

In these examples the italicized Complements are Direct Objects of the verb rather than Subject Complements. We know this for a number of reasons. First, the Complements in (10) do not identify or describe the Subject. They are distinct entities with the semantic role of THEME or STIMULUS, i.e., the source of the sensory impression. Second, they have the syntactic properties of Direct Objects. For example, Direct Objects can be made into Subjects of passive constructions, while Subject Complements may not:

(11) Gas was smelled by us.   *Like prawns was smelled by your Mum.
      The pasta is always tasted by you.   *Heavenly is always tasted by fresh bread.
                                           *An English fruit has been turned into by me.
                                           *A Volvo is been by the estate car.

Furthermore, the examples in (10) differ from those in (9) in that the Subjects in (10) have the semantic role of EXPERIENCER – the animate being who senses the impression. In (9) the Subjects are THEMEs, and the speaker is the default EXPERIENCER.

    Some sensory verbs do not occur in the Subject = EXPERIENCER construction:

(12) Subject = THEME   Subject = EXPERIENCER
      a. The alarm seemed loud.   *They seemed the alarm.
      b. The fire engine looked impressive. *They looked the fire engine.
      c. The assemblies appear identical.   *They appear the assemblies.

Occasionally there may be ambiguity as to whether the Subject of a sensory verb is a THEME or an EXPERIENCER. Consider the following:

(13) a. She smells prawns.   Subject = EXPERIENCER
      b. She smells like prawns.   Subject = THEME
      c. She feels tense.   Subject = THEME or EXPERIENCER

In example (13a), the Subject is an EXPERIENCER – she is the one who experiences the smell of prawns, and *prawns* is a Direct Object of the verb. Prawns cannot be a Subject Complement in this example because it does not refer to or describe the Subject. In (13b), on the other hand, the Subject is the THEME – the source of the prawns smell, and the phrase *like prawns* is a Subject Complement because it describes a characteristic of the Subject. Normally the EXPERIENCER in clauses such as (13b) is understood to be the speaker, e.g., *She smells like prawns* TO ME. If a different EXPERIENCER is intended, it may be specified in another prepositional phrase, as in *She smells like prawns to them*, or as part of the larger context, e.g., *He thinks she smells like prawns*.

Examples like (13c) can be ambiguous as to whether the Subject is an EXPERIENCER or a THEME. The Subject, *she*, could be the EXPERIENCER of the tense feeling, or she could be the source of the feeling sensed by someone else. If a different EXPERIENCER is expressed, this ambiguity is resolved:

(14)   She feels tense to the massage therapist.

In (14), the Subject can only be a THEME – the source of the tense feeling sensed by the EXPERIENCER, in this case the massage therapist. In any case, *tense* is still a Subject Complement. If the Complement is a DP, however, it must be a Direct Object, and the ambiguity is cancelled in favor of the Subject = EXPERIENCER meaning. Example (15) can only mean that the Subject is the EXPERIENCER, and therefore expression of a different EXPERIENCER does not make sense:

(15)   She feels the bumps in the road (*to the massage therapist).

The verbs *taste, smell,* and *feel* seem to be the only sensory verbs that allow both Direct Objects and Subject Complements; therefore they are the only ones that allow both THEME and EXPERIENCER Subjects. The other sensory verbs in (9) allow only Subject Complements, and therefore only THEMEs as Subjects (in their sensory meanings). Others, e.g., *see* and *hear*, allow only Direct Objects as Complements, and therefore EXPERIENCERs as Subjects. You might say that *look* and the sensory meaning of *sound* are the Subject Complement-taking counterparts of *see* and *hear* respectively.

(16)   Subject = THEME   Subject = EXPERIENCER
        +Subject Complement = ATTRIBUTE   +Direct Object = THEME
        The waves looked/*saw beautiful.   They saw/*looked the waves.
        The waves sounded/*heard loud.   They heard/*sounded the waves.

Non-finite clauses can also be Subject Complements (see Chapter 14 on the notion of finiteness in clause combining):

(17)   a.   She <u>seemed</u> *to want everyone to know.*
        b.   My house <u>seems</u> *to have been removed to Paris.*

c.   Well it <u>appears</u> *to fluctuate.*

d.   She ran well, but <u>looked</u> *to be going over the top.*

The italicized portions of these clauses can be considered Subject Complements because, first, the main verbs are sensory verbs that do not take Direct Objects; therefore the infinitive cannot be a clausal Direct Object:

(18)   *?She appeared *a runner.*

If this is grammatical at all – and it isn't for all speakers – *a runner* cannot be a Direct Object, i.e., something separate from and "appeared by" the Subject. At best it can be construed as a Subject Complement. Second, the understood Subject of the infinitive is always the same as the Subject of the sensory verb. In example (19) *him* would be the understood Subject of the infinitive clause if it were different from the Subject of *seem.* This is strictly ungrammatical:

(19)   *She seemed (for) him *to want everyone to know.*

Thus the best analysis of the infinitive clauses in (17) is as assertions made of the Subject participant – in other words, Subject Complements.

The following are some additional examples of stative and inchoative Subject Complements:

(20)   **Stative Subject Complements with *loom***
    a.   Constituency problems now <u>loomed</u> *large.*
    b.   as the day of departure from Framlingham <u>loomed</u> *close,* ...
    c.   Cartmel Fell <u>looms</u> *huge* to the south.
    d.   they have been <u>looming</u> *unnoticed* in the foreground all along.

(21)   **Stative Subject Complements with *prove***
    a.   Getting through the day <u>proved</u> *difficult* for Sandison.
    b.   the jar had a heavy glass base which <u>proved</u> *impossible* to overbalance.
    c.   She may <u>prove</u> *useful* in the future.
    d.   we've been <u>proved</u> *right.*

(22)   **Stative Subject Complements with verbs of position**
    a.   His portrait <u>hung</u> *in the bathroom.*
    b.   by instinct they both <u>crouched</u> *motionless*
    c.   She saw Adam <u>kneeling</u> *erect and motionless*
    d.   people sit, stand, kneel or <u>lie</u> *flat,*

(23)   **Inchoative Subject Complements with *fall***
    a.   Did she <u>fall</u> *asleep* at the wheel?
    b.   But this is where we <u>fall</u> *short.*
    c.   because of the amount of repayments <u>falling</u> *due* on earlier lending.

    d.   She may <u>fall</u> *ill*, or have an accident while you are out.

    e.   Then the workings would <u>fall</u> *silent*.

    f.   And it <u>fell</u> *to bits*.

(24) **Inchoative Subject Complements with *go***

    a.   Her car's <u>gone</u> *completely to bits*.

    b.   And the crowd <u>went</u> *bananas* at Wilko.

    c.   Where did we <u>go</u> *wrong*?

    d.   I'd <u>go</u> *mad*!

(25) **Inchoative Subject Complements with other verbs of motion**

    a.   The cat <u>scurried</u> *under the bed*.

    b.   The children <u>ran</u> *wild*.

Since the Subject Complement function may be filled by a prepositional phrase, a legitimate question arises as to whether a given prepositional phrase is a Subject Complement vs. simply an Oblique "adjunct" functioning as a Modifier. For example, if *in the bathroom* in (22a) is a Subject Complement because it specifies the location of the Subject, and if *under the bed* in (25a) is a Subject Complement because the Subject ends up "under the bed," what about the italicized parts of the following examples?

(26) a.   They talked over their wedding plans *on the bus* to Pembroke.

    b.   most of us slept *with our windows fully open*.

    c.   She coughs *on a shard of matzo*.

    d.   He was found *by police*.

Some of the italicized prepositional phrases in (26) could arguably be interpreted as "referring to or describing the Subject" – "they were on the bus" (26a), and "we were with our windows open" (26b). And if these are Subject Complements, then why not the others as well? Certainly all of these prepositional phrases "enrich the semantic content of the Predicate" in some way.

    As has been mentioned several times in this book, the terms linguists use for linguistic concepts often describe points on a continuous scale, rather than distinct, bounded categories. This is the case with the distinction between Subject Complement and Oblique adjunct. Huddleston and Pullum (2002:215) describe the difference in these terms: "Complements are more central to the grammar than adjuncts: they are more closely related to the verb." Huddleston and Pullum then provide a very nice (and lengthy!) discussion of eight criteria – five syntactic and three semantic – for distinguishing Complements from adjuncts (pp. 219–28), and for distinguishing "core Complements" (Direct and Indirect Objects) from "non-core Complements" (Subject Complements and Object Complements in our terms). This is an excellent discussion, and I encourage interested readers to consult Huddleston and Pullum for the details.

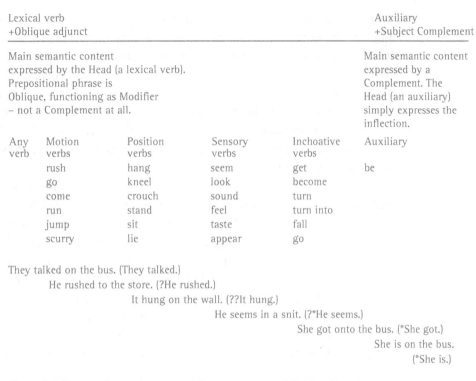

Lexical verb +Oblique adjunct				Auxiliary +Subject Complement
Main semantic content expressed by the Head (a lexical verb). Prepositional phrase is Oblique, functioning as Modifier – not a Complement at all.				Main semantic content expressed by a Complement. The Head (an auxiliary) simply expresses the inflection.
Any verb	Motion verbs	Position verbs	Sensory verbs	Inchoative verbs	Auxiliary
	rush	hang	seem	get	be
	go	kneel	look	become	
	come	crouch	sound	turn	
	run	stand	feel	turn into	
	jump	sit	taste	fall	
	scurry	lie	appear	go	

They talked on the bus. (They talked.)
He rushed to the store. (?He rushed.)
It hung on the wall. (??It hung.)
He seems in a snit. (?*He seems.)
She got onto the bus. (*She got.)
She is on the bus.
(*She is.)

Figure 9.1 The continuum between Oblique adjuncts and Subject Complements

However, for most English language professionals, being able to draw fine distinctions between adjuncts and Complements is not all that central to their everyday work. For the purpose of understanding English grammar, it is important to recognize that Complements and adjuncts are different, but that they describe ends of a continuum that has many intermediate stages.

Here I will briefly characterize the continuum between Subject Complements and Oblique adjuncts in terms of the proportion of semantic content expressed by the Head (a verb or the auxiliary *be*) versus the element in question. Complements contribute relatively more semantic content to the Predicate than do Oblique adjuncts. One syntactic criterion that reflects this scale is obligatoriness – the more obligatory an element is, the more likely it is to be a Complement (Huddleston and Pullum 2002:221–2). Figure 9.1 illustrates the proposed continuum between Oblique adjuncts and Subject Complements.

In Figure 9.1, clear examples of Predicates headed by a lexical verb with an optional Oblique adjunct occur on the left, and the one clear example of an auxiliary with a Subject Complement appears on the right. The columns represent some of the classes of verbs that may take Subject Complements. The examples below the diagram illustrate a rough impressionistic scale of how much semantic content is expressed in the Head vs. the Complement. The more semantic content is expressed in the Complement, the more "obligatory" the Complement seems. Thus, for example, it is very difficult to find situations in which *she got* and *she is* are grammatically acceptable without overt or strongly implied Complements (no examples in the corpora). Whereas at the other extreme a construction headed by any verb, e.g., *talk*, can take an Oblique constituent, e.g., *on the bus*, that just adds some ancillary information, but is not required to complete or "fill out" the semantic content of the Predication itself. The other examples cited in the chart can be considered intermediate stages on the continuum.

The intuition that some Complements are "obligatory" thus depends on how much relative semantic content they express. For example, while *it hung* is a grammatical sentence, the Predicate seems to "want" more semantic content, probably a location where the Subject hangs. However, *they talked* doesn't feel like it "needs" a location to the same extent that *it hung* does. This is because the verb *talk* is potentially semantically rich enough to embody the whole Predication, with no support from a Complement. This is not to say that the Oblique adjunct in *They talked on the bus* is unimportant to the speaker's communicative intent, but only that the Predicate would still express a complete thought (though one quite different from what the speaker intends) without it.

9.3   Object Complements

Constructions that contain Object Complements are transitive – they must have a Direct Object. The Object Complement, then, identifies, or predicates some property of the Direct Object. For example, the underlined part of each of the following clauses is the main verb plus its Object, and the italicized portion is the Object Complement. Like Subject Complements, Object Complements can be stative or inchoative. Stative Object Complements simply assert the state described by the semantic relation indicated in capital letters to the right:

(27)   **Stative Object Complement as noun phrase**
a. They <u>called him</u> *a dunce* at school,   PROPER INCLUSION
b. You still haven't <u>proved yourself</u> *a man.*   PROPER INCLUSION
c. He didn't dislike the man; he just <u>found him</u> *a bore.* PROPER INCLUSION
d. <u>Consider this</u> *your initiation into the Camden family.* EQUATION
e. Nick Farr-Jones <u>rated Rayer</u> *"the best full-back in the world."*
                                                          EQUATION
f. Sage now grandly <u>claims itself</u> *Britain's*   EQUATION
   largest micro software company.

The following is one possible box diagram of (27a) (the abbreviation OC refers to Object Complement):

(28)

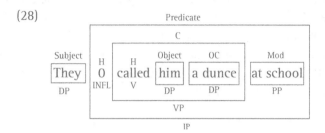

Some linguists argue that the Object, *him*, and the Object Complement, *a dunce*, form a constituent in this type of clause. This constituent is sometimes informally called a "small clause." The idea is that the Object of the verb *call* is not just the pronoun *him*, but the proposition HE IS A DUNCE. This analysis may be diagrammed as follows (the internal structural details of the small clause, labeled S, are left out):

(29)

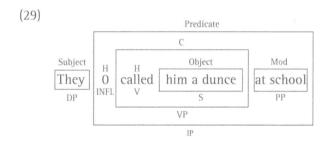

In fact there is some evidence for this analysis. For example, a coherent reply to the assertion in (28) might be:

(30) Him a dunce? No way!

This reply seems to treat *him a dunce* as a clump. Also, the coordination test described in Chapter 7 seems to affirm this:

(31) They called him a dunce and her a genius.

However, the major tests for constituency argue against this analysis. First, *him a dunce* fails the movement test:

(32) *Him a dunce is what they called.
      *It's him a dunce that they called.

Second, *him a dunce* fails the substitution test:

(33) *They called him a dunce and I called that/it/so/such too.

There are several other arguments for and against the "small clause" proposal for Object Complements, but it remains controversial (see, e.g., Aarts 2008). For purposes of understanding English grammar, it is perfectly sufficient and insightful to consider Object Complement to be a syntactic function in its own right, distinct from the Direct Object function, as analyzed in example (28).

The following are additional examples of Object Complements in the corpora (primarily the BNC). When an Object Complement is an adjective phrase, the semantic relation expressed is ATTRIBUTION:

(34) **Stative Object Complements as adjective phrases**
      However, he did <u>consider this event</u> *important enough* to send a report
      I <u>prefer my coffee</u> *black.*
      If you like a single-coloured fish and <u>want something</u> *rare and precious,* then ...
      Hodge <u>did not deem Rhee</u> *essential to a future government* ...

As with Subject Complements, Object Complements can be prepositional phrases. In this case, the semantic relation between the Object Complement and the Direct Object is constrained by the particular preposition chosen:

(35) **Stative Object Complements as prepositional phrases**
      I <u>rated him</u> *as the best British droll comedian we had.*
      we should <u>consider them</u> *as part of our thinking.*
      You got ta <u>treat being down here</u> *as a chance to learn polo.*
      She <u>likes coffee</u> *with cream and sugar.*

Occasionally, an infinitive clause may function as a stative Object Complement:

(36) **Stative Object Complement as infinitive clause**
      The latter provision (s664) <u>will deem the income</u> *to have been paid to the children* ...

The final set of examples in this section involves inchoative (or resultative) Object Complements. These may be noun phrases (determined or non-determined), as in (37), adjective phrases, as in (38), or prepositional phrases. Again, when an Object Complement is an adjective phrase, the semantic relation expressed is always ATTRIBUTION:

(37) **Inchoative Object Complements as noun phrases**
      She's the one who <u>turned you</u> *into this potato that we see*   EQUATION
      before us.
      The people seem to <u>have elected Ahmadinejad</u> *President.*   EQUATION
      Kiplinger Washington Editors Inc. <u>named Jim Ostroff</u>   EQUATION
      associate editor,

Reverend Hewett <u>pronounced them</u> *man and wife*;   EQUATION
He's <u>turned me into</u> *a mime*!   PROPER INCLUSION
They <u>made him</u> *a supervisor*.   PROPER INCLUSION

(38) **Inchoative Object Complement as adjective phrase**
<u>Tie it</u> *tighter*!
They <u>broke it</u> *open*.
I could tell you that he <u>spoiled him</u> *rotten*.[3]
There were only men, and they <u>spoiled me</u> *silly*.
I was <u>driving her</u> *crazy* . . .

(39) **Inchoative Object Complement as prepositional phrase**
They <u>got him</u> *onto the bus*.
We can consciously <u>direct our attention</u> *to certain things* and think about them.

9.4 Summary of Subject and Object Complements

We have seen that Subject and Object Complements are syntactic functions within IPs. These functions are filled by elements that significantly enrich the Predication, and in some sense refer to or describe the Subject or Object respectively. Subject Complements describe or add some significant content to a Predication made of the Subject of an intransitive clause, while Object Complements do the same for the Object of transitive clauses. Both Subject and Object Complements can express a similar range of semantic roles, and both can be stative or inchoative. Table 9.1 summarizes and exemplifies stative and inchoative Subject and Object Complements. The Complements are italicized, and the Complemented Subjects and Objects are underlined in each of the examples in Table 9.1.

Table 9.1 **Stative and inchoative Subject and Object Complements compared**

	Subject Complements	Object Complements
Stative:	<u>I</u> am *a poor wayfaring stranger*.	They consider <u>this</u> *worthless*.
	<u>She</u> looks *interested*.	I prefer <u>my coffee</u> *black*.
	<u>We</u> are *to be married*.	They pushed <u>me</u> *onto the bus*.
	<u>I</u> enjoy *reading Shakespeare*.	Do please change <u>me</u> *into a wolf*.
Inchoative:	<u>She</u> became *a ballet dancer*.	They elected <u>him</u> *man of the year*.
	<u>He</u> turned into *a werewolf*.	Waldo painted <u>the barn</u> *red*.
	<u>Murphy</u> fell *ill*.	She turned <u>him</u> *into a potatoe*.
	<u>The crowd</u> went *bananas*.	Lincoln declared <u>the slaves</u> *free*.

9.5   Subject–Complement inversion constructions

There are several construction types in English that involve post-posing a constituent for special pragmatic purposes. In this section we will briefly discuss a "family" of construction types in which a Subject is post-posed and a Complement, either a Direct Object or a Subject Complement, is preposed. For example, it is very common, particularly in narratives, for direct speech Complements of utterance verbs to invert with the Subject (italicized in the following examples):

(40)   "Oh," <u>said</u> *the bewildered male,*
"How curious," <u>says</u> *Treacher.*
"Found them!" <u>shouted</u> *the Headmaster.*
"Worth looking for!" <u>cried</u> *the squire*, with great enthusiasm.

This same kind of inversion also may occur with "direct thought" Complements of cognition verbs. These can be considered as a kind of utterance Predicate:

(41)   There go the family jewels, <u>thought</u> *Agger* to himself more than once.
"What's the matter with kids today?" <u>wondered</u> *the late Paul Lynde* in Bye Bye Birdie.
"You couldn't have had a golf course made for a man's game more than that golf course for John Daly," <u>observed</u> *the man who has won more Masters than anyone.*

The direct quotes in (40) and (41) are all clausal Direct Objects (see Chapter 14). Like all Direct Objects, they are a kind of Complement because they complete a Predication. In terms of Huddleston and Pullum (2002), they are "core Complements" because they are (somewhat) obligatory, and are very tightly bound semantically and syntactically to the verb. This inversion of Direct Object and Subject only seems to work with utterance and cognition Predicates involving direct quotation. There are other constructions in which an Object is preposed, but the Subject remains in its normal position:

(42)   I like beans. ⇒ Beans I like. / *Beans like I

For all constructions that allow Subject–Complement inversion, "heavier" Subjects (modified full noun phrases) are more likely to invert than "lighter" Subjects (nouns or pronouns only). This is not an absolute requirement, but only a tendency, and is probably a reflection of the functional fact that given and topical information tends to come early in the clause, and new or asserted information tends to come later (see Chapter 15 on pragmatic statuses). Pronouns and other "light" nominals tend to express given information, while longer, "heavier" nominals tend to express new and asserted information (see the studies in Givon 1983):

(43)   Winnie the Pooh cried "Hallo!"   "Hallo!" cried Winnie the Pooh.
       He cried "Hallo!"   ?"Hallo!" cried he.

Other constructions in which a Subject appears after the verb all involve inversion with Subject Complements. Not all Subject Complements may participate in this inversion, but if a post-verbal constituent may invert with the Subject, it must be a Subject Complement:

(44)   **Subject–Complement inversion with *be***
       Marilyn is the best rider on the team. ⇒ The best rider on the team is Marilyn.
       Thy faithfulness is great.   ⇒ Great is thy faithfulness.
       Mrs. Jones is in the kitchen   ⇒ In the kitchen is Mrs. Jones.

(45)   **Subject–Complement inversion with verbs of motion and position**
       Mrs. Jones sits in the kitchen.   ⇒   In the kitchen sits Mrs. Jones.
       The thief crouched behind the counter.   ⇒   Behind the counter crouched
                                                      the thief.
       The rabbit jumped up.   ⇒   Up jumped the rabbit.
       The cat scurried under the bed.   ⇒   Under the bed scurried the cat.

Oblique adjuncts do not easily participate in this inversion:

(46)   The thief wrote on the floor.   ⇒   *On the floor wrote the thief.
       Mrs. Jones is cooking in the kitchen.   ⇒   *In the kitchen is cooking Mrs. Jones.
       The rabbit woke up.   ⇒   *Up woke the rabbit.
       The train stops at Pembroke.   ⇒   *At Pembroke stops the train.
       The cat died under the bed.   ⇒   *Under the bed died the cat.

Similarly, Subject Complements of sensory verbs do not easily invert:

(47)   Phillip felt sick.   ⇒   *Sick felt Phillip.
       Your Mum smells like prawns.   ⇒   *Like prawns smells your Mum.
       Marilyn seems tired.   ⇒   *Tired seems Marilyn.

Finally, inchoative Subject Complements do not easily invert either:

(48)   Mrs. Jones became a doctor.   ⇒   *A doctor became Mrs. Jones.
       The students got into a jam.   ⇒   *Into a jam got the students.
       The milk turned sour.   ⇒   *Sour turned the milk.
       The frog turned into a prince.   ⇒   *Into a prince turned the frog.

All of the inversion constructions discussed in this section are much more common in written than in spoken English.

9.6   Existential and presentational constructions

Existential and presentational constructions share features with Subject–Complement inversion constructions, but also present some unusual syntactic characteristics. They are both PRAGMATICALLY MARKED CONSTRUCTIONS that have very specific discourse functions. In some sense their unusual syntax is an icon of their unusual usage. They function primarily to introduce important participants onto the discourse stage (see Chapter 15, DuBois 1980, and Givon 1983).

Prototypical existential constructions can be thought of as basically locational clauses in which the Subject is indefinite, the Subject and Auxiliary are inverted, a "dummy" Subject *there* appears before the Auxiliary, and the locational Subject Complement follows the post-posed Subject.

(49)   **Locational clause**   **Existential construction**

	Subject$_{indef}$	BE LOC		There BE Subject$_{indef}$ LOC
a.	Ants	are in the syrup!	$\Rightarrow$	There 's ants in the syrup!
b.	A snake	is in the grass!	$\Rightarrow$	There 's a snake in the grass!
c.	Three nuns	are here.	$\Rightarrow$	There are three nuns here.
d.	A big game	is on Tuesday.	$\Rightarrow$	There 's a big game on Tuesday.

Examples (49a)–(49c) are all prototypical existentials. (49d) is slightly less prototypical, since the Subject Complement, *on Tuesday*, is temporal rather than locative. However, since the metaphor TIME IS SPACE is very well established throughout the English language, time expressions are often presented as metaphorical locations.

Other existential constructions are less prototypical.

(50)   a.   There are still some seats available.
        b.   There's always Rick and Susan.
        c.   There's Uncle Albert to consider.

Example (50a) has an adjectival, *available*, rather than a locational Subject Complement. Example (50b) has a definite Subject, and (50c) has a non-finite verb as the Subject Complement.

Finally, existential constructions occasionally have no Complement that is distinct from the Subject NP. These are sometimes called "pure existentials," or "bare existentials," and are often illustrated by the example *There is a god*. However, much more common are bare existentials with Subjects modified by relative clauses. In such cases, the relative clause serves the same communicative function as a Complement, though syntactically it modifies a Head noun:

(51)   There are <u>three reasons</u> *why we should eat more vegetables.*

In this example, the existence of *three reasons* is being asserted, and the three reasons are modified by the italicized finite clause. There are a couple of reasons why I believe this clause is best analyzed as a relative clause inside a noun phrase headed by *reasons*, and not a distinct Subject Complement (see Chapter 14 on relative clauses). First, when there are clear examples of clauses functioning as Subject Complements, they are always non-finite:

(52) a. She seemed *to want everyone to know.*
      b. We are happy *to be here.*

Second, the predicate nominal construction that should correspond to an existential such as (51) is of very dubious grammaticality:

(53) ??Three reasons are why we should eat more vegetables.

Therefore, the most insightful syntactic analysis of (51) is that it is a "bare existential" without a distinct Subject Complement. This does not deny the fact that the relative clause is serving a communicative function that is very similar to that of the Subject Complement in more prototypical existential constructions. This type of "bare" existential (which isn't really very bare, because of the relative clause) is far more common in the corpora than the type represented by *There is a god*, in which there is no Modifying or Complementing element at all.

Another interesting feature of existential constructions from a linguistic perspective is that two elements, the dummy *there* and the post-posed Subject nominal both possess grammatical properties of the Subject relation. For example, the existential *there* inverts with the auxiliary in certain questions, just like Subjects of other types of constructions:

(54) **Subject–auxiliary inversion in non-existentials**
      We should eat more vegetables.   ⇒   *Should we* eat more vegetables?
      They are eating something.   ⇒   What *are they* eating?
      Malcolm loves baseball.   ⇒   *Does Malcolm* love baseball?

(55) ***There*-auxiliary inversion in existentials**
      There are lions in Africa.   ⇒   *Are there* lions in Africa?
      There is something to eat.   ⇒   What *is there* to eat?

Second, to form a TAG QUESTION, the Subject and auxiliary are repeated after the main assertion. In existentials, *there* and the auxiliary are repeated:

(56) **Tag questions in non-existentials**
      We should eat more vegetables, *shouldn't we?*
      Malcolm loves baseball, *doesn't he?*

(57) **Tag questions in existentials**
      There are lions in Africa, *aren't there?* (*aren't lions?)
      There is something to eat, *isn't there?* (*isn't something?)

On the other hand, the nominal that follows the auxiliary in an existential construction controls verb agreement (at least in CSE, but see below). This is strictly a property of Subjects in non-existentials:

(58)   There *is* a cat under the bed.
         There *are* two cats under the bed.

So it seems existential constructions have a "split personality" when it comes to the Subject function. However, in spoken English, it is very common for the verb agreement property to be lost. That is, the inflected auxiliary in the existential tends to be singular even when the Subject is plural:

(59)   There*'s* bears in the forest.
         There*'s* ants in the syrup.
         There*'s* lots of women in linguistics.

Though English teachers may shudder at these examples of agreement "errors," such expressions are extremely common and natural in spoken English. This seems to suggest that the post-posed element is in the process of losing its battle for status as the Subject of the sentence in favor of the existential *there*.

Presentational constructions are syntactically and functionally very similar to existentials. The main structural difference is that the semantic head of the Predicate is a full lexical verb, rather than the auxiliary *be*. The Predicates of presentational constructions are mostly headed by intransitive verbs of motion and position.

(60)   **Typical presentational constructions, with verbs of motion**
         At once <u>there came</u>, clear in the sunny air, *a long piercing scream.*
         There <u>arose</u> *a great and mighty wind.*
         Then <u>there arrived</u> *a rainbow* of stronger colours
         <u>there emerged</u> *a possibility* that the PCP could lose its overall majority
         Occasionally, from out of this matter, <u>there escapes</u> *a thin beam of light.*
         There <u>sailed</u> *a pirate ship* about 10 stories tall.

(61)   **Typical presentational constructions, with verbs of position**
         There <u>sat</u> *an old woman* resting on a stone.
         <u>there stood</u> *a little man*, with a face as grey as morning ashes,
         <u>there rose</u> *three large stone arches,*
         Because from each pole <u>there hung</u> *a robe,*
         Deep in the forest <u>there lived</u> *an old man.*

The main function of both existentials and presentationals is to introduce new relatively "important" participants onto the discourse stage. In other words, participants introduced in existential and presentational constructions are likely to be referred to often in the subsequent discourse (see DuBois 1980). Occasionally, participants that are already on stage can be Subjects of existential or presentational constructions. In particular, when the verb *go* appears in a presentational construction, the Subject is more likely to be definite than indefinite (62). This makes sense, since *go* describes motion *away from* some reference point – normally the current scene on the discourse stage. For something to move away from the discourse stage, it must be present, hence identifiable, to begin with. Therefore, the following serve a DEPARTATIVE rather than presentational function, though structurally they are presentationals according to the definition given above:

(62) **Presentational constructions with definite Subjects expressing departure**
There went *Hansel*. There went *Gretel*.
There went *that little idea.*
"There go *all those little alleyways,*" he said.
There go *the family jewels,* thought Agger to himself more than once.

There are several other situations in which the Subject of an existential or presentational construction can be definite. These are discussed in Huddleston and Pullum (2002:1390–1403). The following is one example from the COCA:

(63) Even in a small boat, there falls over a sailor *the flush* of being master of his own universe.

This is an example of a new, previously unidentified concept – *the flush ...* – rendered uniquely identifiable by the following description – *of being master of his own universe.*
    When verbs that do not describe motion or position occur in presentational constructions, their meanings often can be understood as metaphorical "movement." For example, *appear* can suggest movement into the speaker's field of vision:

(64) There appeared on the horizon *a ship* with billowed sail.

Finally, the examples in (65) illustrate presentationals based on verbs of inception:

(65) there developed *a comparable market* for art
    So behind and above the person of the prince, there formed again *the abstract concept* of "the public person,"
    After a century there began *a long period of sea warfare and skirmishing* over the north of Ulthuan.

Summary

In this chapter we have looked more closely at the syntactic function of Complementation, concentrating on Subject and Object Complements. Complementation is characterized as a syntactic function filled by elements that combine with the Head of a phrasal category to "complete" that category. Complements are distinguished from Modifiers by being more "integral" to the function of the phrasal category. Often this higher degree of functional integration translates into higher "obligatoriness" on the part of Complements.

Both Subject and Object Complements occur within a Predicate, and they refer to or describe either the Subject or the Object of the clause in some way. Either type can be stative or inchoative.

Existential and presentational constructions are variations on constructions with Subject Complements. Existential constructions predicate the existence of the Subject, with the Complement usually expressing a locational or temporal anchor. In "bare" existentials, those with no Subject Complement, the anchor is most often expressed in a relative clause modifying the Subject.

Existential constructions most often serve to introduce new participants onto the discourse stage. Presentational constructions may also have this discourse function, though they have additional uses as well.

FURTHER READING

Huddleston and Pullum (2002:215–28) provide probably the most detailed description of the general function of Complementation in English. The studies in Dixon and Aikhenvald (2006) provide detailed treatments of the structure and function of complement clauses in many diverse languages of the world. Rudanko and Loudes (2005) is an excellent corpus-based study of Predicate Complementation in English.

Exercises

1. The following examples illustrate several types of Predicate Complements. For each example, underline the Predicate Complement, and indicate whether it is a Subject Complement or an Object Complement, and whether it is Stative or Inchoative (examples adapted from Livio 2005, Chapter 1):
   a. An inkblot on a piece of paper is not particularly attractive to the eye.
   b. The interpretation of inkblots forms the basis for the famous Rorschach test.
   c. Why has symmetry become such a pivotal concept?
   d. Da Vinci saw symmetry as the paramount tool for bridging the gap between science and art.

e. When the Greeks labeled a work of art or an architectural design symmetric…

f. This early definition corresponds to our modern notion of proportion.

g. Nature has endowed human beings with the optimal standard configuration.

2. Determine the syntactic function (Head, Modifier, Complement) of each of the underlined constituents and indicate which other constituent it functions in relation to (adapted from Brinton 2000:140).

Example: She got a disappointingly low grade on her term paper.

Answer: *Disappointingly* is a Modifier in relation to *low*. *Term Paper* is the Complement of the DP *her term paper*.

a. She is worried about the water.

b. They didn't seem very happy.

c. He was afraid of earthquakes.

d. McPhail searched for his sweater with the holes in the sleeves.

e. The weeping wound seemed serious.

f. Gregorius told the soldiers what to do.

g. Orna wants to bake us some cookies.

h. They argued over whether to take the high road or the low road.

10 | Modification

> Words are but the vague shadows of the volumes we mean. Little audible links, they are, chaining together great inaudible feelings and purposes.
>
> Theodore Dreiser (2008[1900]:9)

Modification is a very general syntactic function that is relevant at every level of structure. Any syntactic element that is "optional" and which is not a Complement is probably functioning as a Modifier. Since Modification is a *function*, it describes what a linguistic element *does*, and is therefore defined independently of what that element *is*. Thus, the function of Modification can theoretically be filled by elements of any syntactic category. In practice, there are certain categories that seem particularly prone to filling Modification functions, though all of these can fill other functions as well. For example, when we think of Modification of nouns, we immediately think of adjectives. However, as we've seen in Chapter 9, adjectives may serve as Complements, as Heads of NPs, and other functions as well. Furthermore, any number of syntactic categories other than adjectives can also function to Modify nouns in NPs. These include other nouns, prepositional phrases, and whole clauses, as we will see below.

Modification serves an important role in communication. The thoughts that people need to communicate with one another seldom match the idealized conceptual scenes evoked by individual lexemes exactly. Rather, they are rich, nuanced, often unique representations involving detail that may not be a part of the sparse images evoked by particular nouns and verbs. For example, it is one thing to have *a relationship* with someone, but quite another thing to have *a serious relationship* with them. While *Ned's dustbin* evokes a rather mundane, blah sort of image, *Ned's Atomic Dustbin* becomes exciting enough to be a worthy name for a rock band. Part of the art of communication is presenting our thoughts in a way that bends the ideal categories made available by the bare lexemes of our language, and shapes them around the specific scenes in our minds in a way that stimulates the imagination of our audience. Without Modification, linguistic communication would be very stark and dreary indeed.

In this chapter we will look at various kinds of Modification functions, beginning with Modification within noun phrases, and then dealing with Modification functions within an inflected verb phrase (IP). Finally there is a brief section on clause level Modification.

10.1 Modification in the noun phrase

Predeterminer Modification

In this book, we are making a distinction between determined noun phrases (DPs), and undetermined noun phrases (NPs). This is an important syntactic distinction for English, since these two phrasal categories have different syntactic properties (see Section 8.1). Most Modification of nominal phrases occurs within NPs, though there is at least one type that occurs at the DP level. This is sometimes called PREDETERMINER MODIFICATION, and the elements that prototypically fill this function are sometimes called PREDETERMINERS, or PREDETERMINER MODIFIERS (Huddleston and Pullum 2002:433–6).

The special quantifiers *all*, *both*, and *half* are the core members of the class of predeterminers. Other fractions and multiples (*twice*, *thrice*, *three times*, etc.) are marginal members. This set of quantifying elements is distinct from ordinary quantifiers such as *many*, *some*, *much*, and the cardinal and ordinal numerals; therefore we need to give these prototypical predeterminers a special label. Let's call them PDQs, for PREDETERMINER QUANTIFIERS.

PDQs can occur before most forms that function as determiners, including personal pronouns (example 1), genitive pronouns (2), genitive noun phrases (3), and articles (4). In these examples, the PDQ is *italicized* and the determiner is underscored:

(1) Hark *all* <u>you</u> ladies that do sleep,
     She might have *all* <u>us</u> Unionists singing "The Flowers of the Forest."
     All <u>we</u> students pretended we sped to his lectures to imbibe his humanism,
     Half <u>them</u> folks I don't even know.

(2) Nearly *all* <u>my</u> friends were down the pit.
     Both <u>my</u> parents smoke.
     He raised *both* <u>his</u> arms.
     Half <u>our</u> sites are down.
     No, for you are *twice* <u>his</u> age.
     Individual coverage would cost more than *three times* <u>his</u> current $457 premium.
     ... all the graciousness of someone *thrice* <u>her</u> age.

(3) *All* the King's horses and *all* the King's men...
Both the children's mothers...
Half a day's pay...

(4) You can get there on motorway *all* the way.
Both the dishes are simple to make.
The defendant is *both* a teacher and a priest,
I made *half* a pint of white sauce in the measuring jug.
That is *one fourth* the population of the United States.

In addition to PDQs, the word *such* and certain adjectives can serve as predeterminer Modifiers before the indefinite article. In all such cases in the corpora, predeterminer adjectives are themselves modified such that they describe a *relative degree* of some property. For example, something that is *too good* possesses a degree of "goodness" that goes beyond some reference point; *as good* describes a degree of goodness that is equal to some reference point; someone who is *such a bore* exhibits a high degree of borishness, etc. Unmodified adjectives do not occur in the predeterminer position. Therefore, predeterminer adjectives also serve a kind of quantifying function – they describe a relative degree of the property described by the adjective:

(5) He was *too good* a speaker you know.
They did *as good* a job as the crew chiefs.
The plasma membrane is also thought to be *far less rigid* a structure
than originally proposed.
We had *much worse* a problem that day.
Such a convoluted story could not possibly be true.

Predeterminers lie outside the DP, and so must form a constituent at a higher level. Consider the following:

(6) *Both the government and the industry* are committed to boost its software exports

The italicized phrase is a conjunction of two DPs, *the government* and *the industry*. The quantifier *both*, however, must have scope over both DPs, since each one individually is singular. Therefore the tree diagram for this phrase must be something like the following:

(7)

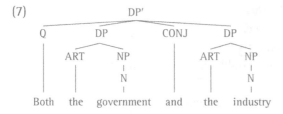

The symbol DP′ can be pronounced "DP prime," and reflects the fact that this is a kind of a DP that has other DPs attached below it (or SUBJOINED to it). The quantifier *both* in this construction is the only element that is serving a Modifying function.[1]

Because of examples like (7), we can conclude that even when the DP that follows the predeterminer does not have two parts, the PDQ must stand outside the DP, as in the following:

(8)

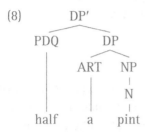

Since the distributional properties of DP′ are the same as those of DP, we can say that the DP is the syntactic (and semantic) Head of the DP′, and therefore the predeterminer is a Modifier. The following is the box diagram corresponding to example (8):

(9)

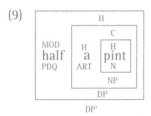

One interesting property of *all* and *both* is that, when the DP′ is a Subject, these predeterminer quantifiers can "float" into the IP, either just before the inflected verb, or between the first AUX (if there is one) and the verb. In Chapter 11 I metaphorically describe this position as the "black hole" of English syntax. It seems that the black hole has the power to "suck" these two predeterminers right off the front of their DP!:

(10)   These people *all* live in Edinburgh.
        The staff should *all* be working in the same direction.
        The papers will *all* be identically punched.
        The Shergolds must *both* be under a great deal of strain.
        The prisoners will *both* profess their innocence.

This construction, often called QUANTIFIER FLOAT, does not occur for predeterminers other than *all* and *both*, and it does not occur when the DP′ modified by the predeterminer is functioning in any role other than Subject of the sentence.

Prenominal Modifiers within the NP

The Determining function was discussed in Section 7.2. Since this chapter is about the Modification function, I will have no more to say about Determiners here, except to reemphasize that genitive pronouns or genitive noun phrases (GPs) function as Determiners, and not as Modifiers.

In this section we will move on to discuss Modification within the noun phrase proper, beginning with PRENOMINAL MODIFIERS, i.e., those that precede the head in a noun phrase, but follow any Determining elements.

Numerals and other quantifiers

The first Modifying element that may appear in a noun phrase is a quantifier. The class of NP quantifiers is distinct from the set of DP quantifiers; therefore we give the former the label Q to distinguish them from PDQs described above. Sometimes NP quantifiers are called POST-DETERMINERS, because they immediately follow any Determiner (i.e., they occur first in an NP), and they precede any other Modifiers. This is evidence that post-determiners "stand outside" the rest of the NP, and so form an NP′ constituent that consists of the quantifier plus an NP:

(11)

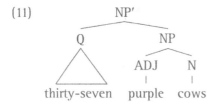

Evidence for this analysis includes the fact that other Modifiers, such as *purple* and *tall*, may occur more than once, and their order of occurrence relative to each other is somewhat free (though see below). However, there can be only one quantifier modifying the head of any given NP, and it is pretty much limited to initial position – except in such poetic expressions as *we travelers three*, and in names such as *Stalag 13*. However, these are very special cases and constitute clear exceptions to the basic generalization that quantifiers occur first in the noun phrase.

Numerals can be CARDINAL or ORDINAL. Cardinal numbers are the ones used in counting – *one*, *two*, *three*, etc. Ordinal numerals are those that specify the numerical position of the head noun in some ordered series – *first*, *second*, *third*, etc. Both types function in the quantifier slot as Modifiers within a noun phrase:

(12)   her *many* accomplishments
       the *several* factors

        the politician's *several dozen* supporters
        the *three* horsemen
        the *third* horseman
        thirty-nine beautiful swans

Examples are attested of multiple quantifiers modifying a single NP head, but in each case, there is some special structure involved. In other words, quantifiers do not just "stack" onto each other like adjectives may. This makes sense in terms of the meaning of quantifiers. While, for example, a dog can be both big and black at the same time, a group of dogs cannot plausibly consist of three and four or few and many at the same time. So *a big black dog* is semantically coherent, while *?three four dogs* or **few many dogs* is not. If someone ever says *three four dogs*, it probably means the speaker is not sure exactly how many dogs there are, and is guessing that there are approximately three *or* four:

(13)   There were three ... four dogs in the yard.

Other apparent examples of multiple quantifiers modifying a single head have similar explanations. In terms of semantics, however, it should be obvious that a quantifier that modifies a noun pretty much excludes the possibility of other quantifiers also modifying the same noun.

    Examples like *Stalag 13* and *zone 2* are interesting cases of cardinal numerals functioning like ordinals. *Stalag 13* means the thirteenth member of a series of Stalags. In order to express this form of Modification, the cardinal numeral must occur after the head. This usage should not be confused with the use of numerals as heads of noun phrases as in *(the) Watergate Seven* or the *Newcastle 9*. These can be paraphrased as "the seven people connected to Watergate" and "The nine people associated with Newcastle" respectively. This is simply another example of how the category membership of an element is logically distinct from its function. A word like *nine* is a numeral. Its prototypical function is to quantify nouns. However, like any tool, it can serve other functions as well when it seems appropriate in communication.

    Another kind of example in which quantifiers can be heads of NPs is when a prepositional phrase headed by *of* follows:

(14)   *Many of* my colleagues
        One of the contestants
        One fourth of the students
        Half of the chickens
        few of us
        both of them

The way we know that the quantifier is the head of these NPs is that the quantifier controls verb agreement when the NP serves as the Subject of a clause:

(15)   One of the contestants has /?have withdrawn.

Though plural agreement (*have*) is often heard in this construction, it is non-standard, and based on proximity, rather than hierarchical structure; the plural word *contestants* is closer to the verb than the head of the phrase, *one*, so speakers tend to "forget" the hierarchical structure and simply inflect the verb in accordance with the most recently mentioned noun. In any case, it is clear that the expression *one of the contestants* refers to one person, and not a group of contestants. Therefore the numeral must be functioning as the head of the NP, and the prepositional phrase is a post-nominal Modifier.

However, when other quantifiers, like *a few*, *a lot*, and (more recently) *a ton* are followed by a prepositional phrase headed by *of*, the Complement of the preposition seems to be the head:

(16)   *A few of* my friends were /*was there.
        A lot of people have /*has come.
        A ton of people were /*was at her party last night.

In these cases, even though the indefinite determiner *a* seems to imply a singular head (*a few*, *a lot*, *a ton*), the plural noun following the preposition controls verb agreement. What seems to be happening is that the expressions *a few of*, *a lot of*, and *a ton of* are so useful and so common that they are being reanalyzed as unified quantifiers, thus shifting the semantic head function to the erstwhile Complement of the preposition. Many of us who comment on student writing are familiar with spellings like "alot" or even "alotta." Most English speakers have no sense of a "lot" as describing a bounded quantity of something, parallel to *a kilo* of bananas, or *a pile* of rocks. We just unconsciously think of "alotta" as one member of a set of quantifiers that also includes *many*, *some*, *thirty-seven*, *much*, etc. I believe the same is happening with "afewa," "atonna," and maybe other quantifiers that derive from quantity nouns (*a few*, *a ton*, etc.). With *a bunch of*, for example, both analyses may be possible:

(17)   A bunch of flowers are/is in the back of the car.

Most English speakers I have questioned about this say that the plural verb form (*are*) is appropriate if just the large number of flowers is being emphasized. The flowers may or may not form a coherent "bunch," but there are "a lot" of them. When the singular form (*is*) is used, it seems to imply that there is one thing in the back of the car – a bunch of flowers. There may not be a huge number of flowers, but they must be bunched together into a coherent bouquet.

Prenominal attributive Modifiers

Between NP quantifiers and the head of a noun phrase there may be one or more elements that serve a Modifying function. Usually we think of these as adjectives, but of course several syntactic categories can serve as prenominal Modifiers:

(18)   This resulted in a *whole new* breed of *machine* tools and techniques.

In this one example, we see two adjectives, *whole* and *new*, modifying the noun *breed*. We also see what looks like a noun, *machine*, modifying *tools* and possibly *techniques*. Some grammarians would say that *machine* in this example is "functioning as an adjective." Well that's true, but just because it's functioning in a way that adjectives often function (i.e., as a prenominal attributive Modifier) doesn't necessarily mean that it has *become* an adjective. As often emphasized in this book, it is important to define syntactic categories distinctly from their syntactic functions. Attributive Modification is one common function of adjectives, but not everything that functions as an attributive Modifier is an adjective, and not every adjective always functions as an attributive Modifier. Using the tools and jobs metaphor, while a screwdriver may prototypically serve to drive screws, it can also be used for a lot of other tasks, such as opening paint cans or scraping dirt out of tight spaces. Similarly, tools designed specifically for other purposes, say knives or even fingernails, may for the nonce be used to drive screws if necessary.

On the other hand, we've also seen that the categorial status of words can change over time. Such change is driven by function. In other words, once a form starts to become useful in a new function, it may, over time, begin to lose its original categorial status, and be reanalyzed in the minds of speakers as belonging to a different category; for example, a verb may become an auxiliary. We will see another example of this in the very next paragraph below. However, until there is *structural evidence* that a shift has taken place, we cannot say for sure that a form has become a member of a new category.

Noun phrases and a few prepositional phrases in fairly fixed expressions can also function as prenominal Modifiers:

(19)   **Noun phrases as Modifiers**
        a *little bit* better deal
        a *High Court* Judge
        a *public house* licence

(20)   **Prepositional phrases in prenominal position**
        That was a rather *off the wall* remark.
        I don't appreciate her *in your face* attitude.
        He always has *on target* comments to make.

Interestingly, when plural NPs like *twenty-four miles* or even *scissors* occur as prenominal Modifiers, they may appear without the plural marking:

(21)   a *twenty-four* mile race.   *a twenty-four miles race
       a *million dollar* house   *a million dollars house
       a *scissor* cut   ?a scissors cut
       a *trouser* hanger   a trousers hanger

This seems to suggest that *scissor, trouser, twenty-four mile,* and *million dollar* have shifted (or are shifting) from being nouns or noun phrases into the category of adjective or adjective phrase. The lack of plural marking is *structural evidence* that these forms have shifted their categorial status. Since adjectives are not marked for plurality, it makes sense that nouns that are being treated as adjectives should also fail to mark plurality as they begin to adapt to a function normally served by adjectives. It should be noted, however, that this is not an absolute rule. Most English speakers seem comfortable with plural nouns as Modifiers in expressions like *trousers hanger, glasses case,* and *sharps receptacle.*

Most adjectives can function equally well as prenominal Modifiers or as Predicate Complements. However, there are some that function only as prenominal Modifiers and others that function only as Predicate Complements:

(22)   Adjectives that function only as prenominal Modifiers:
       He is an *utter* fool.   *That fool is *utter.*
       We were *mere* children.   *Those children are *mere.*
       They caught the *serial* killer. *That killer was *serial.*
       He is an *atomic* physicist   *That physicist is *atomic.*
       She is an *olympic* gymnast   *That gymnast is *olympic.*
       The *frigging* computer has crashed! *This computer is *frigging.*
       The dolphin is a *marine* mammal. *Some mammals are *marine.*

Similarly, while nouns may function as prenominal Modifiers, they often cannot occur as Predicate Complements functioning as Modifiers:

(23)   Shaker furniture   ?Our furniture is Shaker.
       a summer day   *The day is summer.
       a biology teacher   *My teacher is biology.
       a backyard barbecue   *The barbecue was backyard.
       a mother hen   *The hen was mother.

Some adjectives, on the other hand, seem only to function as Predicate Complements, and not as prenominal Modifiers. Most of these begin with the Anglo-Saxon prefix *a-*, which is a reflex of the preposition *on*:

(24) The child is *asleep/awake*
/alive/afraid   *an asleep/awake/alive/afraid child
The building is *ablaze*   *an ablaze building
The ship is *afloat*   *an afloat ship
I am *ashamed*   *an ashamed teacher
My clothes are *awry*   *awry clothes
The child is *well*   ?a well child[2]

The origin of adjectives that begin with *a-* helps explain why they cannot be used in prenominal position. Since the *a-* prefix is an old preposition, and prepositional phrases historically did not appear in prenominal position (though see some recently innovated examples in (20) above), adjectives that derive from prepositional phrases also do not occur in prenominal position.

Adjectives can also be the heads of ADJECTIVE PHRASES. Adjective phrases consist of an obligatory head, plus the possibility of several optional elements serving modifying functions within the phrase. The following are some examples of the kinds of Modifying elements that can occur in adjective phrases:

(25) **Adverbs**
a *very* big dog
quite hard work
a *fairly* tall plant
a *somewhat* useless shovel
an *extremely* unwieldy mattress
an *impressively* benign princess
my *totally* incompetent boss
a *rather* interesting conversation

(26) **Other adjectives**
the *dark green* curtains
the *beady eyed* salesman
the *red roofed* houses
bright green leaves
deep blue sky

Not every contiguous pair of adjectives is an adjective phrase, however. Consider the pair *deep blue sky* and *angry green eyes*. *Deep blue* is probably a constituent that refers to a particular color. It is hard to imagine *deep* as a direct Modifier of *sky*. On the other hand, *angry green* probably does not describe a particular color. Rather, *angry* and *green* are more likely to be separate adjectives that both Modify *eyes* directly. The phrase structure trees for these two noun phrases would be the following:

(27)   a.

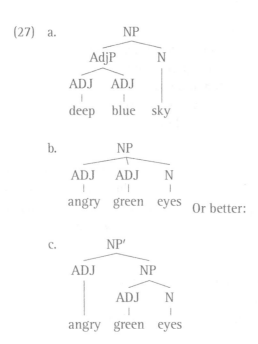

b.

Or better:

c.

Tree diagrams, of course, fail to make syntactic functions explicit. In (27a), *blue* must be the head of the AdjP, and *deep* must be the Modifier, because *deep blue* is a kind of *blue*, rather than a kind of *deep*. In (27b), both *angry* and *green* directly Modify the head noun, *eyes*. In (27c), *angry* is functioning as a Modifier of the NP *green eyes*. There is syntactic evidence for the analysis in (27c), but the syntactic evidence is a consequence of the semantic fact that the color *green* is a property that is more inherently connected to the head than the adjective *angry*. Green eyes are pretty much always going to be green. In addition, green eyes can sometimes be (or at least appear) angry, but *angry* is probably not an inherent quality of the eyes. Therefore *angry* is iconically located syntactically farther away from the head than the more inherent property. If someone were to say *?green angry eyes*, that would seem to imply inherently angry eyes that happen to be green. Most of the "rules" that grammar teachers present for ordering adjectives in the noun phrase boil down to this iconic fact: the more inherent properties (e.g., color, physical characteristics, national origin) come closer to the head than more transitory or debatable characteristics (e.g., dimensions, age, value, and human propensity – see Chapter 3 for a description of semantic types of adjectives).

(28)   an old Prussian soldier   *a Prussian old soldier
a lovely brick building   *a brick lovely building
a big black dog   *a black big dog
a happy French chef   *a French happy chef

Sometimes there may be ambiguity as to whether there is an adjective phrase or simply multiple adjectives in a noun phrase. A *light blue shirt*, could be a shirt that is light blue in color, or a light shirt that is blue (maybe even dark blue) in color. In context, intonation can be used by speakers to make their intentions clear: *a light blue / shirt* vs. *a light / blue shirt*, where "/" indicates a boundary between intonation units. Intonation can be a very important clue to hierarchical structure.

Other syntactic categories that can serve a Modifying function in adjective phrases include the following:

(29) **Nouns**
      a *dog eared* book
      a *moth eaten* sweater

(30) **Comparative and superlative "adverbs"**
      Pat is *more intelligent* than Dale.
      Pat is the *most intelligent* person I know.

Adverbs, especially comparative adverbs, can also themselves be phrasal:

(31) Pat is *far more* intelligent than Dale.
      Pat is *much less* good looking than Dale.

We will close this section by illustrating a few other complex Modifying phrases (italicized) occurring prenominally within noun phrases:

(32) a *thousand dollar a plate* dinner
      a *down and out* trumpet player
      a *dog-eat-dog* world
      a *down in the dumps* attitude
      a *far away* look
      a *two for one* sale

Restrictive vs. non-restrictive Modification

Before discussing post-nominal Modification, I would like to discuss the distinction between restrictive and non-restrictive Modification. In restrictive Modification, the modified element can only be identified by the hearer in terms of the information provided in the Modifier. In non-restrictive Modification, the Modifier enriches the scene by providing information not otherwise provided in the context, yet not essential for establishing the identity of the head. A couple of examples will best illustrate this difference. In spoken English, intonation (represented by accent marks) is the major means of distinguishing restrictive and non-restrictive Modification:

(33) a. My táll sìster can reach the top shelf in the cupoard.
      b. My tàll síster can reach the top shelf in the cupoard.

In (33a) the main word stress in the DP *my tall sister* falls on *tall*, and secondary stress falls on the first syllable of *sister*. In (33b), secondary stress falls on *tall* and primary stress falls on *sister*. In which one do you think the Modifier *tall* is restrictive and in which one is it non-restrictive? If you guessed that (33a) is restrictive, you're right. With the main stress on *tall*, the speaker seems to be saying that the speaker has more than one sister, and the one the speaker means is the TALL one. Thus *tall* restricts the range of possible referents down to exactly the individual the speaker is referring to. If there is no or very little stress on *tall*, as in (33b), the speaker may have only one sister, but may just want to emphasize how tall she is. This is called non-restrictive Modification.

This subtle functional distinction plays a role in the grammar of Modification in noun phrases, both in the spoken and written varieties. In addition to the intonational differences noted above, restrictive vs. non-restrictive Modification can be expressed by placing a Modifier in post-nominal vs. prenominal position respectively. The distinction is *not* absolute, i.e., there is no "rule of grammar" that says prenominal Modification = non-restrictive, post-nominal Modification = restrictive, but there is a tendency in this direction. Consider the following examples:

(34)   a.   *The concerned members* began to shift uncomfortably in their seats.
        b.   *The members concerned* began to shift uncomfortably in their seats.

The difference between these examples is that with the pre-nominal Modifier, *concerned members*, it could be the case that everyone present on stage is a concerned member. The Modifier *concerned* simply adds some information about them that perhaps explains why they might be squirming uncomfortably in their seats. With the post-nominal modifier, *members concerned*, however, the NP seems to single out *some* of the members but not others. Perhaps this is a description of a meeting in which some allegations were raised about certain members. THOSE members, the *ones concerned*, are the ones that began squirming uncomfortably in their seats. This is an example of restrictive Modification because the information in the modifier is needed to single out exactly WHO, among several possibilities, the NP refers to.

It should be pointed out that pre-nominal Modifiers may also serve a restrictive function – see, e.g., (33a) above. However, prenominal Modifiers are generally neutral as to whether they express restrictive or non-restrictive Modification, whereas post-nominal Modifiers are much more likely to express restrictive Modification.

Post-nominal Modifiers

Several classes of Modifiers may follow the head in a noun phrase. These can be called POST-NOMINAL MODIFIERS. In general, relatively "heavy" Modifiers (i.e., those that have lots of syllables, and complex internal structure of their own) are most likely to follow their heads. While this tendency toward HEAVY SHIFTING is optional in most cases, it has become an obligatory grammatical pattern for relative clauses (clauses that serve a Modifying function) – CSE does not admit prenominal relative clauses, no matter how "light" they happen to be. However, other heavy constituents that serve a Modifying function also tend to occur post-nominally. These include prepositional phrases and other oblique adjuncts. In addition to shifting heavy constituents to post-nominal position, there are a few situations in which adjectives alone may occur post-nominally. We will begin with some examples of post-nominal adjectives, then move on to prepositional phrases and relative clauses. The internal structure of relative clauses is discussed in more detail in Chapter 14. In this chapter, the emphasis is on their external function as NP Modifiers.

Adjectives that follow their heads are sometimes considered to be a kind of "truncated relative clause." Consider the following examples:

(35) a. Those members *present* refused to select a candidate.
      b. The man *responsible* was Jason Purvis.
      c. Moscow Centre had facilities in all the countries *concerned*.
      d. A group *concerned with mental and emotional crises*...

In example (35a), the adjective *present* modifies the preceding noun, *members*. This NP would not mean quite the same thing if the adjective preceded the head: *those present members* would mean those individuals who are currently, at the time of speaking, members of whatever organization is being discussed and would possibly be non-restrictive (see above). The phrase *those members present*, however, means the same thing as *those members who were present*, i.e., physically present at the time of the meeting. This is clearly an example of restrictive Modification, and for this reason leads some linguists to conclude that the post-nominal Modifier is a TRUNCATED RELATIVE CLAUSE. The part that has been truncated, of course, is *who were*.

Similarly, the other examples in (35) may be paraphrased with relative clauses: *the man who was responsible*, *the countries who were concerned*, etc. The last example especially resembles a relative clause in that the Modifier is based on a verbal root (*concern*) and itself is complemented by a rather heavy prepositional phrase. This sounds as ungrammatical in prenominal position as a relative clause would:

(36) *The *concerned with emotional and mental crises* group...

Post-nominal prepositional phrases may also modify the head of an NP:

(37) A man *in a coonskin cap*...   *an *in a coonskin cap* man
      A sketch *with a few rough dimensions*... *a *with a few rough dimensions* sketch

      A cat *on a hot tin roof*...   *an *on a hot tin roof* cat

Again, these post-nominal Modifiers serve to restrict the reference of the head noun in much the same way as restrictive relative clauses do.

The next type of post-nominal Modifiers are adjectives following indefinite pronouns. A broad range of adjectives may occur in this position, in spite of the fact that pre-nominal Modifiers are generally not allowed for any pronouns, definite or indefinite:

(38) *Something wicked* this way comes.
They are usually very goodlooking actor types, but *nobody famous.*
... with the help of *someone close and understanding*
I'm never going to meet *anybody nice.*
Anything unusual will do.

Some adjectives require or strongly prefer Complements of their own. Such adjectives overwhelmingly occur in post-nominal position when used attributively. Some examples of these include the following:

(39) Adjectives that take prepositional phrase Complements:
The chairman... issues a report *fraught with absurdities.*
A face *devoid of guile*, the sweetest smile I've ever seen.
To a gentleman *fond of sporting*,...
... or a family *desirous of a truly elegant abode*...
But grammarians *intent on prescribing rules of correct usage*...

(40) Adjectives that take infinitive Complements:
the network includes people *able to translate* for the refugees.
... the corporation or the person *liable to pay.*
A good in-house person makes a list of issues *likely to stir up trouble in the media.*

Most adjectives that take infinitive Complements don't strictly require the Complement, but when they lack Complements they tend to have quite different senses from their use in the construction illustrated in (40):

(41) He is a very *able* assistant.
I'm trying to avoid a *likely* confrontation with Susan.

For this reason, we may consider the infinitive phrases in (40) to be functioning as Complements rather than Modifiers within the adjective phrase.

Finally, relative clauses in English always follow the noun they modify within a phrase. The distinction between restrictive Modification and non-restrictive Modification is particularly relevant for relative clauses. Consider the following:

(42) a. He looks at it, picks it up, throws it to Ros, *who puts it in his bag.*
b. They are not interested in the damage they do to the people *who swallow their pills.*

In example (42a), the character Ros is already fully identified in the context. There is no possibility that a hearer might wonder WHICH Ros is being referred to. Nevertheless, *Ros* is modified by the relative clause *who puts it in his bag*. This is a classic example of a non-restrictive relative clause. The clause just specifies some additional information about Ros. Notice that this information is essential to the communicative act being performed by this utterance, but it is not essential to identifying the unique referent referred to by the head noun *Ros*. In (42b), however, if the relative clause is left out, the reference of the DP remains unclear. WHICH people are intended? Certainly not all people. The relative clause in this example restricts the reference of *people* to a particular group – only those who "swallow their pills."

Traditionally, commas are used to delimit non-restrictive relative clauses in written English. This is probably reflective of an intonational difference in the spoken variety. Consider the following invented examples, culled from my memory of a stand up comedy routine I heard somewhere:

(43)   a.   My wife, *who is a doctor*, immediately began administering first aid.
       b.   My wife *who is a doctor* immediately began administering first aid.

The commas around the relative clause in (43a) reflect intonation breaks – *My wife... who (by the way) is a doctor... immediately...* This relative clause does not help identify WHICH wife is involved; it just gives additional information that may explain why she began to administer first aid. The lack of commas in (43b), then, can be interpreted as a lack of intonation breaks, and the entire DP falls under one long intonation contour – *My wife who is a doctor immediately...* In the comedy routine, the lack of intonation breaks in (43b) is exploited to raise the implication that the speaker has more than one wife, and it was the wife who is a doctor who began administering first aid, not any of the other wives. This is a classic example of restrictive Modification.

10.2   Modification in the Predicate

In Chapter 9 we discussed the syntactic function of Complementation within an IP. We also looked at the difference between Complements in the IP (Objects, Subject Complements, and Object Complements) and what are often called ADJUNCTS or ADVERBIAL ADJUNCTS (Huddleston and Pullum 2002:665–784, Greenbaum and Quirk 2004:162–81, Berk 1999:186–205, among others). To summarize that discussion briefly, elements serving a Complement function are more central to the main idea being predicated than are elements serving an adjunct function (or Modification function in our terms). Some of the same syntactic categories (e.g., adjectives, noun phrases, and prepositional phrases) can serve both Complement and adjunct functions, so at times the distinction can be difficult to maintain. However, parallel to many such "distinctions" in grammatical terminology there are very good examples of Complements, very good examples of adjuncts, and some examples that seem to fall "in between." Figure 9.1 in Chapter 9 illustrates the continuum between Oblique adjuncts (usually in the form of prepositional phrases) and Subject Complements.

In this book we are treating such adjuncts as Modifiers within an IP. Their syntactic function is Modification, while their syntactic category may be an adverb, prepositional phrase, noun phrase, or even a clause. The syntax of adverbial clauses will be discussed in Chapter 14. In the present chapter the discussion will be limited to adverbs, prepositional phrases, and noun phrases.

The prototypical examples of IP Modifiers are adverbs. For this reason, all adjuncts are sometimes called "adverbials," which can be defined as "sort of like adverbs." Adverb as a word class was discussed in Chapter 3. In this section, we will give a few examples of adverbs functioning as Modifiers within the IP. After that we will illustrate some other syntactic categories that serve similar functions.

It is important to remember that all Modifiers are "optional" from the point of view of grammaticality. Ideally, they are not required in order to complete the grammatical coherence of a phrasal category (if they were, they would be Complements rather than adjuncts). Nevertheless, adjuncts do express very important information from a communicative perspective. Since they are part of the IP, they may constitute part of the main ASSERTED information in a declarative clause.

Example (44) illustrates the contrast between Complements and Modifiers in the IP. The basic unmodified, uncomplemented predicate, *fell*, is given along with several examples of the same Predicate with Subject Complements and with IP Modifiers:

(44) Unmodified Predicate	Predicate with Complement	Predicate with IP Modifier (adjunct)
He fell.	He fell *ill*.	He fell *in the living room*.
	He fell in *with a bad crowd*.	He fell *yesterday*.
		He fell *three times*.

In this example it is fairly clear that the Complements (the italicized portions in the center column) *complete* the Predication in a way that the Modifiers do not; *falling ill* is a different kind of event than simply *falling*. The same is true for *falling in with a bad crowd*. On the other hand, the Modifiers (the italicized portions in the rightmost column) simply add information to the basic Predicate *fell*. Falling *in the living room*, falling *yesterday*, and falling *three times* all describe the same basic event of falling, but with additional information enriching the discourse scene.

The following are two box diagrams illustrating the difference between Subject Complementation (SC in (45a)) and Modification (MOD in (45b)) in the IP:

(45)

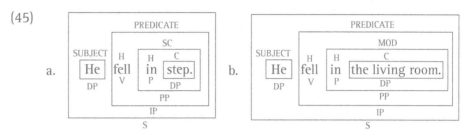

a.   b.

Modifiers functioning in the IP may vary in their position, but are most attracted to two positions:

- The "I" position between auxiliary and Predicating element, or between Subject and inflected verb.
- Final position within the IP.

The following are examples of various syntactic categories serving Modifying functions in these positions. Several examples of adverbs in these roles are found in Section 3.4; therefore in this section we will concentrate on examples of other categories, primarily prepositional phrases and noun phrases[3] serving as Modifiers in the IP. The semantic roles of these adjuncts are given in upper case letters:

(46)   **MANNER adverbs**
This power can not be used *carelessly* or *recklessly*.

(47)   **MANNER prepositional phrases**
I knew the mob wouldn't go down *without a fight*.
I saw them dance *with joy*.
Colonel Llewellyn reacted *in typically robust style*.

(48)   **MEANS adverbs**
You are aware they don't remove it from the cow *surgically*, right?

(49)   **MEANS prepositional phrases**
The Jim Johnson thing was handled deftly *by Obama*.
They were writing Christmas letters *by hand*.
He got into the army *by lying about his age*.
Look what I did to this city *with a few drums of gas* ...

(50)   **PURPOSE prepositional phrases**
Bill Bradley yelled *for help* twice.

(51)   **REASON prepositional phrases**
Human beings, in contrast, interact with one another not only *because of gravity* but *because of dependence, love, envy, hate, etc.*
This position has proven difficult *due to methodological limitations*.

(52)   **EXTENT adverbs** (intensifiers and "downtoners" according to Berk 1999:187)
I'm *really* ashamed of the matter.
The fire *completely* destroyed the main machine shop.
We *badly* need the help of the public.
Our membership slid *somewhat.*
His parents back home in Fiji were *right* behind her decision.

(53)   **EXTENT prepositional phrases**
It doesn't bother me *in the slightest.*
Is your throat *at all* sore?
... a population that's growing *at three percent per year.*
The markings were bizarre *by any measure,*

(54)   **EXTENT noun phrases**
She was only *a bit* older.
This place was about *a quarter of a mile* long.
He used to stammer *a lot.*
Everything she writes sells *a ton.*

TIME, LOCATION, and DIRECTION are also notions often expressed by Modifiers within the IP. These more often occur at the end of the IP rather than in the I position. Here are some examples of these:

(55)   **TIME adverbs**
Yes, she told me about it *yesterday.*[4]
Training courses have been available online *only recently.*
He was *later* arrested for some trifling crime.

(56)   **TIME prepositional phrases**
People start quitting *between now and 3:00 o'clock.*
Etro assumed his role at the family-owned company *in 1990.*
We get up *at three in the morning.*
Dan Nicholson is unable to throw *until May.*
But Mr. Mayor, when I spoke to you *before Christmas...*
The police officer kept him talking *for two hours.*
I'll be there *in ten minutes.*
2,208 students were involved in the experiments *over a period of 20 years;*

(57)   **TIME noun phrases**
So – how is your memory *this morning*?
Coach Jon Gruden felt heat to get team back on track *a year ago.*
What will Wall Street look like *a year from now*?
You'll have to drop by *sometime.*

(58) **LOCATION adverbs**
It will include the functional constraints listed *above*...

(59) **LOCATION prepositional phrases**
He examines the communal framework and its impact *in two areas.*
... people who foolishly keep money *under the mattress* or *in a jam jar.*
A light came on *almost above his head.*
Troops were marching *along both roads.*

(60) **LOCATION noun phrases**
You couldn't do it *anywhere else.*
Strangers make Lincoln jokes *everywhere we go.*
There was a fire *two doors down.*

In Chapter 5, we treated forms such as *anywhere, everywhere, somewhere, anytime,* and *sometime* as indefinite pronouns. Since pronouns are a kind of noun phrase, the examples in (60) are noun phrases functioning as IP Modifiers. Therefore, expressions like *anywhere else, everywhere we go, two doors down,* and *a year ago* are Modified noun phrases.

Finally, we discuss some examples of directional notions expressed in prepositional phrases functioning as Modifiers within the IP. Many of the locational and directional Modifiers are used metaphorically to express a variety of abstract semantic roles. This is the case in both the examples in (61) below. Here *through the corridors of time* expresses a temporal role. Similarly, the phrase *toward their patrons* does not express the literal directional sense of toward, but rather the orientation of the servile attitude on the part of the labouring poets. The prepositions *toward, beyond, against, beside, along,* and *through,* though they may seem to be basically locational or directional, actually occur far more often in the corpora in such extended senses.

(61) **DIRECTION prepositional phrases**
God pursuing men and women *down through the corridors and labyrinths of time,*
Interstate Highway 135 runs diagonally *across the area from lower left to top right.*
Many labouring poets are almost servile *toward their patrons.*

10.3 Modification at the clause level

Modification is a function that also occurs at the clause level. Clause level Modifiers are sometimes termed DISJUNCTS, to distinguish them from "adjuncts" such as those discussed in the previous section (see, e.g. Berk 1999:208–10, Greenbaum and Quirk 2004:181–4). In this book we will consider these to be filling the general syntactic function of Modification. Their distinctive properties stem from their position in the hierarchical structure of a clause, rather than in any inherent characteristics they may possess. Roughly the same set of syntactic categories can serve the Modifying function at the clause level as at the IP level.

The following is a sparse box diagram indicating Modification at the clause level:

(62)

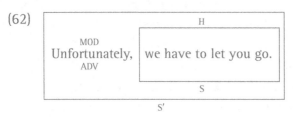

Clause level Modifiers metaphorically encase the main assertion within a "modal bubble" defined by how the speaker chooses to present the information in the clause. The same kinds of notions expressed by the modal auxiliaries and diagrammed in Figure 11.2 in Chapter 11 can be expressed by clause level Modifiers. In fact, the possible modal notions that can be expressed by clause level Modifiers are much more varied than those expressed by modal auxiliaries. This is because the auxiliaries express particular categories, mostly within the domain of modality, that are so useful that a well-oiled *grammatical system* has developed for expressing them. Only a very limited number of modal categories have attained such status. The notions expressed by clause level Modification, on the other hand, are much more open-ended. A fitting analogy may be the distinction between the grammaticalized tenses and aspects of English (past, present, and future; perfect and progressive), and the time adverbials discussed in the previous section. Time adverbials and the tense/aspect system express the same *kinds* of information, but the tense/aspect categories are much more discrete and categorical, whereas the adverbial temporal Modifiers are more open-ended and flexible.

The following are a few examples of the kinds of semantic roles that are expressed by clause level Modifiers. Prototypical examples of clause level Modifiers occur at the beginning of clauses, and may be set off by a slight intonation break, often indicated in writing with a comma. However, they also occur in the I position or at the end of the clause. In example (63a) (a quote from the film *The Hitchhiker's Guide to the Galaxy* – 2005) the clause level Modifier *curiously enough* appears in the I position of the relative clause indicated in brackets.

(63)   **SPEAKER ATTITUDE clause level Modifiers**
   a.   The second most intelligent creatures were of course dolphins [who, *curiously enough*, had long known of the impending destruction of the planet earth.]
   b.   *Luckily* the restaurant was open.

  c. *Oddly enough*, it was also the most obscure.

  d. *Curiously*, Lucius, several of them were under the impression...

SPEAKER ATTITUDE Modifiers are perhaps the most prototypical of the clause level Modifiers. Their meanings can usually be paraphrased with a proposition like "I (THE SPEAKER) CONSIDER IT X THAT Y," where X describes a quality of the situation expressed in the clause Y. For example, (63b–d) could be paraphrased as:

(64) I CONSIDER IT lucky THAT the restaurant was open.

   I CONSIDER IT odd enough THAT it was also the most obscure.

   I CONSIDER IT curious THAT, Lucius, several of them were...

The latent (unspoken) proposition is the "modal bubble" that encases the main assertion for each of these utterances.

 MANNER OF SPEAKING Modifiers describe the speaker's assessment of the manner in which the speech act itself is being asserted, whether it is expressed *honestly*, *frankly*, *in confidence*, etc.

(65) **MANNER OF SPEAKING Modifiers**

  a. *Frankly*, my dear, I don't give a damn.

  b. *Confidentially*, Hawkeye, I couldn't hit a bullet with the side of a barn.

  c. *Honestly*, I'm more concerned about the guy you are now.

  d. *In confidence*, I will tell you that your tie is not in good taste.

MANNER OF SPEAKING Modifiers also encase the asserted proposition in a modal bubble, but the bubble has a different character than that of SPEAKER ATTITUDE Modifiers. Instead of I CONSIDER IT X THAT Y, the latent proposition that underlies MANNER OF SPEAKING Modifiers may be paraphrased as I SAY TO YOU IN A X WAY THAT Y. For example, in (65a) the speaker isn't saying that he considers it frank that he doesn't give a damn. He is asserting that he is acting in a frank manner when he makes this devastating assertion. Similarly, examples (65b, c, and d) can be paraphrased as follows:

(66) I SAY TO YOU IN A confidential WAY THAT Hawkeye, I couldn't hit a bullet with the side of a barn.

   I SAY TO YOU IN AN honest WAY THAT I'm more concerned about the guy you are now.

   I SAY TO YOU IN A confidential WAY THAT I will tell you that your tie is not in good taste.

 Finally, EPISTEMIC clausal Modifiers create the same sorts of "modal bubbles" as epistemic modal auxiliaries do, though again the possibilities are much more open-ended with the Modifiers. EPISTEMIC modality has to do with the speaker's assessment of how likely, possible, or necessary a situation is, and/or how the speaker learned the information:

(67) **EPISTEMIC clausal Modifiers**
    a. *Apparently* people have been hiding them.
    b. *Supposedly*, a telephone call was made by a phone by the pool.
    c. This letter had *purportedly* been written by his wife.
    d. I'm *probably* going to collapse in about 10 minutes.
    e. *Maybe* we will go through the actual ceremony at some point.
    f. *Conceivably*, this could have influenced some participants' responses.

These Modifiers can be distinguished between EVIDENTIAL Modifiers – those that express something about the source of the information expressed in the clause – and VALIDATIONAL Modifiers – those that express something about the speakers assessment of how likely the information expressed in the clause may be.

(68) **Evidential Modifiers**
    Apparently: I have reason to believe this information is true, but it may not be.
    Supposedly: I got this information from some dubious source.
    Purportedly: I got this information from some dubious source.

    Validational Modifiers
    Probably: This information is more likely to be true than not true.
    Maybe: This information is roughly as likely to be true as not true.
    Conceivably: This information is less likely to be true than not true.

These characterizations of "the meanings" of these Modifiers are very rough out of context. Recall that all linguistic elements, including the sentence level Modifiers discussed in this section, affect and are affected by the contexts in which they are used. They are generalized tools that speakers use in a number of ways to accomplish specific communicative tasks.

Finally, CONJUNCTIVE clausal Modifiers relate the information in the modified clause to some other proposition, usually expressed in the immediately previous clause:

(69) **CONJUNCTIVE clausal Modifiers**
    a. *However*, we'll never know the outcome of that argument.
    b. The house seemed *nevertheless* to have a special weight inside it.
    c. That day has, *therefore*, always meant something to me.
    d. *In spite of this*, we never complained about the food.
    e. *First* she would stand at the corner of the yellow house, watching me.

Summary

In this chapter we have looked at the syntactic function of Modification. Like Complementation, Modification is relevant to many different phrasal categories. The main divisions of the presentation are:

- Modification in noun phrases
- Modification in Predicates
- Modification at the clause level

Some syntactic categories, in particular adverbs, noun phrases, and prepositional phrases, can serve as Modifiers at more than one level.

In Section 10.1 the structure of the noun phrase, including semantic types of Modifiers and the orders in which they may appear, was described. In general, Modifiers that describe more inherent properties of an entity occur closer to the head of a noun phrase than Modifiers that describe temporary characteristics.

Several different semantic roles expressed by Modifiers in the predicate were discussed and exemplified. These include: MANNER, MEANS, PURPOSE, REASON, EXTENT, TIME, LOCATION, and DIRECTION. Direction and location Modifiers are particularly likely to be extended metaphorically to express a variety of abstract relations.

Finally, three general semantic roles of clause level Modifiers were discussed and exemplified. These are SPEAKER ATTITUDE, MANNER OF SPEAKING, and EPISTEMIC.

FURTHER READING

Ferris (1993) is a thorough treatment of form, meaning, and use of adjectives in English. Thompson (1988) argues for the discourse basis for the distinction between attributive and predicative uses of adjectives. Langacker (1995) and Taylor (2006) discuss genitive constructions from a Cognitive Grammar perspective.

Exercises

1. Each of the following phrases contains one or more Modifiers. For each word in these examples, indicate the syntactic category below the word, and the syntactic function above it. The first example is done for you. (Note: Remember that syntactic functions of individual words are always in relation to the immediate level of syntactic structure. For example, in an NP like *an extremely beautiful nose*, the syntactic function of *beautiful* is Head of the adjective phrase *extremely beautiful*. The adjective phrase, then, is a Modifier of *nose*. *Beautiful* does not modify *nose* directly.)

a. MOD   D   Mod   Head
   all   the   following   phrases
   PDQ   Article PresPart   Noun
b. so utterly carefree
c. has recently joined the army
d. very tall and lanky
e. the cat in the hat
f. three strikingly intelligent students in her class
g. his recently divorced girlfriend
h. once in a great while
i. formidable and loyal bodyguards

2. The following sentences contain IP Modifiers (adjuncts) or Clause level Modifiers (disjuncts). The Modifiers may be noun phrases, adverbs, prepositional phrases, or even clauses. Underline all the adjuncts and circle the disjuncts you find. Then give the semantic role each one expresses. The first example is done for you:

   a. Unfortunately, the students arrive next week for classes.
      Unfortunately is a disjunct expressing SPEAKER ATTITUDE. *Next week* is an adjunct expressing TIME. *For classes* is an adjunct expressing PURPOSE.
   b. By the way, have you ever been to Bujumbura?
   c. Marilyn, much to my surprise, steadfastly refused to attend our concert.
   d. She finally came to a conclusion concerning Michael.
   e. Finally, we need to think about tomorrow's meeting.
   f. Silvia was otherwise occupied.
   g. Otherwise one or both of us would have pulled off the silly things.
   h. In fact I was not even allowed to play outside when he came.
   i. I felt flattered, as she expected.
   j. As a rule, I've felt less wary with men.

11 Auxiliaries and the "black hole" of English syntax

"Anything that crosses the boundary of a black hole cannot get back. Things can go in, but nothing can get out. Is that clear!" "Yes, Uncle," she said. "I shall remember."

from *Black Holes and Uncle Albert* (Stannard 2005:115)

At several points in this book I have mentioned the importance of auxiliaries in understanding English grammar. In Chapter 3 we discussed the distinction (really a continuum) between grammatical functors and lexical vocabulary, and I argued that auxiliaries are grammatical functors, quite distinct from lexical verbs. This is because auxiliaries have all the characteristics of grammatical functors, e.g., they form a relatively small, closed set and express very limited semantic features. Verbs, on the other hand, have all the properties of full lexical words; for example, they form an open class of words that tend to express rich (complex) semantic content.

In this chapter we will look at constructions that contain auxiliaries, and will see how the "Inflection position" right after the Subject and before the main Predicate of basic English clauses is metaphorically speaking a "black hole" that has the power to suck lexical verbs into itself and convert them into the grammatical functors that grammarians call auxiliaries.

Later in the chapter I will suggest on the basis of the formal and functional properties of constructions that contain auxiliaries two major revisions to a traditional approach to English grammar. These suggestions, if taken seriously, significantly simplify the tasks of teaching, learning, and understanding English grammar. The two suggested revisions are:

1. "Copular be" is an auxiliary, not a lexical verb.
2. *Inflection* (i.e., tense, aspect, and/or mode), not a verb, is the defining property of a Predicate.

Suggestion 1 is actually fairly easy to argue for – copular *be* has all the morphosyntactic properties of prototypical auxiliaries (see Section 11.3 below). There is, in fact, a lexical verb *be*, but the *be* that occurs in copular constructions is not the lexical one. Lexical *be* is an *active* verb, while copular *be* is a stative auxiliary.

Suggestion 2 is intended to clarify the status of *be* in so-called "copular" constructions. While it is true that most Predicates contain lexical verbs, there are some that do not. In particular, "copular *be*" constructions (Predicates with Subject Complements following *be*) do not contain a lexical verb. Rather, the Complement of the auxiliary *be* is the major predicating element in such constructions – the auxiliary simply expresses the required Inflectional information.

11.1 Types of auxiliaries

All auxiliaries have the syntactic properties described below in Section 11.3 as the "NICE properties" (Huddleston and Pullum 2002:92–112). Within this general commonality, there are several divisions and subdivisions of auxiliaries. The major subdivision is between MODAL AUXILIARIES and non-modal or INFLECTABLE AUXILIARIES. Within the modal auxiliaries, there are what I would like to call PLAIN MODAL AUXILIARIES and SEMI-AUXILIARIES. The term "semi-auxiliary" is sometimes used by other grammarians (see, e.g., Berk 1999, Greenbaum and Quirk 2004), though the items considered to be members of this class vary from one author to the next. Greenbaum and Quirk (2004:39–40) add a category of "marginal modal auxiliaries." This intermediate category, however, has only slightly different syntactic properties from plain modal auxiliaries, and their properties vary considerably from one variety of English to another, as we will see below.

Plain modal auxiliaries are non-inflectable, and most of them (all except *need*) do not function as lexical verbs in Modern English. The following are examples of the modal auxiliaries, divided between plain modal auxiliaries and semi-auxiliaries:

(1) **Plain modal auxiliaries**

can:	I *can* see clearly now.
may:	*May* I help you?
need (negative):	You *needn't* come. *You *need* come.
will:	*Will* you have a seat?
shall:	*Shall* I wrap it for you?
must:	They *must* be there by now.
could:	I *could* be married for all you know!
would:	*Would* you give your daddy a message for me?
had better:	You*'d better* just get used to the idea.

(2) **Semi-auxiliaries**

ought to (*oughta*):	There *oughta* be a law.
have to (*hafta*):	They *hafta* file for a permit.

used to (*useta*):	We *useta* buy wienerschnizel right here.
want to (*wanna*):	It doesn't *wanna* come out.
need to (affirmative or negative):	The activities (don't) *need to* be planned.
dare:	One *dared* not mention any topic at all.
be going to (*gonna*):	I'm gonna *get you!*
be supposed to:	We're *supposed to* be communicating with the parents!
be bound to:	Things *are bound to* work out.
be sure to:	You're *sure to* meet a fiendish surprise.

The term "modal" is used for this set of auxiliaries because most of their semantic functions fall in the category of MODALITY (see below, and Chapter 12, for a discussion of modality), though they cohere as a class more because of their formal properties than their semantic functions. Since it is a general principle of language that forms hardly ever have an absolute, one-to-one relation to functions (see the Introduction), some of the modal auxiliaries express meanings that do not really fit very well into the semantic domain of modality. For example, *will* expresses something more similar to TENSE, and *useta* (*used to*) expresses a conceptual category that is more similar to ASPECT than modality. Nevertheless, these forms all have some structural features in common (described in Section 11.3), and so can be insightfully grouped together on formal grounds.

The non-modal auxiliaries are *do*, *have*, and *be*. Each of these has a variety of uses that will be discussed at different points in this chapter:

(3)	"Dummy" *do*:	She *did*n't tell me anything.
		So what *do* you think?
	"Emphatic" *do*:	I *DID* see a pussy cat!
	"Pro-verb" *do*:	Just *do* it.
		I will oppose it and I hope every member of this Council *does* too.
	"Perfect aspect" *have*:	*Have* you guys tried it yet?
		Catherine *had* disappeared.
	"Progressive aspect" *be*:	She'll *be* comin' round the mountain.
		I'm looking for a good book.
	"Passive voice" *be*:	She *was* accosted in the market place …
		I *was* smeared by the Pentagon.
	"Copular" *be*:	We *are* the world.
		They *were* hilarious.
		Marion *is* in the kitchen.

The non-modal auxiliaries are distinguished from the modals in that they all function as main lexical verbs as well as auxiliaries. Whether they are functioning

Table 11.1 **Sequencing of modal and non-modal auxiliaries**

	May follow:			
Non-modal auxiliary	Modals	have (perfect)	be (progressive)	be (passive)
do	no	no	no	no
have (perfect)	yes	no	no	no
be (progressive)	yes	yes	no	no
be (passive)	yes	yes	yes	no

as main lexical verbs or as auxiliaries, all the non-modals are Inflectable (note the capital "I," explained below in Sections 11.2 and 11.3) with tense and Subject Inflection (see also Chapter 4 on verbal inflection). Modal auxiliaries, on the other hand, are not themselves Inflectable. Rather, the mere presence of a modal auxiliary constitutes the required Inflection for any given clause.

Within the class of non-modal auxiliaries, *do* is the odd one out in the sense that it may not follow any other auxiliaries. *Be* and *have* may both follow modals. In addition, *be* may follow *have* (*have been*) and passive *be* may follow progressive *be* (*was being considered*). Table 11.1 summarizes the sequencing possibilities for these major auxiliary types.

Another way of describing the sequencing of auxiliaries is with a linear diagram as follows. The dummy auxiliary *do* does not cooccur with any other auxiliaries, and so lies outside the scope of this diagram:

(4)   Modal > Perfect > Progressive > Passive

The way (4) can be read is Modal auxiliaries precede all other auxiliaries (except the dummy *do*, which does not figure in this diagram); the perfect auxiliary (have) precedes the Progressive and Passive auxiliaries (*be*), and Progressive *be* may precede Passive *be*. Thus, up to four auxiliaries may occur in any given clause:

(5)   By then the bill *will have been being* considered.

Note that each auxiliary governs the form of the auxiliary or verb to its right. *Will* governs the bare form of the perfect aspect auxiliary *have*; *have*, in turn, governs the past participle form of the progressive aspect auxiliary *be* (*been*); progressive aspect *be* governs the present participle form of *be* to its right (*being*); this *be*, in turn, is the passive auxiliary, which of course governs the past participle form of the verb *consider* (*considered*). Only the first auxiliary, *will*, expresses the Inflection for the clause (future tense).

Some varieties of English allow double modals, but these are considered non-standard in CSE:

Table 11.2 **Comparison of frequency of double-modal constructions**

	had ought (including 'd ought)	might could	will shall (including 'll shall and 'll sha)
BNC	1	2	32
COCA	8	58	4

(6)   And I felt like I *might could* help contribute to that. (From a television interview)
(He said) I*'d ought* to return home and stop acting contrary. (From a novel)
She's never raised her voice to me, even when she *ought should* have. (Novel)
Maybe you *had ought* to take such a famous person right on over to Hattiesburg. (Novel)
well I*'ll shall* have to take you out there won't I? (Conversation)

The sequence spelled *had better* is best treated as a single auxiliary, rather than as an example of double modals for a couple of reasons. First, neither *had* nor *better* exist as modal auxiliaries on their own. Second, the whole construction *had better* functions as a unit for purposes of negation. In (7) the negative particle *not* follows *better*:

(7)   I*'d better not* ask you your age.

In other double modal constructions, as in multiple auxiliary constructions in general, the first modal is treated as distinct from the rest:

(8)   I *shouldn't ought* to of let no stranger shoot my dog.

In example (8), the negative particle intervenes between the two modals. There are four examples of this in the COCA. However, the negative never intervenes between *had* and *better* in their auxiliary function. This is in spite of the fact that there are 3,870 examples of *'d better*, and only 9 examples of *should ought* in the COCA (13 including the negatives cited above). Therefore we conclude that *had better* is a single, compound modal auxiliary.

Table 11.2 presents the raw numbers of occurrences of the most common double modal constructions in the BNC and the COCA. It seems from these figures that *will shall* is a (marginal) feature of British English while *might could* is more characteristic of (some forms of) American speech. All of these, however, are considered non-standard on both sides of the Atlantic.

The following are examples of the Inflectable auxiliaries in their functions as lexical main verbs:

(9)   *do*:   I already *did* the dishes.
       She *does* very nice work.

She *did* a figure-8 on the ice.

have: They *have* three children.

I *had* a dream last night.

We should *have* a party.

be: Why don't you *be* the leader?

Don't *be* silly.

He just *be's* himself. (non-standard)

He will just *be* quiet.

The lexical verb *be* is an active verb, and as such can follow any other auxiliary, including *do*. In some contexts, lexical *be* can be regular, taking the present tense form *be's* (pronounced "bees") and the past tense form *beed*. This non-standard phenomenon is discussed in more detail in Section 11.4 below. The verb *have* for some speakers has the syntactic properties of all auxiliaries (e.g., inversion with the Subject in a yes/no question: *Have you a match?*) even when functioning semantically as a lexical verb expressing possession.

11.2   The black hole

The metaphor of a "black hole" is an image that may (or may not) be helpful in understanding the importance of the "Inflection position" in basic English clauses. The term "Inflection" has a slightly different meaning here than in some other parts of this book. As mentioned in Chapter 7, "Inflection" with an upper case "I" is a syntactic category. An "Inflectable element" is an element in phrase structure that can express the Inflection for the clause. Inflection in this sense essentially means tense/modality and agreement with the Subject. This is different from "inflection" (in all lower case) as in "inflectional morphology" (Chapter 4).

All independent clauses in English must have one element that expresses the *Inflection* for the clause. As outlined in Chapter 7, the Inflection may reside in an Inflectable auxiliary (*be*, *have*, or *do*), or a main verb. Also, a modal auxiliary may itself constitute the required Inflection for the clause. In any case, there is, at least in the standard varieties, only one Inflectional element in any given independent clause. If a modal auxiliary occurs, the non-modal may not be Inflected:

(10)   He *should be* here by now.   *He should is here by now.

She *might have been* there.   *She might has been there.

*She might had been there.

*She might have is there.

Similarly, if an Inflected auxiliary occurs, the main verb that follows may not carry Inflection:

(11)   He is running.   *He is ran.
       They were given to me by Orna.   *They were gave to me by Orna.

So, Inflection can be expressed by one and only one of the following:

- A (plain) modal auxiliary: They *should* withdraw.
- An Inflected auxiliary: He *is* running away.
- An Inflected lexical verb: He *ran* away.

The Inflection position is so central to the clause structure of English that it has become kind of a "black hole" into which lexical verbs have been being "sucked" for at least a thousand years. Once a verb gets sucked into this hole it never returns. It just becomes an empty shell of its former self, a "zombie verb" expressing only very specialized meanings, and having few of the morphosyntactic properties that characterize real, live verbs. This is just a metaphor, and if it helps you understand English grammar better, then it has done its job. If not, then you may ignore it entirely!

Let's look at the properties of elements that occur in this "black hole" in order to get a feel for why it is so important. The auxiliaries listed above are a mixed bag that have different syntactic properties from verbs and from one another. The reason for this is that there is a historical path whereby certain lexical verbs in certain constructions over time tend to be subconsciously reanalyzed by speakers as modal auxiliaries. As this reanalysis takes place, verbs in those constructions tend to lose their semantic and morphosyntactic properties as lexical vocabulary items, and begin to look more like grammatical functors. The further along on the path from full lexical verb to auxiliary a form is, the fewer verbal properties it tends to have. Since this is a continuous process, different constructions are at different "stages" in the journey, and so exhibit different clusters of morphosyntactic properties. The forms that are classified in this book as plain modal auxiliaries have been functioning in the Inflection position for centuries, and by now have lost most of their properties as lexical verbs. The semi-auxiliaries have not been in that position for quite as long, and so retain some of their verbal character.

For example, *will* is a word that once was a full main verb that meant pretty much the same thing as *want* does in Modern English. The older usage can still be found in literary texts:

(12)   Nor that I *will to* borrow his messenger without his knowledge.

In this usage, *will* means *want* or *be willing to*. Now, if someone "wants" to do something in the present, the thing she wants to do hasn't happened yet. It is still in the future at the time of wanting. So there is an element of futurity inherent in the notion of wanting. For some reason over the years, the futurity component began to take over as the main element of meaning expressed by the form *will to*. This form thus became very useful as a way of expressing a certain kind of futurity, with the element of desire or willingness gradually becoming less salient. As this usage became more frequent, the natural process of grammaticalization kicked in and the form became shorter, the *to* component was lost, and people started to unconsciously think of *will* as one of the auxiliaries. In other words, *will* was reanalyzed as an auxiliary rather than a full lexical verb.

As *will* lost the meaning of "conscious desire," the verb *want*, which at the time meant "lack," stepped in to take over the job of expressing the important concept of conscious desire. Even today, *want* still can be used to mean "lack," though I suspect it sounds a bit archaic to most speakers:

(13)   Surely all this frost must be owing to the *want* of fire.

Furthermore, some verbs continued in their functions as lexical verbs in some constructions, while becoming auxiliaries in others. This has happened, for example, with the auxiliary *can*. This auxiliary derives historically from the same Germanic root as the modern verb *know*. This root occurred in at least three types of constructions: one with a noun phrase Object, one with a finite clausal Object, and another one with an infinitive Complement. The form *ken* survives to this day with all these uses in Scottish English:

(14)   Construction 1: *ken* + NP: D'ye *ken* anyone who can boast of that?
        Construction 2: *ken* + CP: And you *ken* they used to lift it off . . .
        Construction 3: *ken* + INF: He *ken* to do it?

The verb *know* in other varieties of Modern English continues in constructions 1 and 2. It appears before a nominal element and has all the morphosyntactic properties expected of verbs, including all five verb forms. In construction 3, however, this verb appears between the Subject and a verb – the *black hole*! This is the position where auxiliaries are found, and so it was reasonable for speakers to begin thinking of it (unconsciously, of course) as an auxiliary, *in that particular construction*. As it was reanalyzed, its meaning began to specialize such that the component of ABILITY became more prominent, and the senses of "recognize," "understand," or "be acquainted with" gradually disappeared. Parallel to this semantic shift, its formal properties began to be "stripped away." At the present point in history, the auxiliary *can* has lost all of its morphosyntactic properties of verbs – it has only one form, and does not stand on its own as a separate verb. Though the form *could* derives historically from the past tense of *ken/can*, in the modern language its meaning and use is so different from that of *can* that it must be considered a separate auxiliary.

The story is similar for the other forms that we are calling "plain modal auxiliaries." They all started out as full lexical verbs (except the *better* part of *had better*), but when they found themselves in that dangerous Inflection position, they started to whither away and become less than full verbs. The "semi-auxiliaries" are forms that have begun that process, but have not functioned long enough in that black hole to lose all of their verbal character. Some of them still have a reflex of a past tense form (*used to*), or have an Inflectional *be* element of their own (as in *be going to* or *be bound to*). They also lack some of the syntactic properties described in the following section. However, they are still tenaciously hanging on to the edge of the hole, maintaining some of the trappings of their former glory as full verbs.

No one can predict precisely which lexical verbs will become auxiliaries in the future. When we look to the past, however, we see that there are certain semantic classes of verbs that have tended to become auxiliaries, and of course as linguists we want to try to understand why this should be the case. The kinds of lexical verbs that are most likely to be coopted as auxiliaries are those that express meanings that cluster around the domain of "modality" (see Chapter 12). Modality has to do most generally with a speaker's attitude toward the information being expressed, including how confident the speaker is in the truth of the information, the speaker's emotional commitment to the information, or how necessary the information is. Verbs expressing meanings in the domains of DESIRE, CERTAINTY, DOUBT, ABILITY, POSSIBILITY, NECESSITY, and others have tended in the past to become auxiliaries, so we might look at these semantic domains for verbs that may potentially become auxiliaries in the future. Though again I want to stress that no one can predict with precision what will happen in the future course of language change. It's just that when a language gets into the "habit" of changing in a certain way, that habit pattern tends to influence, though not absolutely determine, the course of language change on into the future.

11.3   Morphosyntactic properties of auxiliaries

In the following paragraphs I will briefly describe a few of the morphosyntactic "tests" for distinguishing lexical verbs from auxiliaries. These tests involve four syntactic properties deemed the NICE properties by Huddleston and Pullum (2002:92–112). NICE is an acronym for Negation, Inversion, Code, and Emphasis.[1] Auxiliaries have the NICE properties, while lexical verbs do not. These constitute the standard syntactic arguments that auxiliaries and full lexical verbs are two distinct types of syntactic entities.

Many approaches to English grammar identify two "*be* verbs" – one a lexical or copular verb and the other an auxiliary (see Azar 2002:A6, Berk 1999:151, Böjars and Burridge 2001:166–7, Celce-Murcia and Larsen-Freeman 1999:53, Greenbaum and Quirk 2004:36, Teschner and Evans 2007:51, to name a few). Common textbook examples of these two uses of *be* are given in (15a) and (15b) respectively:

(15)   a.   **"COPULAR"** *be* **(a lexical verb)**
             She *is* a doctor.
             They *are* hilarious.
             Malcolm *was* the leader.
             This *is* for you.
             We*'re* in the kitchen.
             There *were* three dogs in the yard.
       b.   **AUXILIARY** *be* **(a grammatical functor)**
             She *is* waiting.
             The vase *was* broken by the workers.
             We *were* devastated by the tragedy

In the following section, I will show that copular *be* as illustrated in (15a) has all the properties of auxiliaries, and none of the properties of lexical verbs.

The NICE properties

Negation

In negative clauses, the negative particle *not* follows an auxiliary (the first, if there are more than one in a Predicate):

(16)   **AFFIRMATIVE**   **NEGATIVE**
       She should eat more kimchi.   →   She should *not* eat more kimchi.
       She is eating kimchi.   →   She is *not* eating kimchi.
       The vase was broken by the workers. →   The vase was *not* broken by the workers.
       We have lived in Paris.   →   We have *not* lived in Paris.

The same is true of *be* in Copular constructions:

(17)   She is a doctor.   →   She is *not* a doctor.
       They are hilarious.   →   They are *not* hilarious.
       Waldo was the leader.   →   Waldo was *not* the leader.
       They are in the kitchen. →   They are *not* in the kitchen.

In Modern English, lexical main verbs do not allow the negative particle to follow them:

(18)   *She eats not kimchi.
       *The workers broke not the vase.
       *We live not in Paris.

Rather, if there is no auxiliary in the corresponding affirmative clause, the "dummy" auxiliary *do* is inserted, and the negative follows it:

(19)   She eats kimchi.   →   She *does not* eat kimchi.
       The workers broke the vase.   →   The workers *did not* break the vase.
       We live in Paris.   →   We *do not* live in Paris.

This is not true of *be* in copular constructions, or of any of the other auxiliaries:

(20)   *She does not be a doctor.
       *They do not be hilarious.
       *They do not be in the kitchen.

With respect to negation, therefore, copular *be* functions like auxiliaries rather than full lexical verbs.

Inversion

In certain questions the first auxiliary and the Subject must invert (exchange positions):

(21)   **DECLARATIVE**   **Yes/No INTERROGATIVE**
       She should eat more kimchi.   →   *Should she* eat more kimchi?
       She is eating kimchi.   →   *Is she* eating kimchi?
       The vase was broken by the workers.   →   *Was the vase* broken by the
                                                                            workers?
       We have lived in Paris.   →   *Have we* lived in Paris?
       WH-INTERROGATIVE (non-subjects)
       What *should she* eat more of?
       What *is she* eating?
       Who *was the vase* broken by?
       Where *have we* lived?

The same is true of *be* in Copular constructions:

(22)   She is a doctor.   →   *Is she* a doctor?
       They are hilarious.   →   *Are they* hilarious?
       Waldo was the leader.   →   *Wasn't Waldo* the leader?
       They are in the kitchen. →   *Aren't they* in the kitchen.

Lexical main verbs do not exhibit this property:

(23)   *Eats she kimchi?
       *Broke the workers the vase?

*What broke the workers? (trying to mean "What did the workers break?")
*Where live we?

Instead, if the declarative Predicate is headed by a lexical verb, the dummy auxiliary *do* must be inserted before the Subject:

(24)   **YES/NO INTERROGATIVE**
Does she eat kimchi?
Did the workers break the vase?
Do we live in Paris?
WH–INTERROGATIVE (non-subjects)
What *does* she eat?
What *did* the workers break?
Where *do we* live?

Again, copular *be* is like auxiliaries in that it does not require the insertion of *do* (though see below for a discussion of situations where it is allowed):

(25)   *Is she* a doctor?   *Does she be a doctor?
Are they hilarious?   *Do they be hilarious?
Is this for me?   *Does this be for me?
What *is she*?   *What does she be?
Who *is this* for?   *Who does this be for?
Where *are we*?   *Where do we be?

Code

In constructions that "stand for" or "code" a previously mentioned verb phrase, the first auxiliary is repeated (and inverted with the Subject). The ungrammatical examples illustrate the fact that lexical main verbs do not have this property:

(26)   **TAG QUESTIONS**
She should not eat kimchi, *should she*?
*She should not eat kimchi, *eat she*?
*She eats kimchi, *eats not she*?
The vase was broken by the workers, *wasn't it*?
*The workers broke the vase, *broken't they*?
ELLIPSIS
I should see the doctor, and *so should she*.
*I saw the doctor, and *so saw she*.
Who should eat kimchi? *She should*.
Who ate kimchi? *She ate.
We were eating kimchi, and *so was she*.
*We eat kimchi and so eats she.

Copular *be* follows the pattern of auxiliaries, and not lexical verbs:

(27)   **TAG QUESTIONS**
     She is a doctor, *isn't she?*
     They aren't hilarious, *are they?*
     Waldo isn't the leader, *is he?*
     That was in the kitchen, *wasn't it?*
     ELLIPSIS
     She is a doctor, and *so is* he.
     Who is the doctor? She *is*.

Emphasis

In constructions in which the truth of the proposition is emphasized, the first auxiliary receives emphatic stress. Again, the nonsensical examples show that lexical main verbs do not possess this property (note that the symbol ☺ indicates that the following sentence is not ungrammatical, but would not make sense in the context provided):

(28)   She should eat more kimchi. Yes she SHOULD.   ☺Yes she should EAT.[2]
     The vase was broken by the workers. Yes it WAS. ☺Yes it was BROKEN.
     We have lived in Paris. Yes we HAVE.   ☺Yes we have LIVED.

If there is no auxiliary in the original clause, the dummy auxiliary *do* occurs and receives the emphatic stress:

(29)   She eats a lot of kimchi.   Yes she DOES.   ☺Yes she EATS.
     The workers broke the vase.   Yes they DID.   ☺Yes they BROKE.
     We live in Paris.   Yes we DO.   ☺Yes we LIVE.

Yet again, copular *be* follows the pattern of auxiliaries. It is stressed in these emphatic constructions, and does not require the insertion of *do*:

(30)   She's a doctor.   Yes she IS.   ☺Yes she DOES.
     We were in Paris.   Yes we WERE. ☺Yes we DID.

Notice that other copular (or "linking") verbs that take Subject Complements, such as *seem*, *become*, or *resemble*, do not have the NICE properties, and do require the presence of *do* in NICE constructions. Therefore they are lexical verbs, and as such are syntactically distinct from copular-*be*:

(31)   N: They don't seem hilarious.   *They seem not hilarious.
         She didn't become a doctor.   *She became not a doctor.
     I: Does she resemble her mother? *Resembles she her mother?
         What did she become?   *What became she?

C: She became a doctor, and so did he.   *She became a doctor, and so
                                             became he.

The situation turned ugly, didn't it?   *The situation turned ugly, turned
                                             not it?

E: They seem happy. Yes they DO.   *Yes they SEEM.

Among "copular" verbs, then, only *be* has the NICE properties otherwise only attributed to auxiliaries. We can conclude, then, that copular *be* belongs to the same syntactic class as auxiliaries.

The myth of "lexical verb" *BE*

If copular *be* is so clearly a member of the class of auxiliaries, why have pedagogical and more linguistically oriented works on English grammar insisted on calling it a lexical main verb? It is my contention that this strange phenomenon can largely be explained by a pervasive myth of traditional grammar that has been perpetuated by generations of English teachers. This myth is expressed in (32):

(32)   Every independent clause in English must have a lexical verb.

Starting from this assumption, all the instances of copular *be* we've seen so far must be lexical verbs, since the only other element in the Predicate is the non-verbal Subject Complement. What I would like to suggest is that (32) is an unnecessary and ungrounded assumption. The more insightful generalization, I contend, is the following:

(33)   Every independent predication in English must have tense, aspect, and/or mode *Inflection*.

There are other reasons for replacing (32) with (33), in addition to resolving the status of copular *be*. First, as we've seen in Chapter 7, theoretical approaches to English grammar, including recent versions of Generative Grammar, affirm the assertion in (33). The *Inflection* is the syntactic Head of a Predicate, not necessarily a verb. In fact, in the minimalist paradigm (represented by Radford 1997), the "Sentence" is no longer the highest node in a syntactic tree. Rather, the Inflectional Phrase is the highest node. This reflects the fact that, within 1997 minimalism, the category that is the syntactic "Head" of a sentence is its "I-node," or Inflection. In other words, the properties of a sentence are projected from its Inflection – if there is no Inflection, there is no sentence. The actual arguments for this determination are quite compelling, if rather complex. Readers are referred to Radford (1997:61ff.) for the details.

Second, the Complement of *be* is always non-verbal anyway, whether the construction is copular, progressive, or passive. The special forms traditionally termed present and past participles that follow *be* in progressive aspect and passive voice constructions are all DEVERBAL in that they have lost most of the syntactic properties of verbs; in particular, they cannot be Inflected. Therefore, just like

other non-verbal categories (nouns, adjectives, and prepositional phrases), participial forms must rely on some other element (an auxiliary) to express the important
Inflectional information when the participle itself expresses the main semantic
content of a Predicate.

Let's look at some examples that may help illustrate this fact. Basic passive
constructions are isomorphic with copular predicate adjective constructions in
which the adjective happens to be a past participle:

(34)   a.   The vase *was broken* when the workers moved the piano.
       b.   The vase *was beautiful* when the artisan finished painting it.
       c.   As soon as I walked into the room, I noticed that the vase *was broken.*

Many traditional grammar books would say that *was* in (34a) is an auxiliary
because the construction is a passive. On the other hand, *was* in (34b) and (34c)
is claimed to be a lexical verb because the construction is a predicate adjective.
Clearly there is a difference in meaning between the passive and attributive senses
of the Complements of *be* in these sentences, but that difference can be attributed
to the nature of the Complements, not necessarily to any syntactic categorial
difference between the two uses of *be*.[3]
Similarly, consider the following two examples:

(35)   a.   That person *is annoying* me.
       b.   That person *is annoying.*

Again, many grammar books and linguists would say that (35a) is a progressive
aspect construction with auxiliary *be*, while (35b) is a predicate adjective construction with a lexical copular *be*. Of course, there is no doubt that there is a semantic
difference between the senses of *annoying* in these two examples, and semantic
differences are significant since language is primarily a tool for communicating
meaning. Nevertheless, if the distinction between auxiliary and main lexical verb is
supposed to be a distinction between two syntactic classes of items, there should be
some *syntactic* correlate to the semantic distinction. Otherwise, there is no reason
to posit anything other than garden variety POLYSEMY (multiple meanings). As we
saw in Chapter 10, *be* + Complement constructions may be polysemous in a
number of ways, but in every case the polysemy stems from the syntactic construction or the discourse context (as in (34a and c)) rather than the syntactic
category of the form of *be*:

(36)   **Polysemy of "copular *be*"**
       a.   That person *is tall.*   ATTRIBUTIVE
       b.   That person *is a teacher.*   EQUATIVE
       c.   That person *is in the kitchen.*   LOCATIVE
       d.   There *is a person* in the kitchen. EXISTENTIAL

    e.   This *is for you*.   BENEFACTIVE

    f.   This *is mine*.   POSSESSIVE

(37) **Polysemy of auxiliary *be***

    a.   That person *is eating* a banana.   PROGRESSIVE ASPECT

    b.   That banana *was eaten* by someone.   PASSIVE VOICE

Looking first at the examples in (36), we see that the semantic relations expressed are significantly different from one another, yet traditional and pedagogical grammars typically find no reason to posit syntactically distinct "copulas" for each relationship.[4] Similarly, in (37) two quite distinct meanings are expressed, both of which depend on the semantic properties of the Complements, rather than on any syntactic category difference among the forms of *be* – the present participle form of a verb expresses an ongoing action, while a past participle refers to a resultant state. The auxiliary in all these examples is functioning in exactly the same way – to carry the all-important Inflectional information required of every English independent clause.

    In summary, insisting that there is a fundamental syntactic difference between copular *be* and auxiliary *be* introduces a number of unnecessary analytic and pedagogical complexities. Adopting the alternative assertion, suggested in (33), resolves these complexities. From this point of view, every main clause must contain an element that is "Inflectable" with whatever Inflectional information is appropriate for that clause's function (e.g., as an independent assertion, a question, a relative clause, an adverbial clause, etc.). One job of an auxiliary, then, is to express the necessary Inflectional information. Since only one instance of Inflection is required, only one auxiliary – the first one – expresses the Inflection. Any additional auxiliaries just occur in the deverbal form required of the auxiliary that precedes them. Most auxiliaries participate in expressing various aspectual and modal categories as well, but *be* basically just serves as a "platform" for Inflection when the lexically rich element – the one responsible for most of the semantic content of the Predicate – is non-verbal, and therefore cannot express the Inflectional information directly. This function unites the uses of *be* in copular as well as progressive aspect and passive constructions.

11.4   Lexical *be* as an active, regular verb

In the previous section, I have outlined the properties of core auxiliaries in English, and have shown that the distinction between "copular *be*" and "auxiliary *be*" is spurious. That is a fairly easy claim. The only arguments against it are based on different interpretations and properties that arise because of different semantics of the Complements that follow *be*. But, as I have shown, many semantic differences may arise between *be* and its Complement that traditional grammars do not attribute to a syntactic category difference between types of *be*. Given the fact that "copular *be*" and "auxiliary *be*" have the syntactic properties of core auxiliaries, there is no reason to suggest that the different uses of *be* are due to a categorial distinction between two lexemes.

The more difficult assertion I would like to make is that in fact there are two syntactically distinct *be* verbs in English, and that one is a lexical main verb and the other is the auxiliary. Furthermore, I will claim that the syntactic distinctiveness of these two *be*s (evidenced by *syntactic* properties) is motivated by the semantic difference between *stativity* and *activity*. The reasons that this assertion is more difficult are (1) a cursory reading of the argument may give the impression that the harder claim actually contradicts the easier claim. In fact it does not, but a full reading is necessary to put the issue in perspective. (2) Corroborative evidence for the harder claim is based on data from "non-standard" forms of English. Some of the examples given below would definitely be "ungrammatical" to most English teachers. However, the fact that such examples are frequently attested in natural discourse, and are logically coherent, lends additional support for the hard claim, though it does not constitute the major evidential basis.

Semantic stativity vs. activity

The semantic distinction between STATES and ACTION is mostly determined by volitionality and change (see Chapter 6). Situations that are presented as involving change, and are normally initiated and controlled by some entity acting with volition (on purpose) are ACTION. Situations that do not involve change, and have no controlling entity are STATES. This is a very general characterization. As with any semantic distinction, there is in fact a continuum between prototypical states and prototypical actions – there are very good examples of states and very good examples of actions, but a large number of situations fall somewhere in between (see Vendler 1967, Chafe 1970, and Comrie 1989 for fuller characterizations). However, the grammar of English tends to discretize (make distinct) the semantic difference between stativity and activity in a number of significant ways. In this section I will describe two of the "tests" for whether a situation is being presented as a 'state' or an 'action.' These I will refer to as the habitual test and the progressive test.

The habitual test

When an independent clause occurs in the so-called "present" tense form, the temporal reference may be interpreted as habitual aspect or as a "true present," i.e., a situation that is in effect at the time of utterance (see Chapter 12). Actions are normally understood as habitual (42), while states are normally understood as true present (43):

(38)   HABITUAL

     They sometimes *build* their eyries on inland lava pinnacles.
     You *exercise* to look good.

In the senses intended in the examples given in (38), *build* and *exercise* describe actions in that they refer to situations that involve intentionality, volition, and change. When occurring in the "present tense," as in these examples, these verbs do not assert that the actions are taking place "now," i.e., at the time of speaking (though they incidentally may be), but rather that they occur from time to time over a long period that includes the time of speaking. No particular finite event of building or exercising is referenced.

On the other hand, the examples in (39) below express STATES in that no movement or change is asserted. In the present tense, these examples assert that the state holds "now." The specific current instance of the state is being referenced, rather than the possibility that the state holds true from time-to-time:

(39)   TRUE PRESENT

     I *see* you are troubled at something.
     I *love* you.
     Mm. the room *is red* now.

Thus "present tense" for actions expresses "habitual aspect," while "present tense" for states expresses a true present, in the sense that it is used when the speaker wishes to assert that a state holds true at the time of speaking. In order to express the idea that an action is taking place "now," a special construction must be employed. This constitutes the next test for whether a situation is being presented as a state or an action.

The progressive test

As we will see in more detail in Chapter 12, there is an apparent semantic anomaly between stative situations and the English progressive aspect construction. This is because in English the progressive aspect construction evokes an image that involves "progression," i.e., progressive change and/or movement. A state, by definition, does not involve movement or change; therefore prototypically stative situations are not semantically amenable to expression in the progressive aspect:

(40)   I see the airplane.   ?I'm seeing the airplane.
      She likes ice-cream.   ?She is liking ice cream.

We know the answer.   ?We are knowing the answer.
The barn is red.   *The barn is being red.

However, the first three examples in the right hand column of (40) are not completely "ungrammatical." Rather, they constitute less-than-prototypical expressions of the stative concepts of *seeing*, *liking*, and *knowing*. In fact, stative concepts can be expressed in the progressive, but when Predicates that normally express stative concepts do occur in the progressive aspect construction, a different, non-stative sense is implied. Because of the cognitive schema evoked by the progressive aspect construction, the construction itself imparts the notion of activity to the assertion. In Chapter 12, this phenomenon is described and exemplified in more detail.

Another piece of evidence that *be* in the progressive aspect is active is the fact that it doesn't seem to work with Subjects that are incapable of acting with volition. The following are examples from Partee (1977):

(41)   a.   John is being noisy.
       b.   *The river is being noisy.

Thus we see that, like other stative verbs, when *be* appears in the progressive aspect it takes on an active, volitional meaning. But wait – isn't this a syntactic property of lexical verbs that distinguishes this *be* from auxiliaries? I don't think any other auxiliaries can occur in the progressive aspect:

(42)   *They are shoulding eat more kimchi.
       *They are having eaten more kimchi.
       *They are doing eat more kimchi.
       etc.

Furthermore, active *be* can occur with the auxiliary *do*, as in the following:

(43)   Careful! No *don't be silly* Amy.   DON'T ACT SILLY
       Don't *be stupid* Stuart!   DON'T DO SOMETHING STUPID
       My dear, *do be quiet* –;
       he may be listening now!   CEASE MAKING NOISE
       Do be careful, love . . .   ACT CAREFULLY

This is another property that the active *be* does not share with other auxiliaries.

(44)   *Do should eat more kimchi!
       *Do have eaten more kimchi!
       *Do do eat more kimchi!
       etc.

Finally, compare the true lexical *be* examples in (43) above to the following stative situations expressed with the same lexical items, but without the presence of *do* or progressive aspect:

(45)   They're *silly* buggers though *aren't they?*
They *are stupid* that lot!
Of course, I'm *stupid*.
Toads *are quiet* and *harmless* and *nice*.
Usually she *is careful,*

While it may be a stretch to think of states as being "habitual," it should be clear that the examples in (45) make assertions about the general character of their Subjects, rather than to any particular instance of their acting *silly, stupid, quiet,* etc. that is asserted to be true at the moment of speaking. This seems to me to be the stative equivalent of habitual aspect.

These examples show that indeed there is something "odd" about *be.* So-called "copular *be*" has all the properties of auxiliaries, but it can occur in the progressive aspect and it can follow the dummy auxiliary *do.* It just so happens that whenever *be* occurs in the progressive aspect, or follows *do,* it expresses an action rather than a state.

Stative *be* vs. Active *be*

In the above section we have seen that *be* in copular constructions that express STATES has all the properties of auxiliaries. However, *be* may have properties of lexical verbs exactly in those situations that express ACTIVITIES – *acting* quiet, *acting* silly, or *acting* stupid, etc. It passes the syntactic tests for lexical verbs exactly and only when the semantics involves an ACTIVITY, usually initiated and controlled by an AGENT acting with volition. This is the basis of the claim that in fact there are two syntactically distinct *be*s in English, one stative/auxiliary *be* and another active/lexical *be.*

In addition to the evidence presented so far, is there any independent evidence for the distinction between the two *be*s? Consider the following naturally occurring example from one of my daughters when she was 12 years old. The context was the behavior of one of her friends who attended a birthday party:

(46)   He's not silly; he just *bes* silly when he's around girls.

The form *bes* (pronounced "bees"), though utterly non-standard, is logically coherent in this context. It shows that this native speaker has two *be*s in her lexicon. The stative *be* is the irregular one that is really an auxiliary whenever it occurs (as demonstrated earlier). The active *be,* on the other hand, is morphologically regular, taking the regular third person singular present tense *-s* ending. Thus active *be* and stative *be* are formally, as well as semantically, quite distinct. This example is particularly telling in that it explicitly contrasts stative *be* – *He's not silly* – with active *be* – *he just bes silly,* thus showing that the speaker had internalized both *be*s in her lexicon, and considered them to describe distinct states of affairs, one of which she presented as true and the other not.[5]

Example (46) seemed so sensible to me in this context that I was curious to determine how widespread this usage was. Unfortunately, the BNC and COCA provide no clear examples of the "regular" active *be* illustrated in (46). So, I turned to an even larger corpus – the Internet. There I found much more fertile ground. Below are a few of the several hundred examples of the morphologically regular, active *be*. Examples (47) through (49) are a few of the results of a Google search for "he just bes" (845 total hits – accessed June 24, 2009):

(47)   Sometimes he just *bes* like that.
(preggersinlalaland.blogspot.com/2008/09/sometimes-he-just-bes-like-that.html)

(48)   he dosent really dress up he just *bes* himself and wears bermuda shorts, headband, sandles and plain shirts sometimes sleeveless
(littlemisssavannah.buzznet.com/user/journal/2021051/)

(49)   He doesn't hold one side or the other, he just *be's* himself and I admire that.
(www.populistamerica.com/not_blood_not_color_people_one_nation)

The following is from a Google search for "she just bes" (428 total hits):

(50)   If she just *be's* herself ... people will stay add her!
(www.myrefresh.com/showthread.php?t=38608andpage=4)

Clearly "X just be's Xself" is a relatively common construction. Other examples of morphologically regular *be* used in an active sense are also attested on the Internet. However, they are eclipsed by many instances of the regularization of auxiliary *be* in AAVE (African American Vernacular English). While the regularization of active *be* may or may not have originated with AAVE, it is a totally reasonable formation based solely on the internal syntactic character of so-called Standard English. Consider the following example:

(51)   If she just *bes* herself, she'll do fine in the debate.
(mikerupert.newsvine.com/_news/2008/09/28/1924839-sarah-palin-contra-dicts-mccain-on-pakistan-seems-to-back-obamas-position-)

The "standard" way of expressing this would be:

(52)   If she just *is* herself, she'll do fine in the debate.

According to my native speaker intuition, this just doesn't capture the sense of volitionality and activity that is nicely expressed in (51). This distinction is reminiscent of the distinction between other pairs contrasting stative and active *be* (constructed examples):

(53)   a.   Why aren't you the leader?   STATIVE/AUXILIARY BE
     b.   Why don't you be the leader?   ACTIVE/LEXICAL BE

In example (53a) the speaker just questions a state of affairs, while (53b) is a suggestion that the addressee act in some volitional way to take a leadership position. Again, this illustrates that auxiliary *be* (53a) is stative, while lexical *be* (53b) is active.

Example (54) is one last example of regular active *be*, this time occurring in the major-class past tense with -*ed*:

(54)   I gave the monitor to her while she "beed the doctor" using the monitor to poke around my feet.
    (www.tertia.org/so_close/2007/07/well-there-you-.html)

This is an example of an adult quoting a child, and so may be dismissed as a simple morphological overgeneralization. Nevertheless, it is significant that this usage clearly implies the child was actively acting like a doctor. The standard form, *she was the doctor*, simply would not have expressed the same sense. An expression such as *she pretended to be the doctor* would have been needed.

11.5   Consequences for pedagogy

The consequences for English grammar pedagogy of spuriously uniting copular *be* with the lexical copular verbs and distinguishing it from auxiliaries are manifold. In particular, every discussion of the NICE constructions must be qualified in a disjoint way: auxiliaries and copular *be* work one way; lexical verbs except copular *be* work the other way. If ESL/EFL teachers and grammar books would consider copular (i.e., stative) *be* to be an auxiliary, the number of special cases that students would have to learn and assimilate would be reduced by almost half. After all, a significant number of rather complex constructions are sensitive to the auxiliary/lexical verb distinction as manifested by the NICE properties, including clausal negation, *yes/no* questions, non-subject *Wh*-questions, emphatic constructions, imperatives, *do-so* (recapitulated verb-phrase) constructions, and others.

Another consequence of calling copular *be* a lexical verb is that it renders the basic clause structure of English mystifying to many SLLs. My contention and my experience as a TESOL and EFL teacher is that the assertion given in (33) (repeated and slightly modified here for convenience) goes a long way in helping students conceptualize and internalize basic English clause structure:

(55)   Every independent clause in English must have ONE EXPRESSION of tense, aspect, and/or mode Inflection.

There are several reasons for the assertion given in (55). First, many languages do not employ auxiliaries to the extent that English does. Such languages (Russian,

Hebrew, Burmese, Tagalog, and Indonesian, to name a few) require no lexical verbal element in at least some copular constructions (predicate nominal, predicate adjectival, locational, and existential constructions in unmarked tenses). Typologically, the clause structure of English (and some other Indo-European languages) is rendered quite "exotic" by the supposition that a lexical verb is used in such constructions. This is a major and unnecessary conceptual hurdle for many SLLs.

Second, *be* is so common in English that many students become confused as to when to include *be* and when not to, as well as when to inflect it and when not to. For example, the use of spurious *be* is common, as well as double Inflection constructions such as the following (actual examples from advanced Korean SLLs of English):

(56)   Did you brought the forms?
       She is went to the store.
       They already were came.

A strong emphasis on the centrality of the Infl (Inflection) slot in English goes a long way toward helping students overcome such difficulties. In many ways the initial position in the Predicate is the pivot, as well as the "Black Hole" of English syntax. Part of mastering the "character" of English, and thereby developing fluency, is capturing a sense of how special that Infl position is. Of course, it is not necessary to emphasize the unity of "copular *be*" and "auxiliary *be*" in order to help students assimilate this important fact about English. However, keeping the two distinct actually introduces unnecessary confusion, which makes understanding of the overall clause structure of English much more difficult.

Finally, this approach underscores the profound importance of the distinction between activities and states for English grammar. While this is a semantic distinction that can undoubtedly be expressed in every language, not every language pays quite so much attention to it grammatically as does English. In this chapter we have seen how the activity/state distinction helps explain the different usages of the "present tense" and "progressive aspect" forms. In addition to this well-known feature of English grammar, activity vs. stativity helps to explain the use of perfect aspect forms in discourse. In particular, the distinction between simple past and present perfect is one that many SLLs find perplexing. This distinction can largely be understood in terms of the difference between an active event and a resultant state – the simple past tends to express an active event, while the perfect expresses a state that results from an earlier event.

11.6   Conclusion

The different morphosyntactic properties of the various types of auxiliaries can be explained historically in terms of grammaticalization. The bare bones of the scenario is the following: the auxiliary position, right between the Subject and the Predicate is, metaphorically speaking, a "black hole" that over time tends to "suck" verbs, especially those that are useful for expressing temporal, aspectual, or modal meanings, into itself. The modals are the forms that have been in this black hole the longest, and therefore have lost most or all of their verbal properties. The aspectual auxiliaries and the semi-auxiliaries have been occupying the hole for less time, and therefore still show signs of their earlier verbhood (though even they are spiraling downward into lexical oblivion). Still other verbs are "hovering on the edge" of the black hole waiting for speakers to deem them useful enough as auxiliaries to fall into the hole, from which there is no return. These potential auxiliaries include *keep on*, *finish*, *start*, *think*, *believe*, and perhaps others. These are not yet auxiliaries by any means, but they are among the prime candidates for future auxiliaryhood, if English continues to develop in the direction it has been going for the last thousand years or so.

In conclusion, I have tried to show that the assumption that every English clause requires a lexical verb is unfounded. Like most languages of the world, the lexically rich predicating element in copular constructions is not a verb at all, but the non-verbal Complement. The copular *be* that occurs in such constructions functions mostly as a "platform" for expression of the important Inflectional information. As such, it has all the syntactic properties of core auxiliaries, and none of the properties of lexically rich verbs. Thus, copular, passive, and progressive aspect constructions are unified in requiring an auxiliary *be*.

The second, related claim is that there is, in fact, a lexical verb that, in its base form, is phonologically identical to auxiliary *be*. Semantically, it has lexical content in that it expresses activity; in most cases it may be paraphrased with the lexical verb *act*. However, for some speakers lexical *be* belongs to the major inflectional class, taking the present tense form *bes* and the past tense form *beed*. This non-traditional, but syntactically and semantically highly motivated, approach to the basic clause structure of English significantly simplifies the conceptualization and teaching of English grammar.

Summary

In this chapter we have discussed the very important auxiliary, or Inflectional, position in English syntax. First several types of auxiliaries were distinguished, including:

- plain modal auxiliaries
- semi-auxiliaries
- non-modal, or Inflectable, auxiliaries (*do*, *have*, and *be*)

The interactions among the members of these subclasses of auxiliaries were described, including their sequencing and cooccurrence possibilities.

In Section 11.2, the "Inflectional position," occurring between the Subject and the Predicate of a basic clause, was described as a "black hole" that is so powerful a pivot for English syntax that it metaphorically sucks unsuspecting verbs into itself and turns them into auxiliaries.

In Section 11.3, auxiliaries were distinguished from full lexical verbs. A major conclusion of this section is that so-called "copular *be*" is best treated as an auxiliary.

In Section 11.4, arguments were presented that there is a lexical verb *be*, but it has very different syntactic properties from the copular/auxiliary discussed in Section 11.3. In particular, lexical *be* is an active verb, whereas auxiliary *be* simply carries the required Inflectional information for stative Predicates in which the main semantic content is expressed in a Subject Complement.

Finally, it was argued that an approach that treats Inflection as the main defining property of an independent clause in English, rather than a verb, goes a long way toward helping SLLs understand and use English grammar.

FURTHER READING

The best treatment of the morphology and syntax of auxiliaries in Modern English is Huddleston and Pullum (2002). At several points in this monumental work, the special characteristics of auxiliaries are mentioned and discussed. See especially pp. 92–112. Warner (1993) is also a thorough treatment of auxiliaries in English, including their historical sources.

Exercises

1. Find an excerpt of 200 words or more of English narrative (a story) on the Internet, and print it out. Then underline the primary (non-modal) auxiliaries, circle the modal auxiliaries, and draw a rectangle around the semi-auxiliaries.

2. Find and print another excerpt of 200 words or more on the Internet. This does not need to be a story, but should be some form of coherent English discourse. Circle the element that expresses the INFLECTION in each finite clause.

3. Fill in each blank in each of the following examples with a modal auxiliary that expresses the meaning indicated in parentheses:

    a. George __ play the guitar.   (is able to)
    b. Sheila __ have more biscuits if she wants to.   (is allowed to)
    c. The river __ overflow its banks.   (is possible)
    d. Matthew __ swim when he was two.   (was able to)
    e. Theodore __ study Swahili.   (has an internal obligation to)
    f. I __ be glad if they were to visit us.   (contingent on X)
    g. He __ practice the guitar.   (I insist)
    h. It __ rain this afternoon.   (I predict)
    i. The red stuff __ be pepper sauce.   (I assume)

12 Time and reality

... human kind
Cannot bear very much reality.
Time past and time future
What might have been and what has been
Point to one end, which is always present.

T. S. Eliot (1944)

Every speech community needs to be able to anchor the situations and actions communicated in language according to the parameters of time and reality. In addition to adverbial Modification as described in Chapter 10, languages tend to have well-oiled grammatical systems for accomplishing these important functions. In English there are three grammatical paradigms that relate to the domains of time and reality. These paradigms are usually described as TENSE, ASPECT, and MODE (TAM for short) – tense expresses the time of discourse world situations in relation to some reference point, usually the time of speaking; aspect describes the internal temporal "shape" of a situation; while mode relates the speaker's commitment to the probability that the situation is real, necessary, or likely. It is reasonable to treat these three paradigms together for a couple of reasons. First, they constitute the main categories of Inflection on verbs and auxiliaries. Second, these paradigms interact with each other significantly, as we will see in the following pages. It would be very difficult, and even misleading, to treat each of them separately without mentioning the others.

Figure 12.1 illustrates in a general way the relationship between the conceptual domains of relative time, temporal "shape," and reality on the one hand, and the grammatical categories of tense, aspect, and mode on the other. As with all relationships between form and meaning, there is much variation and overlap among the formal categories and the concepts that they express. Figure 12.1 represents the prototypical relationships – the ones that define the *main uses* of the grammatical tools known as the tense, aspect, and modal systems of English grammar. Like any tools, of course, these forms can and are used to accomplish other tasks as the need arises in the course of communication.

Conceptual Domains (meaning)	Time of the situation expressed relative to the time of utterance	Internal temporal "shape" of the situation expressed	Modality – speaker's evaluation of the reality or necessity of the situation expressed
Grammatical Categorization (form)	Tense (past, present, future)	Aspect (progressive, perfect)	Mode (various epistemic and deontic categories expressed by modal auxiliaries)

Figure 12.1 The relationship between form and meaning in the TAM systems of English

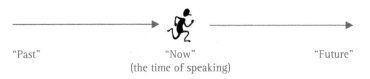

"Past"   "Now"   "Future"
                  (the time of speaking)

Figure 12.2 The conceptual domain of tense

12.1   Tense

Tense is the grammatical expression of relative time. Situations being communicated in clauses are often anchored in relation to a reference point, usually the moment the clause is spoken, i.e., "now." If we think of time as a line, with "now" represented by a point moving from left to right, we can imagine relative time in terms of Figure 12.2.

Time that is on the left side of now is past, and time on the right side of now is future. Now is, of course, the present.

In terms of grammatical expression, English verbs have three morphological forms that are usually described as "present tense" (two forms) and "past tense" (see Section 6.3 for a description of the verb forms of English). These are reasonable terms, since most of the uses of the present tense forms include the time of speaking, and most of the uses of the past tense form have something to do with past time. However, we must keep in mind that these grammatical tenses are only loosely related to the conceptual domain of relative time, as diagrammed above. In particular, the reference point can be shifted to some other point in time, or reality (see below). Furthermore, "now" is constantly changing. Really, the only kinds of situations that can truly be said to hold "now" are enduring situations. An action that occurs in an instant in time cannot easily be referred to in the present, since by the time you refer to it, it's already past!

The following examples illustrate some of the usages of the morphological present tense, as represented in the BNC. The examples in (1), in which present tense really does refer to the moment of speaking, illustrate the major usage. The others are also very common.

(1)   **Present tense = "now"**
      You *know* how much I *love* you.   STATES
      His ears *are* huge.
      The angles of a triangle *add up* to 180 degrees.
      Pele *kicks*; he *scores*!   ACTIONS (Online narration)

(2)   **Present tense = "performative present"**
      This, madam, you left last night, and I *take* the liberty to restore it to you.
      I hereby *move* that we do similarly.

(3)   **Present tense = "habitually over a period of time that includes 'now'"**
      My son *walks* to school.
      He sometimes *kicks* his legs when he *doesn't know what I'm doing.*

(4)   **Present tense = "future, the planning of which includes 'now'"**
      Tomorrow I *leave* for Cambridge.
      I mean he *kicks* them out in two weeks.

(5)   **Present tense = "possible/probable conditional future situation"**
      If he *sees* you wearing that he'll have a cow!
      I'll have to tell him when he *comes.*
      I'm taking it with me when I *leave.*

(6)   **Present tense = "vivid narrative past"**
      Casey *lashes* out as he *kicks* his legs free. I *duck* and *come* inside. He *tries* a head-butt which I *dodge*, and I *clip* a neat jab across his chin which *rocks* but *doesn't fell* him. From somewhere down round his ankles he *heaves* a massive haymaker punch, using the dead pistol as a knuckleduster. If it had landed, my head would have flown like a shied coconut. But I *sway* back and *mop* another satisfying crosspunch on his ear to send him stumbling after his haymaker … (from a description of a fistfight in a novel, Russell 1989).

Similarly, the "past tense" verb forms can be used in a number of ways. The most common function of past tense is clearly to refer to completed situations presented as occurring before the time of speaking, as represented in the examples in (7):

(7)   **Past tense = "before now" or "true past"**
      You *knew* that they both had to agree.   STATES
      It *was* rather short notice.
      We *were* at the last meeting.
      and I *told* them where they can get it.   ACTIONS
      This, madam, you *left* last night …

(8)   **Past tense = "polite request for a reminder"**
      What *was* your name again?
      Whose turn *was* it this time?

(9) Past tense = "hypothetical conditional (past)"

They were told that the government would not bail them out if things *went* wrong.

They knew they could not replace anybody if they *gave* the sack.

If you *asked* for trouble, you got it.

(10) Past tense = "hypothetical conditional (present)"

I wouldn't live with your father if he *took* drugs.

(11) Past tense = "hypothetical conditional (future)"

If we *went* back to nineteen seventy eight, we'd pick up all the Selby drawings.

The doctor could examine me if you *wished*.

If you *gave* me a fiver I'd be grateful.

I expect you could really make a mess if you *tried*

As we've seen above, the grammatical "present tense" of English is often used to refer to situations that are in the future (cf. the examples in (4) and (5) above), or the past (6). Future time is also part of the meaning of most of the modal auxiliaries discussed below. In CSE, future time is the main meaning of the modal auxiliary *will*, and the semi-auxiliary *be going to* or *be gonna* in most spoken varieties (see Chapter 11 on the different subtypes of auxiliaries). These analytic future tense constructions combine relative time with a bit of modality, and so are somewhat hybrid in the meanings they express.

In many cases, the future with *will* and the future with *be going to* express little or no difference in meaning, and simply reflect free variation or stylistic preference on the part of the speaker. Other times, one of these analytic futures seems more appropriate than the other. There are also contexts in which only one makes sense, and the other would be either ungrammatical or would mean something quite different.

The following little experiment was conducted to try to get a sense of how *will* and *be going to* are understood and used by CSE speakers. Three (American) English speakers were presented with pairs of examples that contrasted only in the use of *will* or *be going to* to express future time. One of the examples in each pair was a direct quote from the spoken corpus of the BNC, and the other was the same except the future construction was changed. Subjects were given one whole paragraph of context for each example. They were told that the difference between *will* and *be going to* was the focus of the study, but they were not told which example of each pair was actually attested in the corpus, and which had been "doctored." Subjects were then asked to judge whether the two examples were "equivalent in the context," whether both examples were acceptable but one "sounded better," or whether only one was "acceptable or reasonable" in the context. Approximately eighteen pairs were presented to each subject. Only pairs on which there was unanimity among the three speakers are documented here.

In the pairs in (12), the example with *will* occurs in the BNC spoken corpus, and the contrasting example with *be going to* was unanimously judged to be fully equivalent in the same context:

(12) a.   There is the almost paranoiac feeling that the machines *will* take over.
      b.   There is the almost paranoiac feeling that the machines *are going to* take over.
      c.   We *will* take our petition with us on that one.
      d.   We *are going to* take our petition with us on that one.

In the pairs in (13), the example with *be going to* occurs in the BNC spoken corpus, and the contrasting example with *will* was judged to be fully equivalent:

(13) a.   … if we're prepared to accept that we'*re going to* lose money.
      b.   … if we're prepared to accept that we'*ll* lose money.
      c.   I'*m going to* ask the general assembly to turn their mind to quite a different subject now.
      d.   I'*ll* ask the general assembly to turn their mind to quite a different subject now.

The next set of pairs illustrates situations where either *will* or *be going to* would be acceptable, but the one that actually appears in the corpus "sounds better" to all three English speakers consulted. The "odd" example is indicated with a question mark:

(14) a.   So *will* you all get round to your limerick's please ladies.
      b.   ?So *are* you all *going to* get round to your limerick's please ladies.
      c.   And if I'*m going to* be leafleting thousands of people in conferences …
      d.   ?And if I'*ll* be leafleting thousands of people in conferences …

Finally, the last set of pairs illustrate situations where only one of the analytic future forms seems fully appropriate. The unacceptable (i.e., not equivalent in the context) example is indicated with two question marks:

(15) a.   Right and you'*ll* be reading that other report *will* ya?
      b.   ??Right and you'*re going to* be reading that other report, *are* ya *going to*?
      c.   Jessie *is going to* have a baby.
      d.   ??Jessie *will* have a baby.

The general conclusion from this little study and various searches of the BNC is that there appear to be general principles that influence the choice between the two analytic futures of English, but that there are few absolute laws regarding their usages. The general principles that seem to emerge are the following:

Table 12.1 **Distribution of *will* and *be going to* in the BNC**

	will		going to VERB	
Spoken	19,501 *will*	7,862 (14%)	59,082 (100%)	
	31,719 *'ll*			
	51,220 (86%)			
Written	89,878 *will*	10,156 (8%)	129,532 (100%)	
	29,498 *'ll*			
	119,376 (92%)			

- The future *will* is more common overall than *be going to* in both spoken and written British English (see Table 12.1).
- There is a higher proportion of *will* in written British English than in spoken (equivalent statistics for American English have not been calculated). Table 12.1 displays these statistics.
- *Will* is even more common in questions, especially questions expressing indirect commands, than it is overall (see (14a) above, and the following):

(16) **Indirect commands**
Will you continue Simon.
Will you be able to provide me with a erm WordPerfect package?

- *Will* is preferred when referring to a human's willingness or decision to do something:

(17) Speaker expresses a decision concerning how to celebrate a colleague's promotion:
I know! We*'ll* have a party. (??We*'re going to* have a party.)

- *Be going to*, though not strictly preferred, is likely to occur when a prediction is made about the future behavior of some inanimate Subject:

(18) It*'s going to* be a beautiful day today.
I don't know what*'s going to* happen.
It*'s going to* get worse before it gets better.

- *Be going to* is more appropriate when describing future actions that are already planned, or which steps have been taken toward their realization:

(19) Speaker referring to someone who is pregnant:
She*'s going to* have a baby! (cf., ??She*'ll* have a baby!)
Speaker A arrives at friend B's house to find the house decorated for a birthday party:
A: Wow, what's happening here?
B: We*'re going to* have a party. (cf. B: ??We*'ll* have a party.)

Statistics are not available for the last three of these assertions, as they rely on data not recorded in the published corpora (e.g., animacy and willingness of the Subject). However, they have emerged from inspection of the data in the corpora and in everyday conversation.

One characteristic of *be going to* that distinguishes it from *will* is that it has a clear past tense form. This allows it to be used for "future in the past" situations that are not, strictly speaking, available for *will*:

(20)   a.   what I *was going to* suggest is that we should seek to negotiate with them
       b.   But he said he *was going to* ask for two.
       c.   we knew we *were going to* have a speaker
       d.   They *were going to* have a concert weren't they?

Fully one quarter of the *be going to* future constructions in the BNC are in the past tense. This allows speakers to refer to a time in the past when a particular action was still in the future. The action that was future in the past, may or may not be future at the time of speaking. Historically, the form *would* is the past tense of *will*. However, in most cases, substituting *would* for *was/were going to* in (20) results in quite a different modal sense (see the discussion of modality below):

(21)   a.   what I *would* suggest is that we should seek to negotiate with them
       b.   But he said he *would* ask for two.
       c.   we knew we *would* have a speaker
       d.   They *would* have a concert wouldn't they?

It is clear that *will* and *would* have diverged in meaning to such an extent that *would* can no longer be considered the past tense form of *will*. *Will* is the form that has become grammaticalized as an expression of future tense, and like other modal auxiliaries, such as *must* and *had better*, no longer has a past tense form.

12.2   Aspect

Aspect refers to the internal temporal "shape" of actions or states (Comrie 1976). It refers to the time dimension, but is not anchored relative to a particular point in time, as is tense. Particular kinds of situations can have their own INHERENT ASPECT, or AKTIONSART. For example, certain situations are inherently stative, others are processes, some are more dynamic (involve change and/or movement), while some are relatively static (see Chapter 6 for a discussion of these different situation types). English has two constructions whose prototypical function is to adjust the aspect of an expression. These will be termed the PROGRESSIVE CONSTRUCTION and the PERFECT ASPECT CONSTRUCTION. Clauses that do not occur in either of these constructions still "have aspect," but their aspect is determined by other factors,

Table 12.2 **Grammatical tense and grammatical aspect in English**

	Progressive construction	Perfect aspect construction
Past tense	I was just tending my cows.	I had just tended my cows.
Present tense	I am just tending my cows.	I have just tended my cows.
Future tense	I will just be tending my cows.	I will have just tended my cows.

such as the inherent aspect of the situation described, the syntactic context, the characteristics of the participants involved, and the presence of adverbial elements, such as particles, adverbs, and prepositional phrases.

While the conceptual domains of relative time and temporal shape are related, their expressions are largely independent of one another in English. For this reason, both of the aspect constructions can be used in any of the three tenses. This defines a six-celled matrix as presented in Table 12.2. The structures in Table 12.2 are not six different "tenses," nor are they six different "aspects." They are three tenses and two aspects in all their possible combinations.

The progressive construction can be diagrammed according to the following general pattern:

(22)   be VERB-ing

In this pattern, *be* refers to a form of the auxiliary *be*. VERB refers to any verb stem. Tense may be expressed via the auxiliary. Sometimes you will hear or read the terms past progressive, present progressive, and future progressive. These can be understood as combinations of the progressive aspect construction (given in (22)), plus the tense of the auxiliary *be*. The "-*ing* form" of the verb is usually called the present participle (see Section 6.3).

Similarly, as shown in Table 12.2, the perfect aspect construction can occur in all three tenses. The construction itself can be diagrammed as follows:

(23)   have VERB-en

The pattern in (23) is an abbreviation for a form of the auxiliary *have*, plus the past participle of any verb. Sometimes you may hear or read terms like PRESENT PERFECT, PAST PERFECT, PLUPERFECT, or FUTURE PERFECT. Again, these are just combinations of the perfect aspect construction (given in (23)) plus the three grammatical tenses. Past perfect and pluperfect are just two ways of describing the combination of past tense and perfect aspect.

Progressive and perfect are the only constructions of English specifically dedicated to the function of adjusting the aspect of clauses. This does not mean that other English clauses "have no aspect," or that aspectual notions cannot be expressed in other ways. It just means that these are the only well-oiled grammatical means of expressing aspectual variation. Other aspects can be expressed, but they require tools from other grammatical systems. For example, inception and completion (the initial and final phases of actions) can easily be expressed in English, but they are not fully grammaticalized as aspectual categories (see the discussion of "phasal aspects" below). Rather, they are expressed by analytic structures involving a lexical verb plus an infinitive or participle Complement: *I started to work, I finished working.* Other aspectual notions are expressed in a number of different ways, such as particles, adverbs, and prepositional phrases.

In the following paragraphs, examples of how English expresses a few of the universal aspectual categories mentioned by Comrie (1976) are presented. In the diagrams below, the following notation is used:

- time line
← → unbounded time
| boundary of an action
( ) boundaries of a state
x a punctual action, i.e., an action that occurs instantaneously and therefore has no internal temporal structure.

The major division in the conceptual domain of temporal shape is between **perfective, imperfective,** and **perfect aspects.** First we will discuss these three major categories, and then fill in some of the aspectual categories that fall under these headings. Figure 12.3 summarizes the relationships among all of these terms.

Perfective

In perfective aspect a situation is viewed in its entirety, including its beginning, middle, and completion. The main actions of a story are normally recounted in perfective aspect, whereas secondary, explanatory, and descriptive material occurs in various non-perfective aspects (e.g., imperfective, progressive, or habitual):

(24) |————————| 'He wrote a letter.'

English does not have a specific grammatical form dedicated to expressing perfective aspect. Rather, actions that inherently have a beginning and an ending, like writing a letter, particularly when they are expressed in the simple past tense, as in (24), are by default understood to be perfective. In the present tense, actions such as *write a letter* may involve a couple of different aspectual qualities, to be described below, but perfective is not one of them. This makes sense, since writing a letter takes some time, and one can't possibly start, continue, and finish writing a letter in the instant in time known as "the present." In the future, however, we can again talk about perfective aspect, since if you say *he will write a letter* you certainly do have in view the inception, continuation, and completion of the action.

Without an Object expressed, the clause *he wrote* could express perfective, habitual, iterative, or almost any other aspect. This is because writing is a process that does not have a logical endpoint (a linguist would say it is ATELIC). The verb form simply expresses tense, leaving the aspectual properties to be gleaned from the context. On the other hand, *he wrote letters* is probably iterative (an action repeated several times) even though the verb still simply expresses past tense.

Imperfective

In imperfective aspects a situation is viewed from the "inside," as an ongoing state or process. Habitual, progressive, and iterative aspects are all subtypes of imperfective.

(25) $\longleftrightarrow$ 'He writes letters.'

Perfect

It is perhaps unfortunate that the terms perfective and perfect are so similar, as the concepts they refer to are very different. If I were a grammar dictator, I would immediately decree different terms for these two very different concepts. But, alas, for some obscure reason these are the terms that have emerged and have been used by generations of English grammar teachers and students, and so we are destined to deal with them.

Perfect aspect normally describes a currently relevant *state* that results from the situation (normally an action) expressed by the verb:

(26) $-x|\ (-\overset{\text{\Large\char"2660}}{?}-)$ 'He has come from Houston.'
              "now"

In this clause, the action of coming is in the past (x), but the clause describes the state that currently holds as a result of that action. The action itself is not in focus, but rather the state that results from the action. For this reason, the sentence *he has come* likely implies "he is here now." The perfective *he came*, on the other hand, involves no such implication. He may be here now or he may have come and then left again.

Furthermore, because perfect aspect primarily asserts a state, and only incidentally an action, it does not make sense to recount a series of actions in the perfect aspect:

(27)   ??He has come in, and then has sat down, and then has started to read.

The perfective, on the other hand, primarily expresses actions themselves. For this reason it is much more reasonable for series of actions to be expressed in perfective aspect: *He came in, sat down, and started to read.*

As mentioned above, past perfect, or "pluperfect," is not a separate aspect. Rather, it refers to the combination of perfect aspect and past tense. The effect of this combination is to shift the reference time (RT) from "now" to some point in the past. That is, the state that results from an earlier action is presented as occurring at some point in the past:

(28) $-x$ $(-$ RT $-)$ $-$ "now"   'I had entered a congested zone.'

This example is from a motorist's explanation of how a small traffic accident occurred. The action of entering the congested zone occurred at time x. The reference time describes the state of being in the congested zone that resulted from the entering action. "Now" is the time of speech (in this case, writing), at which point the motorist is no longer in the congested zone, so the state is no longer relevant. Since that state is in the past at the time of writing, the whole perfect aspect construction is presented in past tense by the use of the past tense form of the auxiliary, *had.*

Completive

COMPLETIVE ASPECT expresses the completion of an action. Sometimes completive and inceptive are called phasal aspects, because they refer to different temporal "phases" of the action described by the verb:

(29)   ←——————┤   'She finished working.'

Inceptive

Similarly, **inceptive aspect** expresses the starting phase of an action:

(30)   ├——————→   'She began to work.'

The phasal aspects are mostly expressed in English via lexical verbs such as *finish, stop, start, begin, commence,* and perhaps *keep on* plus a clausal Object (see Section 14.3 on clausal Objects). Since there is no evidence that these MATRIX VERBS have been grammaticalized as aspectual auxiliaries, we can't really say these constitute part of the grammaticalized aspectual system of English. As discussed in Chapter 2, the signs of grammaticalization include: (1) structural simplification and (2) semantic shift. The matrix verbs that express the phasal aspects neither simplify structurally nor express any idiosyncratic semantic senses when occurring in inceptive or completive constructions. They sound the same and mean essentially the same thing as they do when used in ordinary transitive clauses, like *He finished the bookcase* or *They began the Mozart Requiem.* Contrast this with the difference in form and meaning between, say, the lexical use of *have* in *I have a new car*, and its use as an auxiliary in *I've been to Paris* or *I have to* [*hafta*] *write this chapter.*

The fact that *have* in these contexts reduces to -*'ve* and *hafta* and doesn't really mean "have," as in "own," is evidence that this use of *have* has been reanalyzed as an auxiliary. There is no such evidence in the case of the phasal verbs. The lexical phasal verbs are tools that, because of their particular basic meanings, can be adapted to express notions that verge on the domain of aspect. They are not, however, dedicated "aspect markers."

Phasal aspects can be considered to be subtypes of perfective, since they view particular phases as complete wholes. Like perfective aspect, clauses in phasal aspects can be presented in other aspect constructions, such as progressive (31a), or even other phasal aspects (31b):

(31)   a.   **Progressive of inceptive aspect**
              I'*m beginning* to see the light.
       b.   **Inceptive of completive aspect**
              I *began to finish* writing an important letter that I had started three days ago.

Inchoative

Inchoative aspect describes the event of entering into a state:

(32)   ———⟨———⟶   'She got tired.'

The terms inchoative and inceptive often confuse English grammar teachers and students, but English grammar itself makes a very clear distinction. First, the matrix verbs that express these two notions are entirely distinct. Inception is expressed by *begin, start, commence,* and maybe a few others. Inchoation is expressed by *become, fall, get, turn, grow,* and *wax.* I don't believe there is any overlap between the sets of forms that express these two ideas. Contrast this, for example, with the amount of overlap that exists between the ways present, future, and past time are expressed (see examples (4)–(6) above). Apparently the grammar of English considers inceptive and inchoative to be even more distinct than present vs. future and past time! Second, as we have seen, the distinction between states and actions is a very important conceptual distinction in many areas of English grammar. It is not surprising, then, that entering into a state (inchoation) and the beginning phase of an action (inception) should be expressed in very different ways. The following are a few more examples of inchoative clauses from the BNC:

(33)   The possibilities for error *become* enormous.   STATE = BE *enormous*
       Malekith *became* his personal ambassador   STATE = BE *his ambassador*
       We haven't *got* there yet.   STATE = BE AT *there*

Thou'rt *got* into a fool's paradise.	STATE = BE IN *a fool's paradise.*
Things can only *get* worse then.	STATE = BE *worse*
The audience *turned* sour.	STATE = BE *sour*
It'd be heartbreaking to see it *turned* into a car park.	STATE = BE *a carpark*
he'd *become* more conscious of it as he *grew* older	STATE = BE *more conscious*
	STATE = BE *older*
You won't *grow into* a big strong girl	STATE = BE *a big strong girl*
One fisherman *waxed* lyrical.	STATE = BE *lyrical*

There are, of course, different nuances of meaning among these inchoative verbs. For example, *get* seems to imply more volition than most of the others (except *wax*), and *get* also is the only one that can easily take a locational Complement (*get there, get to London, get on the bus,* etc.). *Grow* seems more gradual than most of the others, while *turn* implies a more punctual transition. The verb *wax* almost always refers to a speech act (*wax lyrical, wax eloquent, wax enthusiastic,* etc.). What they all have in common, however, is that they all express entry into a state of some sort. That state can be the state of being a thing (*become a doctor*), having a property (*turn sour*), being located somewhere (*get off the table*), or displaying some characteristic (*wax eloquent*).

Punctual

PUNCTUAL actions are those which have no internal temporal structure because they occur in an instant in time.

(34) x 'He sneezed.'

Sometimes this aspect is referred to as instantaneous. This is an aspect which is inherent to particular kinds of actions, and has no dedicated mechanism for grammatical expression in English, except perhaps via adverbs such as *instantaneously* or *all at once*:

(35) She is *instantaneously* assimilated.
      When *all at once* I heard above the throng Of jocund birds a single plaintive bleat.

Progressive

PROGRESSIVE (or continuative) aspect is a subtype of imperfective. Actions in progressive aspect are ongoing, dynamic processes. They prototypically involve movement and change.

(36) →——————→ 'He is writing letters.'

Progressive aspect is distinguished from habitual aspect in that progressive refers to actual message-world actions, whereas habitual aspect asserts that some action takes place from time to time. Habitual does not assert any specific actions (see below). Progressive aspect is directly expressed in English via the progressive construction described earlier.

Because the progressive construction expresses the idea that an action is ongoing and dynamic, it often sounds pragmatically odd when it is used with stative verbs, like *know*:

(37)   ??Waldo was knowing the answer.

A stative situation is one in which there is no movement or change (see Chapter 6). Therefore, putting a stative verb into the progressive construction sets up a logical contradiction – an action cannot be both dynamic and stative at the same time! This is not to say that the stative verbs are *ungrammatical* in the progressive construction. Remember that language is a tool for communication; therefore if someone has a need to express a stative idea in a dynamic way, they will find a way to do so. Here are some examples from the BNC of stative verbs in the progressive construction. The active interpretations of these situations, as made clear by the context, are given in caps following each example:

(38)   We*'re seeing* already, that Health Authorities   LEARNING
       haven't got the money ...
       The last time we *were seeing* each other it Oh!   DATING
       all ended in tears.
       Yes they *were seeing* how much more they
       could eat and take home.   DETERMINING
       I *was seeing* them one after the other.   INTERVIEWING

(39)   Football is a game of chance and I *am*   ENJOYING PARTICIPATING
       loving every minute of it.

(40)   They*'re being rude* up that end.   ACTING RUDELY
       they*'re being silly*.   ACTING SILLY
       I*'m being honest*.   SPEAKING HONESTLY
       I thought I'd persuaded him that he *was*
       being foolish.   ACTING FOOLISHLY

These examples clearly show that stative concepts can be presented as active by use of the progressive construction.

Iterative

ITERATIVE ASPECT is when a punctual action takes place several times in succession.

(41)   >-x-x-x-x-x-x-x-x-x-x-x-> 'He is coughing.'

This is another case in which the progressive construction is used where it may seem to set up a logical contradiction. If an action is punctual, it takes place in an instant in time. However, the progressive construction describes actions that involve motion and change over a period of time. Nevertheless, speakers do use the progressive construction to express punctual actions, and when they do, they are asserting that the action takes place several times in succession. This is called the iterative aspect:

(42) And you*'re coughing* all night, keeping everybody awake?
      I *was coughing* at work.

The verb *cough* describes a punctual action. So if someone *is coughing* that can't possibly refer to one long cough, in the same way that, say, *is singing* can mean someone is singing one song. Other means of expressing iterativity include adverbials such as *over and over again* and *repeatedly*.

Habitual

As mentioned above under progressive, HABITUAL ASPECT asserts that a certain action, such as Waldo walking to school, regularly takes place from time to time. It does not assert that an instance of the action is taking place at the time of speaking, or any other specific reference time, though it may incidentally.

(43) $\longleftrightarrow$ 'Waldo walks to school.'

The temporal shape of the situation described in (43) is very different from iterativity or progression. Iterative aspect asserts a particular series of actions: *he coughed for an hour*. Progressive aspect expresses one dynamic action taking place over a period of time – *she's painting the barn*. Habitual aspect does not assert any particular action or series of actions – it simply asserts that such actions occasionally occur. Habitual is the default aspect expressed by the simple "present tense" for dynamic verbs in English.

Stative verbs on the other hand, such as verbs of sensation and mental state, describe situations which do not involve movement or change, e.g.:

(44) She *knows* the answer.
      He *sees* a bear.
      I *wonder* what happened to Jane?
      You *know* how much I *love* you.
      etc.

For such verbs, the present tense form actually does anchor the situation to the time of utterance. These are not normally understood as describing situations that occasionally occur once in a while, but rather states that are asserted to be true at the time of speaking.

While habitual aspect is the default interpretation of the present tense of dynamic actions, there are also ways of forcing a habitual interpretation of actions in the past. The past form of habitual aspect is often expressed by the semi-auxiliary *used to*:

(45)   Your mother *used to* sleep like a log.
       People *used to* whitewash their ceilings.
       my father *used to* bath us six kids in front of the fire.

These utterances describe situations that occurred habitually in the past, but no longer. Other, less grammaticalized, ways of expressing the idea of habitual actions in the past include the modal auxiliary *would*, and using the simple past with adverbials like *often* or *regularly*:

(46)   My father *would* never give my mother any money.
       Edna *often* took Celia down there,
       He *regularly* attended sessions of the House of Commons

Finally, when a transitive verb with a plural Object occurs in the simple past, a habitual interpretation is often possible:

(47)   Q: What did your father do when you lived in Seattle?
       A: He *built houses.*

There are, apparently, no dedicated ways of forcing a habitual interpretation on future actions. This sort of makes sense, since the future is unknown (or "irrealis"; see the discussion of modality below), so it is hard to predict whether actions will become habitual patterns or not. Of course, adverbials of various sorts are always available to bend the expression of actions as needed, but there are no constructions that seem to specifically assert "habitual in the future":

(48)   We will *regularly* attend Herrick Chapel.
       He will *often* walk to school.

Finally, it is worth mentioning here that there is a historical and contemporary connection between the conceptual domain of aspect and grammatical expression of location and direction marking. A few examples will suffice to illustrate this point.

Historically, the progressive construction described above arose from a locational construction NP *be on* LOCATION, as follows (de Groot 2007):

(49)   Stage 1:   She is on dancing. (Locational construction)
       Stage 2:   She is a-dancing. (Still heard in some dialects/contexts)
       Stage 3:   She is dancing. (Progressive aspect)

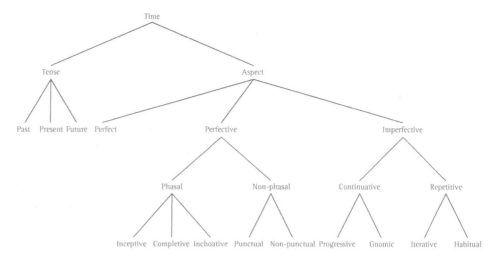

Figure 12.3 Conceptual categories in the domain of time

This is a classic example of grammaticalization. Back in the eleventh century or so, as English was losing its robust system of verb inflections, the need for a new way of expressing the idea of progressive aspect arose. Since being in the process of doing something can metaphorically be described as being "on" or "at" that activity, the locational construction was available to be co-opted for that purpose, with the present participle of the verb describing the metaphorical "location" of the action. This usage became so useful and frequent that it began to be shortened phonologically, until the locational meaning was eventually lost (de Groot 2007).

Other respects in which location and direction marking verge on the domain of aspect include the use of the directional verbs *come* and *go* to express certain aspectual nuances:

(50)   I *came* to understand …
        The radio *came* on.
        The idea *came* clear and brilliant!
        He's *going* crazy.
        The electricity *went* off.

In other cases, locational and directional prepositions function as post-verbal particles to express or reinforce certain aspectual notions:

(51)   He chopped *away at* the log.   away (at) = imperfective
        Tom drank the Pisco sour *down*.   down = perfective/completive
        I ate *up* all the ugali.   up = perfective/completive

This concludes our discussion of the ways in which English expresses notions relating to time. Figure 12.3 gives a tree diagram of the various conceptual notions associated with temporal grounding and temporal shape mentioned in this section. As emphasized in this chapter, not all of these notions are specifically grammaticalized in regular, well-entrenched paradigms in English, but they all may be expressed in some way. Also, as you can see from this diagram, the terms linguists use to describe various aspectual notions are not mutually exclusive categories. Rather, they constitute points on a hierarchy. For example, progressive and habitual are types of imperfective aspect. Another important point to remember is that tense and aspect are logically independent of one another. Theoretically, at least, any given aspect can occur in any given tense. The grammaticalized aspect constructions termed progressive and perfect may each occur in any of the three grammaticalized tenses, as indicated in Table 12.2.

12.3 Modality

MODALITY is a complex conceptual domain that covers a wide range of possible speaker's attitudes or orientations toward a situation. These include the speaker's belief in the reality, necessity, or likelihood of the situation described. In English, modality is expressed most directly by the modal auxiliaries (see Chapter 11). The terms MODE and MOOD are often used interchangeably to refer to the grammatical categories that relate to the conceptual domain of modality. In this book, however, we will use the term *mode* for the grammatical expression of modality, and *mood* to refer to the traditional distinction between declarative, imperative, and interrogative speech acts. These *moods* are discussed in Chapter 15, and are quite different conceptually and grammatically from the *modes* as discussed in this section. Like the terms perfect and perfective, inchoative and inceptive, this is yet another situation where two quite different concepts are referred to with similar terms. Sigh.

Linguists often recognize two subdivisions within modality:

- EPISTEMIC MODALITY describes the speaker's perception as to how "real" a situation is, or how confident the speaker is in the truth of the assertion.
- DEONTIC MODALITY describes the speaker's perception as to how "necessary" a situation is. A way of remembering this is that the word "deontic" comes from the same root as "debt." Think of DEONTIC MODES as expressing the speaker's obligation or debt to do something.

Most of the modal auxiliaries in English have both epistemic and deontic functions, though some tend to express one more than the other. Here is a selection of examples of each modal auxiliary, functioning to express a variety of modal notions:

Epistemic modality

Possibility:	I *might* borrow Slumbat's car this weekend.
	It *might* rain tonight.
	They *may* just want to ask us some questions.
Probability:	They *should* be here by 3:00.
Prediction:	They *will* be here at 6:00 pm.
Ability:	Mariela *can* sing the alto part to the Hallelujah chorus.
Contingent/conditional:	I *could* make spaghetti, if you make a salad.
	Give her that gift and she *would* be in seventh heaven.
Assumption:	They *must* be in Cincinnati by now.
	That *ought to* be enough curry for this recipe.
	The output *has to* equal the input.

Deontic Modality

Permission:	You *can* go now.
	The defendant *may* be seated.
Suggestion:	You *might* just send her a card.
Slight obligation:	I *should* eat more green vegetables.
	You*'d better* pick somebody else.
Stronger obligation:	They *ought to* be more polite to her family.
Insistence:	He *must* stop chewing his fingernails.
	They *have to* submit the application by next Tuesday.
	You*'d BETTER* get over here right now!

The expressions *to have to do* something and *ought to do* something are "semi-auxiliaries," i.e., historically recent additions to the list of modal auxiliaries. For this reason, they have not lost all of their full verbal character the way most of the other modals have. However, they clearly belong to a different word class than the corresponding verbs (*have* and *owe*).

The expression *had better* (usually *-'d better* or even just *better*, as in *you better do it*) can express a very mild sense of obligation, or a strong sense of insistence, depending on the degree of stress applied to the word *better*. To a certain extent this is true of *should* and *ought* as well, but seems to be particularly salient for the form *-'d better*.

Modal auxiliaries sometimes express the speaker's estimation of the relevance of the situation to him or her self:

(52) The airport *can't* be closed! (It is a serious inconvenience *for me* if the airport is closed.)

That *shouldn't* be too hard. (I guess this is easy *for me* to do.)

Both epistemic and deontic modalities can be located on a continuum between REALIS and IRREALIS. Prototypical realis modality strongly asserts that a specific action or state of affairs has actually happened, actually holds true, or is very imminent or necessary. Prototypical irrealis modality makes no such assertions whatsoever. Irrealis modes do not necessarily assert that an action did not take place or will not take place; they simply make no claims with respect to the actuality of the action or situation described. Negative clauses assert that actions or situations do not hold, but these are subject to the same realis–irrealis continuum as are affirmative clauses. For example, I can assert the reality or necessity of the proposition HE DOES NOT CLEAN THE KITCHEN just as weakly or strongly as I can assert the reality of its affirmative counterpart.

Modality interacts significantly with aspect and tense (see Wallace 1982). For example, habitual aspect clauses are less realis than perfective aspect clauses since habitual aspect describes an action *type* that is instantiated from time to time by actual actions, but does not itself assert the occurrence of any particular action. Similarly mode interacts with the REFERENTIALITY and IDENTIFIABILITY of the noun phrases associated with a verb. For example, entities that are part of a highly realis assertion are more likely to be refer to specific, identifiable things than those that are part of an irrealis assertion:

(53)   Waldo ate the cheerios that were in the cupboard.

However, a less realis mode with a specific referential Object is logically odd:

(54)   ??Waldo always eats the cheerios that were in the cupboard.

Irrealis modality can refer to an situation which is presented as occurring in a contingent world. For example:

(55)   *If you eat your cheerios*, you'll be like the big boys.

In this clause the condition, *if you eat cheerios*, is irrealis. Similarly, interrogative and imperative clauses are irrealis, since they do not assert that X did happen, but order it to come about, or question something about how or whether it will or did come about. Various kinds of assertions that are fall under irrealis modality include the following:

(56)   Optative: I wish I had a million dollars.
       I want to earn a million dollars.

(57)   Potential: I might earn a million dollars.
       I can/am able to earn a million dollars.

(58)   Hypothetical: Let's suppose that I had a million dollars ...
       Now if it were possible to earn a million dollars as a university professor ...

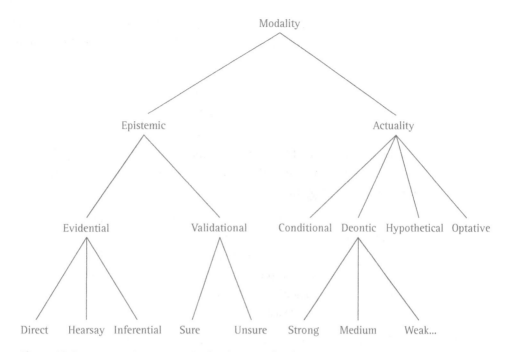

Figure 12.4 Conceptual categories in the domain of reality

> If you had eaten your cheerios as a child, you would be
> doing better in school today.

(59)   Conditional: If you eat your cheerios, you will be strong.
        If you come home before six, we can go to the movie.

EVIDENTIALITY has to do with how speakers let hearers know how they obtained the information expressed in a clause. It has been called "the linguistic coding of epistemology" (Chafe and Nichols 1986). People have different attitudes toward knowledge partially because they obtain knowledge from different sources. For example, I am more certain of things I have experienced directly or have reliable evidence for. I am less certain of things I have heard second-hand, or have ambiguous evidence for. In English, evidentiality is not grammaticalized. Rather it tends to be expressed periphrastically by clause combining (*it seems that . . . , they say that . . .*) or adverbial expressions (*purportedly, apparently,* etc.).

It should also be clear that evidentiality is closely tied to tense, aspect, and mode. We are more likely to be sure of past actions than future actions, the completion of perfective actions than of actions still in process, realis assertions than irrealis assertions.

In summary, Figure 12.4 illustrates the hierarchical relationships among the various modal notions mentioned in this section. The modal auxiliaries constitute one major way that these dimensions are communicated in English, though of course other communicative choices (such as the use of auxiliaries, articles, various construction types, etc.) also impinge on the semantic domain of modality.

Summary

In this chapter we have discussed three interrelated grammatical systems that anchor discourse world situations in terms of time and reality. Two such systems, tense and aspect, relate to the dimension of time, while the third, mode, relates to the dimension of reality.

- Tense – expression of the time of a situation in relation to a reference point, usually the time a clause is uttered (the present)
- Aspect – expression of the internal temporal "shape" of a situation
- Mode – expression of the speaker's "attitude" toward the information expressed in a clause, particularly the speaker's commitment to the situation's truth, likelihood, or necessity.

It is important to recognize that all of these systems are grammatical categorizations that relate to infinitely variable conceptual dimensions. In addition to the well-grammaticalized categories in the tense, aspect, and modal systems, fine nuances of temporal sequence, temporal shape, and modality can be expressed via adverbial elements and a variety of other lexical and constructional choices.

FURTHER READING

Comrie (1976, 1985) and Palmer (2001) are foundational works in the typology of aspect and tense and modality respectively. Binnick (2006) and the references cited therein discuss the form, meaning, and use of tense and aspect in Modern English. The studies in Facchinetti *et al.* (2003) provide broad perspectives on modality in English.

Exercises

1. The following examples from second language learners of English illustrate non-standard (or non-idiomatic) uses of Inflection. For each example, indicate whether the problem is in the domain of tense, aspect, or mode, and rewrite the example in a more natural way. The first example is done for you:

   a. Yesterday I meet my friend downtown.
      Tense: Yesterday I met my friend downtown.
      OR Tomorrow I meet my friend downtown.

b. That professor is often arriving late to class.

c. She doesn't be happy today.

d. Yesterday we could climb Mt. Seorok.

e. If I don't pass this test, my father must be angry.

f. Where did you found your keys?

g. I can see her now – she walks toward us.

h. I have gotten up and then ate breakfast.

2. Describe the probable difference in meaning and/or use, if any, between the following pairs of sentences (adapted from Radden and Dirven, 2007:199):

a. I see Jane. / I'm seeing Jane.

b. Melvin understands the problem. / Melvin is understanding the problem.

c. Constantine is foolish. / Constantine is being foolish.

d. Gonzaga reads French. / Gonzaga is reading French.

e. I felt threatened. / I was feeling threatened.

f. In just a few minutes, we'll sing the chorus. / In just a few minutes, we will be singing the chorus.

g. I will probably ask him to review that book. / I will probably be asking him to review that book.

3. Describe the probable difference in meaning and/or use between the following pairs of sentences:

a. I saw that film. / I have seen that film.

b. I appreciate Ken Russell films. / I have appreciated Ken Russell films.

c. They wandered through the desert. / They had wandered through the desert.

d. They wandered through the desert. / They have wandered through the desert.

e. At three o'clock they will play the national anthem. / At three o'clock they will have played the national anthem.

13 Voice and valence

It is a matter of perspective, Doctor.
Lt. Cmdr. Data, in *Star Trek: The Next Generation*

In Section 2.3 we discussed how speakers can present situations in different "argument structure frames." In Chapter 2, the emphasis was on the relationship between the meanings of individual verbs and the frames in which they may occur. Every verb evokes one or more idealized "scenes" in the discourse world, and conventionally occurs in a certain limited number of argument structure frames. Sometimes two or more verbs evoke essentially the same scene but differ in the set of frames in which they may couch the scene. Some pairs of verbs that vary according to the frames in which they present an event include *buy/sell, borrow/lend, comprise/consist of, own/belong, rob/steal,* and many more. In terms of communication, argument structure frames are ways speakers impart different perspectives on situations in the discourse world.

In this chapter we will discuss several grammatical means of accomplishing perspectivizing functions. Some such grammatical constructions are referred to as VOICES. For example, a typical ACTIVE VOICE construction is a frame in which an AGENT-like participant is the Subject of the clause and a PATIENT-like participant is the Object. The PASSIVE VOICE is a construction that realigns the AGENT and PATIENT roles, placing the PATIENT in the Subject position and the AGENT in an oblique role. This can be represented in terms of argument structure diagrams introduced in Chapter 6 as follows:

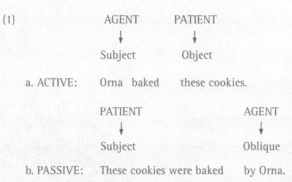

(1)
               AGENT   PATIENT
                 ↓   ↓
               Subject   Object

a. ACTIVE: Orna baked   these cookies.

               PATIENT   AGENT
                ↓   ↓
               Subject   Oblique

b. PASSIVE: These cookies were baked   by Orna.

In (1b), the passive voice is a grammatical means of adjusting the argument structure frame in which the verb *bake* is presented. The passive allows the speaker to present the event of baking in terms of what happened to the cookies, rather than what Orna did. In other words, in (1a) the AGENT is in primary perspective, while in (1b) the PATIENT is in primary perspective. It's all a matter of perspective.

13.1   Valence theory

In the following pages, we will use the concept of VALENCE to discuss several constructions that adjust the argument structure frame in which a discourse world situation is presented. These include constructions that traditionally fall under the heading of voice, though there are several valence-related constructions that are not normally considered voices. Nevertheless, because of their functional commonalities, it is convenient to group them together for analytic and expository purposes.

Valence in linguistics is always a number from one to three. It can be thought of as a semantic notion, a grammatical notion, or a combination of the two. Valence-adjusting constructions are morphosyntactic constructions that affect the *semantic* and/or the *grammatical* valence of a clause. SEMANTIC VALENCE refers to the number of participants in the discourse world scene conventionally evoked by a verb. For example, the verb *eat* in English has a semantic valence of two, since for any given event of eating there must be two participants – something that eats and something that gets eaten. If one of these is missing from the scene itself, then the scene does not describe an event of eating. Of course, more participants, such as a LOCATION or an INSTRUMENT, *may* be relevant to an eating event, but these participants do not define an eating event in the same way as an "eater" and an "eaten thing" do.

GRAMMATICAL VALENCE (or SYNTACTIC VALENCE) refers to the number of core arguments present in any given clause (see Section 7.2 for discussion of the term "argument"). The verb *eat* in English may occur in a clause with a grammatical valence of one or two depending on how the verb is used. In a clause like *Calvin already ate* there is no Direct Object, so the only core argument of the verb refers to the "eater." Nevertheless, in the scene expressed by this clause, it is understood that something got eaten. It's just that the identity of the eaten thing is not known or is unimportant for the communicative task at hand.

(2)   EVENT OF EATING (semantic valence = 2):   AGENT   PATIENT
                                                  ↓   ↓
                                               Subject   Ø
      (grammatical valence = 1):   Calvin already ate Ø.

Similarly, in a clause like *She ate away at the bone*, there is only one core argument of the verb. *Bone* is an Oblique, and therefore is not a core argument:

(3)   EVENT OF EATING (semantic valence = 2):   AGENT   PATIENT
                                                           ↓   ↓
                                                       Subject   Oblique
                    (grammatical valence = 1):   *She* ate away at the bone

Before we go any further, we need to discuss an important difference between the omission of a verbal argument and the use of a ZERO PRONOUN. In a clause like (2) above, there is arguably a "zero" (the absence of an expected noun or pronoun) following the verb *ate*. In (4) there is another kind of "zero" preceding the verb *grabbed*:

(4)   EVENT OF GRABBING (semantic valence = 2):   AGENT   PATIENT
                                                               ↓   ↓
         (grammatical valence = 2):   Subject   Object
                              Calvin came in and . . . *Ø* grabbed *Hobbes*.

In this example the zero preceding the verb *grabbed* refers to a specific participant that is mentioned in the previous clause. It is so obvious who that participant is that you would hardly ask *Who grabbed Hobbes?* after someone utters this sentence. Sometimes this kind of zero is called a ZERO PRONOUN, because it does the same kind of job as a regular pronoun – it mentions or refers to some discourse world participant. Therefore the second clause in example (4) still has a grammatical valence of 2, as well as expressing a situation that has a semantic valence of 2.

On the other hand, example (2) represents a valence-decreased construction (sometimes called "Object omission"). It has a grammatical valence of 1, while expressing a situation that has a semantic valence of 2. The zero after *ate* does not refer to any particular entity. You could very naturally ask *What did he eat?* after someone says *Calvin already ate*.

So there are at least two kinds of "zeros" – zero pronouns, which refer to participants on the discourse stage, and omitted arguments, which do not refer to anything. In many languages (notably East-Asian languages, including Chinese, Japanese, and Korean) zero pronouns (also referred to at times as "zero anaphora" or "pro-drop") are much more common than they are in English. Speakers of these languages often have difficulty deciding when to leave a pronoun out, and when to put one in when speaking and writing English. Therefore, it is important for English language professionals to be able to distinguish constructions with omitted arguments from those with zero-pronouns, and incorporate this distinction into their teaching and writing.

The notion of valence is closely connected with the traditional idea of TRANSITIVITY. Even as there is a distinction between semantic and grammatical valence, so there is a difference between semantic and grammatical transitivity – a semantically TRANSITIVE situation is a relation between two participants such that one participant acts toward or upon the other. A semantically INTRANSITIVE situation is a property, state, or other situation involving only one participant. A grammatically transitive clause, on the other hand is a construction in which there are at least two arguments. Again, semantic transitivity relates to situations in the discourse world, while grammatical transitivity refers to grammatical constructions.

Sometimes intransitive situations are called UNIVALENT, i.e., they have a semantic valence of one. Similarly, transitive situations such as *HE KILLED A BEAR* are called DIVALENT, because there are two participants – HE and A BEAR. TRIVALENT situations are those that involve three participants, e.g., *HE GAVE US THE GATE KEY*. Sometimes trivalent situations are perhaps confusingly called DITRANSITIVE or BITRANSITIVE. These terms are based on the fact that verbs like *give* can take two Objects – the given thing and the recipient. Valence is more general, however, looking at all the participants – not just those expressed as Objects. From this point of view there are potentially three core arguments, including the Subject, for a verb like *give* that expresses a trivalent situation.

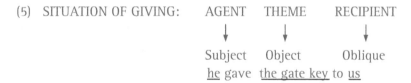

(5) SITUATION OF GIVING: AGENT   THEME   RECIPIENT

                                   ↓   ↓   ↓

                                 Subject   Object   Oblique
                                 <u>he</u> gave <u>the gate key</u> to <u>us</u>

Grammarians do not always distinguish semantic transitivity from grammatical transitivity consistently. So, for example, there are some who would say that *eat* is always a transitive verb – you don't have an event of "eating" if you don't have an "eater" and an "eaten thing." These grammarians use the term transitive in the sense of *semantically* transitive. Others would say *eat* is sometimes transitive and sometimes intransitive. These grammarians are most likely referring to *grammatical* transitivity. Still others would say that there are two related verbs *eat* in the lexicon of English, one of which is transitive and the other intransitive. In this book we are taking the perspective that grammatical valence (hence transitivity) is a property of constructions and not individual verbs. Individual verbs tend to evoke scenes that have a given number of participants (semantic valence), but speakers choose the argument structure frame in which to couch any verb according to the specific perspective they need to express.

Valence-related constructions can be categorized in terms of how they affect the presentation of the scene evoked by verbs. The communicative effect of increasing grammatical valence can be characterized most generally as bringing a participant that is normally not part of a scene, or on the margin of a scene onto "center stage." The effect of decreasing grammatical valence, on the other hand, is to downplay a normally center stage participant to marginal status, or eliminate it from the scene altogether. Furthermore, the participants brought onto or taken off of center stage can be controllers, i.e., AGENTs or AGENT-like participants, affected or PATIENT-like participants, or they may have any number of other peripheral roles, such as RECIPIENTS, INSTRUMENTS, or BENEFACTEES (see Chapter 6 on semantic roles).

With the metaphor of the "discourse stage" in mind, we can begin to sketch out a functional typology of valence adjusting constructions. Following this we will present a way of modeling the adjustments that argument structures may undergo.

13.2 A functional typology of valence-adjusting constructions

The highest level distinction in valence-adjusting constructions is between those that decrease valence and those that increase valence. Remember that valence is a number. A valence-decreasing construction takes a scene that requires two participants and presents it in a frame in which only one participant is in perspective $(2 \rightarrow 1)$, or it presents a scene with three participants in a frame with only two in perspective $(3 \rightarrow 2)$. On the other hand, valence-increasing constructions take a scene that has one or two participants, and present it in a frame in which two or three are in perspective $(1 \rightarrow 2, 2 \rightarrow 3)$. There are also valence-adjusting constructions that do not actually change the number of participants in perspective, but simply adjust the alignment between the semantic roles of the participants and the grammatical relations in the syntactic frame.

Within valence-decreasing constructions, there are constructions that reduce semantic valence by expressing the idea that the two semantic roles required in a semantically transitive scene are actually filled by the same discourse-world entity. These are called REFLEXIVES, RECIPROCALS, and MIDDLE CONSTRUCTIONS. Then there are constructions that reduce grammatical valence by "de-perspectivizing" or "downplaying" a controlling participant (an AGENT or Agent-like participant), and those that de-perspectivize or downplay an affected participant (a PATIENT or Patient-like participant).

Within valence-increasing constructions, English grammar provides ways of perspectivizing or "upgrading" a controlling participant, and ways of perspectivizing or upgrading a peripheral participant. Table 13.1 summarizes the constructions that we will be discussing according to how they affect the valence of a clause.

Table 13.1 **A functional typology of valence-adjusting constructions**

Valence-decreasing constructions:

Those that "combine" controlling and affected participants into a single participant:	REFLEXIVES RECIPROCALS MIDDLES
Those that downplay a controlling participant:	PASSIVES IMPERSONALS
Those that downplay an affected participant:	OBJECT OMISSION OBJECT DEMOTION OBJECT INCORPORATION

Valence-increasing constructions:

Those that add a controlling participant:	CAUSATIVES
Those that upgrade a peripheral participant:	DATIVE SHIFT

Consistent with the general typology of English, these jobs are accomplished either lexically or analytically. There are no productive morphological valence-adjusting constructions in Modern English. As mentioned in earlier chapters, this can be a challenge for second language learners who come from L1 backgrounds in which more communicative work is accomplished morphologically than it is in English.

13.3   Valence-decreasing constructions

Reflexives

A REFLEXIVE construction presents a two-participant scene in which both participants are the same entity, e.g., *She saw herself.* All true reflexive constructions reduce the semantic valence of a transitive scene by specifying that there are not two separate entities on stage. Rather, one entity both acts and is acted upon. With lexical reflexives, the reduction in semantic valence is reflected in a corresponding reduction in grammatical valence. The analytic reflexives do not reduce grammatical valence, as we will see below.

A LEXICAL REFLEXIVE[1] is one which is tied to the lexical meaning of a particular verb. For example, the verbs *dress*, *shave*, and a few others, when used intransitively imply that the AGENT and PATIENT are the same entity, e.g.:

(6)   Calvin shaved, washed, and dressed.

This sentence implies that Calvin shaved himself, washed himself, and dressed himself. If some other Object is intended, it must be explicitly mentioned, e.g.:

(7)   Calvin shaved Hobbes.

The argument structure of a lexical reflexive construction can be represented as follows:

(8)   AGENT = PATIENT

Subject
Calvin shaved. AGENT=Subject, PATIENT=Subject

The equals sign in this example indicates that the two semantic roles are filled by the same discourse world entity. The arrows indicate that the semantic roles of AGENT and PATIENT are both expressed by the only argument of this intransitive clause.

English also has ANALYTIC REFLEXIVES. These may also be referred to as SYNTACTIC or PERIPHRASTIC REFLEXIVES. Analytic reflexives are expressed by the REFLEXIVE PRONOUNS *myself, yourself, himself, herself, ourselves, yourselves, themselves,* and *itself* in an Object or Oblique role. For example:

(9)   AGENT = PATIENT
                                                      ↓   ↓
                                                  Subject   Object

Do you have any control over how creepy <u>you</u> allow *yourself* to get?

This is an analytic reflexive because reflexivity is expressed by a separate word that is distinct from the verb. From a purely syntactic point of view, the analytic reflexive construction of English is not a valence-decreasing construction. This is because there are still two syntactic arguments – *you* and *yourself.* We may want to say, however, that this clause is semantically intransitive because the two syntactic arguments refer to a single entity. This semantic identity is indicated by the equals sign in example (9).

Since English has two types of reflexive constructions, lexical and analytic reflexives, the question arises as to what difference in meaning is expressed by the two, when both are possible. This of course only occurs with verbs that are potentially lexically reflexive, principally the "grooming" verbs such as *shave, bathe, shower, wash up, undress,* and *dress.* Consider the following:

(10)   a.   So *he* shaved *himself* in a great hurry.
       b.   Next, *I* bathed *myself* with a soapy cloth in the appropriate hygienic order.
       c.   The photographer *had* dressed *himself* in clothes that were less foppish than his usual attire.

d. Wasn't that where some bakery foreman dressed *himself* up in a turban, …?
e. [He] dressed *himself* in period costume.
f. For posterity he had dressed *himself* in the imperial style of one hundred and ten years earlier.

All of these examples could have been expressed without the reflexive pronoun, since these are all lexically reflexive verbs. However, what all of these have in common is that they express some "special" act – not the simple "grooming" acts of *shaving, bathing,* or *dressing* that one might do on an everyday basis. For example, (10a) occurs in a limerick in which the Subject shaves his chest hair quickly in order to avoid being eaten by a bear. The normal lexical reflexive use of *shave* is to describe a man shaving his face as part of a regular daily routine. Shaving one's chest to avoid being eaten is certainly out of the ordinary! The other examples in (10) (indeed, all the clear examples occurring in the BNC) also describe "special" situations – bathing in appropriate hygienic order, dressing up in a turban, in period costume, imperial style, etc.

In most cases, reflexive pronouns indicate COREFERENCE between the performers of two discourse world roles – two roles filled by one entity. Usually one of these roles is the controller of the event and the other an affected participant of the same event. There are situations, however, when the coreferential participants fill roles in different events:

(11) a. Yanto watched the smoke from his cigarette drift lazily up the shaft of the sunbeam which bathed Molly and *himself* through a gap in the greenery above.
      b. You give me a sad opinion of *myself.*
      c. But a chemist, wondering how the rather fetching picture of *myself* (below) might be affected by being doused in nitric acid …

In example (11a), the reflexive pronoun *himself* refers to one of the affected participants in the event of bathing, but it indicates coreferentiality with the controller of the event of watching, namely Yanto. In (11b), the coreferent of *myself* is the affected participant of the main verb, rather than the controller. However, in an underlying or semantic sense, the sentence includes a state with the coreferent as the THEME: "I have a sad opinion of myself." In (11c), the referent of *myself* isn't even mentioned in the sentence at all. This is a relatively common use of the form *myself,* though it is considered non-standard in CSE. It seems to "work" functionally because in any conversation, the speaker is always highly topical, and hence available to be referred to with a reflexive pronoun. It is as though the whole sentence has an "underlying" preceding clause like: "I tell you that …" The form *myself* makes sense in (11c) because it signals coreferentiality with the controller of this abstract predicate of utterance.

Another extended use of reflexive pronouns is to indicate counterexpectation (12), or to emphasize the individuality of the referent of the reflexive pronoun (13):

(12)   Edsel washed the car *himself.*   (Rather than someone else.)

(13)   Mercedes washed the car all by *herself.* (No one helped her.)
       The car *itself* is worth $10,000.   (Not including the accessories.)
       Celica paid $10,000 for the car *itself.*   (Not including taxes, insurance, etc.)

RECIPROCAL constructions are very similar conceptually to reflexives. A prototypical reciprocal has a plural Subject, and indicates that the two or more Subject participants interact symmetrically, e.g., both are AGENT and PATIENT, both are EXPERIENCER and THEME, etc. For example, *they saw each other* is a reciprocal construction. Reciprocals are conceptually similar to reflexives in that both indicate that the controller and some other participant in the situation are coreferential (they refer to the same entity), though in a different way. There are still two distinct participants on stage, but both of them equally control and are affected by the situation.

LEXICAL RECIPROCALS are verbs for which reciprocity is a built-in component of their meaning. Some lexically reciprocal verbs in English are *kiss, meet,* and *shake hands with*; e.g., *Matilde and Mary met* usually means *Matilde and Mary met each other.* This can be diagrammed as follows. Notice that both *Matilde* and *Mary* refer to the AGENT and the PATIENT:

(14)   AGENT   PATIENT

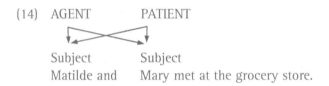

       Subject   Subject
       Matilde and   Mary met at the grocery store.

If some other situation is to be communicated, the Object must be explicitly mentioned, e.g., *Matilde and Mary met Grandma at the grocery store.* Notice that there is no equals sign between the roles of AGENT and PATIENT in the semantic structure of this scene. This is because there are still two distinct participants on stage. The four arrows, however, indicate that these two participants are both equally AGENT and PATIENT.

In English, there are analytic as well as lexical reciprocals. Analytic reciprocals use the special anaphoric expressions *each other* or *one another*:

(15)   They are helping *each other.*
       Byzantine and Fatimid vessels resemble *one another* in appearance.

As with reflexive pronouns, the reciprocal expressions can be used when any clause constituent is coreferential with the Subject of the clause:

(16) a. ... if <u>people</u> stayed away *from one another,*
      b. The way <u>fans</u> climbed *over one another* during the Fourth of July weekend ...
      c. ... the <u>Persian Gulf states</u> would not just cooperate *with one another,*
      d. [We] should not be judged simply by how <u>we</u> relate *to one another.*
      e. Four <u>tourists</u> took pictures *of one another*

In example (16a) the expression *one another* follows the preposition *from,* indicating that the participants who are the Subject are also Objects of the preposition with respect to one another. The same is true for the other examples in (16).

Sometimes it appears that the coreferential participants signaled by the reciprocal form are not the grammatical Subject of the clause. Consider the following examples:

(17) a. ... it is [the exclusive and permanent commitment of <u>the marriage partners</u> *to one another*] that is the sine qua non of civil marriage.
      b. ... he had to accept amendments limiting <u>the clubs</u> to two per ward, [not within 1,200 feet of *one another* ...]

In (17a), *the marriage partners* is not the Subject of the sentence, since it is preceded by the preposition *of.* However, the bracketed portion of this sentence is a nominalization of a clause in which *the marriage partners* are the Subject:

(18) <u>The marriage partners</u> are committed *to one another.*

Similarly, in (17b) *the clubs* seems to be the Object of the participial relative clause modifying *amendments.* However, again in the semantic structure of the bracketed phrase, *the clubs* may be considered a kind of Subject:

(19) <u>The clubs</u> are not within 1,200 feet *of one another.*

Thus the reciprocal form indicates coreferentiality of the Subject participants according to an "underlying" or semantic level rather than directly to surface grammatical relations.

Middle constructions

The term MIDDLE construction or MIDDLE VOICE has been used in a variety of ways in the linguistics literature. What all such constructions have in common is that they involve a reduction in valence. The motivation for the term is that these constructions are neither passive nor active – they are in between, or "middle." We will consider a middle construction to be one that expresses a semantically transitive situation in terms of a process undergone by a PATIENT, rather than as an action carried out by a distinct AGENT.

As with reflexives and reciprocals, English has certain verbs that can be considered to be LEXICAL MIDDLE verbs. Sometimes verbs of this class are called LABILE VERBS (Haspelmath 1993). For examples, used transitively, *change* expresses an AGENT as the Subject and a PATIENT as the Object. When used intransitively, however, the PATIENT rather than the AGENT is the Subject, and the situation is expressed as a process rather than as an action. The AGENT may not be expressed as part of a middle construction:

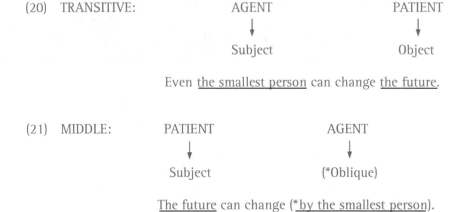

(20) TRANSITIVE: AGENT   PATIENT
                                        ↓   ↓
                                     Subject   Object

Even <u>the smallest person</u> can change <u>the future</u>.

(21) MIDDLE: PATIENT   AGENT
                        ↓   ↓
                     Subject   (*Oblique)

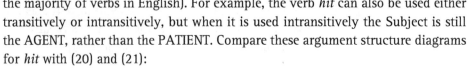

<u>The future</u> can change (*<u>by the smallest person</u>).

This property distinguishes verbs like *change* (including *break*, *grow*, *melt*, and many others) from other verbs that can be either transitive or intransitive (probably the majority of verbs in English). For example, the verb *hit* can also be used either transitively or intransitively, but when it is used intransitively the Subject is still the AGENT, rather than the PATIENT. Compare these argument structure diagrams for *hit* with (20) and (21):

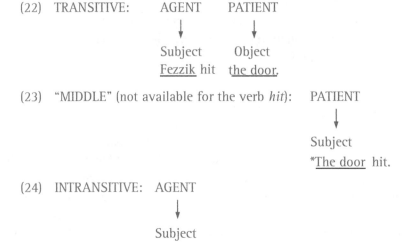

(22) TRANSITIVE: AGENT   PATIENT
                        ↓   ↓
                     Subject   Object
                     <u>Fezzik</u> hit <u>the door</u>.

(23) "MIDDLE" (not available for the verb *hit*):   PATIENT
                                                         ↓
                                                      Subject
                                                      *<u>The door</u> hit.

(24) INTRANSITIVE: AGENT
                        ↓
                     Subject
                     <u>Fezzik</u> hit.

English also employs an analytic (or periphrastic) middle construction, though it is not all that common. Almost any transitive verb that can reasonably be modified with a manner adverbial can be used in a middle construction, if an adverb or prepositional phrase expressing the manner follows:

(25) a. This soup eats *like a meal.*
      b. These trousers wear *well.*
      c. That old Volvo of his drove *like a tank.*
      d. Vygotsky's books read *easily.*

These are *analytic* middle constructions because separate words – the manner adverbial element, italicized in these examples – must be present for this construction to be grammatical (c.f. *this soup eats, *his Volvo drove*, etc.).

There is significant functional similarity between middle constructions and passives (discussed in more detail below). The only functional difference is that a passive treats the situation as an action carried out by an AGENT but with the identity of the AGENT downplayed. A prototypical middle construction, on the other hand, treats the situation as a process, i.e., it ignores the role of the AGENT entirely. Notice that the Subject in the examples in (25) is the participant that undergoes the action expressed by the verb. However, these cannot be passives, because the AGENT may not be expressed in a "*by* phrase" (e.g., *This soup eats like a meal by children*). Any causal action on the part of a distinct AGENT is not part of the scene evoked by middle constructions.

Passives

A prototypical PASSIVE construction is characterized both in terms of its morphosyntactic form and its discourse function. Morphosyntactically, a prototypical passive is a semantically transitive (two participant) construction which has the following three properties:

- The AGENT (or most AGENT-like participant) is either omitted (*not* zero-pronominalized, see above) or demoted to an Oblique role.
- The other core argument (the Object) becomes the Subject of the clause.
- The verb becomes intransitive.

In terms of communicative function, a prototypical passive is used in contexts where a controller is deperspectivized, or downplayed. In the following paragraphs we will first discuss prototypical passives, sometimes called "personal passives." Then we will briefly discuss some less prototypical constructions whose functions overlap considerably with passives. These are sometimes called IMPERSONAL constructions.

PERSONAL PASSIVES are constructions for which some specific AGENT is strongly implied, but either is not expressed, or is expressed in an oblique role. Personal passives in English are all analytic. In English passives, an auxiliary (*be* or *get*) plus the past participle of the active verb must be used:

(26) TRANSITIVE:

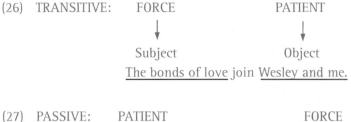

(27) PASSIVE: PATIENT   FORCE

Subject   Oblique

Wesley and I are joined (by the bonds of love).

Example (27) is an analytic passive because it requires the presence of a distinct word – the auxiliary *be* (of which *are* is one form). It is also somewhat morphological in that the verb, *join*, occurs in the past participle form.

English also has a common passive that employs the verb *get* as the auxiliary:

(28) a. I *got* well paid for it on both occasions.
      b. We are *getting* bogged down by this textbook.
      c. *Get* paid more interest by First National Bank!

Get passives imply that the PATIENT retains some degree of control over the event. This is evidenced by the fact that a *get* passive can be used in the imperative (28c). *Be* passives, on the other hand, cannot easily be used in the imperative. This is obviously due to the pragmatic fact that you can't command someone to do something they have no control over:

(29) a. ??*Be* well paid!
      b. ??*Be* bogged down by this textbook!

Like personal passives, IMPERSONAL CONSTRUCTIONS deperspectivize an AGENT-like participant. However, in impersonals, the downplayed AGENT is not a specific individual. It is usually a non-identifiable, unknown and/or vague entity. Impersonal passives can be formed from semantically intransitive as well as transitive verbs. The following examples of impersonal constructions are based on other clause patterns, namely an ordinary active verb with a third person plural Subject for (30a) and an existential construction in (30b):

(30) a. *They* say it can puncture the skin of a rhino.
      b. *There* will be dancing in the streets.

Object demotion and omission

While passive and impersonal constructions decrease valence by deperspectiviz-
ing a controlling participant, OBJECT DEMOTION and OBJECT OMISSION are valence
decreasing constructions that deperspectivize an affected, or PATIENT-like, participant. Because these constructions are the functional "mirror image" of a passive
construction, some linguists refer to these as "antipassives" (Heath 1976).[2] Here is a
simple example of a transitive clause, and a corresponding Object demotion and
Object omission construction:

(31) TRANSITIVE: The hunter shot the deer.

(32) OBJECT DEMOTION: The hunter shot at the deer.

(33) OBJECT OMISSION: The hunter shot.

The English Object demotion construction tends to express a situation in which a
PATIENT-like participant is less involved or less affected by the action of the verb
than in the transitive construction. Similarly, Object omission suggests that the
identity of the PATIENT-like participant, if any, is totally irrelevant.

Object incorporation

Noun incorporation is any construction in which a nominal (noun-like) element of a
clause becomes "attached to" or "incorporated into" the verb. Nouns of pretty much
any semantic role and grammatical relation can participate in incorporation constructions, but OBJECT INCORPORATION (incorporation of the Object of a verb) is the
only one that occurs with a wide range of verb and noun combinations, and which
qualifies as a valence decreasing construction. All noun incorporation constructions
in English exhibit the characteristics of compounding in general, namely: (1) a stress
pattern characteristic of words rather than phrases, (2) unusual word order, (3)
morphophonemic patterns characteristic of words rather than phrases, and (4)
meanings that may be more specific than the meanings of the individual parts.

In English both Subject and Object incorporation may occur, but neither is fully
productive, with Subject incorporation being very marginal (in these examples the
abbreviation "Incorp" refers to an incorporated element that has lost its status as an
independent verbal argument):

(34) OBJECT INCORPORATION: AGENT   PATIENT
                                 ↓   ↓
                              Subject   Incorp
                              We went trout fishing.
                              (From: *We fished (for) trout.*)

(35)   SUBJECT INCORPORATION: PATIENT   AGENT

                                    ↓   ↓

                              Subject   Incorp
                          This medicine   is   FDA approved.

                          (From: *The FDA approved this medicine.*)

The reason that these examples are called "Object" and "Subject" incorporation is that the incorporated element is the Object and Subject respectively of the transitive clauses that "underlie" these incorporated structures. These are given in parentheses following the examples.

Evidence that the incorporated element in each of these examples is not an independent argument of the verb includes the fact that they have none of the properties of independent noun phrases. For example, they cannot take plural marking, Determiners, etc. (36a, b, c). Also, incorporated Objects may not be promoted to Subject status in a passive (36d):

(36)   a.   *We went the trout fishing.
       b.   *We went trouts fishing.
       c.   *This medicine is the FDA approved.
       d.   *Trout was gone fishing by us.

Incorporated forms in English are either lexicalized expressions such as *baby sit*, or they are severely restricted with respect to their syntactic possibilities; e.g., *to trout fish* as a verb may only appear in the special progressive form with *go* illustrated in (34). Similarly, *to FDA approve* only seems to appear in the passive (cf. example (35)):

(37)   *We trout fished all morning.
       *They FDA approved this medicine.

Many examples of noun incorporation have become fixed compounds that can be used in all five forms that ordinary verbs occur in:

(38)   a.   I'd love to *go ice skating.*   We *ice skated* all morning.
       b.   At least I'm *going Christmas shopping* tomorrow.   We *Christmas shopped* all day.
       c.   we were going to Nantes to *go sight seeing* and shopping.   We love *to sight see.*

However, Object incorporation appears to be about the only kind of noun incorporation that is at all productive, i.e., that can occur with a wide variety of verb+noun combinations. I'll end this section with an interesting example of incorporation from a university accounting department memo:

(39)   Please settle this account immediately or you will *be pay deducted.*

13.4   Valence-increasing constructions

In addition to the several valence-decreasing constructions discussed above, English has two constructions which fall into the category of valence-increasing constructions. These are causatives and dative shift.

Causatives

CAUSATIVE CONSTRUCTIONS are very common in the world's languages. Prototypical examples express a simple event or situation with the addition of a causer, i.e., an AGENT that is external to the situation itself. By "external" I mean the AGENT of a causative is not an essential part of the caused event. The event can be fully described even with no mention of the causal AGENT. For example, consider the following clause:

(40)   Calvin broke the vase.

This is a kind of causative because the AGENT (Calvin) is the causer of an event of breaking, yet the event would still be complete if the AGENT were not present on the scene:

(41)   The vase broke.

     Now consider the following:

(42)   Cortez ate possum.

This clause expresses an event that has an AGENT (Cortez). However, this clause would not adequately describe an event of eating if the AGENT were left out. You don't have an event of "eating" if you don't have an eater! So (42) is not a causative – Cortez did not cause the possum to eat. We can make a causative out of (42) by adding a separate verb that expresses the idea of cause:

(43)   Montezuma made Cortez eat possum.

This is a causative because it takes the event expressed in (42) and adds an external causer, Montezuma.

     The parts of a causative construction are:

- The effect: *ate possum* in example (43).
- The cause: *made (something happen)* in example (43).
- The causee (or AGENT of effect): *Cortez* in example (43).
- The causer (or AGENT of cause): *Montezuma* in example (43).

Causatives in English are either lexical or analytic. All causatives increase semantic valence by adding a new participant (the causer) to the scene evoked by the verb. Lexical causatives also increase grammatical valence, in that they add one argument (a Subject) to the argument structure frame in which the verb appears. In the following paragraphs we will give examples and argument structure diagrams of all three types.

Lexical causatives

Each of the three subtypes of lexical expression discussed in Section 3.5 are employed to express causation in English. The three types are:

- **(Strong) suppletion (completely distinct verbs)**
  non-causative: *Inigo's father died.*
  causative: *You killed Inigo's father.*
  also: *see/show, learn/teach, eat/feed*, etc.
- **Weak suppletion (some idiosyncratic difference between verbs)**
  non-causative: *The tree fell.* (verb = 'to fall')
  causative: *Bunyan felled the tree.* (verb = 'to fell')
  also: *rise/raise, lie/lay, sit/set*, and possibly others.
- **Isomorphism (no difference between non-causative and causative verb)**
  non-causative: *The vase broke.*
  causative: *Calvin broke the vase.* (i.e., Calvin caused the vase to break)

Notice that lexical causatives can be considered the "mirror image" of lexical middle constructions (see Section 3.2). For this reason, middle constructions are sometimes called "anticausatives." With "labile" verbs like *break*, *change*, move, and *stop* the question of whether the intransitive construction is a middle, or the transitive construction is a causative, rests on whether one believes the "basic" form is transitive or intransitive. What do you think? Is there any objective way of deciding which of the two forms of each of these verbs is the "basic" or "underlying" form, and which one is the "valence-adjusted" version?

(44)		Transitive (causative?)	Intransitive (middle?)
	break	Waldo *broke* the bottle.	The bottle *broke* against the wall.
	change	The mayor *changed* the city.	The city *changed*.
	move	The cowboy *moved* the herd.	The herd *moved* to greener pastures.
	stop	Millicent *stopped* her car.	The car suddenly *stopped*.

In fact it is not particularly useful to declare which frame is "basic" to these verbs. As discussed in earlier chapters, principally Chapter 3 on the lexicon, individual forms do not necessarily belong to basic or inherent word classes or subclasses. Rather, they evoke certain semantic features, but acquire many of their structural and semantic characteristics in constructions. Sometimes the semantic features a form evokes make it much more likely that speakers will use it in a particular kind of a frame. In such cases, e.g., verbs like *grow*, *melt*, and *explode*, we may be tempted to assign them a "basic" frame (intransitive in these cases), but still this is a judgment call, and doesn't really help very much in understanding English grammar. These verbs also may occur in transitive frames if it suits the speaker's needs.

Analytic causatives

Many causatives in English are analytic in that they involve a separate causative verb, e.g., *make, cause, force, compel*, etc.

(45) He *made* me do it.
      Gloucester *caused* Aileron to die.
      Melinda *forced* her hairdresser to relinquish his position.
      Marie *compelled* Taroo to dance with her.

In most cases analytic causatives consist of a MATRIX VERB expressing the notion of CAUSE whose Complement (see Chapter 14 on clause combining) refers to the caused event. They are not normally considered to be valence-increasing constructions, because they do not increase the grammatical valence of a single clause. Rather, they accomplish the task of adding a controlling AGENT by adding a verb (the matrix verb) that contributes its own arguments to the valence of the whole construction. Therefore you may say that analytic causatives increase the semantic valence of a scene, but not the grammatical valence of an individual clause.

Dative shift

Trivalent situations usually involve an AGENT, a THEME (an item that moves, physically or metaphorically, from one place to another), and a RECIPIENT. English verbs that often express trivalent propositions include *show*, *give*, *tell*, *offer*, and *send*, though many other verbs can be used in a trivalent frame (see, e.g., Goldberg 1995). In an English trivalent construction the RECIPIENT occurs sometimes as a Complement of the preposition *to* or *for*, and sometimes with no preposition. The construction in which the RECIPIENT does not take a preposition is sometimes termed the DATIVE SHIFT construction. There are many ways that different grammar books describe this phenomenon, including "dative alternation" or "dative advancement." The examples in (46) illustrate the basic dative shift constructions:

(46)   "to" construction: a.   Ugarte gave the exit visas *to Rick* for safe keeping.
       Dative shift: b.   Ugarte gave *Rick* the exit visas for safe keeping.
       "for" construction: c.   My main concern is to find a proper place *for the child.*
       Dative shift: d.   My main concern is to find *the child* a proper place.

When the preposition in the prepositional construction is *to*, the semantic role of the Complement is limited to RECIPIENT, either directly or metaphorically. If the preposition *for* is used, the Complement can also be a BENEFACTEE. However, not every BENEFACTEE can undergo dative shift; only BENEFACTEEs that are also RECIPIENTS qualify:

(47)   a.   She mowed the lawn for *me.*
       b.   *She mowed *me* the lawn.

In example (47a), the pronoun *me* is the Complement of the preposition *for*, signaling that the mowing of the lawn was done for the benefit of the speaker, not that the lawn was physically transferred to the speaker. Thus *me* refers to a BENEFACTEE but not a RECIPIENT. In this case, dative shift is not allowed, as (47b) shows. In (46c), however, *for* indicates, in addition to the fact that the child will benefit from the speaker's finding a proper place, that the place will then "belong to" the child. In other words, the child is the RECIPIENT of the proper place, and not just the BENEFACTEE of the act of "finding" a proper place.

Similarly, if the Complement of the preposition *to* is an inanimate GOAL or endpoint rather than an animate (usually human) RECIPIENT, dative shift is much less likely:

(48)   a.   She sent the package to France.
       b.   ??She sent France the package.

Examples such as (48b) are reasonable if *France* is understood metaphorically from the context to refer to a person or group of people who are RECIPIENTS of the package, e.g., the branch office of a company located in France. But if France is just the place where the package was sent, then dative shift is very odd.

The THEME in a dative shift construction can be a concrete moving object, e.g., *the exit visas* in example (46b), or it can be an abstract idea such as a speech act, a visual impression, or an activity:

(49)   a.   They were *telling you a lie* earlier on.   THEME = *a lie*
       b.   *Show me your books.*   THEME = (a view of) *your books*
       c.   *Give him a kick* in the pants.   THEME = *a kick*

Examples (47) through (49) show that the semantic role of RECIPIENT is a crucial prerequisite to dative shift construction. (49) additionally shows that the RECIPIENT can metaphorically "receive" an abstract concept such as a speech act (*a lie* in (49a)), a visual impression (49b), or a nominalized activity (49c).

Dative shift can be considered a valence-increasing construction because it is a means of bringing a participant with a peripheral semantic role, e.g., RECIPIENT, onto center stage by making it into an Object of the verb. It presents a major problem for second language learners of English for several reasons.

First, trivalent constructions are actually very useful and common in everyday speech – they are impossible to avoid. Yet there are subtle differences in meaning between using a preposition and a dative shift construction to express a trivalent situation. Sometimes the difference is between "caused motion" and "caused possession":

(50) a. Orual threw the discus to Psyche.
      b. Orual threw Psyche the discus.

According to Goldberg (1995), these clauses do not mean the same thing. Example (50a) can be paraphrased as "Orual caused the discus to move along a path in the direction of Psyche" (caused motion), whereas (50b) can be paraphrased as "Orual caused Psyche to have the discus by throwing" (caused possession). It does seem to be the case that in (50a) Psyche may or may not actually receive the discus – all the speaker asserts is that Orual threw the discus with the intent that it reach Psyche. In (50b), on the other hand, Psyche definitely ends up with the discus. This is similar to the distinction between other argument structure alternations in which a Direct Object alternates with an Oblique participant (see, e.g., the difference between (31) and (32) above). There is a general iconic tendency for Direct Objects to be more completely, directly, or confidently affected by the action of the verb than Complements of prepositions.

In terms of the "discourse stage" metaphor that we are using in this chapter, in example (50a) Orual and the discus are "on center stage" – the assertion primarily describes what Orual did with the discus. In Example (50b), on the other hand, Orual and Psyche are in perspective – the assertion is primarily about what Orual did to Psyche.

The second reason dative shift constructions pose a problem for second language learners is that some trivalent situations can be expressed in both constructions, while others cannot. Consider the following:

(51) a. You do not have to <u>give</u> one of your boyfriends *to Daphne*.
      b. You do not have to <u>give</u> *Daphne* one of your boyfriends.
      c. You do not have to <u>donate</u> one of your boyfriends *to Daphne*.
      d. *You do not have to <u>donate</u> *Daphne* one of your boyfriends.

Even though the scenes evoked by the verbs *give* and *donate* are very similar, *give* allows dative shift (51b), while *donate* does not (51d).

A "rule of thumb" suggested by many grammar teachers is that one-syllable verbs allow dative shift, while multisyllable verbs do not. Surprisingly, this rule of thumb works fairly well most of the time. The following is a short list of verbs that occur in trivalent constructions. I have tried to put verbs that evoke similar scenes beside one another in these columns:

(52)

Allow dative shift:	Do not seem to allow dative shift:
give her the money	donate *her the money
hand them the pamphlets	distribute *them the pamphlets
tell me a story	recount *me a story
tell me the solution	explain *?me the solution
tell me your idea	express *me your idea
show them your answer	demonstrate *them your answer
	reveal *them your answer
	expose *them your answer
	project *them your answer
buy her a birthday cake	purchase ?her a birthday cake
get me a new car	obtain *me a new car
	acquire *me a new car
lend the College some money	contribute *the College some money
find yourself a new job	discover *yourself a new job
make me a sandwich	assemble *me a sandwich
build them a new home	construct *them a new home
fling me the ball	catapult *me the ball
toss me the ball	propel *me the ball
hurl me the ball	etc.
bowl me the ball	
pitch me the ball	
heave me the ball	
lob me the ball	
fetch me the ball	
roll me the ball	
shoot me the ball	
sling me the ball	
push me the ball	
kick me the ball	

While grammaticality judgments vary somewhat with some of these verbs, there is a clear and strong correlation between the number of syllables in a verb and its ability to occur in a dative shift construction, though there are exceptions. The "real" story is that verbs that allow dative shift are all of Anglo-Saxon origin, and those that don't are all of Latin origin – it just so happens that most Anglo-Saxon verbs have only one syllable, and Latinate verbs tend to be multisyllabic. The reason for this, briefly, is that Old English (Anglo-Saxon) had a distinct dative case form for nouns that expressed RECIPIENTS (53a). Norman French, on the other hand, expressed RECIPIENTS with a preposition (53b), and no special dative case form:

(53)   **Old English**
   a.   Ġif   *ðǽm*   *cyninge*   his   sweord.   'Give the king his sword.'
         give the.DAT king.DAT 3SG.GEN sword
   b.   French
         Donnez   *au*   *roi*   son   épée.   'Give (to) the king his sword.'
         give   to.the king   3SG.GEN sword

So, for a long time the RECIPIENT of a trivalent situation would appear with a preposition when the verb was in French, and without a preposition when the verb was in English. In the Middle English period, the dative case merged with the accusative. By this time, people were used to expressing RECIPIENTS in a prepositional phrase, so a preposition (*to* or *for*) began to substitute for the lost dative case endings. However, people were still in the habit of using English verbs, like *give*, with no preposition marking the RECIPIENT. Thus there arose two possible argument structures for verbs that derived from Old English, while French verbs continued to occur only in the frame in which the RECIPIENT was expressed with a preposition.

   In addition to the fact that many verbs simply do not allow dative shift, for other verbs some situations seem to *require* dative shift. For example, if there is direct physical contact between the AGENT and the RECIPIENT, dative shift is much more natural than the prepositional alternative:

(54)   Orual gave Psyche a bath.
         ?Orual gave a bath to Psyche.
         Orual gave Bardia a kiss.
         ?Orual gave a kiss to Bardia.

Furthermore, if the THEME is an abstract condition, dative shift is preferred:

(55)   Orual gave Psyche a sense of dread.
         ?Orual gave a sense of dread to Psyche.
         Orual gave Psyche the flu.
         ?Orual gave the flu to Psyche.
         Orual gave Psyche an idea.
         ?Orual gave an idea to Psyche.

Many traditional grammars use the term "Indirect Object" for the RECIPIENT in both the prepositional construction and the dative shift construction. This is a bit misleading, as the term Indirect Object sounds like a grammatical relation, and there can be no doubt that the RECIPIENT in a prepositional construction has a different grammatical relation to the verb than the RECIPIENT in a dative shift construction. This can be expressed in argument structure diagrams as follows:

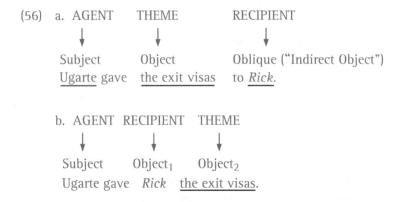

(56) a. AGENT   THEME   RECIPIENT

Subject   Object   Oblique ("Indirect Object")
Ugarte gave   the exit visas   to *Rick*.

b. AGENT RECIPIENT THEME

Subject   Object₁   Object₂
Ugarte gave   *Rick*   the exit visas.

In the prepositional construction (56a) the RECIPIENT, *Rick*, comes at the end of the clause, and is preceded by a preposition – exactly the grammatical properties of Oblique roles. In the dative shift construction (56b), the RECIPIENT comes right after the verb, and takes no preposition – exactly the overt grammatical properties of Direct Objects. Because of these distinct *grammatical* properties we must say that *Rick* in these two constructions occurs in two different *grammatical* relations. It is the semantic role, RECIPIENT, that remains the same. Therefore, the traditional notion of Indirect Object, which would be applied to *Rick* in both constructions, must refer to the semantic role of RECIPIENT, rather than to any coherent grammatical relation. While there are grammatical differences between the first Object in dative shift constructions (Object₁) and other Direct Objects (see, e.g., Huddleston and Pullum 2002:249–50), these differences are very minor compared to the grammatical differences between the expression of *Rick* in (56a) and (56b). Such subtle grammatical differences can for the most part be explained by the fact that Object₁ has the semantic role of RECIPIENT, and Object₂ has the semantic role of THEME or PATIENT.

It is important to remember that semantic roles are roles that participants play in discourse world situations, while grammatical relations are relations between words in linguistic structures. It is not at all unusual, of course, for participants that fill particular semantic roles to be expressed in different grammatical relations depending on the construction. In fact, that is the main function of voice and valence constructions – to adjust the "alignment" between semantic roles and grammatical relations in order to express different "perspectives" on discourse world scenes. Consider again the active/passive voice alternation. In the scene described by the active construction *Orna baked these cookies* the person Orna has the semantic role of AGENT. In the construction, the word *Orna* has the grammatical relation of Subject. In the passive voice construction *These cookies were baked by Orna*, Orna is still presented as the AGENT in the scene, but the word *Orna* has been "demoted" to a different grammatical relation – an Oblique. We know this because *Orna* appears after the verb, and is preceded by a preposition. Something similar happens in the dative shift construction illustrated in (56). The person Rick is presented as the RECIPIENT in the scenes described in (56a) and (56b), but the word *Rick* has the grammatical relation of Oblique in (56a) and Object in (56b).

Summary

In this chapter we discussed the notion of valence as a way of describing a "family" of grammatical constructions that adjust the argument structure frames within which scenes may be communicated. These constructions allow English speakers to impart different "perspectives" on discourse world situations.

Valence in linguistics is always a number from one to three, and can be characterized in terms of meaning or form. Semantic valence (meaning) refers to the number of central participants in a discourse world scene. Grammatical valence (form) refers to the number of core arguments in linguistic expressions of those scenes.

The different valence-adjusting grammatical constructions available in English were described in terms of the following hierarchy.

- Valence-decreasing constructions
  - constructions that grammatically "combine" a controller and an affected participant
    - reflexive constructions
    - reciprocal constructions
    - middle constructions
  - Constructions that "downplay" or omit a controlling participant
    - passive voice constructions
    - impersonal constructions
  - constructions that grammatically "downplay" or omit an affected participant
    - Object omission
    - Object demotion
    - Object incorporation
- Valence-increasing constructions
  - those that add a controlling participant
    - causatives
  - those that upgrade a peripheral participant to center stage
    - dative shift

FURTHER READING

Tesnière (1959) first applied the concept of valence (from chemistry) to linguistic structures. Foundational work on voice and valence from a cross-language functional perspective include the articles in Shibatani (1988) and Dixon and Aikhenvald (2000). Wanner (2009) presents a corpus-based analysis of the form and function of the passive voice construction in English.

Exercises

1. Valence-decreasing constructions
    Each of the following pairs of English clauses contains an intransitive clause (a) which may or may not be construed as a valence-decreased version of the other clause (a') in the pair. Your tasks are:
    A. Indicate which valence-decreasing construction, as discussed in this chapter, is represented by the first member of the pair.
    B. Indicate whether the first member of the pair can be construed as a valence-decreased version of the second member or not ("Yes" or "no" are fine answers).
    C. Indicate the kind of expression involved in the first construction (lexical, morphological, or syntactic/analytic). Occasionally more than one kind of strategy is used. Indicate at least the main strategy.

    a. This hammer broke.   A: Middle
    a'. This hammer broke the window.   B: No
                                                  C: Lexical

    b. Daisy got hit by that taxi.   A:
    b'. That taxi hit Daisy.   B:
                                                  C:

    c. The granola burned quickly.   A:
    c'. Wesley burned the granola.   B:
                                                  C:

    d. Wesley and Buttercup kicked.   A:
    d'. Wesley and Buttercup kicked each other.   B:
                                                  C:

    e. Buttercup and Wesley hugged.   A:
    e'. Buttercup and Wesley hugged themselves.   B:
                                                  C:

    f. We went impala hunting.   A:
    f'. We hunted impala.   B:
                                                  C:

    g. The students were finished.   A:
    g'. The students finished the assignment.   B:
                                                  C:

2. **Valence-increasing constructions**

   Each of the following pairs of English clauses contains one clause (a) which may or may not be construed a "valence-increased" version of the other clause (a') in the pair. Your tasks are:

   A.   Indicate which valence-increasing construction, as discussed in this chapter, is represented by the first example of each pair.

   B.   Indicate whether the first example could normally constitute a description of the same scene as the second example ("Yes" or "no" are fine answers for part B).

a.	Rick gave Ugarte the exit visas.	A: Dative shift
a'.	Rick gave the exit visas to Ugarte.	B: Yes
b.	Rembaldi fed Sydney piroshki.	A:
b'.	Sydney ate piroshki.	B:
c.	Sydney's mother made her write a letter.	A:
c'.	Sydney wrote a letter to her mother.	B:
d.	Sydney made her mother a bed.	A:
d'.	Sydney made her mother's bed.	B:
e.	Igor slowly opened the casket.	A:
e'.	The casket slowly opened.	B:
f.	Jack made Sydney become a spy.	A:
f'.	Jack made a spy out of Sydney.	B:

14 | Clause combining

Language is wine upon the lips.
  Virginia Woolf

Every language provides ways of combining basic clauses to form more complex structures. Most of the constructions described in this chapter involve combinations of two or more clauses – one INDEPENDENT clause and one or more DEPENDENT clauses. An independent clause is one that is fully Inflected and capable of being used in discourse on its own. A dependent clause is one that depends on some other clause for at least part of its Inflectional information. For example, (1a) below is an independent clause, while (1b) is dependent. We only know who locked the door and when it was locked because the Subject and tense are expressed in clause (a):

(1) a. Oddmund came in,   Independent clause
    b. locking the door behind him.   Dependent clause

In example (2), on the other hand, each clause has its own Subject (*he* in both clauses) and is inflected for past tense:

(2) a. After he came in,   Dependent clause
    b. he locked the door.   Independent clause

We still say that (2a) is dependent because the SUBORDINATOR *after* makes it difficult to use this clause to express a complete thought on its own. Logicians would say that clause (2a) expresses a PRESUPPOSITION and not an independent ASSERTION. If someone just walks up to you and says *After he came in*, it sounds like you, the hearer, should already know that he came in, and the speaker is using that known (presupposed) fact to set the stage for some newsworthy assertion about to be made. So clauses can be dependent either because they depend on some other clause for some or all of their Inflectional information (Subject, tense, aspect, mode), or because they express presupposed information, and therefore do not add anything new to the discourse scene.

In this chapter we will discuss several construction types that involve combinations of verbs or combinations of clauses. First we will discuss a couple of constructions that consist of verbs combined into one clause. These are important, but carry relatively little functional "weight" in the toolbox known as English grammar. Later, we will discuss a structural typology of dependent clauses. There are seven clause types in English that function in dependent roles. Consistent with the perspective taken throughout this book, we will discuss the forms of these clauses (what they *are*) independently of how they are deployed in communication (what people *do* with them).

14.1   Monoclausal verb combinations

Verb–verb compounds

In Chapter 3 we discussed compounding as a morphological process. Occasionally two verb roots are combined to form one stem. The resulting compound has all the characteristics we expect compounds to have (intonation characteristic of a single word, and a meaning that is not the simple sum of the two compounded roots), yet expresses one multifaceted event:

(3)   Heat the butter and *stir fry* the courgettes, red peppers, sweetcorn and garlic . . .
       He's calling for a change in direction to *kick start* the economy.
       Skiing is just like windsurfing, except the water's been *freeze dried*, spread around a mountain side and bashed into submission.

In some sense verb–verb compounding is the "tightest" form of clause combining, since two verbs are merged into one unit. In each of these compounds the first part, *stir*, *kick*, and *freeze* can be thought of as describing a manner in which the second part is carried out. In other words *stir frying* is a kind of frying accomplished by stirring, *kick starting* means starting something by "kicking," etc.

However, it is clear that all of these examples are MONOCLAUSAL, i.e., they constitute one clause with a single compound verb, rather than two clauses in combination. The evidence for this includes:

• Both verbs have to have the same Subject and Object.
• Both verbs are understood to have the same tense, aspect, and modal qualities.
• Only one negation is needed to negate both verbs – it is impossible to negate one without negating the other.
• The whole construction has an intonation contour characteristic of single clauses, and not multiclause constructions.

- The compound functions like a single verb in passive voice: *These vegetables have been stir fried.*
- Elements can be extracted from the very end of the clause to the very beginning: *It was the vegetables that they stir fried.*

Serial verbs

English also has a rather marginal serial verb construction. This is a construction that involves one or more verbs of motion, followed immediately by another verb. This is most common in imperatives, such as the following:

(4)   *Come see* me on Tuesday.
        Run go get your mother a newspaper.
        Go play on the freeway!

Some speakers find these marginal, but they are well attested in both the BNC and the COCA. Serial verbs can also occur in other constructions where a bare verb form is appropriate:

(5)   She's the professor I want to *go see.*
        Don't make me *come get* you!
        They will *come see* me tomorrow.

Serial verbs are clearly monoclausal for some of the reasons stated above for verb–verb compounds. However, there is other semantic and structural evidence that they are not compound verbs.

First, serial verbs do not consist of a head verb preceded by another verb expressing manner. In other words, *going* is not a kind of *seeing* in example (5) in the same way that *stirring* is a kind of *frying* in example (3). Structurally, unlike verb–verb compounds, serial verbs do not occur in any forms other than the bare form (which, of course, is also the imperative). To put these constructions into any other form a clause combining construction is needed:

(6)   She came and saw me.   *She come saw me. (cf. They stir fried the vegetables.)

        He ran, went and got a newspaper.   *He run go got a newspaper.
        She is going to see him.   *She is go seeing him. (cf. She is stir frying them.)

        She has gone to see him.   *She has go seen him. (cf. She has stir fried them.)

Verb–verb compounds and serial verbs are two constructions that combine verbs into very "tight" grammatical constructions. They can be considered "verb-combining" constructions rather than "clause-combining" constructions, since

High degree of grammatical dependence			Low degree of grammatical dependence
Non-finite clauses:	Semi-finite clauses:		Finite clauses
• Bare form infinitives	• Present participles	• Present subjunctive	
• "to" infinitives	• Past participles	• Past subjunctive	

Figure 14.1 The scale of grammatical dependency

the result is a single clause. This is all we will have to say about verb–verb compounding and serial verbs. In the rest of this chapter we will focus on true clause-combining constructions.

14.2   The forms of dependent clauses – the scale of grammatical dependency

In this section we will discuss seven types of dependent clause in terms of a scale of grammatical dependency (Figure 14.1). At one end are NON-FINITE CLAUSES, and at the other end are FULLY FINITE CLAUSES. There are two points in between these two extremes – participial clauses and subjunctive clauses. Both of these may be considered to be SEMI-FINITE CLAUSES. Non-finite clauses are clauses that express no tense, aspect, or modal information, and therefore are highly dependent on some other clause. A finite clause is one that expresses all of its tense, aspect, or modal inflection directly, and is therefore capable of being integrated into discourse independently. Semi-finite clauses express *some* tense, aspect, or modal information, yet still cannot comfortably be integrated into discourse on their own.

Non-finite clauses

Non-finite clauses express no tense, aspect, or modal information. Verbs that are the main predicators in non-finite clauses are often called INFINITIVES. In Modern English there are two structurally distinct infinitives, which we will term bare form infinitives and *to*-infinitives.[1] The following are examples of these two infinitive forms in various non-finite clauses:

(7)   **Bare form infinitives**
      He didn't see her *cross* the road to the wine bar
      The piglet choir has come along so we can hear them *sing* our song.
      Two things made him *slow down* as he came to the entrance.
      We helped the neighbors *build* their deck.
      Rather than Kim *give* the introductory lecture, why don't you do it yourself?[2]

(8)   *To*-**infinitives**

Would you like *to get* me some coffee?

She's a very good person *to work* with.

I've asked Jeffrey *to ask* a friend.

To keep the water clean, you've got *to keep* the pressure up.

The taxi was able *to move*.

It was the war *to end* all wars.

Semi-finite clauses

The first type of semi-finite clause we will discuss are PARTICIPIAL CLAUSES. These are clauses in which the main predicator is a present or past participle verb form (see Section 6.3). We consider these to be semi-finite because the participle forms help express aspectual nuances. The clearest case of this is probably in the use of participles as noun-phrase modifiers:

(9)   a falling star   Present participle
      a fallen star   Past participle

The present participle modifies the noun *star* in terms of an ongoing process, while the past participle modifies the star in terms of the result of some completed event. This semantic nuance is the source of the terms "present" and "past" participle for these word forms, though "ongoing" vs. "resultative" would be more accurate. This nuance carries over into the uses of these forms as predicators as well:

(10)   a.   There they go, *blasting* a new tunnel through the mountain.
       b.   There it is, a new tunnel *blasted* through the mountain.

Even though the tense of both of these clauses is present, the dependent clause in (10a) describes an ongoing situation, whereas the same verb in the past participle form in (10b) is RESULTATIVE. So, in this sense there is arguably some tense or aspectual information expressed by these different verb forms.

Two other semi-finite clause types are SUBJUNCTIVES. These clause types are somewhat archaic for many speakers, but are still recognized by most. Subjunctives are semi-finite because some of the aspectual and modal information that can be expressed in finite clauses cannot be expressed in the subjunctive, though present and past tenses are still distinguished:

(11)   **"Present" subjunctive (identical to bare form of the verb)**
       She insisted that he *wash* the dishes.
       Their main requirement is that the lawsuit *be* dropped.
       The suggestion that *he leave* was taken badly.

(12)   "Past" subjunctive (evident for *be* only)
   a.   If I *were* a carpenter, and you *were* a lady, would you marry me anyway?
   b.   He had treated her as though she *weren't* a normal girl.
   c.   She wished she *weren't* so aware of the sarcasm that lay behind his words.

The past subjunctive usually expresses COUNTERFACTUAL MODALITY. That is, it describes situations that are not true. For example, (12a) implies "I am not a carpenter, and you are not a lady." (12b) implies that "she is a normal girl," and (12c) implies that "she is aware of the sarcasm." This is different from HYPOTHETICAL MODALITY, which describes situations that may or may not come true at some point. The examples in (11) are hypothetical, while those in (12) are counterfactual.

The past subjunctive allows no aspectual or modal information other than the expression of counterfactual modality. In contexts in which the present subjunctive may be used, structures with modal auxiliaries can usually also occur. However, the present subjunctive does not easily occur in progressive aspect, and is totally unacceptable in the perfect:

(13)   She insisted that he *may wash* the dishes.   Mode
       ?She insisted that he *be washing* the dishes.   Progressive aspect
       *She insisted that he *have washed* the dishes.   Perfect aspect

Because participial clauses and subjunctive clauses are able to express only a limited number of tense, aspect, and modal distinctions, we can say that both these clause types are semi-finite. Subjunctives are actually a little more finite than participial clauses, since participials only express a distinction between present and past, while subjunctives express hypothetical vs. counterfactual modality as well.

Fully finite clauses

The last structurally defined group of dependent clauses are fully finite in that they allow the full range of tense, aspect, and modal possibilities that main independent clauses allow. In most cases, the only respect in which they are grammatically dependent is that they normally occur following a SUBORDINATING CONJUNCTION or COMPLEMENTIZER (underlined in the following examples):

(14)   a.   They will be easy to upgrade by fitting new chips as *they become available.*
       b.   If *you blink a lot* that helps to wash it out.
       c.   That *this is all militarily justified* is questionable.
       d.   it is a subjective experience that *is intertwined* with other aspects of existence;

e.   Comparable statistics in Canada show <u>that</u> *over 600,000 people have visual disabilities*

f.   This study examined coping behaviors <u>because</u> *they lead to positive and negative outcomes.*

In all of these examples the clause in italics is formed around a fully finite verb – one that could be expressed in any tense, any aspect and take any modal auxiliary. In fact, all of them except (14d) could be fully independent clauses, if they did not have a subordinating conjunction (*as, if, because*) or complementizer (*that*) preceding them.

14.3   The functions of dependent clauses

The seven types of dependent clauses just described in terms of their forms all have multiple syntactic functions in clause combinations. In this section we will discuss four functions that have played a particularly important role in the linguistics literature:

- clausal Subjects
- clausal Objects (also called Complement clauses)
- relative clauses
- adverbial clauses

Clausal Subjects

A prototypical CLAUSAL SUBJECT is a clause that functions as a Subject of another clause, sometimes called the MAIN or MATRIX clause. The following are examples of clausal Subjects:

(15)   Clausal Subject

[[That Lord Oberon trod on his toe] stunned the Duke of Wimple].

◄─────── Subject ───────►

◄──────────── Main (matrix) clause ────────────►

In example (15) what stunned the Duke of Wimple is the entire proposition expressed by the clause *that Lord Oberon trod on his toe.* Therefore this clause is the Subject of the verb *stunned.*

   The following tree diagram illustrates the syntactic position of the clausal Subject in (15). The form *that* is called a COMPLEMENTIZER. Since it determines the syntactic behavior of the clause that follows it, it may be considered to be the syntactic Head of its syntactic category. Therefore the phrasal node immediately above the COMP is a CP, or COMPLEMENT PHRASE:

(16)

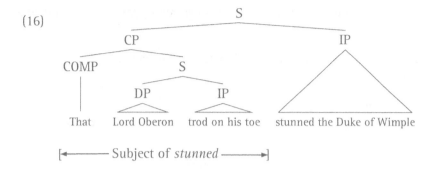

In English, clausal Subjects usually come after the verb and the "dummy" pronoun *it* appears in the preverbal position:

(17)   It stunned the Duke of Wimple that Lord Oberon trod on his toe.

Notice that this clause means the same thing as example (15). In (17), the clause *that Lord Oberon trod on his toe* is still the Subject (expressing the event that stuns the Duke), even though it comes at the end of the clause. This is called a POST-POSED or EXTRAPOSED clausal Subject. The dummy pronoun *it* then takes the normal place of the Subject. Post-posing of clausal Subjects is an instance of a general tendency in English syntax to place "heavy" constituents later in the construction. This is sometimes called HEAVY SHIFTING. We will be seeing other examples of this tendency at various points in this chapter.

The following are a few examples of clausal Subjects from the corpora for this study. Notice that all the structural types of dependent clause, except bare infinitives and past participial clauses, can function in this role:

(18)   **Non-finite clausal Subjects**
   a.   *To cook a meal like that* requires a lot of patience.
   b.   It isn't easy *to get this kind of job* without having had previous experience.
   c.   Do you think it bothers ATandT *to jettison Unix*?

Example (18a) illustrates a clausal Subject in the normal Subject position, preceding the main verb. Examples (18b) and (18c) illustrate post-posed clausal Subjects.

(19)   **Present participial clausal Subjects**
   a.   *Pushing my luck* is my favourite occupation.
   b.   *Breaking the habit* would be easier.
   c.   It isn't easy *coping with a person who is twice your age*.

Examples (19a) and (19b) illustrate present participial clausal Subjects in the normal Subject position, while (19c) illustrates a post-posed participial clausal Subject.

Example (20) illustrates a post-posed clausal Subject in the present subjunctive:

(20)   **Subjunctive clausal Subject (uncommon in the corpora)**
It is important *that policy be anchored to some identifiable and acceptable theoretical basis.*

Finally, the examples in (21) illustrate finite dependent clauses functioning as clausal Subjects:

(21)   **Finite clausal Subjects**
a.   *That it was David Mellor,* a Major crony, has reinforced fears ...
b.   *That this is possible* reflects the fact that ...
c.   It is important *that we are there.*

In the corpora, it is difficult to find examples of non-post-posed finite clausal Subjects (presumably because of the tendency toward heavy shifting described earlier). Examples (21a and b) are from tabloid newspapers. Example (21c), illustrating a post-posed finite clausal Subject, is more typical.

Finally, I'd like to illustrate a distinct type of clausal Subject which has the form of an adverbial clause:

(22)   a.   *Just because it's not warm* doesn't mean you can't have custard with it.
b.   *Just because he was a policeman* didn't mean she couldn't go out with him.
c.   *Just because you're married* doesn't mean you've got to be Siamese twins.

This is a fixed construction consisting of a clausal Subject introduced with the subordinating conjunction *just because*, a main clause built around the verb *doesn't mean* and a clause functioning as the direct Object. This construction may be schematized as follows:

(23)   Just because FINITE CLAUSE$_1$ doesn't mean FINITE CLAUSE$_2$.

Finite clause 1 is clearly the Subject of *doesn't mean*; therefore it is a clausal Subject. Interestingly, finite clause 2 often occurs in the negative (22a) and (22b), which can set up rather convoluted strings of negatives.

Clausal Objects and other Complement clauses

Even as some clauses can be Subjects of other clauses, so clauses can be Complements of other clauses. As mentioned earlier, "Complement" is a general term for all syntactic functions filled by elements that "complete" other elements. For example, direct Objects "complete" transitive VPs, DPs "complete" PPs, etc. Example (24) illustrates a clausal Object, which is the major type of Complement clause:

(24)   [Lord Oberon wants [to tread on the Duke of Wimple's toe]].

The proposition LORD OBERON WANTS is not complete. It needs a semantic THEME in order to be a complete thought. The THEME of the verb *want* shows up as the grammatical direct Object, whether it is a thing, e.g., *a new scepter*, or a proposition, as in (24). So we can say that (24) expresses the complex proposition in (25):

(25)   LORD OBERON WANTS THAT LORD OBERON TREADS ON THE DUKE OF WIMPLE'S TOE.

A clausal Object is a clause that functions as the logical Object of some other clause. As with clausal Subjects, the term "matrix clause" is sometimes used to refer to the large clause which contains another clause as its Complement. Linguists also say that a Complement clause is EMBEDDED within a matrix clause.

    A possible tree diagram for example (24) is given in (26):

(26)

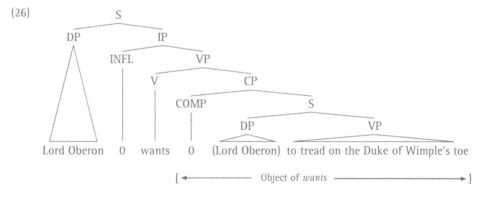

In this structure, the verb *want* is the MATRIX VERB or the COMPLEMENT-TAKING PREDICATOR (CTP). The S under the CP node is the EMBEDDED CLAUSE. Notice that there are several constituents of this phrase structure that do not have any overt realization. First, there is the empty Inflectional element (Infl) of the main clause. As we've seen in Chapter 8, when a verb phrase does not contain an overt auxiliary, yet has the properties of a fully inflected verb phrase (e.g., present tense on *want*), the standard way of describing this is that the Inflection has "migrated" to the main verb. One can also say that there is a "null auxiliary" in the matrix clause, and the Inflection that is normally carried by the auxiliary has been absorbed by the main verb *wants*.

    The next constituent that has null realization is the complementizer. English has several types of clausal Objects, and one structural parameter by which they vary is the complementizer that they employ. The following examples illustrate the various possible complementizers of English:

(27) *Null* complementizer: I know ⊘you are left-handed.
      That complementizer: I know *that* you are left-handed.
      If complementizer: I don't know *if* he is coming.
      WH complementizer: I know *where* you are going.

Finally, the Subject of the embedded clause is omitted. This is indicated in (26) by putting *Lord Oberon* in parentheses following the Comp node. Again, this is a consequence of the fact that the Subject of both clauses is the same. If the Subject of the embedded clause is different, then of course it must be expressed:

(28) Wesley wants Buttercup to tread on the Duke of Wimple's toe.

If *Buttercup* were left out of this clause, it would be understood that Wesley wants himself (Wesley) to tread on the poor Duke's toe.

A clause can be both a clausal argument *and* a matrix clause, i.e., it can function within one clause and at the same time have a third clause as its own Complement. For example:

(29) [Oberon wants [to believe [that that oaf is the Duke of Wimple]]].

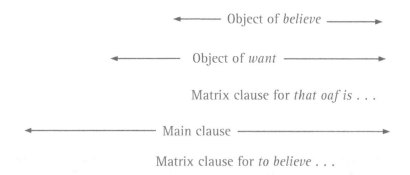

Not every Complement clause is a clausal Object. For example, some predicates allow or require Complement clauses, even if they don't allow DP direct Objects. For example, a thought like I AM WILLING is not complete. The Subject has to be willing TO DO or TO BE SOMETHING:

(30) a.   I am willing *to write a letter of reference.*   Complement clause
      b.   I am willing *to be a referee.*   Complement clause
      c.   *I am willing *a letter of reference.*   DP Complement (not allowed)

The Complement clauses in (30a and b) are not, strictly speaking, direct Objects since *be willing* does not take a direct Object (as shown in (30c)).

Clausal Objects and other Complement clauses are extremely common in spoken and written discourse, and have been the topic of much discussion and theorizing in the philosophical and linguistics literature. This is partly because of the EPISTEMOLOGICAL implications of complementation, and partly because of the challenge complementation presents for second language learners. We've already encountered epistemology in our discussion of the modal auxiliaries in Chapter 11. Complement clauses provide many ways of expressing epistemological possibilities, simply because the class of predicators that may take Complement clauses is open ended. In fact, the modal auxiliary constructions are all historically derived from predicates involving Complement clauses, and this process continues to add auxiliaries to the lexicon in the present day. The established "modes" simply represent epistemological categories that have proven to be so useful and so common over the centuries that they have become entrenched in the grammar as specialized grammatical structures – the modal auxiliaries. Predicates that take Complement clauses, then, are nascent auxiliaries, and the modal auxiliaries are erstwhile Complement-taking predicators (CTPs).

The second reason complementation is such an important area of study is that it presents major challenges for second language learners. We've already seen (Section 14.2) that there are at least seven structurally distinct dependent clause types in English. All of these may occur as Complement clauses, but not all CTPs allow all types. Thus students must learn which structural types of Complement go with each Complement-taking predicate. Furthermore, when a CTP allows more than one Complement type, major meaning differences are often expressed by the different possibilities. Several examples of this phenomenon are discussed below (see, e.g., the examples in (44)).

The forms of Complement clauses are highly dependent on the semantics of the main verb or other CTP in the construction. For example, utterance verbs tend to take finite complements (in the following examples, the main verb is underlined, and the Complement clause is in italics):

(31) **Finite Complement clauses with utterance verbs (speaking, shouting, etc.)**
Did I ever <u>tell</u> you *I was struck by lightning seven times*?
Then he <u>goes</u>, *"what are you doing?."*
She <u>shouted</u>, *do you want a cup of tea?*
Phillips and Drew <u>emphasized</u> that *there was no finance director* to look after investors' money.

On the other hand, CTPs that involve someone trying to get someone else to do something (manipulation or causation CTPs) tend to take non-finite Complements:

(32) **Non-finite Complements with manipulative CTPs**
She <u>urged</u> me *to sell my Volvo.*
the Judge will <u>compel</u> him *to learn it by heart.*

It was <u>making</u> her *feel sick.*
The Zoo had <u>helped</u> Mr Wolski *find rooms nearby.*
<u>Let</u> him *grow stronger* before you break the news.
They <u>had</u> them *scurrying all ways.*

CTPs of cognition (*know, think, understand, believe,* etc.) tend to take finite Complements:

(33)   **Finite Complements with verbs of cognition**
You <u>knew</u> that *they both had to agree* before anything was done.
I don't <u>see</u> why *we shouldn't give it a try.*
My dear Pamela, I <u>believe</u> *he loves you.*
I <u>understood</u> *he was nearer thirty.*

Some CTPs that express hypothetical, but possible, situations allow present subjunctive Complements.

(34)   **Present subjunctive (semi-finite) Complement clauses with CTPs expressing hypothetical situations**
My mother <u>insisted</u> that *she have a chaperon.*
I <u>insisted</u> that *he attend.*
They <u>insisted</u> *he take down his flag pole.*

The italicized clauses in (34) are all Complements, but they are not clausal Objects, since the verb *insist* does not take a direct Object:

(35)   *My mother insisted a chaperon.   *I insisted him.

The only kind of "Object" the verb *insist* can occur with is a Complement clause preceded by the complementizer *that* or zero (34d).[3]

Emotion predicates (*like, enjoy, be happy, sad,* etc.) take participial or infinitive Complements:

(36)   **Participial Complements with CTPs expressing emotion**
I <u>enjoy</u> *picking wildflowers.*
He <u>liked</u> *playing the acoustic guitar.*
Whoever it is certainly <u>likes</u> *having fun.*
They're <u>happy</u> *being here.*

(37)   **Infinitive Complements with CTPs expressing emotion**
Whoever it is certainly <u>likes</u> *to have fun.*
They're <u>happy</u> *to be here.*
but:
*I <u>enjoy</u> *to pick wildflowers.*

CTPs that express various "aspectual" or "modal" ideas, but which have not yet become auxiliaries, typically take participial or infinitival Complements:

(38) **Participial Complements with "aspectual" or "modal" CTPs**
      I <u>started</u> *making them* quite a while ago.
      We've <u>finished</u> *playing games* now.
      He doesn't <u>want</u> people *buying his gear* for conversation pieces.
      The barn <u>needs</u> *painting.*
      The barn <u>needs</u> *painted.* (Acceptable in some varieties only)
      but:
      *I <u>expect</u> *returning* on Tuesday.

(39) **Infinitival Complements with "aspectual" or "modal" CTPs**
      I <u>started</u> *to make them* quite a while ago.
      He doesn't <u>want</u> people *to buy his gear* for conversation pieces.
      I <u>expect</u> *to return* on Tuesday.
      They <u>need</u> *to get up a bit earlier.*
      I haven't <u>managed</u> *to get all of them.*
      She's <u>got</u> George *to thank.*
      He is <u>eager</u> *to please.*
      but:
      *We've <u>finished</u> *to play games* now.

Finally, CTPs that express simple sensory perception take bare form or participial Complements:

(40) **CTPs of perception taking bare form Complements**
      I <u>heard</u> him *cut down the trees.*
      They <u>saw</u> you *stagger into the party.*

(41) **CTPs of perception taking participial Complements**
      I *heard* him *cutting down the trees.*
      They *saw* you *staggering into the party.*

The correlation between the semantic type of CTP and the grammatical form of the Complement is understandable to a large extent in terms of the IMPLICATIONAL RELATIONS between the main Predicator and the Complement clause. For example, a person can say, think, or believe anything – there is no implicational relationship between an act of utterance or cognition and the content of what is uttered or thought; e.g., *I believe there is a unicorn in the garden* or *Mary said there is a unicorn in the garden* do not imply whether there actually is a unicorn in the garden or not. Verbs of utterance and cognition, therefore, are NON-IMPLICATIVE CTPs. CTPs of manipulation, emotion, aspect, and perception, on the other hand,

Strong implicational constraints: (CTPs of aspect, modality, emotion)	No implicational constraints: (CTPs of utterance, cognition)
Grammatically very dependent complements	Grammatically independent complements

Figure 14.2 Scale of semantic dependency correlated with the scale of grammatical dependency

normally imply that the Complement is true – e.g., *He made me do it* implies that I did it, *I like picking wildflowers* implies that I pick wildflowers from time to time, *I started working* implies that indeed I worked, and *I saw you smiling* implies that you in fact smiled. These CTPs, then, are IMPLICATIVE.[4]

Thus there is a scale of semantic dependency (interpreted as degree of implicational constraint) that correlates generally with the scale of grammatical dependency described at the beginning of this chapter. The correlation is diagrammed in Figure 14.2. The correlation between semantic dependency and grammatical dependency in complementation (first noted by Givón 1980 and termed "the binding hierarchy") not only helps explain the use of particular Complement types with particular kinds of Predicates, but also helps clarify the different nuances of meaning expressed by one Complement type or another for CTPs that allow more than one. In the following examples, the more grammatically dependent the Complement is, the more complete, direct, or strong the implicational relationship between the two clauses:

(42) a. The police <u>observed</u> the culprit *get onto the train.*
      b. The police <u>observed</u> the culprit *getting onto the train.*
      c. The police <u>observed</u> that *the culprit got onto the train.*

In (42a), the Complement is totally non-finite (bare form infinitive), and the implication is that the police actually observed the whole event. The Complement in (42b) is a little more finite, employing a present participle as the main verb. The implication of (42b) seems to be that the police saw the event in progress, but may or may not have seen the whole event. In (42c), the implication is that the police observed something that led them to believe that the culprit got onto the train, but not that they saw the event at all. For example, they could have seen a punched ticket stub with the culprit's fingerprints on it, or something like that.

The examples in (43) illustrate another sensory perception CTP with a participial and finite Complement:

(43) a. I've <u>noticed</u> you smoking one of those filthy things.
      b. I've <u>noticed</u> that you smoke one of those filthy things.

In (43a) the implication is that the speaker actually saw the addressee smoking "one of those filthy things." In (43b), the speaker may have seen indirect evidence but not an actual event of smoking.

The examples in (44) illustrate three distinct Complement types with the utterance verb *ask*:

(44) a. She <u>asked</u> him *to leave.*   Direct request for action (manipulative)
      b. She <u>asked</u> for him *to leave.*   Possibly indirect request for action
      c. She <u>asked</u> that *he leave.*   Definitely indirect request for action
                                                  (MANDATIVE)

Example (44a) illustrates the "tightest" grammatical connection of the three. The Complement is a *to*-infinitive, and expresses the strong implication that the Subject spoke directly to someone and gave him no option but to leave. (44b) is also an infinitive Complement, but the particle *for* distances the Complement from its matrix verb a little bit in terms of structure. The semantic effect of this increased grammatical distance is that the request to leave may be indirect, i.e., directed to some third person, with reference to the person who needs to leave. Example (44c) even more strongly suggests that the request is directed to a third person. The request is also a bit less strong, allowing the possibility that "he" may or may not actually leave.

Finally, the examples in (45) illustrate an emotion or cognition CTP with infinitive and finite Complements:

(45) a. He <u>is afraid</u> *to be alone.*
      b. He <u>is afraid</u> *that he is alone.*

Example (45a) implies that being afraid to be alone is a permanent characteristic of the Subject. Example (45b), on the other hand, does not imply that this is a permanent characteristic at all. In fact, he may or may not be alone. It is just the prospect that he *might* be alone that is frightening to him.

In addition to non-implicative and implicative CTPs, there are also CTPs that are NEGATIVE IMPLICATIVE or SEMI-IMPLICATIVE. Negative implicative CTPs strongly imply that the Complement is false. These would include ideas expressed by the verbs *fail*, *pretend*, and *prevent*. Semi-implicative CTPs imply that the Complement is possibly true, but not necessarily. These would include *try*, *want*, the manipulative senses of *ask* and *tell*, etc.

(46) **Negative implicative CTPs**   Implication
      Other problems <u>prevent</u> us from *charging.*   We don't charge.
      Long was <u>prevented</u> from *driving his 72-seat*   Long didn't drive the bus.
      National Express double-decker.
      The scheme <u>fails</u> *to attract anybody.*   Nobody is attracted.
      We just <u>pretended</u> *to take a photo.*   We didn't take a photo.

(47) **Semi-implicative CTPs**
      I <u>tried</u> *staying in town overnight and then driving home during the day.*
      She <u>tried</u> *to drag Michael from off the road.*
      The CEC <u>asked</u> you *to support composite twelve.*

The italicized portions of these clauses may or may not be true, if the CTP is true.

We will end this discussion of Complement clauses with a brief description of the difference between DIRECT and INDIRECT SPEECH. Sometimes direct and indirect speech taken together are referred to as REPORTED SPEECH. Direct speech (or direct quotation) is when a speaker reports the exact words of another person. Indirect speech (or indirect quotation) is when a speaker reports the content of what someone said, but not necessarily the exact words. For example, (48a) illustrates direct speech, while (48b) illustrates indirect speech:

(48) a. Walter said "I love Taiwan."   DIRECT SPEECH
      b. Walter said he loves Taiwan.   INDIRECT SPEECH

Complements of direct speech CTPs are always the most independent Complement type in any language. This is because the content of what someone says is in no way constrained by someone else's report of what they say. The reported discourse can be distant in time and space from the act of reporting, and there is no necessary implication that the quoted speech is true or not.

Adverbial clauses

ADVERBIAL CLAUSES function to modify verb phrases or whole clauses (see Chapter 10 on modification, and Thompson *et al.* (2007)). They are not arguments or Complements of some other clause. Sometimes adverbial clauses are termed adjuncts (as opposed to arguments). "Adjunct" is a good term since the term "Complement" implies completion, and a phrase or clause does not express a complete thought until all its Complement positions are filled. On other hand, adverbial clauses and phrases attach to already complete clauses. The adverbial clause simply adds some additional information to what is expressed in the other clause.

Adverbial clauses can appear in all seven dependent clause forms identified in Section 14.2:

(49) He ran *to get help.*   to-infinitive expressing PURPOSE
      Rather than Kim give the introductory lecture, why don't you do it your-self?   Bare infinitive expressing ALTERNATIVE
      In giving, we are fulfilled.   Present participle expressing MEANS
      Warmed and filled by Anna Mae's hot chicken soup, the pilgrims resumed their journey.   Past participle expressing CIRCUMSTANCE
      Were he a carpenter, I would marry him.
                          Past subjunctive expressing CONDITION
      Be he alive or be he dead, I'll grind his bones to make my bread!
                          Present subjunctive expressing CIRCUMSTANCE
      We're sorry *that you feel that way.*   Finite clause expressing REASON

The semantic relations expressed in adverbial clauses are the same kinds of relations expressed by adverbs, e.g., TIME, PLACE, MANNER, MEANS, CIRCUM-STANCE, PURPOSE, REASON, etc., plus a few others, notably various kinds of CONDITIONAL information and CONCESSION. In the following examples, the adverbial clause is given in italics, and the independent clause in normal text.

TIME adverbial clauses

(50)   *When I was your age*, television was called books. (also *before, after*)
       While (we were) eating, we heard a noise outside the window.

PLACE adverbial clauses

(51)   I'll meet you *where the statue used to be.*

MANNER adverbial clauses

(52)   a.   She talks *like she has a cold.*
       b.   Carry this *as I told you.*

PURPOSE adverbial clauses

(53)   He stood on his tiptoes *in order to see better.*

REASON and cause adverbial clauses

(54)   Sleep soundly young Rose *for I have built you a good ship.*
       Languages need to be documented *because they are supreme achievements of a uniquely human collective genius.*

CONCESSIVE clauses

(55)   So *even though the whole thing is in fairly dark tones*, there's still plenty of detail.

The semantic relation of CONCESSION is the idea that the speaker believes the information expressed in the adverbial clause may lead the audience to doubt the assertion in the main clause. Nevertheless, the speaker wishes to assert the information in the main clause *in spite of* or *conceding* the evidence to the contrary expressed in the adverbial clause. In example (55), the speaker believes the audience might think that since a particular work of art is in dark tones, there won't be much detail. But the speaker wishes to assert that it does have plenty of detail, while conceding the fact that it is in dark tones.

Conditional clauses

CONDITIONAL CLAUSES express situations that may or may not hold true in the message world. Whether a conditional clause is understood as true or not determines or influences the truth value of the independent clause in the construction:

Simple CONDITIONAL clauses

(56)   *If you haven't got your health*, you haven't got anything.
       If you make her laugh, you have a life.
       If you stare at someone long enough, you discover their humanity.

HYPOTHETICAL CONDITIONAL clauses

(57)   *If I (were to see) David*, I would speak Quechua with him.

COUNTERFACTUAL CONDITIONAL clauses

(58)   *If you had been at the concert*, you would have seen Ravi Shankar.

NEGATIVE CONDITIONAL clauses

(59)   *Unless it rains*, we'll have our picnic. (i.e., If and only if it does not rain, we will have our picnic)

CONCESSIVE CONDITIONAL clauses

(60)   *Even if it rains*, we'll have our picnic.

English employs the morphosyntax of conditional clauses in a number of fascinating rhetorical ways. For example:

(61)   *If you're thirsty* there's coke in the refrigerator.

This is not a classic conditional clause in that even if the hearer is *not* thirsty, presumably the situation expressed in the main clause would still be true. Rather, this complex construction can be paraphrased as "You may be thirsty, and in order to solve this hypothetical problem, I hereby give you permission to drink some of the coke that you will find in the refrigerator."

Here's another example of a clause that is in the form of a conditional, but which accomplishes a speech act that has nothing to do with conditionality:

(62) *If there's a mental health organization that raises money for people like you,* be sure to let me know.

The communicative effect of this kind of clause is to insult the hearer, rather than set up a condition under which the situation in the independent clause holds true.

Relative clauses

A RELATIVE CLAUSE has the syntactic function of modification within a noun phrase (Keenan 1985). For example:

(63) The *oaf that* [Ø trod on Lord Oberon's toe] ...

In terms of syntactic structure, a relative clause is a clause that is embedded within a noun phrase. This may be diagrammed as follows:

(64)

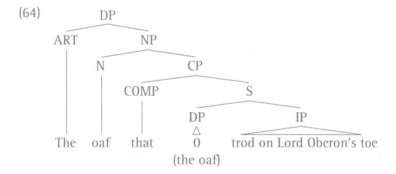

The important parts of a relative clause are the following:

- The HEAD is the noun phrase that is modified by the clause. In (63) the Head is *oaf.*
- The RESTRICTING CLAUSE is the relative clause itself. In (63) the restricting clause is surrounded by brackets.
- The R-ELEMENT is the element within the restricting clause that is coreferential with the head noun. In (63) the R-element is represented as Ø (a zero, or "gap").[5]
- The RELATIVIZER is the morpheme that sets off the restricting clause as a relative clause. In (63) the relativizer is the complementizer *that.* If the relativizer reflects

some properties of the R-element within the restricting clause (e.g., humanness, grammatical relation in the restricting clause, etc.), then it can be termed a RELATIVE PRONOUN.

Notice that in (64), the full embedded clause is *The oaf trod on Lord Oberon's toe*. The Subject of this clause is omitted because it is coreferential with the Head of the relative clause.

Most of the dependent clause types exemplified in Section 14.2 can occur in relative clauses. In the following examples from the corpora for this study, the Head is underlined and the relative clause is italicized:

(65) **Finite relative clauses**
  <u>people</u> *who were here when this presentation was last given*
  <u>products</u> *upon which Mellor built his reputation*
  the last <u>time</u> *I saw him*
  <u>things</u> *I didn't want*
  the <u>hope</u> *that she would turn to him*
  the <u>reason</u> *why that group was set up*

(66) **Present participial relative clauses**
  the <u>woman</u> *sleeping under the apple tree*
  <u>people</u> *working in branch meetings*
  an old <u>man</u> *sitting in a chair*

(67) **Past participial relative clauses**
  the <u>road</u> *less traveled*
  a new <u>tunnel</u> *blasted through the mountain*
  <u>entertainment</u> *held in the lower cafe part of the Priory*

The participial relative clauses in (66) and (67) have several properties that distinguish them from other relative clauses. For this reason, they may more insightfully be analyzed as a distinct class of phrasal Modifier. Their syntactic function is clearly Modification, and they do at some level express a proposition (a "complete thought"), so they have the functional properties of relative clauses. However, they have enough formal distinctives that many grammarians reasonably treat them as participial phrases rather than clauses.

The first distinctive of participial relative clauses is that they do not allow the full range of relativizers that other relative clauses do.

(68) the princess *who/*that/ *which sleeping under the apple tree

Second, participial modifiers may precede their Heads, as in *sleeping woman* or *broken dishes*.[6] It is only when a participial verb form heads a phrase with other constituents that they quickly become awkward in the pre-Head position:

(69)   The sleeping princess ...
       The deeply sleeping princess ...
       ?The sleeping under the apple tree princess ...
       ??The sleeping for 100 years in a glass case princess ...

The fact that such phrases are more comfortable following the Head of the NP may simply be another instance of "heavy shifting" described earlier – the heavier the constituent, the more likely it is to be shifted to the end of its phrasal category. However, as discussed in Chapter 10, even rather "light" relative clauses are ungrammatical if they precede their Heads.

For these reasons, and perhaps others, the forms we are calling "participial relative clauses" may be considered to be a different class of phrasal Modifier. However, according to the functional definition given in Keenan (1985) of a relative clause as a "clause that modifies a Noun Phrase," participial clauses must be considered a type of relative clause.

Subjunctive verb forms are also possible in relative clauses, though they probably sound seriously archaic and stilted to most modern speakers:

(70)   **Present subjunctive relative clauses**
       a.   There's a <u>book</u> *what be quite good, Sooty.* (Non-standard)
       b.   the <u>things</u> *that be Caesar's*

In addition to the subjunctive verb form, example (70a) employs the WH-word *what* as a relative pronoun. This usage is very non-standard.

Relative clauses can also be built around *to*-infinitives:

(71)   **Non-finite relative clauses**
       a.   the proper senior <u>*officer*</u> *with whom to make contact*
       b.   The electorate knows <u>*who*</u> *to blame.*
       c.   he knew exactly <u>*where*</u> *to locate the top button,*
       d.   We don't quite know <u>*what*</u> *to do.*

These also have some unusual syntactic properties in comparison to other relative clauses. In particular, the last three of these examples have no overt head. The head is "fused" with the relative pronoun (so they are italicized *and* underlined). In other words, the DPs that contain the relative clauses in (71b), (71c), and (71d) might be paraphrased as: *the person who to blame, the place where to locate ...*, and *the thing what to do* respectively. Sometimes these are called HEADLESS RELATIVE CLAUSES or FUSED RELATIVE CLAUSES (Huddleston and Pullum 2002:1068–79). Other kinds of relative clauses can be fused, but in the corpora non-finite relative clauses are much more likely to be fused than finite relative clauses are.

It is important to note that the R-element and the Head of a relative clause are different syntactic entities, even though they are COREFERENTIAL, i.e., they refer to the same discourse-world entity. The Head noun itself has a function in the main clause, and it always has a COREFERENT within the relative clause (the R-element in our terms). The role of the R-element can be different from the role of the Head noun within the main clause. For example, in (72a) *the alligator* is the Subject of the main clause verb *ate*. It is also the Subject of the relative clause verb *saw*. In (72b), however, *the alligator* is still the Subject of *ate*, but it is now the Object of the relative clause verb:

(72) a.   The alligator [that Øsaw me] eats tofu.
      b.   The alligator [that I saw Ø] eats tofu.

These clauses can be diagrammed as follows:

(73) a.

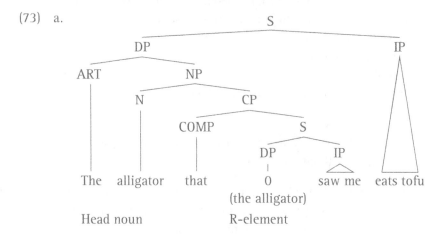

      b.

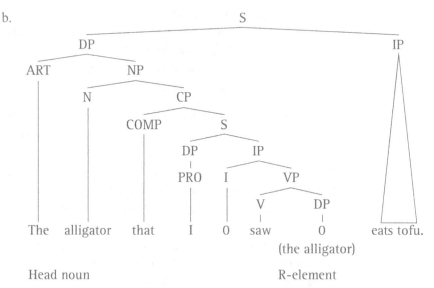

Since the R-element is left out in the surface structure of these clauses (72a, b), a problem arises as to how the hearer is to identify the grammatical relation of this invisible noun phrase within the bracketed clause. English solves this problem by simply leaving a conspicuous gap in the position where the R-element would be if it were overtly expressed. This is called the GAP STRATEGY. This strategy works because English has a fairly rigid constituent order; since grammatical relations are expressed by the position of the core nominals in a clause, a missing argument is very obvious.

If the relative clause is very complex, however, sometimes the gap strategy is insufficient to allow the hearer to figure out what the grammatical relation of the R-element is. In such cases, speakers sometimes use PRONOUN RETENTION. In this strategy a pronoun that explicitly expresses the grammatical relation of the R-element is retained within the relative clause:

(74)   That's the guy who [I can never remember *his* name].

In this example, the R-element is expressed by the genitive pronoun *his*. Here is another example I recently heard in a television news interview:

(75)   We've got 16 drums here that we don't even know what's in *them*.

In (75), the retained pronoun, *them*, occurs in the accusative form and follows the preposition *in*. This shows that the grammatical relation of the R-element is oblique.

Relative clauses with pronoun retention are non-standard in written Englishes, but are common in oral speech, at least in the USA. The preferred way of expressing example (74) in CSE would be to use PIED-PIPING. This cute term refers to the legend of the Pied Piper, a character who enticed rats and other beings out of the village of Hamlin by playing a magic pipe. The idea is that the head of the possessed noun follows the relative pronoun to the front of the clause, just like the rats followed the Pied Piper:

(76)   That's the guy *whose name* I can never remember ∅.

In this example, there is still a gap where *his name* would be, but instead of just moving the pronoun to the front of the clause, the speaker must move the pronoun and the possessed noun as well.

As for example (75), there seems to be no CSE way to express this idea without resorting to two independent clauses. With or without pied-piping, the gap strategy does not work at all when the R-element is so deeply embedded in the relative clause:

(77)   *We've got 16 drums here that we don't even know what's in ∅.
       *We've got 16 drums here in which we don't even know what's ∅.

The only way to "save" this sentence, apparently, is to abandon the relative clause approach altogether, and break it up into separate coordinate clauses:

(78)   We've got 16 drums here *and* we don't even know what's in them.

Relative clauses may employ the form *that* (normally unstressed) as an introducer. This is the same form that we have called a complementizer, but in a relative clause it may be called a RELATIVIZER:

(79)   The people *that* I saw.
       The people *that* saw me.
       The bed *that* I slept in.
       The house *that* I went to.

Technically, *that* is not a relative pronoun in these examples, because it does not refer to the R-element or the head. This is evidenced by several facts:

- The form of *that* does not change when the head is plural: **the people those I saw.*
- *that* cannot participate in pied-piping

(80)   *The bed *in that* I slept.
       *The house *to that* I went.

Instead, in such circumstances a relative pronoun must be used:

(81)   The bed *in which* I slept.
       The house *where* I went.

Relative pronouns can be thought of as combining the functions of a plain relativizer and a clause-internal pronoun that refers to the R-element. English allows the relative pronoun strategy (Rel Pro), a relativizer plus gap strategy (Rel + gap), and an unmarked "no relativizer" plus gap strategy (No Rel). Sometimes all three are allowed in the same environment, and it is difficult to determine what semantic nuances are expressed, if any, by the various allowable structures. The following illustrate some English possibilities and impossibilities:

(82)   a.   Rel Pro: The man who saw me
       b.   Rel + gap: The man that saw me
       c.   No Rel: *The man [0 saw me]

(83)   a.   Rel Pro: The man whom [I saw]
       b.   Rel + gap: The man that [I saw 0]
       c.   No Rel: The man [I saw 0]

(84)   a.   Rel pro: The place where I live
       b.   Rel + gap: ?The place that I live
       c.   No Rel: The place I live

(85) a. Rel pro: The reason why I came
      b. Rel + gap: The reason that I came
      c. No Rel: The reason I came

(86) a. Rel pro: *The way how he did it (acceptable to some)
      b. Rel + gap: The way that he did it
      c. No Rel: The way he did it

(87) a. Rel pro: The table which he put it on
      b. Rel + gap: The table that he put it on
      c. No Rel: The table he put it on

14.4   Coordination

COORDINATION is a type of grammatical construction in which two syntactic elements that have the same syntactic function are linked. It is distinct from SUBORDINATION, in which one element is grammatically dependent on the other. All of the dependent clause types discussed in the previous sections (i.e., clausal arguments, adverbial clauses, and relative clauses) may be considered to be examples of subordination.

In spoken discourse some kind of morphosyntactic clause linkage, either coordination or subordination, may be evident at nearly all clause junctures. Many readers will be familiar with the colloquial narrative style that inserts *and* or *and then* after each clause. In general, the fact that two elements are grammatically coordinated simply asserts that (1) the two elements have more or less the same function in terms of the event structure of the text (e.g., they both express events, they both express non-events, they both express foregrounded information, or they both express background information, etc.) and (2) they are presented as being conceptually linked in some way.

The following paragraph from a movie script (Roth 2008) includes several examples of clause coordination. The conjunctions are given in bold and are numbered so that we may refer to them below:

(88) When the package was wrapped, the woman, who was back in the cab, was blocked by a delivery truck, all the while Daisy was getting dressed. The delivery truck pulled away (1) **and** the taxi was able to move, while Daisy, the last to be dressed, waited for one of her friends, who had broken a shoelace. While the taxi was stopped, waiting for a traffic light, Daisy and her friend came out the back of the theater. (2) **And** if only one thing had happened differently: if that shoelace hadn't broken; (3) **or** that delivery truck had moved moments earlier; (4) **or** that package had been wrapped and ready, because the girl hadn't broken up with her boyfriend; (5) **or** that man had set his alarm (6) **and** got up five minutes

Table 14.1 **Summary of English dependent clause forms and functions**

Syn. form	Syn. function			
	Adverbial	Clausal subject	Complement Clause	Relative clause
Finite	*As soon as Taroo arrives,* Miyoko will dance with him. After Taroo arrived, Miyoko danced.	It bothers me *that she enjoys Bartok.*	She thinks *that he was a dancer.*	The man *who thinks he is a hat* was hanging on the coat rack in the entryway.
Present participial	She went out, *locking the door behind her.* After closing the door, she locked it securely.	*Walking the dog* gives her great pleasure.	She enjoys *walking the dog.*	I know the girl *sleeping under the apple tree.*
Past participial	*Warmed and filled by Anna Mae's chicken soup*, the pilgrims resumed their journey.			They saw a tunnel *blasted through the mountain.*
Present subjunctive	*Though he have riches untold*, she still wouldn't marry him.	*That he have a place to stay* is very important to us.	Obama demands *that he be scrutinized and questioned by the American people.*	They *who be great in riches* also are great in sadness.
Past subjunctive	*If I were a carpenter*, she would marry me.		I wish *I were a rich man.*	
To-infinitive	He climbed the mountain *to see what was on the other side.*	*To throw a log of that size* requires great strength	She likes *to walk the dog.*	That was the war *to end all wars.*
Bare form infinitive	*Rather than me give the lecture*, why don't you do it?		They made him *eat the turnips.*	

earlier; (7) or that taxi driver hadn't stopped for a cup of coffee; (8) or that woman had remembered her coat, (9) **and** got into an earlier cab, Daisy and her friend would've crossed the street, (10) **and** the taxi would've driven by. (11) **But** life being what it is – a series of intersecting lives and incidents, out of anyone's control – that taxi did not go by, (12) **and** that driver was momentarily distracted, (13) **and** that taxi hit Daisy, (14) **and** her leg was crushed.

Much could be said about the use of coordination to set up a hierarchical structure in this excerpt. Most of the highlighted conjunctions conjoin pairs of clauses that have similar functions in terms of the structure of the text. For example, *and* #1 conjoins two clauses that both express foregrounded events in the text. Similarly the series of *or*s from (3) to (8) conjoin clauses that all express alternative conditions under one *if*. One particularly notable example is *and* #2. The units that it conjoins are two major sections of the text. The first part describes a series of events, and are narrated mostly in the simple past. After *and* #2, the perspective shifts to hypothetical mode until *but* #11 is encountered. Then the perspective shifts back to narrative (factual story telling) mode. So, we can see how coordination can involve units at multiple levels of structure, and need not be limited to conjoining words, phrases, and clauses.

It is important to note that apparently any phrase or clause type can enter into a coordinate structure. It is not necessarily the case that both clauses must be independent. The important feature that the coordinated elements must have in common is their syntactic function. The following examples illustrate various pairs of coordinate structures observed in the corpora for this study:

(89) **Conjoined participial Complement clauses (in this case, complements of the preposition *of*)**
   It's just a case of *diving in the bag <u>and</u> looking for whatever you want.*

(90) **Conjoined participial adverbial clauses expressing simultaneous actions**
   Delaney bent over them, *adjusting a lamp <u>and</u> using a magnifying glass.*

(91) **Conjoined independent clauses with coreferential Subjects** (very common)
   I moved from Alderton <u>and</u> went to Bingham.
   The Council went ahead <u>and</u> looked at Wordsworth Road.

(92) **Bare form Complement clauses** (of the preposition *to*)
   It's more important to *dry things <u>and</u> keep them dry* for a while ...

14.5 Forms and functions of dependent clauses summarized

Table 14.1 summarizes the distribution of the seven dependent clause types and four dependent clause functions outlined in this chapter, with simple examples illustrating all the combinations that have been found in the corpus. Blank squares in Table 14.1 indicate that no example was found of that particular combination of syntactic type and syntactic function.

Summary

In this chapter we have looked at several constructions that involve combining verbs or clauses. First, two monoclausal constructions were described. These are:

- compound verbs
- serial verbs

Then two "typologies" of dependent clauses were outlined – a formal typology and a functional typology. The formal typology describes the forms of the clauses themselves, and consists of:

- non-finite clauses (*to*-infinitives and bare form infinitives)
- semi-finite clauses (participial clauses and subjunctive clauses)
- fully finite dependent clauses.

The functional typology describes what dependent clauses do in larger structures. Types of dependent clause functions include:

- clausal Subjects
- clausal Objects and other complements
- adverbial clauses
- relative clauses

Finally, clause coordination was described as a clause combining construction that involves no grammatical asymmetry. Neither clause in a coordinate structure is necessarily dependent on the other.

FURTHER READING

Noonan (2007) provides an excellent basic treatment of clausal arguments from a cross-language perspective. The other studies in Shopen (2007b) provide similar general introductions various types of dependent clauses in the world's languages by leading researchers in the field. Mair (1990) studies English infinitival Complement clauses from a functional and communicative perspective. Verstraete (2007) provides a refreshing new analysis of adverbial and coordinate clauses in English.

Exercises

1. In the following passage, underline all dependent clauses. Because of the possibility of multiple embeddings, some clauses may have two or more underlines.

    Example: <u>Because of your essay</u>, I believe <u>you think</u> <u>the world will end tomorrow</u>.

    I have admitted that there are very few women who would put their job before every earthly consideration. I will go further and assert that there are very few men who would do it either. In fact, there is perhaps one person in a thousand who is passionately interested in his job for the job's sake. The difference is that if that one person in a thousand is a man, we say, simply, that he is passionately keen on his job; if she is a woman, we say she is a freak. From *Dorothy Sayers – Are women human? (1938)*

2. In each of the following examples, there is one dependent and one independent clause. Underline the dependent clause, and give its form (bare form infinitive, *to*-infinitive, present participial, past participial, present subjunctive, past subjunctive, or finite) and its function (clausal Subject, clausal Object, adverbial clause, relative clause). The first example is done for you;

   a. I want <u>you to read this book</u>. Clausal Object, *to*-infinitive
   b. Felicia said they have to replace the copy machine.
   c. It's clear that he wants a new computer.
   d. They organized a farewell party because three students were leaving.
   e. Just because she is a doctor doesn't mean I have to obey her.
   f. Driving to work is such a pain!
   g. He stood on his tiptoes in order to see better.
   h. The man wearing the black top hat is Abraham Lincoln.
   i. If I were you, I'd lose the moustache.

3. The following sentences all contain relative clauses. For each relative clause, circle the head (if present), and <u>underline</u> the R-element. If the R-element is expressed as a gap, insert an X at that point. The first example is done for you (examples adapted from "Child's play" by Alice Munro, in Rushdie 2008:201–29).

   a. I never had to go past the yellow (house) that <u>X</u> reminded me so much of Verna.
   b. The old building where the Special Classes had been held was condemned.
   c. Its pupils were transferred to the Bible Chapel, now rented on weekdays by the town.
   d. There were a couple of ways that Verna could have walked to school,
   e. but the way she chose was past our house.
   f. I would always look in the direction from which she might be coming.
   g. I was the one she had her eye on.
   h. We had an understanding between us that could not be described.
   i. Then we would line up at the Tuck Shop, which opened every day at one o'clock.
   j. The Specials appeared to be trying to figure out what they were doing here.

15 Pragmatic grounding and pragmatically marked constructions

I personally think we developed language because of our deep inner need to complain.

Jane Wagner (1986:133)

Pragmatics is the practice of utterance interpretation (Levinsohn 1983). Speakers and hearers are continuously engaged in pragmatic interpretation of contexts and utterances whenever they participate in communication, whether it be conversing with friends, reading a textbook, complaining, or engaging in any other form of communication. Utterances are actual instances of language in use; therefore they always occur in a context and their interpretations always affect and are affected by the context (Sperber and Wilson 1995). While semantics has to do with the propositional *meaning* of linguistic structures, pragmatics has to do with the *use* of structures in actual contexts. A well-formed and meaningful utterance may have very different pragmatic interpretations depending on how it is used in different contexts. Take for example, a simple utterance like:

(1) I like vegetables.

In reply to the suggestion "Let's have steak for dinner!" the utterance in (1) may be understood as a negative response. However, following the suggestion "Let's have ratatouille for dinner!" the same utterance will probably be understood as affirmative agreement. The propositional meaning of the utterance is the same in both cases, but the pragmatic effect is quite different, simply because of the context.

When communicating with other people, normal language users constantly (1) assess the audience's current mental state, e.g., what they probably already know, what they are currently attending to, what they are interested in, etc., and (2) construct messages so as to help the audience revise their mental state in a particular way. The study of how these kinds of INFERENCING tasks affect the structure of linguistic communication is the subject matter of linguistic pragmatics.

In this chapter we will look first at some of the PRAGMATIC STATUSES of information in the contexts of communication. Just as parts of linguistic utterances have grammatical relations (form) and semantic roles (meaning), so they have pragmatic statuses (use). Pragmatic statuses are particularly tricky because they involve speakers' and hearers' assumptions about what is going on in each others' minds. This process is a matter of "educated guessing" (inferencing), and thus always involves a measure of subjectivity.

After the discussion of pragmatic statuses, we will present a few constructions of English that are considered to be PRAGMATICALLY MARKED. Markedness is a general term in linguistics that refers to the fact that some linguistic elements are unusual, unexpected, or striking in some way. The unmarked (normal, ordinary, default) pragmatic function of an utterance is unemphatic, non-contrastive, affirmation – in other words, "blah." If all our utterances were of this sort, language would be very flat and boring indeed. Fortunately, all languages, including English, provide structural ways of livening up conversations with pragmatically varied constructions. These include special intonation patterns, constituent order variation, and CLEFT CONSTRUCTIONS of various sorts. Later in this chapter we will also discuss negation, questions, and imperatives, all of which belong to the class of pragmatically marked constructions.

15.1 Pragmatic statuses

PRAGMATIC STATUSES have to do with choices speakers make about how to efficiently adapt utterances to the context, including the hearer's presumed mental state. Like semantic roles, pragmatic statuses can be thought of as characteristics of participants in the discourse world. However, semantic roles are features of the *meaning* of utterances (see Section 6.1), while pragmatic statuses relate to choices speakers make as to how to *use* utterances in particular contexts. Labels that describe various pragmatic statuses of participants include: PRESUPPOSED, ACTIVATED, NEW, FOCUS, TOPIC, IDENTIFIABLE (or DEFINITE), and REFERENTIAL.

Careful expression of pragmatic statuses is extremely important to communication. If a speaker misjudges the pragmatic status of information in the hearer's mind, a perfectly well-formed and meaningful utterance may be uninterpretable. Consider the following hypothetical exchange:

(2) Q: "What are you eating?"
     A: "I'm EATING them."

The clause *I'm EATING them* (with extra stress on the word *eating*) is completely grammatical and meaningful, in the right context. However, as an answer to the question "What are you eating?" it comes across as "unpragmatical" (that's a word

I just made up). The use of the unstressed pronoun *them* implies that the identity of the food eaten is already known, and is "activated" on the discourse stage, yet the question makes it clear that the hearer cannot identify the food. Also, the use of extra stress on *eating* implies that the verb is the main piece of new information that is being communicated. But the question actually treats *eating* as presupposed information. The questioner seems to assume that the other person is *eating* something, so to treat *eating* as new information in the response results in "unpragmaticality" in that context.

Most of us have been in situations where someone answers a different question than we have asked. Usually this just means our question was not fully understood by the other person, but it can result in an awkward moment while both interactants readjust their model of the conversation in order to come to some level of agreement.

It should be pointed out that grammatical relations are one major means of expressing pragmatic information about nominal elements in discourse (see Section 7.2). For example, Subjects tend to be identifiable, activated, topical, and already available in memory. Direct Objects are either activated or new in about equal proportions (see, e.g., Chafe 1976). Obliques (nominal clause elements that bear no grammatical relation to the verb) tend to express either new information or activated information that is not central to the ongoing development of the discourse (Thompson 1997). Also, the pragmatic status of a nominal correlates in a general way with semantic roles. So, for example, people are likely to choose AGENTS as the main topics of their discourses. This is because there is a human tendency to talk more about things that exercise power and control than things that don't.

In addition to the grammaticalized pragmatic statuses accorded to nominal elements in clauses by grammatical relations, English expresses a number of pragmatic statuses via specialized grammatical tools. Such tools include contrastive stress, determiners, clefts, and variation in the orders of words. In the subsections below, various pragmatic statuses and their grammatical expression will be briefly described.

Identifiability

DEFINITE noun phrases refer to entities that the speaker judges should be IDENTIFIABLE to the hearer. The article *the* is one means of expressing identifiability in English:

(3)   *The* man has a broken thigh and *the* woman severe concussion.

The use of *the* in this example is an instruction to the hearer to identify a particular man and woman based on the current scene on the discourse stage. Upon hearing *the*, the hearer will immediately attempt to identify the man and the woman, searching the immediate discourse stage first. If that does not yield appropriate REFERENTS, the hearer will then scan contextual features that are related to the discourse stage, but not actively "on stage" at the moment; then, if necessary, the physical situation of the speech act, including the room, the town, the country, and even the planet. If no plausible referents can be identified within a second or two, the hearer is likely to assume that communication has broken down. If the communication is important enough, the hearer may stop the speaker, and say "Hold on; *which* man and woman are we talking about?" The use of the question word *which* is a good clue that someone needs to have a particular referent identified more clearly.

If the article *a* were used in place of *the* in (3), quite a different instruction would be presented to the hearer. The INDEFINITE article tells the hearer "Don't bother looking for the referent for this NP; just put one on stage starting now." The effect, then, would be to set up a particular man and a particular woman on the discourse stage. There would be no expectation that the hearer should be able to identify *which* man and *which* woman at the point in the discourse where such UNIDENTIFIABLE (or indefinite) participants are introduced. However, from that point on, the use of *the man* and *the woman* would be coherent, as there would now be a particular man and a particular woman set up "on stage" to be referred to over and over again.

In addition to the definite article, noun phrases can be presented as identifiable in several ways. In the following paragraphs, some of these ways will be discussed.

Proper names

The use of a proper name normally implies that the speaker assumes the hearer can uniquely identify the referent:

(4)   Jacques embraced Barack.

Here the speaker probably assumes that there is no need to "set the stage" by saying "There was a guy named Jacques ..." or "Do you remember that Barack guy we met at the party last weekend?" to establish the identity of the participants. Somehow the speaker assumes they must already be uniquely ACCESSIBLE or AVAILABLE in the hearer's memory. Similarly, upon hearing a clause like (4), any hearer will assume the speaker is referring to identifiable referents, and will quickly attach the name to some referent if at all possible. If a plausible referent is not identified, the hearer is likely to protest: "Hey wait a minute. Who's Jacques?" or "Which Barack are you talking about?" Such protests are a clue that the expectations of speaker and hearer do not match sufficiently. We can say, then, that proper names are "automatically definite" or that they have a "null definite determiner."

Vicarious identifiability

Often identifiability is expressed in a noun phrase by its association with some other already identified noun phrase. For example:

(5)   Bernadette's husband embraced Barack.

In this clause the identity of the referent of the noun *husband* is grounded via its association with the proper name *Bernadette*. Since *Bernadette* is presented as identifiable, and since presumably Bernadette has only one husband, then her husband should also be identifiable. So, NPs that are grammatically possessed by identifiable NPs are also identifiable. For this reason, genitive noun phrases (or GPs: see Section 8.2) and pronouns serve a determining function in clause structure. The following is a box diagram of example (5) showing the relevant syntactic categories and syntactic functions. Since *Bernadette's* is the Head of a DP, its syntactic function is DETERMINATION:

(6)

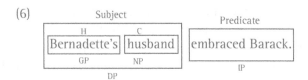

Identifiability is in practice always significant only in relation to the communication situation. That is, something is treated as identifiable if its referent is *explicit enough* for the speaker's current purposes. For example, consider the following utterance:

(7)   I got mad at Joe for writing on the living room wall.

Here the phrase *the living room wall* is treated as identifiable even though most living rooms have more than one wall. It is just not relevant for the speaker's purpose in this case to distinguish exactly *which* living room wall is being referred to (see Du Bois 1980 and Sperber and Wilson 1995 for further discussion). Similarly, even *Bernadette's husband* in (5) may not in itself identify a specific message – world entity (i.e., in a situation in which Bernadette is known to have more than one husband). However, an utterance such as (5) would still be interpretable if either (a) it just didn't matter which husband were involved, or (b) the particular husband were identified in terms of the context, e.g., only one of Bernadette's husbands visited Barack; therefore it could only plausibly be that husband who embraced Barack.

Unique referents

Certain items are always identifiable, because there is only one of them within a relevant context, and so there is no possibility of confusion:

(8)   The moon looks lovely tonight.

We can say that *the moon* (and a few other expressions, like *the earth*, *the sun*, the *north pole*, etc.) can always be treated as identifiable as long as the communication is taking place on Planet Earth. In a conversation on Jupiter, *the moon* may have to be identified more explicitly, since the speaker would probably need to identify *which* of the sixty-three moons she means.

Situationally identifiable items

While "Planet Earth" is the most general context for most conversations in English, every communicative act takes place within more specific contexts. Consider the following:

(9)   Shall we gather at the river?

In this utterance, *the river* is treated as identifiable, implying that there is a river, probably somewhere close by, that the hearer can identify as a place where the speaker may plausibly be suggesting that "we" gather.

The following examples are from a reality TV interview over a scene in a restaurant. One of the interview participants is the fiancé of the woman mentioned in the text below. There is a lot of evaluative material that intervenes between (10a, b, and c), but these extracts will serve to illustrate several ways in which participants are treated as situationally identifiable:

(10)   a.   That's her at the corner table getting awfully cozy with this stranger, ...
       b.   He's holding her hand the whole time across the table. ...
       c.   It's time to tell our cheaters to get the check and head for the door, ...

In (10a), *the corner table* is treated as identifiable in the context of a restaurant. The audience for this TV show can be expected to know that restaurants are likely to have tables and probably corners. If someone doesn't know this, this clause could constitute a clue that *this* restaurant has tables and corners. In any case, upon hearing this DP, the hearer immediately starts scanning the context for the particular corner table (there may be several) where the speaker is directing the hearer's attention.

Similarly, in example (10b) *her hand* and *the table* are treated as identifiable. *Hand* is identified by relating it to the already identified participant, *her*. Since most people have two hands, one might ask "Which hand?" Apparently, however, it doesn't matter for the purposes of this communicative act which of the woman's two hands is intended (like *the living room wall* in example (7)). Perhaps in another situation, such as a courtroom, it may be relevant to clarify *which* hand were involved for some reason. But in this case it doesn't seem to matter. In fact if the speaker did specify "her right hand" it may be a potential distraction. The hearer may legitimately wonder why the speaker is mentioning her *right* hand. There must be some relevance to that detail, and the hearer, being a cooperative conversationalist, would try to identify the relevance of the right vs. left hand. Also, *the table* in (10b) can be considered identifiable because there is a table that is present in the scene. Yes, *the corner table* is mentioned previously, but it is not necessarily just because of that first mention that the table can be considered identifiable in (10b). It is identifiable because it is *on stage*, however it got there in the first place.

Finally, in (10c), the expression *our cheaters* refers to the couple mentioned previously. The word *cheater* had not been used before in the text, but it is treated as identifiable in terms of its relation to "us," presumably the people discussing the scene before them. The genitive pronoun *our* certainly doesn't express the semantic role of POSSESSOR in this case – the discussants don't "own" the cheaters. Rather, the audience is being instructed to identify some set of participants on the discourse stage as "cheaters" by associating them with "us" in some way. The most likely referents would be the fiancé and the stranger who have been central characters throughout this text. They are "our" cheaters because "we" (the interview participants) have discovered them flirting with one another over dinner. Finally, *the check* and *the door* in (10c) can also be treated as identifiable in the context of a restaurant even though they have never been mentioned in the discourse.

The key to understanding identifiability (or definiteness) in English, then, is the discourse stage metaphor (see the Introduction). People engaged in communication collaborate to create a unique cognitive "scene" that serves as the basis for communicating thoughts, emotions, and other meaningful subject matter in a particular context. Communication succeeds or fails to the extent that participants subconsciously "agree on" the details of the scene or scenes being elaborated. A speaker will treat a referent (a participant or prop) as identifiable if there is some reasonable expectation that the hearer can pick out a particular referent. There are many ways that referents may be rendered identifiable. Most good English grammar books will give rather long lists of situations in which a noun phrase can be treated as definite. What all these situations or usages have in common, however, is that the speaker can assume that, given the information that the hearer already has access to, either from previous experience, general knowledge, or the current state of the discourse stage, the hearer is able to *identify*, i.e., establish a referential link, between that noun phrase and a particular referent.

Referentiality

Referentiality is similar, but not identical, to identifiability. Here I will briefly contrast two approaches to the notion of referentiality. The first approach I will term OBJECTIVE REFERENTIALITY. The second is DISCOURSE REFERENTIALITY (Givón 1979, Du Bois 1980).

An entity is objectively referential if it exists as a bounded, individuated entity on the discourse stage. Sometimes referentiality in this sense is referred to as SPECIFICITY. The italicized noun phrases in the following clauses refer to objectively referential participants:

(11) *Those men* are ridiculous.
      Someday I'd like to buy *your cabin* by the seashore.

This definition excludes the following:

(12) Generics: *All men* are ridiculous.
      Non-specifics: Someday I'd like to buy *a cabin* by the seashore.

Notice that objective referentiality is not the same as identifiability. A generic referent can be identifiable in the sense that the speaker assumes the hearer can identify the genera (e.g., *all men* in example (12)), though there is no specific individual being referred to. This fact is reflected in English grammar in that the particle *the* can mark generic noun phrases:

(13) *The elephant* is a huge mammal.

Here the speaker instructs the hearer to identify the generic class referred to by *elephant* but not necessarily to single out any particular (objectively referential) elephant or elephants.

Similarly, non-identifiable entities may be referential. To understand this, consider the following example:

(14) Arlyne would like to marry a Norwegian.

This clause is ambiguous in English. It could mean that Arlyne would like to marry anyone that happens to be Norwegian (non-referential), or it could mean that Arlyne has a specific (referential) Norwegian in mind but the speaker just doesn't assume that the hearer can identify that particular Norwegian. In either case *Norwegian* is treated as non-identifiable (as expressed by the article *a*). In the first case it is non-referential (or non-specific) because there is no particular person "on stage." In the second case "Norwegian" is objectively referential (or specific), because it refers to a particular person in the world of the discourse.

Table 15.1 summarizes the relationships between referentiality and identifiability, giving examples of all four possibilities. Notice that English has grammatical means for distinguishing identifiability from non-identifiability (the Determining function), but objective referentiality is largely left to interpretation based on contextual factors. For example, DPs like *the elephant* or *a Norwegian* are grammatically specified as being identifiable and non-identifiable respectively, but each

Table 15.1 **Objective referentiality and identifiability**

	Identifiable	Non-identifiable
Referential	He's holding *her hand*.	I read *a good book* today.
Non-referential	*The elephant* is a large mammal.	I'm looking for *any good book*.
	Elephants are large mammals.	

may be ambiguous as to referentiality. The Determiner *any* in *any good book* is one way of specifying that its Complement, *good book*, is non-referential, but this is optional in English. Expression of referentiality is not as essential to English grammar as expression of identifiability.

In contrast to objective referentiality, discourse referentiality has to do with continuing presence on the discourse stage over a portion of text (Du Bois 1980). In general this is a more restrictive concept than is objective referentiality. That is, while it is common for objectively referential entities not to be discourse referential, it is difficult to conceive of discourse referential entities that are not also objectively referential. For example, any prop in a story might be objectively referential, as in the following:

(15)   Minimal detective work pinned him to *a P.O. box* in Hastings-on-Hudson.

In this clause *a P.O. box* is treated as objectively existing on the discourse stage. However, if the box is never mentioned again, it would not be discourse referential in terms of Du Bois (1980), because it would not have a continuing presence.

Wright and Givón (1987) have shown that demonstrative determiners (*this, that, these, those*) in spoken English are, among other things, indicators of discourse referentiality. In spoken narratives, participants may be introduced onto the discourse stage for the first time with the demonstratives *this* or *these* as well as with *a(n)* or *some*. At the point they are introduced, such participants are non-identifiable, or "indefinite," because the speaker cannot assume that the audience can "pick out" the referents based on what the audience already knows. But when such indefinite participants are introduced with a demonstrative determiner, they are much more likely to be mentioned repeatedly in the subsequent discourse than are items introduced with *a(n)* or *some*. Consider the following example from a novel, depicting an emergency phone call to the police:

(16)   We just arrived at my cabin and found *this guy* hanging from my garage rafters.

In (16) the speaker is very likely to continue talking about the referent of the expression *this guy*. To the extent that the number of times a participant is mentioned in a conversation is an indication of how *important* that participant is, we can say that *this* introduces participants that are "destined" to be central, important characters in the subsequent text. In this sense *this* is a marker of discourse referentiality.

Other terms that have been used for the concept of discourse referentiality are MANIPULABILITY (Hopper and Thompson 1984) and DISCOURSE DEPLOYABILITY (Jaggar 1988). The reasoning behind these terms is the idea that certain participants tend to be referred to repeatedly, i.e., "manipulated" or "deployed" in a discourse, while others are not. So, *a P.O. box* as introduced in example (15), having been introduced in an Oblique role, is not likely to be referred to very often in the discourse following this example. It would, in fact, sound quite strange if (15) were followed by the following invented narration:

(17)   It was a very beautiful box with bevelled glass and neo-Grecian highlights.

A participant is simply not very *deployable* if it is mentioned as an indefinite NP in an Oblique role. On the other hand, introducing a participant with *this* makes it statistically much more likely to be referred to repeatedly in the following discourse. Of course, this is not a matter of grammaticality *per se*. If one wants to introduce a participant as an indefinite NP in an Oblique role, there is no strictly grammatical prohibition against referring to that participant over and over again in the rest of the text. However, it might sound "unpragmatical" (English teachers may just say "awkward") to do so.

Focus

The following is a brief overview of ways in which the term "focus" (and various expansions of that term) have been used in the recent linguistic literature. This typology is adapted from Chafe (1976), Dik (1981), and Lambrecht (1996).

There are two general approaches to the term focus. These are:

- "focus" as a pragmatic status of one element of every clause. This definition can be termed the FOCUS OF ASSERTION.
- "focus" as a special pragmatic status assigned only to some elements in certain PRAGMATICALLY MARKED clauses.

The first approach to focus stems from the work of the FUNCTIONAL SENTENCE PERSPECTIVE linguists of the PRAGUE SCHOOL (e.g., Mathesius 1939). According to these scholars, every sentence ("clause" in our terminology) has two parts; the part that refers to what the hearer is presumed to already have in mind, and the part that adds some new information. Some clauses may consist entirely of new material. Although the early Prague School linguists did not use the term "focus," they are to be credited with the *concept* of focus as the part of the clause that expresses the new information.

One way to determine which part of a clause is focused in this sense is to imagine the clause as an answer to a WH-question. The focus is the part of the answer that fills in the information requested in the prompting question. In the examples below, the words in italics represent the focus of assertion. The underlining indicates that sentence stress falls on the stressed syllable of the underlined word (see Celce-Murcia *et al.* 1996 for an excellent discussion of sentence stress in English):

(18)　a.　What happened?　　　　　　　　　*Barack invited Jacques to Washington.*
　　　　　　　　　　　　　　　　　　　　　　　(Whole clause)
　　　b.　What did Barack do?　　　　　　　　He *invited Jacques to Washington.*
　　　　　　　　　　　　　　　　　　　　　　　(Predicate focus)
　　　c.　Who invited Jacques?　　　　　　　　*Barack* invited Jacques.
　　　　　　　　　　　　　　　　　　　　　　　(Subject focus)
　　　d.　Who did Barack invite?　　　　　　　He invited *Jacques.*　(Object focus)
　　　e.　Where did Barack invite Jacques?　　He invited him *to Washington.*
　　　　　　　　　　　　　　　　　　　　　　　(Location focus)

The second conception of the term focus takes focus to be a special pragmatic status that is not evident in all clauses. Sometimes this conception is termed MARKED FOCUS. Clauses that are "focused" or have a "focused constituent" in this sense are PRAGMATICALLY MARKED. That is, they deviate in their pragmatic nuances from most other clause types in the language. Many authors (e.g., Chafe 1976) use the term FOCUS OF CONTRAST to describe this pragmatic status.

A major distinction in the typology of marked focus involves SCOPE OF FOCUS. The scope of focus of a clause is either the truth value of the entire clause (TRUTH-VALUE FOCUS, or TVF) or a particular constituent of the clause (CONSTITUENT FOCUS, or CF).

Truth-value focus (or VERUM FOCUS in some traditions) strongly asserts the truth of the proposition. In the following example, upper case letters indicate extra stress, or what is sometimes called CONTRASTIVE STRESS (as distinct from ordinary sentence stress), on the syllable in question.

(19)　Speaker A:　Barack never invited Jacques to Washington.
　　　Speaker B:　Barack DID invite Jacques to Washington.

Contrastive stress on the dummy auxiliary *DID*, in Speaker B's response indicates that Speaker B wishes to assert the truth of the proposition in contrast to Speaker A's expressed belief.

In constituent focus (CF), the scope of focus is a particular constituent, e.g., a noun phrase, verb phrase, or some other part of the clause. In this type of focus the speaker asserts the identity of a particular constituent against a background of a set of other possible referents. So, for example, the clause 'SALLY made the salad' (with stress on Sally) implies that:

(a) Sally was the person who made the salad, and
(b) No one else made the salad (e.g., Harry, Mary, or Larry ...)

Not every instance of constituent focus will have all of these characteristics, but this is common.

Topic

Like the term "focus," the term "topic" has been defined in many ways, including:

- the topic as a pre-posed clause constituent. Sometimes such elements are said to be "topicalized." This is a definition based entirely on *form*.
- the topic as a clause level notion that can be paraphrased "what the clause is about." Every (or almost every) clause has a topic in this sense (Reinhart 1982).
- the topic as a discourse level notion that can be paraphrased "what the discourse is about." Not every clause in a discourse may mention the topic in this sense.
- the topic as "the [conceptual or referential] frame within which the rest of the predication holds" (Li and Thompson 1976).
- topicality as a scalar discourse notion. Every nominal participant is topical to a certain degree. Relative topicality may be inferred in terms of how often various participants are mentioned over a span of text (Clancy 1980).

The notion of topic as a clause level pragmatic notion probably stems from the work of the Prague School linguists (see above). Like the term "focus," the term "topic" was not used by these early linguists. Nevertheless, they came up with the *concept* that part of every (or almost every) clause must be "old," or already known information, and another part must be "new," or asserted information.

15.2 The morphosyntax of focus, contrast, and "topicalization"

Probably the most common way of adjusting the pragmatic status of particular pieces of information is INTONATION – English speakers draw special attention to parts of their utterances by pronouncing those parts more loudly, and/or at a higher pitch. Other common means of expressing various pragmatic statuses are word-order variations (see Section 9.5 on Subject–Complement inversion), various CLEFT constructions, and the use of different kinds of determining elements.

The use of intonation is fairly self-evident. Occasionally tempo or vocalization type are used for pragmatic purposes. For example, slow staccato speech can suggest an intensive assertion in English: "Wé ... háve ... nó ... móre ... móney!"

Screaming and whispering are obvious ways of achieving special pragmatic effects via vocalization type.

There is a large literature on the use of intonation and vocalization type in English to express pragmatic nuances of meaning. Good places to start to investigate these topics include Lambrecht (1996), Brazil *et al.* (1997), and Selkirk (2002). In the following sections we will provide additional discussion and examples of three types of "fronting" constructions and cleft constructions.

Constituent order variation

There are at least three constructions which exploit the clause-initial position for ascribing special marked pragmatic statuses to clause elements. These we will term clause-internal FRONTING, LEFT-DISLOCATION, and APPOSITION. These three constructions differ in how the initial element relates to the rest of the clause. In fronting, a non-Subject is simply placed in front (to the "left") of the Subject within the boundaries of the clause. In left-dislocation a pronominal "copy" of the fronted element remains in the clause proper. In apposition, there is no syntactic relation between the fronted element and the rest of the clause. These statuses can be schematized as follows. The notations will be discussed further below:

(20) a. [NP ...]$_s$ Clause-internal fronting – the NP is still entirely within S.
      b. [NPi [... NPi ...]$_s$]$_{s'}$ Left dislocation – there is a copy of the NP in S.
      c. [NP] [S]   Apposition – the NP is not represented in S at all.

In other words, noun phrases that are placed in clause-initial position can be an integral part of the clause (20a), grammatically adjoined to the clause but not an integral part of it (20b), or grammatically separate from the following clause (20c).[1]

The following are some invented examples of each of these constructions:

(21) Fronting: *Money* you can't live without.
      Left-dislocation: *Money.* She would have to get some.
                          As for money, it's the root of all evil.
      Apposition: *Money.* What a waste of energy!

The following is an example of clause-internal OBJECT FRONTING for expressing a particular kind of contrastive focus:

(22) Beans I like; carrots I don't.

There is no corresponding "Subject fronting" construction, since immediately preverbal is the normal position for Subjects; therefore that position does not attribute any marked (i.e., "special") pragmatic status beyond that of Subjects in general.

Though constituents other than Objects may be fronted in this way, Object fronting is perhaps the most striking case, probably because IP Complements, such as Direct Objects, are "normally" quite rigidly fixed following the predicating element. Other examples of clause-internal fronting constructions include the following:

(23)　**Fronted IP modifier**
　　　　Carefully they crossed the river.
　　　　With his head down he twists to look at Guil.

(24)　**Fronted predicate Complement**
　　　　A doctor she became.
　　　　Into the woods he went.

Note that these are not "inversion" constructions as described in Section 9.5. In those constructions the Subject "inverts" (exchanges places with) a Complement in the predicate. In these constructions the Subject remains in position, right before the Predicating element.

In these fronting constructions, the fronted element remains inside the boundaries of the clause proper. Constructions known as LEFT-DISLOCATION place a clause element outside the syntactic boundaries of the clause. Sometimes left-dislocation is called EXTRAPOSITION, PREPOSING, or LEFT-DETACHMENT. In terms of structure, the dislocated element occupies a constituent structure position that is adjoined to the clause at a higher level. In the generative tradition, that position is sometimes referred to as the TOPIC position. This analysis may be displayed in the following way:

(25)　　　　　　S′
　　　　　　　╱‾‾╲
　　　　TOPIC　　S

Here S′ is pronounced "S prime" or "S bar" and refers to a grammatical structure that is larger than a clause. S refers to a simple clause, while TOPIC refers to a structural position that is outside S, but still grammatically associated with it.

The TOPIC position, then, serves as a site where various elements can be "copied" out of S. For example:

(26)　a.　My father, he likes Beethoven.
　　　　b.　Beethoven, now I enjoy his music.
　　　　c.　As for kabbalah, I found it utterly incomprehensible.
　　　　d.　As for working the ebony, it blunts tools very rapidly.

This notion of topic is strictly structural. Whatever functional (i.e., communicative) properties may be associated with topicalization constructions in this tradition are tangential to their structural status.

Cleft constructions

A CLEFT CONSTRUCTION is an equative predicate nominal consisting of a noun phrase (NP$_i$) and a relative clause whose R-element is coreferential with NP$_i$ (see Section 14.3.4 on relative clauses). NP$_i$ is commonly referred to as the CLEFTED CONSTITUENT, and is normally found to the left of the rest of the clause, though it may appear in other positions. Cleft constructions can be formulated most generally as follows:

(27)   DP$_i$ *be* [[... DP$_i$ ...]$_{RelCl}$]$_{DPj}$

The two DPs (DP$_i$ and DP$_j$) in this construction can occur in either order.

In a corpus study of spoken American English, Piotrowski (2009) shows that there are four main types of cleft construction; those she terms IT-clefts, WH-clefts, REVERSE WH-clefts, and existential THERE-clefts (examples from Piotrowski 2009:1):

(28)   a.   It's an apartment that I want to rent.   IT-cleft
        b.   What I want is a good apartment to rent.   WH-cleft
        c.   An apartment is what I want to rent.   REVERSE WH-cleft
        d.   There's an apartment that I want to rent.   THERE-cleft

Piotrowski studies the uses of these construction types and concludes, among other things, that REVERSE WH-clefts are the most common cleft constructions in spoken English. Furthermore, clefts in general do not typically express contrastive focus, as is often claimed in traditional grammars. In other words, these constructions are not used only to "correct" a presumed false assumption on the part of the hearer, as described above for fronting constructions, but also to refer to participants that are highly relevant to the preceding text. For example, a speaker is likely to use example (28c) when there is a possible set of alternatives to the proposition I WANT TO RENT AN APARTMENT, but the speaker wishes to assert that THIS alternative is the most relevant to the current conversation.

15.3 Negation

A NEGATIVE clause is one which expresses the idea that some event, situation, or state of affairs does *not* hold. Negative clauses usually occur in the context of some presupposition, functioning to negate or counterassert that presupposition. For example, if I say *Jorge didn't clean up the kitchen* I probably assume the hearer presupposes that Jorge did, or should have, cleaned up the kitchen. In this respect, negative clauses are functionally similar to contrastive focus clauses.

Clausal negation

Prototypical negative constructions are those that negate an entire proposition. These we will describe as CLAUSAL NEGATION, e.g., *I didn't do it*. Other types of negation are associated with particular constituents of clauses, e.g., *I have no bananas*. This will be referred to as CONSTITUENT NEGATION. In this section we will primarily discuss clausal negation. Toward the end we will deal briefly with constituent negation, and some other types of negation in English.

Standard clausal negation involves the insertion of the negative particle *not* in the I position, after an auxiliary and before the main predicating element (see Section 11.3).

(29)   It *is not unique* to the industrial sector
       Karpov *did not reach* that standard until 15
       they *had not given* the subject much thought
       Was it not a drunken pedlar in a parson's habit?

Derivational negation

English grammar has several ways of negating a root by using derivational morphology. Several negative prefixes, including *un-*, *non-*, *il-/ir-/in-*, *de-*, and *a-*, can be interpreted as "negative" in some way, though they each have their own individual meanings and spheres of applicability:

(30)   **un**happy   **non**-smoker   **il**legal
       unselfish   **non**-past tense **ir**reverant
       unreasonable **non**-entity   **in**tolerant
       untie   **im**possible
       unglue

       deregulate   **a**moral
       deescalate   **a**historical

Negative quantifiers

In addition to these examples of DERIVATIONAL NEGATION, individual constituents may be negated using the negative forms *not* and *no*. The particle *not* negates DPs, while *no* negates NPs:

(31)   *Not* negating DPs (not NPs)   *No* negating NPs (not DPs)
         *not student   not the students   no students   *no the students
                         not my student   no student   *no my students

Because *no* negates NPs, rather than DPs, it falls into the category of quantifiers serving determining functions, such as *every*, *all*, *some*, *any*, etc.

The following are examples of *no* negating clause constituents of various categories:

(32) **Negation of Subject Complement**
It's *no problem.*
I'm *no good at thinking of names.*

(33) **Negation of Object**
We were getting *no money* from anywhere.
I mean she's got *no children.*

(34) **Negation of Subject**
No children would want to see the film.
Secondly, *no component* in this programme should be seen in isolation.

(35) **Negation of Complement of preposition**
Not quite the poverty of *no shoes*, ...
With *no berries* to pick, nor game to hunt, food would soon be a problem.
No lover did she tryst with. (Fronted Complement of the "stranded" preposition *with.*)

Not as a constituent negator freely occurs with DPs that are Subjects:

(36) **Constituent negation of Subject**
Not a soul would speak English, ...

DP negation with *not* of non-Subjects is overwhelmingly used in the corpora as a kind of negative conjunction (see, Huddleston and Pullum 2002:1313). These are situations in which the negative is being contrasted with an affirmative conjunct:

(37) a. They saw it as a land that could produce a commodity, *not a country.*
b. ??They saw it as *not a country.*
c. They are leaving not on Friday, but on Saturday.
d. ??They are leaving not on Friday.

Example (37a) (from the COCA) is very representative of examples of DP negation in the corpora. The negated DP, *not a country*, is conjoined to the Complement of the preposition, and contrasted with it. The corresponding form without the other conjunct (37b) is nearly unacceptable. The pair in (37c) and (37d) (from Huddleston and Pullum 2002:1313) illustrates the same phenomenon. This usage of *not* as a conjunction also occurs with modifiers (38):

(38) And investors benefit if companies are clearly, *not hazily*, understood by the City.

In CSE there is a prescriptive norm that says there should be only one negative marker in a clause – either clausal negation, or constituent negation, but not both.

For example, the following attested examples are considered non-standard in many varieties:

(39)   I don't see nothing.
He never had no patience,
I've not had none for so many hours now.
We're not putting nobody down..

15.4   Non-declarative speech acts

Normally we think of language as functioning to express information. In fact, this is only one of the functions of language. Language is a tool for accomplishing many social tasks. Some of these include apologizing, promising, naming, greeting, complaining, etc. These are "speech acts" (Austin 1965), i.e., sociocultural tasks normally accomplished using speech.

A PERFORMATIVE utterance is one which simultaneously describes and enacts a speech act. In order to qualify as a performative, the main verb has to describe a speech act, it has to be in the present tense, and have a first person Subject. For example:

(40)   a.   I apologize for being late.
        b.   He apologizes for being late.

In the right context, example (40a) counts as an apology. (40b), on the other hand, is *not* an apology – it is a description of an apology. Similarly:

(41)   a.   I promise to be there at eight.
        b.   I promised to be there at eight.

Example (41a) may be a promise, while (41b) does not count as a promise, but as a description of an earlier promise.

Some acts may or may not be accomplished with speech, e.g., helping, or entertaining. You can help someone, or entertain someone using language as a tool, but these acts can also be performed without language. There are some social acts, however, for which language is particularly useful. These include:

* expressing information
* requesting information
* getting other people to do something

Because these acts are so common, and so useful, all languages have "well-oiled" (i.e., fully habitualized, automated, and regular) grammaticalized structures to express them. In order to perform these acts, we don't need to use an overt "performative" construction, although we can if we want to. For example:

(42)   a.   I declare that Oregon is a beautiful state.
       b.   I ask you where the honey is.
       c.   I command you to finish your peas.

Example (42a) accomplishes the act of declaring that Oregon is a beautiful state. It doesn't make Oregon a beautiful state, but it does count as a declaration of that idea. (42b) counts as an act of requesting information, and (42c) would count as a command in the right context.

However, the acts of declaring, commanding, and requesting are so common, so useful, that speakers rarely need overt performative verbs in order to accomplish them. Rather, they are more typically accomplished with grammaticalized clause types often called moods. The typical moods that languages express grammatically are:

* DECLARATIVE: Prototypically function to declare information.
* INTERROGATIVE: Prototypically function to request information.
* IMPERATIVE: Prototypically function to get someone to do something.

Although the prototypical functions of the moods are as given above, they are so useful that they can be used to accomplish other speech acts as well. When a given mood is used to accomplish an act that is not prototypical, we call that an INDIRECT SPEECH ACT (Searle 1975). Indirect speech acts are particularly useful when it comes to getting other people to act (the imperative function). In many circumstances it is considered impolite to simply command someone to do something. Therefore declarative and interrogative moods can be used to accomplish manipulative functions, depending on the context:

(43)   a.   It's cold in here.
       b.   Can you close the window?
       c.   Please close the window.
       d.   Close the window!

In the right context, an utterance such as (43a) may be understood as a request for someone else to close a window. (43b) is more direct, but is still in the form of a question. (43c) is no longer in the form of a question. It is a direct, but polite, command, and would be appropriate if the speaker has some kind of established authority over the addressee. (43d) is very direct, and would be impolite, unless there were some kind of emergency that required the window to be closed immediately.

The term "declarative" in traditional grammar refers to clauses that simply assert information. Often the term "declarative mood" or even "declarative mode" will be found in the literature. In this book, and in linguistics in general, declarative is not a mode (see Section 12.3 for a linguistic treatment of mode and modality). In the tradition of speech act theory, the term ASSERTION most closely approximates the traditional notion of declarative mood.

Since declarative clauses have constituted the majority of the examples already presented in this book, the remainder of this section will discuss various kinds of non-declarative speech acts.

Interrogatives

Within the class of interrogative clauses, languages typically distinguish two subtypes: those for which the information requested is a simple affirmation or disaffirmation (yes or no), and those for which the requested information is more elaborate, either a phrase, a proposition, or an entire discourse. In the following two subsections these two general types of interrogative clauses will be discussed.

YES/NO QUESTIONS

In English, YES/NO QUESTIONS are prototypically expressed with a combination of intonation and Subject/auxiliary inversion (see Section 11.3.1), as in examples (44a and b). If the corresponding assertion contains no auxiliary, the "dummy" auxiliary *do* is inserted (44c):

(44) a. Will he arrive on time?
       b. Can they bite corn nuts?
       c. Do you want to subsume these clause types?

In all varieties of English, simple Subject–auxiliary inversion occurs in predicate nominal, existential, and locational clauses (45a, b, and c). In some varieties, chiefly in British English, this extends to possessive constructions (45d):

(45) a. Is he a ringmaster?
       b. Are there cats under your flowerpots?
       c. Were you in the butterscotch pudding?
       d. Have you a match?

A TAG QUESTION is a yes/no question consisting of a declarative clause plus a "tag" that requests confirmation or disconfirmation of the declarative clause. Spoken English uses tag questions in particular pragmatic environments. For example:

(46) She's leaving, *isn't she?*
       She's leaving, *right?*

These questions seem to imply that the speaker expects an affirmative answer. The basic yes/no question strategy described earlier does not carry this pragmatic expectation.

In English, as in most languages, the morphosyntax of yes/no questions is used in several different ways in discourse. These include:

1. **To solicit information.** This is the basic use of yes/no questions:

(47)   Is it time for class?

2. **To request action.** This is quite different from soliciting information, and can be considered an indirect speech act:

(48)   Could you close the window?

3. **For rhetorical effect.** Rhetorical questions expect no answer:

(49)   Are you always such a slob?

4. **Confirmation** of information already possessed by the speaker:

(50)   You're going, aren't you?
       Aren't you going?

5. **Intensification:**

(51)   Did he ever yell!

Although the clause type illustrated in (51) does not typically have question intonation, it does exhibit Subject/auxiliary inversion common to yes/no questions, and therefore is in the syntactic form of a question.

WH-QUESTIONS

Questions that expect a more elaborate response than simply an affirmation or disaffirmation are called WH-PRONOUN QUESTIONS, CONTENT QUESTIONS, INFORMATION QUESTIONS, or simply WH-QUESTIONS. The last term reflects the fact that in written English the WH-pronouns all contain a *w* and an *h*. These are the WH-pronouns described in Section 5.3.

The WH-pronoun in a question accomplishes two tasks: it marks the clause as a question, and it indicates what information is being requested. For example, (52b) through (52f) are questions formed from the declarative clause in (52a):

(52)   a.   Zebedee threw stones at the herring.
      b.   *Who* threw stones at the herring?
      c.   *What* did Zeb throw 0 at the herring?
      d.   *What* did Zeb throw stones at 0?
      e.   *What* did Zeb do to the herring?
      f.   *Why* did Zeb throw stones at the herring?

The presence of the WH-pronoun at the beginning of the clause marks the clause as a question. The actual WH-pronoun chosen, plus a "gap" somewhere in the clause (indicated by a zero in examples (52c and d)) or the "pro-verb" *do* (52e), specify what information the speaker is requesting the hearer to fill in.

WH-pronouns can occur with adpositions. When a nominal in an oblique role is questioned, the adposition may remain with the gap (53a) or it may go along with the WH-pronoun (53b):

(53)   a.   What did you eat with 0?
       b.   With what did you eat 0?

Imperatives

IMPERATIVES are construction types that are used to directly command the hearer to perform some actions, e.g., *Eat this!* Usually imperatives are understood to refer to second person Subjects. Because it is so common and expected for the intended Subject of an imperative clause to be the hearer, reference to the Subject is not necessary and so the Subject is often omitted. Imperatives also are not open to tense and aspect contrasts available in other construction types. This is because it is simply pragmatically impossible to command someone to perform acts with certain tense/aspect categories, e.g., **Ate that!*, **be having fun!*, etc. In the following paragraphs we will discuss and exemplify certain functional and formal properties of imperative constructions.

The forms of imperatives in English are very straightforward; it's the uses that are complicated. The imperative form is simply the bare form of a verb:

(54)   *Give* me a break!
       Toss me that hammer, will ya?

There are also so-called first and third person imperatives:

(55)   a.   Let's go!   First person (plural) imperative
       b.   May they go!   Third person imperative

In any speech community, getting other people to behave in a certain way is always fraught with complicated social implications. As we've seen in the previous section, questions are often used to accomplish the function of getting people to do things without using a direct imperative. On the other hand, the imperative form is often used for purposes other than to get someone else to do something. Here we will describe a few of the ways in which English speakers use the form of imperative clauses.

The prototypical function of imperatives is to command someone to do something. For this type of imperative to be FELICITOUS (i.e., interpretable, acceptable, or "happy" in the context), the speaker must have some clear authority over the hearer:

(56)   a.   "Awright, lads," he had cried, smiling over the fifty new airmen. "We're just going to trot round to the park, *so follow me.*" (a commander to subordinates)
       b.   Now, *turn over your papers.* (a teacher to a class)

However, people rarely "command" other people to do things. More common are situations in which someone tries to help, encourage, or give advice to someone else. Imperative constructions can be a good way to do this:

(57) a. To get to the downtown station, *take the 33 bus*. (instructions)
b. If you need anything, just *holler*! (permission, enablement)
c. *Melt two ounces of butter* ... (a step in a process in a recipe)
d. *Listen* Mark; I know what it's like to feel pain. (advice)

There are also many situations in which imperative constructions cannot literally be taken as attempts to get someone to do something:

(58) a. That's right. *Misinterpret everything I say*! (sarcasm)
b. *Get well soon.* (good wishes)
c. *Get outta here!* (I don't believe what you just said)
d. *You go girl!* (encouragement, or congratulations)
e. *Have a good day.* (leave taking)

Advertising is a particularly rich domain for imperative and imperative-like constructions. Advertisers often evoke an encouraging, advice-giving stance when issuing instructions to potential customers. Here are a few examples:

(59) *Work hard. Be successful. Go someplace* where none of that matters.

Example (60) consists of three imperatives in a row from an advertisement for a luxury sports utility vehicle. They are couched as advice directed to people who probably think of themselves as already working hard and being successful (otherwise they wouldn't be able to afford the vehicle advertised). Of course, this is accompanied by a picture of the vehicle and its hard-working, successful owner in a pristine, natural setting.

A large number of imperatives in advertising evoke the friendly advice-giving stance when they inform potential customers of the steps they may take to buy the advertised product:

(60) *see your dealer* ...
Go to www.myproduct.com for further details.
Follow the "seek it local" signs.

In addition to the advice-giving stance, imperative constructions in advertising can inform potential customers of the benefits enjoyed by users of the products:

(61) *Keep* DVDs as long as you want.
Get over 100 channels!
Compete for the grand prize ...
Save money!

Finally, the function of getting people to behave in a certain way can be couched as statements and questions. In the previous section we described some "indirect imperatives" based on an interrogative model. Here are some in the form of statements:

(62)   I'm gonna need a key for that room. (give me a key)
        I want you to call me Crystal. (call me Crystal)
        You don't have to tell your therapist everything. (don't tell her about this)
        Better head for Jerry's. (head for Jerry's)

Summary

In this chapter several "pragmatic statuses" were defined and illustrated, including principally:

- identifiability
- referentiality
- contrastive focus
- topicality

Two categories of contrastive clauses were then discussed:

- "fronting" constructions
- cleft constructions

Finally, several pragmatically marked construction types were described, both in terms of their grammatical form, and in terms of how they are used in communication. These are:

- negative constructions
- yes/no questions
- WH-questions
- imperatives

FURTHER READING

The best solid overview and introduction to linguistic pragmatics is Levinson (1983). Classic readings on speech act theory include Austin (1965) and Searle (1975). Grice (1975 and 1981) are foundational articles in conversational implicature. Sperber and Wilson (1995) elaborate an entire theory of communication, Relevance Theory, based on Grice's insights. Lambrecht (1996) analyzes several grammatical constructions in terms of information structure, including speakers' assumptions about hearers' state of knowledge and consciousness. Chesterman (2005) proposes a refreshing approach to definiteness in language, focusing on English and Finnish. Lambrecht (2001) and Calude (2009) are recent works dealing with cleft constructions. Calude specifically treats cleft constructions in spoken English.

Exercises

1. State the presupposed part of each of the following sentences.
   Contrastive stress is indicated by all uppercase letters. The first example is done for you. (Hint: See if you can identify and describe the trick in the last example.)

   a. Is Molly's father playing that loud music? Presupposition: Someone is playing loud music.
   b. The figure that Kate saw behind the omnibus looked familiar.
   c. SORIA wandered off into the bush.
   d. It was inspector Clouseau who finally solved the mystery.
   e. When did you stop smoking those filthy things?
   f. Carver sold BEVERLY that heap of junk.
   g. What I don't understand is why you didn't call the police immediately.
   h. Where did Soria go?
   i. I don't spank my children because I love them.

2. The following paragraph contains several constructions that clash in terms of the pragmatic statuses of various pieces of information. This manipulation of the information structure renders it almost incoherent. Rewrite the paragraph using more natural information structure. In your rewrite, try to reconstruct what the original author probably wrote. This is the first paragraph of a mystery novel:

   > It was Kate Adleigh who glanced warily over her shoulder. The pit was what the late-summer night was as black as, and stormy, the glare of lightening flashes that were blue-white and intermittent lighting it. Like a mad thing skittered the wind through the nearly empty streets of Manhattan, about her ankles twisting the sensible skirt of Kate and flapping the sign of the vendor of chestnuts. The sort of wild night which Kate's upstairs neighbor, Pearl St. John, had been kidnapped less than a month earlier on it was. And in just such a street that was shadowy it was that poor Pearl was apprehended by the kidnappers and they bore her off to the fate that was hers.

Glossary

ablaut   A morphological process involving changing a vowel in a stem, e.g., *sing*, *sang*, and *sung*.

accessible   Available to be referred to in discourse. A referent is accessible if the hearer is able to establish a referential link to it; in other words, if the hearer knows what or whom the speaker is talking about.

accusative case   In English, personal pronouns that refer to Complements are said to be in the accusative case. These are *me*, *you*, *him*, *her*, *us*, and *them*. The forms *you* and *it* are both nominative and accusative case; *her* is both genitive (possessor) and accusative case.

action nominalization   A noun that derives from a verb and refers to the action described by a verb, e.g., *dancing*, *destruction*, or *laughter*.

activated   A referent is activated if it has already been introduced onto the discourse stage, either directly or indirectly.

active voice   A grammatical construction in which a very AGENT-like participant is expressed as a Subject, and a very PATIENT-like participant is expressed as a Direct Object. Active voice contrasts with passive voice.

action   An event type controlled by a AGENT or FORCE, but not necessarily involving an affected patient, e.g., *Sally danced and danced.*

action-process   An event type in which an actor (AGENT or FORCE) causes a change in an affected participant, e.g., *The king's stinking son fired me.*

adjective   A grammatically distinct word class that consists mostly of words that express property concepts, such as color, size, shape, value, human propensity, etc.

adjective phrase   A phrase headed by an adjective, e.g., *very good*, *uncomfortably hot.*

adjunct   Clause elements that are "optional." Usually adjuncts have the syntactic function of Modification.

adposition   A cover term for prepositions and postpositions.

adverb   A grammatically distinct word class that typically express such notions as time, manner, purpose, reason, likelihood, etc. Examples include *later*, *earlier*, *surely*, *quickly*, *defiantly*, and *very.*

adverbial adjuncts   Modifying words or phrases within the verb phrase.

adverbial clauses   A type of dependent clause that fulfills an "adverb" function within another clause.

affix/affixation   A bound morpheme that always attaches to the same class of words. Affix is a cover term for prefix and suffix in English.

agglutinative/agglutinating   A language in which morphemes can be easily divided, and which tends to express only one meaning per morpheme is of the agglutinative type.

agreement   A conceptual category which reflects the person and/or number of an element in a syntactic relation with the word that expresses the category. For example, present tense verbs agree with their subjects in English.

aktionsart   See "inherent aspect."

allomorph   A systematic variant pronunciation of a morpheme.

ambiguous   When a structure (a word, a phrase, or a sentence) expresses more than one meaning, it is ambiguous, e.g., *the right bank.*

analytic expression   The expression of a conceptual category that involves the addition of separate words, or adjustments in word order. These are sometimes called "syntactic" or "periphrastic" expressions.

analytic/syntactic/periphrastic reflexive   A reflexive construction expressed by adding a distinct reflexive pronoun, e.g., *He tied himself to a tree.*

anaphoric device   Any grammatical functor (pronouns or certain zeros) that refer to a *thing.*

Anglophone   Countries in which English is the main *lingua franca* are called *Anglophone countries.*

apposition   Two units in a syntactic structure are "in apposition" if there is no hierarchical relationship between the two, and they refer to the same message world entity or situation. For example, in *my son John, my son* and *John* are in apposition.

arbitrariness   One of the properties of the bond between form and function in a symbolic system. Linguistic signs can be arbitrarily related to their meanings.

argument   A noun phrase that has a grammatical relation to something else. For example, Subjects and Objects are arguments of verbs.

argument structure   The particular relationship between semantic roles and grammatical relations in a construction. For example AGENT→Subject, PATIENT→Object is one argument structure for the verb *break* (*Jeremy broke the stick*). PATIENT→Subject is another (*the stick broke*).

articles   "Small" words that express pragmatic status, such as identifiability. English has three articles *the*, 'definite,' *a(n)*, 'indefinite singular,' and zero 'indefinite plural.'

aspect   Grammatical expression of the internal temporal "shape" of a situation or event, whether it is ongoing, completed, instantaneous, iterative, etc. Aspect refers to the grammatical constructions that reflect this semantic domain.

assembly   A combination of two or more form–function composites.

asserted/assertion   A speech act in which information is expressed. This contrasts, for example, with commands and questions. Assertion is the prototypical function of declarative mood clauses.

atelic   The inherent aspect (cf.) of situations that do not have logical endpoints, e.g., READING, PLAYING. (See also "telic.")

attributive function of adjectives   Adjectives that occur within NPs to modify the head noun are in the attributive function (*beautiful dreamer*). This contrasts with the predicative function of adjectives (*that dreamer is beautiful*).

autosegmental   A morphological process whereby some feature other than consonant or vowel quality is changed in order to express a conceptual category. Stress shift is an autosegmental process in English.

auxiliary   Auxiliaries are grammatical functors that express tense, aspect, mood, and/or other notions, but do not express the main semantic sense of the verb phrase. In traditional English grammar auxiliaries are sometimes called "helping verbs."

auxiliary stacking   The use of multiple auxiliaries, where each auxiliary is the Complement of the previous one, as in *They will have been traveling for three days*.

available   See "accessible."

backformation   A word form resulting from a speaker's subconscious application of a spurious morphosyntactic rule, e.g., *clo* is a backformation from *clothes*.

bare form   A word form that includes no affixation. For example, the bare form of a verb in English expresses present tense, non-third person singular.

bitransitive   See "ditransitive."

borrowing   When speakers of a language treat a word, morpheme, or construction from another language as a lexical item in their own language. For example, the modern English words *thug, pajamas, chic, canoe, tomatoes*, and thousands of others are borrowed.

bound morpheme   A morpheme that is not normally pronounced as a separate word, but must be attached phonologically to some other word. Examples include the *-ed* and *-s* suffixes, and the "articles" *a/an* and *the*.

bound root   A word root that depends on another root or morpheme in order to be incorporated into discourse, e.g., *duce* in *reduce*, or *cran* in *cranberry*.

bounded   Having distinct boundaries. Prototypical nouns refer to clearly bounded entities, such as rocks, trees, and cars.

branch   The lines that connect nodes in a syntactic tree.

cardinal numbers   The numbers used in counting: *one, two, three*, etc.

case frame   See "argument structure."

causative construction   A grammatical construction that increases transitivity by adding a controlling participant to the scene evoked by a verb, e.g., *Alice made the cat smile* (analytic causative) or *Bunyan felled the tree* (lexical causative of *the tree fell*).

clausal argument   A clause that functions as an argument of another clause, e.g., *We know where you live*.

clausal Subject   A clause that functions as the Subject of another clause, e.g., *It bothers me that they always have loud parties*.

clause   The grammatical instantiation of a proposition.

cleft construction   A special pragmatically marked predicate nominal construction involving a relative clause, e.g., *What I want is another cup of coffee*.

clefted constituent   The constituent in a cleft construction that is coreferential with the head of the relative clause, e.g., *What I want is another cup of coffee*.

clitic   A bound morpheme that functions at a phrase or clause level, rather than attaching only to words of a particular word class.

cognitive model   An idealized mental representation that serves as a basis for understanding and storing knowledge.

coining   The act of inventing new words.

colexicalization   The lexicalization of multiple form–function composites into a single lexeme, e.g., *by the way*, meaning "I'd like to change the topic of our conversation."

collective noun   A noun that refers to a recognized group of individuals, e.g., *flock, herd, band, team, committee,* etc.

collective plural   One of a set of six plural nouns that refer to well defined groups: *people, cattle, fowl, swine, vermin, kine.*

comparative construction   A construction in which two items are compared according to some property, e.g., *My daddy is bigger than your daddy.*

Complement-taking predicator   A predicator, usually a verb, that may or must take a clause as its Complement, e.g., *I think Tiffany is coming to dinner.*

Complementation   If the syntactic Head of a phrasal category is not also the semantic head, it must have a Complement. The Complement is the semantic head of the phrasal category. It "completes" the meaning of the category.

complementizer   A word that introduces a whole clause when it is embedded within another clause or phrase. Unstressed *that* is a complementizer: *The book that I read.*

completive   An aspectual category that expresses the ending phase of an action, e.g., *He finished writing his dissertation.*

compound words   Words that result from the colexicalization of two other words.

conceptual category   An element of meaning that is expressed by systematic grammatical variation.

conditional clause   A type of adverbial clause that expresses conditions under which other situations may or may not hold true in the message world. For example, *if I were a carpenter* ... (distinct from traditional "conditional mood").

conjunction   A word class consisting of "small" words that join two larger constituents. Coordinating conjunctions in English include *and, or,* and *but.* Subordinating conjunctions include *because, so,* and *if.*

constituency   Elements in a syntactic structure exhibit constituency when they "merge" or "clump together" syntactically.

constituent focus   A pragmatic status that applies only to certain constituents of a clause. This contrasts with *verum focus.*

constituent order typology   The division of the languages of the world into "types" depending on how the major constituents, usually Subject, Object, and verb.

constructions   Well-established morphosyntactic patterns (see, e.g., Goldberg 1995).

content questions   See "WH-questions."

contextual meaning   Meaning that derives from the context in which a form is used.

contrastive focus   A pragmatic feature of participants in the message world, as presented by a speaker. For example, *SALLY made the salad* (with extra stress on SALLY) is likely to be used when the speaker believes the hearer thinks someone other than Sally made the salad.

contrastive stress   See "contrastive focus."

coordination   A grammatical construction in which two syntactic elements are combined with no asymmetry between them. Words, phrases, or clauses can be coordinated, but only elements of the same category may be combined in this way.

core grammatical relations   Subject, Object, and Indirect Object.

coreferential   Two anaphoric devices are coreferential if they both refer to the same discourse-world entity.

countable noun   A noun that refers to items that can be easily and usefully counted, e.g., *keys*, *oysters*, or *cabbages*.

counterfactual modality   A modal category that implies that the information expressed is contrary to fact, e.g., *If you had been there* ... implies that you weren't there.

dative shift   A construction that upgrades an Indirect Object to Direct Object status without requiring any other morphological adjustments in the clause: *I gave Mildred the book*. In this example, *Mildred* has undergone dative shift.

declarative mood   A grammatical form specifically adapted to accomplish the speech act of assertion.

defective   A morphosyntactic paradigm is defective if one or more logically possible members are missing.

definite   See "identifiability."

deictic center   The reference point for a deictic relation, e.g., the time of speaking is usually the deictic center for tense.

demonstrative pronouns   Words that imply "pointing" (demonstrating). Demonstratives may occur within noun phrases, as in *these* houses, or can themselves be heads of noun phrases: *I'll take three of those*.

deontic modality   Modal categories that express the relative necessity of the information expressed in the clause, e.g., *I should do it* and *I must do it* express two degrees of deontic modality.

dependent   A clause that cannot normally be integrated into discourse without occurring in construction with some other clause is a dependent clause.

derivation/derivational categories/derivational morphemes/derivational processes   In contrast with inflection, derivational morphology creates new stems from simpler stems or roots. For example, the suffix often spelled *–able* in English creates adjectives based on verb roots – *questionable*, *reliable*, etc.

Determination   A syntactic function that "grounds" a noun phrase in pragmatic space.

determiner   A grammatical element that "grounds" a noun phrase in pragmatic space, including the articles (*a/an*, *the*, Ø), demonstratives (*this*, *that*, *these*, *those*), all possessors, some question words, pronouns, etc. Determination is the syntactic function filled by determiners.

determiner phrase   A syntactic "clump" headed by a determiner. Abbreviated DP, determiner phrases can also be thought of as "determined noun phrases."

deverbal   When a verb is used as a noun, adjective, or some other function, that verb has become deverbal, e.g., the suffix *-able* is a deverbalizer, because when it attaches to a verb, the resulting word becomes an adjective: *a believable report*.

Direct Object   See "Object."

direct speech   A quotation in which the exact words of a speaker are reported, e.g., *Walter said "I love Taiwan."*

discourse   The act of communication. Sentences may exist in isolation, divorced from any actual function. Discourse, however, involves actual linguistic acts performed in order to accomplish real social tasks.

discourse manipulability/discourse manipulable/discourse deployable   A pragmatic property of prototypical nouns; entities in the discourse world that can be referred to repeatedly as "the same" are discourse manipulable.

discourse-pragmatic properties   The properties of a linguistic element that relate to that element's use in communication, e.g., topicality, contrastiveness, referentiality, identifiability, etc. See also "pragmatic statuses."

discourse referentiality   Having continuous presence on the discourse stage.

discourse stage/discourse world   A metaphor often used by linguists to represent how communication occurs. People communicate with one another by setting up mental "scenes" that have "participants," "acts," "scripts," "climaxes," etc.

discretize   Convert a continuous scale into discrete categories, e.g., the vocabularies of all languages discretize the color spectrum into a small number of basic color terms.

distribution   (also "distributional properties") The distribution of a morphosyntactic unit is the list of syntactic contexts in which it may appear.

ditransitive   One term used to describe a situation that involves three obligatory participants, or a clause that has three core arguments, for example *Alice gave the Mad Hatter a stern look.*

divalent   See "transitive."

dummy pronoun   A pronoun used to occupy an obligatory position in clause structure, even though there may be no concrete referent, e.g., *it* in *It's raining.*

dynamic   A type of situation that involves motion and/or change. Verbs that describe such situations are sometimes called "dynamic verbs," in opposition to "stative verbs."

echo questions   Questions used for clarification, that retain the constituent order of the clause being clarified, e.g., *You bought a what???*

ellipsis   The obvious omission of some element of clause structure. For example, answers to questions sometimes contain ellipsis: *Where are you going? To the store.*

embedded   Clauses that occur within other units in syntactic structure are embedded: *The horse I ride is fast.*

enclitic   A clitic that follows its host.

epistemic modality   Conceptual categories that express the speaker's commitment to the truth of an utterance are epistemic. For example, *may, might,* and *will* are epistemic modal auxiliaries.

equative clauses   Predicate nominal clauses in which the subject is asserted to be identical to the Predicate Complement, e.g., *Marianne is the teacher.*

evidential/evidentiality   Conceptual categories that express the source of the information contained in an utterance: *I hear you're getting married.*

existential construction   A clause that expresses the existence of a particular entity, e.g., *There once was a king* or *There's ants in the syrup!*

expression types   Structural ways that languages express conceptual categories. There are three groups of expression types discussed in this text: lexical, morphological, and syntactic.

extraction   The metaphorical "movement" of a unit out of its normal position in a syntactic structure. For example, *Beans I like.*

extraposed   A nominal element that appears outside the boundaries of a clause. For example, *My father, what a great guy!*

finite   Any verb or auxiliary that has its own Inflection and Subject is finite.

flat structure   A syntactic structure in which all nodes are at the same hierarchical level. In other words, a structure that does not involve "nesting."

focus/focus of assertion The pragmatic status usually associated with the asserted information in a clause. In addition to this basic use of the term "focus" in linguistics, there are also several special kinds of focus, such as contrastive focus.

frame See "argument structure."

free morpheme/free root A word root that does not have to attach to some other morpheme in order to be understood. Words such as *dog* and *cat* are free roots.

fronting The placement of a constituent, such as a direct object or prepositional phase, at the beginning of a clause. A fronted element remains inside the boundary of the clause, in contrast to left-dislocated elements, e.g. *Beans I like.*

full lexical words Words that have rich semantic content, such as *incredible*, *garden*, and *Wonderland*. These are in contrast to grammatical morphemes.

fully finite clauses Clauses that have all the tense, aspect, modality, and subject reference information needed for independent assertions, e.g., *I know that Mildred cares about her garden.*

function The syntactic, semantic, pragmatic, and social "tasks" performed by linguistic structures.

functional sentence perspective The name applied to a theoretical framework originating with a school of linguistics known as the Prague School, *ca.* 1939–60.

fused relative clauses Relative clauses in which the Head and the relative pronoun are the same element. Also known as headless relative clauses, e.g., *Whoever goes to the store should buy bread.*

fusion/fusional The degree to which a language tends to express one meaning per morpheme. A language which employs fusion extensively is of the fusional morphological type.

gap strategy One of the ways in which the role of the R-element in a relative clause can be expressed, e.g., *The guy that my sister married 0 is a doctor.*

Generative Grammar A linguistic theory, originating in the 1950s and 60s, associated with the linguist Noam Chomsky. In Generative Grammar, a language is conceived as an infinitely large, but highly constrained, set of grammatical sentences. Grammar is understood as a "machine" that "generates" all of the grammatical sentences and none of the ungrammatical sentences of a language.

genitive noun phrase/genitive phrase A noun phrase that bears the genitive relationship to another noun phrase, e.g., *the queen's*, or a genitive pronoun, e.g., *their house.*

gloss A convenient abbreviation for the meaning of a morpheme, used in linguistic examples to help readers understand the structure of the language being described even if they have no previous knowledge of the language.

grammatical functors Grammatical functors express limited "grammatical" meanings (such as "third person singular" and "past tense").

grammatical relations Grammatically instantiated relations between words in phrases or clauses. Some typical grammatical relations are Subject, Object, and Indirect Object.

grammatical valence The number of core arguments in a clause. This contrasts with semantic valence.

grammaticalization The historical process whereby full lexical words become grammatical functors.

habitual aspect The aspectual category that describes actions that regularly take place from time to time, e.g., *My son walks to school every day.*

head In this book the unmodified term "head" is shorthand for "syntactic head."

headless relative clause See "fused relative clause."

heavy shifting The tendency for "heavy" constituents (those with several syllables) to appear late in a clause, e.g., *It'd be nice <u>for you come over sometime</u>* in place of *For you to come over sometime would be nice.*

helping verbs A term from traditional grammar that corresponds to the use of the term auxiliary in this book.

hierarchical structure The characteristic of syntactic structures whereby units occur "nested" within larger units.

hortatory A discourse genre in which the speaker tries to persuade the audience to be or act in a particular way.

host The free morpheme that a bound morpheme attaches to.

hypothetical modality Any modal category that expresses a situation that may or may not conceivably be true, e.g., *<u>If I see David</u>, I'll tell him you called.*

iconicity A property of the bond between form and function in a symbolic system. Signs are iconic to the extent that they constitute a "picture" of their meanings.

idealized A concept in which the details are left vague is idealized. The meanings of words are often stored in memory in terms of idealized images.

identifiable A pragmatic feature of participants in the message world, as presented by a speaker. Participants are treated as identifiable if the speaker assumes that the hearer can uniquely identify the referent.

idiosyncratic Unpatterned, random. For example, the plural of *child* is idiosyncratic, *children*, in that there are no other nouns in the modern language that form their plural in precisely this way.

imperfective An aspectual category that describes a situation as an ongoing activity, rather than as a completed whole.

impersonal construction A passive-like construction in which no specific AGENT is implied, e.g., *she was considered lost* or *they say there'll be snow tomorrow.*

implicative CTPs that normally imply that their complements are true are implicative, e.g., *He made me do it* implies that I did it.

inchoative The aspect that describes the Subject of a clause as entering into a state, e.g., *The milk turned sour.*

indefinite If a speaker judges the audience cannot establish a referential link to a particular discourse stage participant, the speaker may present that nominal as indefinite, e.g., *There's <u>a cat</u> under the bed.*

indefinite pronoun A pronoun that refers to an indefinite entity, e.g., *someone, somewhere, sometime.*

index of fusion See "fusion."

index of synthesis See "synthesis."

Indirect Object A term from traditional grammar that refers to the semantic RECIPIENT in a ditransitive clause. In this book, Indirect Object is the grammatical relation of the RECIPIENT in a ditransitive clause only when it is preceded by *to*: *We gave the printer to Michael.*

indirect speech   A clause in which the words of a speaker are reported but not directly quoted, e.g., *Walter said he loves Taiwan.*

individuated   The property of being distinct from other entities. Prototypical nouns refer to individuated entities, such as cars and birds. Unindividuated entities include such notions as mud, ants, and marksmanship.

inference   Guessing with evidence.

infinitive   A verb form that expresses no inflectional information (see "inflection").

inflectable auxiliaries   The auxiliaries *be, have, do, need,* and *dare* are inflectable because they take tense and Subject Inflection. These contrast with the modal auxiliaries which, for the most part, do not inflect.

inflected verb phrase   A syntactic category that consists of a verb phrase with a (possibly zero) auxiliary. See also "Inflection."

inflection   See also "derivation," above. Inflectional categories are conceptual categories that do not create new stems. Rather, they add specific "grammatical" information to already existing stems. Inflectional categories tend to occur in "paradigms."

Inflection   (note upper case "I") Morphosyntactically expressed information about the tense/aspect/mode and Subject that is required of every independent clause in English.

inflectional categories   Conceptual categories that are expressed by inflectional morphology (see "inflection").

inflectional phrase   See "inflected verb phrase."

inflectional processes   See "inflection."

inherent aspect   (also "aktionsart") The aspectual characteristics of an event or situation independent of any grammatical expression, e.g., FLASH is an inherently punctual concept, while KNOW is inherently stative, and CREATE is inherently dynamic.

interlanguage   The internal grammar developed by a second language learner who has not become fully proficient in the second language.

interposition   One of the minor "tests" for constituency. If an adverb or other variable-position element of a syntactic structure may occur between two other elements, chances are there is a syntactic boundary at that point.

interrogative pronouns   Pronouns that replace the missing information in content questions. All interrogative pronouns contain the letters "w" and "h" in written English.

intransitive verb/intransitive clauses   A verb is intransitive if its basic, unmarked argument structure contains only one participant on stage. A clause is intransitive if it does not contain a direct object, either expressed or implied.

inversion   A syntactic construction in which two elements appear in the opposite order from their "normal" position. See "Subject-AUX inversion."

irrealis   A high-level modal category that indicates that the information expressed in the clause has not happened yet, and may not ever actually happen.

isolating language   A language that tends to express only one meaning per morpheme is of the isolating type.

isomorphism   A kind of lexical expression in which a stem expresses a conceptual category by conspicuously failing to undergo any morphological or syntactic change. For example, the past tenses of the verbs *hit, cut, shed,* and others are the same as the bare forms.

iterative aspect   The aspectual category that describes multiple occurrences of a normally punctual action, e.g., *He was coughing all night.*

labile verb   See "lexical middle."

left-dislocation/left-detachment   The placement of a nominal constituent outside of a clause, while leaving a pronominal "copy" within the clause boundary, e.g., *Money, it's what I want.*

lexeme   A memorized unit in the lexicon.

lexical ambiguity   When a structure is ambiguous because it contains a polysemous word. For example, *Let's try another bank* is lexically ambiguous because the word *bank* can refer to the edge of a river or a financial institution.

lexical categories   The lowest (terminal) nodes on a phrase structure tree refer to lexical categories. They consist of units that do not have internal syntactic structure themselves.

lexical causative (also "inherently causative verb")   A verb whose lexical entry expresses the meaning of cause and effect, e.g., *kill* means 'cause to die.'

lexical content   The rich (detailed) semantic features associated with a lexical vocabulary item like *rabbit* or *underwear.*

lexical entry   See "lexeme."

lexical expression   A way of expressing a conceptual category that cannot be predicted by a pattern or rule. Strong suppletion, weak suppletion, and isomorphism are the general subtypes of lexical expression.

lexical middle (also "inherently middle verb" or "labile verb")   A verb that describes a situation that normally involves an AGENT and a PATIENT, but when used intransitively places the PATIENT in the subject relation, e.g., *The window* broke, *The city* changed.

lexical reciprocal (also "inherently reciprocal verb")   A verb that is understood as reciprocal when occurring in an intransitive frame and a plural subject, e.g., *Lynn and Cory hugged, … shook hands.*

lexical reflexive (also "inherently reflexive verb")   A verb that is understood as reflexive when occurring in an intransitive frame. These all seem to be "grooming" verbs, like *dress, bathe, shave,* etc.

lexicalization   The process of becoming a lexical item.

lexical typology   A way of classifying languages according to how they characteristically bundle semantic features into particular lexical items.

lexicon   The store of all memorized words, pieces of words, and regular patterns of word formation and combination that are available to a language user.

lingua franca   A language used over a wide area by people who speak various other languages as their mother tongues.

locative clause   A clause that expresses the location of the subject, e.g., *The broom is in the kitchen.*

main clause   In a clause combining construction, the main clause is the clause on which all dependent clauses rely for at least some of their inflectional information.

mandative   A manipulative construction in which the subject is presented as indirectly commanding someone to do something, e.g., *They had him wash their car, We insisted he wash the car.*

manipulative   A class of CTPs that describe activities in which the actor attempts to get another person to do something. e.g., *force, make, compel, command, urge, ask to, ask that, request.*

mass noun   A noun that refers to a substance, and therefore is not normally used in the plural, e.g., *air, sand, water.*

matrix clause   A clause that has another clause embedded within it, e.g., *I wonder who's coming to dinner?*

matrix verb   The main verb in a matrix clause.

middle construction/middle voice   A grammatical construction that removes an AGENT from the scene evoked by a verb, places the PATIENT in the subject role, and presents the situation as a process undergone by the PATIENT, with no mention or implication of the presence of a distinct AGENT, e.g., *This Volvo drives like a dream.*

minimalism   A recent approach within the Generative tradition that stresses the importance of simplicity in syntactic analysis (Chomsky 1995, Radford 1997). The "minimalist criterion" states that, given two analyses that adequately account for the same range of data, the simpler analysis is preferred.

modal auxiliaries   A class of auxiliaries that express various modal categories, e.g., *could, should, would, might, may, can, will, must, ought to,* and *have to.*

modality   (also "mode") A set of conceptual categories that express various speaker attitudes or perspectives on an event. Mode is grammaticalized in English mostly via the modal auxiliaries.

Modification   A very general syntactic function filled by words that are syntactically "optional," but are important for enriching the scene elaborated in the discourse.

monoclausal   Consisting of one clause. Compound verbs and serial verbs are monoclausal.

mood   The moods of English are the grammaticalized ways of expressing the very common and useful speech acts of stating propositions (declarative mood), requesting information (interrogative mood), and manipulating other people (imperative mood).

morpheme   A linguistic unit that contributes meaning to an utterance, but cannot itself be divided into smaller meaningful parts. For example, *dog, -ed, -s, the,* and *almanac* are all morphemes.

morphological causative   A causative construction that is expressed primarily by a morphological process applied to a verb. There are no productive morphological causatives in Modern English.

morphological expression   A way of expressing a conceptual category by altering the shape of a word.

morphological typology   A classification of languages according to how much "work" is accomplished by morphology, vs. the syntax and lexicon. Also, how distinct the morphemes are from one another.

morphology   The study of the shapes of words, or, more specifically, how words are constructed out of smaller meaningful pieces (see "morpheme") in order to express conceptual categories.

morphophonemic processes   Systematic adjustments in pronunciation.

morphosyntax   The part of grammatical knowledge that involves how conceptual categories are expressed structurally.

mother tongue   An individual's first language – the language one learns at home from birth to about six years of age.

motion+manner language   A category within lexical typology that describes languages that characteristically combine the semantic features of motion and manner of motion in individual verbs. English is a motion+manner language.

motion+path language   A category within lexical typology that describes languages that characteristically combine the semantic features of motion and path in individual verbs. Spanish is more of a motion+path language.

motivated   A linguistic phenomenon is motivated if it makes sense in terms of the function of language as a tool for communication.

narrative   A discourse genre that describes events in time sequence, e.g., stories and descriptions of personal experiences are narratives.

negative implicative   A kind of CTP that implies that its complement is false, e.g., *pretend, fail, prohibit.*

node   A labeled branching point on a constituent structure tree.

nominalization   Nouns or noun phrases that are built on roots that prototypically belong to other word classes or syntactic categories, e.g., *the collapse of the empire.* This is a noun phrase that refers to the ACTION of the empire collapsing.

nominative case   Personal pronouns that refer to subjects are in the nominative case, e.g., *I, you, she, he, we,* and *they.*

non-count nouns/non-countable nouns   Nouns that refer to items that cannot easily be counted. These include mass nouns, abstract nouns, and action nominalizations.

non-finite clauses   Dependent clauses that carry no inflectional information at all. Non-finite clauses are built around bare infinitives or *to*-infinitives.

non-implicative   CTPs that do not imply anything about the truth of their Complements, e.g., *say, think,* and *believe.*

noun   The word class that prototypically expresses bounded, individuated entities. Defined in English by a cluster of morphosyntactic properties, including the ability to function as Subject or Object of a verb.

noun phrase   A "clump" in constituent structure that is headed by a noun, and which may or may not contain other elements.

Object (also Direct Object)   A core grammatical relation, defined in English by the following properties: (1) position immediately following the verb in pragmatically neutral, transitive clauses, (2) when pronominalized, non-Subject pronouns are used, and (3) absence of a preceding preposition.

Object Complement   A clause element that functions as a Complement and refers back to the object of the clause, e.g., *I consider him a bore.*

Object demotion   A grammatical construction that demotes a participant that is "normally" (i.e., in a prototypical scene evoked by the verb) the Direct Object to an oblique role. The semantic effect of Object demotion is to "downplay" the PATIENT, and/or render it less wholly affected by the action of the verb: *Aileron kicked at the Duke.*

Object incorporation   A kind of compounding that downplays (or "deperspectivizes") the PATIENT of an event by expressing it as part of the verb, rather than as an independent noun. For example: *We went fox hunting.*

Object omission   A construction that downplays (or "deperspectivizes") an Object by simply omitting it: *Calvin already ate.*

objective referentiality   An entity is objectively referential if it exists as a bounded, individuated entity on the discourse stage.

oblique   A nominal element of a clause that does not bear a core grammatical relation to the verb.

open class   A word class is "open" if it easily admits new members. In general, lexical vocabulary consist of open classes, while grammatical functors do not.

ordinal numbers   Numbers referenced according to their position in a series, e.g., *first, second, third,* etc.

paradigm   A related set of conceptual categories. For example, the tense paradigm of English consists of past tense, present tense, and future tense.

paradigm leveling   The diachronic (over time) process of filling in "gaps" in morphosyntactic paradigms. For example, the many vernacular ways of expressing second person plural (*y'all, youse, yinz,* etc.) are examples of paradigm leveling.

participial clauses   Dependent clauses that are headed by verbs in the present or past participle forms. Such verbs are semi-finite.

participant reference   The job of referring to or mentioning participants in the discourse world.

passive/passive voice/passive construction   A grammatical construction that upgrades (or "perspectivizes") a PATIENT to the subject position and either omits or demotes the AGENT to an oblique role: *The baby was named Jane (by her parents).*

past participle   A deverbalized form of a verb. English has present participles, marked with the suffix *-ing,* and past participles marked in various ways, but most commonly with *-ed* or *-en.*

perfect aspect   An aspect that expresses a state as the result of an earlier event. The perfect aspect construction in English involves the auxiliary *have*: *I have been there before, They had entered Albanian airspace.*

performative   An utterance that simultaneously describes and enacts a speech act, e.g., *I hereby christen thee the HMS Pinafore.*

periphrastic expression   See "syntactic expression."

periphrastic reflexive   See "analytic reflexive."

perfective aspect   An aspect that expresses a situation as a completed whole.

personal passive   A passive construction in which a specific AGENT is clearly implied or present, e.g., *he was attacked by a mad dog.*

personal pronoun   The ordinary pronouns that constitute arguments of clauses in the declarative mood, e.g., *I, you, she, he, we, they, me,* etc.

perspective/perspectivization   The point of view a speaker chooses to take with respect to a message world situation. For example, the same situation can be described with an AGENT in perspective, *Orna baked these cookies,* or with a PATIENT in perspective, *These cookies were baked by Orna.*

phonosemantic processes   Word building processes based on how pieces of words sound, e.g., a word ending in a plosive consonant plus *-le* probably refers to small, repetitive actions, *wiggle, wobble, babble, jingle, whittle,* etc.

phrasal categories Syntactic categories that are not lexical categories. Phrasal categories (DP, NP, IP, VP, PP, etc.) are defined by the word class of the syntactic head.

phrasal nodes Points where a phrase structure tree branches such that one branch leads to the "head" of the phrase.

phrasal verb Many verbs in English consist of two parts: a verb root plus a preposition-like particle or two, e.g., *look up, figure out, boogie down, etc.*

phrase A syntactic "clump" consisting of one or more words that function together in some way.

pied-piping When a Complement of a preposition is extracted to the front of the clause, the preposition may come with it. This is sometimes called pied-piping, e.g., *To whom have I the pleasure of speaking?*

plain modal auxiliaries Modal auxiliaries that do not inflect, e.g., *can, might, must, could, should, would, will, shall,* and *may.*

plosive consonant A consonant in which pressure is built up in the mouth and suddenly released. The plosive consonants (or plosives) of English are /p, t, k, b, d, g/.

pluperfect A traditional grammar term for perfect aspect plus past tense, e.g. *I had already seen that movie.*

polysemy/polysemous A form is polysemous if it has more than one meaning, e.g., the word *bank* can refer to several quite distinct discourse-world items.

polysynthetic A language in which words tend to have many morphemes is of the polysynthetic type.

post-nominal modifiers Modifiers that occur after the head in a noun phrase, e.g., *There weren't very many people present.*

post-posed A syntactic unit is post-posed if it comes at the end of a clause, rather than in its normal, or "unmarked," position.

postposition An adposition that follows its related noun phrase. For example, if English had postpositions instead of prepositions, the expression *the house to* would mean 'to the house,' and *my mother with* would mean 'with my mother.'

pragmatics The study of how context affects and is affected by linguistic communication.

pragmatic statuses The statuses that pieces of information have in the minds of speakers and hearers. Speakers are constantly inferring what the pragmatic status of information is in the minds of their audience. See also "discourse-pragmatic properties."

pragmatically marked A clause is pragmatically marked if it expresses some unusual pragmatic function, such as a question, negation, contrastiveness.

Prague School A community of linguists located in Prague, Czechoslovakia, ca. 1939–60. The Prague School devised the theoretical framework known as Functional Sentence Perspective, which is the precursor to most modern theories of pragmatics.

predeterminers/predeterminer quantifiers Elements that can precede a determiner in a determined noun phrase, e.g., *all my children.*

predicate adjectives Constructions in which an adjective is the main predicating element, e.g., *You are just wonderful.*

Predicate Complement A Complement of the main predicator of a clause, e.g., *She loves karaoke* or *We are happy to be here.*

predicate locative   Constructions in which a locational expression is the main predicating element, e.g., *The bananas are in the kitchen.*

predicate nominals   Constructions in which a noun phrase is the main predicating element, e.g., *You are just the person I'm looking for.*

predicate possessive   Constructions in which a possessor is the main predicating element, e.g., *This hammer is mine.*

predicating element   The part of a Predicate that expresses its main semantic content. This is usually a verb, but may also be a noun phrase, adjective phrase, or any number of other syntactic categories.

Predication   The syntactic function prototypically filled by verb phrases.

prefix/prefixation   A morpheme that attaches to the beginning of a word, e.g., the negative *un-* (*unlovely, unsuccessful, uncola*) or repetitive *re-* (*reconsider, recook, reengineer*) are prefixes in English.

preposing   See "extraposition."

preposition   An adposition that precedes its related noun phrase, e.g., *to the house, with my mother.*

present participle   A kind of deverbalization that refers to an ongoing action, e.g., *a falling leaf.*

presentational   A construction that functions primarily to bring a new participant onto the discourse stage, e.g., *On the horizon there appeared a ship.*

presupposition   A proposition that is assumed when asserting some other proposition.

primary word stress   One syllable in every full lexical word of English is pronounced with a higher pitch and higher volume than the other syllables. Word stress contrasts with contrastive stress, which is phonetic stress that is even higher in energy that primary word stress. This is indicated at times with an acute accent, e.g., *háppy, convért.*

proclitic   A clitic that attaches to the beginning of its host. These contrast with enclitics, which attach to the ends of their hosts.

productive   A morphological process is said to be very productive if it has the same effect every time it applies, and it applies to all members of a well-defined class of stems.

pro-form   A linguistic unit that "stands for" another, larger, unit. Pronouns are the major type of pro-form, though pro-verbs and perhaps other pro-forms also exist. See "substitution."

progressive aspect   The semantic aspectual category that involves ongoing, dynamic processes, e.g., *My son is walking to school.*

progressive construction   A construction of English formed with the inflected auxiliary *be* plus a present participle of a verb, often used to express progressive aspect, e.g., *We are growing tomatoes.*

projection/projection principle   A phrasal category is the projection of its syntactic Head. In other words, the syntactic Head of a phrase determines its syntactic properties.

pronoun retention   One strategy for referring to the R-element in a relative clause. For example: *that's the guy who I can never remember his name.*

pronoun   A free grammatical functor that refers to a thing but is not a full lexical noun, e.g., *he is clearly overreacting.*

proper inclusion   One semantic function of predicate nominal constructions. A construction expresses proper inclusion if it predicates that the Subject is a member of a group represented in the Complement, e.g., *Marianne is a teacher.*

proposition   A semantic notion that involves one or more entities (or participants) and a property or relation that involves them. Propositions are the semantic bases for grammatical clauses.

prototype   The member of a category that best instantiates the entire category. For example, a sparrow is probably the prototype for the category of "bird" for most English speakers.

pro-verb   A pro-form that "stands for" a verb or verb phrase. See "substitution."

punctual aspect   The inherent aspect of events that have no internal temporal structure because they occur in an instant in time, e.g., *sneeze, flash*, and *trip*. This is sometimes referred to as "punctiliar aspect" or "semelfactive aspect."

quantifier float   The phenomenon whereby certain predeterminers can "float" off of a Subject noun phrase into the Infl position, e.g., *My children will all wear t-shirts.*

quotative   A construction or particle used to describe someone's actual words, e.g., "*Why are we in this handbasket?" asked Alice.*

realis   A modal category that describes situations that are asserted to be true. Realis contrasts with irrealis.

reanalyzed   A structure is reanalyzed if speakers unconsciously assign it to a new syntactic category. For example, the verb *go* is currently being reanalyzed as a future auxiliary, e.g., *We're gonna get married.*

reciprocal   A construction that expresses a semantically transitive situation in which the two participants are distinct but their roles as controller and affected participant are "combined," e.g., *Lynn and Cory hugged* or *Lynn and Cory hugged each other.*

referent   A discourse-world entity that may be referred to by any participant reference form, such as a noun phrase or pronoun. For example, the referent of the phrase *my grandmother* is a person in the message world – the speaker's grandmother.

referential   See "objective referentiality."

reflexive   A valence-decreasing construction that expresses a semantically transitive situation in which the controller and the affected participant are the same entity, e.g., *Mildred loves herself.*

reflexive pronoun   A special pronoun whose main function is to indicate that the subject and object of a transitive clause refer to the same entity, e.g., *myself, yourself, herself,* etc.

relative clause   A clause that is a constituent of a noun phrase, and which modifies or characterizes the head of the noun phrase, e.g., *the Duke who trod on Aileron's toe.*

relative pronoun   A special pronoun that introduces a relative clause and simultaneously expresses the relativized element. In English, as in many other languages, the set of relative pronouns is similar, but not identical, to the set of interrogative pronouns.

relativizer   A special particle, such as *that* (unstressed) in English, that introduces a relative clause. It contrasts with a relative pronoun in that a relativizer does not reflect any features (animacy, case, etc.) of the relativized element.

R-element   The constituent within a relative clause that is coreferential with the head noun. In English the R-element is usually expressed by a zero or a relative pronoun.

reported speech   A cover term for direct and indirect speech.

resultative   A construction that expresses the idea that the subject is in a particular state as a result of the action described in the construction, e.g., *She has skinned her knee.*

root   A morpheme that expresses the basic meaning of a word, and cannot be further divided into smaller morphemes.

schema   One way in which the human mind stores and categorizes information. Schemata are conventional images involving generalized entities and relationships used as bases on which to build specific messages.

scripts   Common, prototypical sequences of events that can be used to store and communicate knowledge. For example, in most cities there is a script for riding a bus, so once a speaker sets up the "bus ride" frame, she can say *when I went to pay, I couldn't find my pass* without having to explain why she would pay, or what a "pass" is.

secondary word stress   In words of three or more syllables, there is one primary word stress, and possibly a secondary word stress. This is indicated at times with a grave accent, e.g., *cìrcumstànce, felícitỳ*.

semantic head   The semantic Head of a noun phrase is the noun that refers to the same thing that the whole phrase refers to, for example *man* in *the tall handsome garbage man who lives next door*. Quite often, semantic Heads and syntactic Heads are the same, but not always.

semantic properties   The meaning characteristics of a lexical item. Full lexical words, like *linguistic* and *participant*, are rich in semantic properties, while grammatical functors, such as *it* and *-ed*, tend to have restricted semantic properties.

semantic roles   The roles that participants play in message world situations, e.g., AGENT, PATIENT, etc. These exist independently of linguistic structure.

semantic valence   The number of required participants in a scene.

semelfactive aspect   See "punctual aspect."

semi-auxiliaries   A set of verbs that are being reanalyzed as auxiliaries, but have not yet lost all of their verbal properties. These include *used to, be going to*, and *ought*.

semi-finite clauses   Clauses headed by subjunctive or participial verbs are semi-finite in that they may express only a limited number of tense/aspect categories. They are not infinitives, but neither are they fully finite.

semi-implicative   CTPs that imply that their Complement clauses are probably true, e.g., *try to, ask to*.

sentence   There are two major definitions of the term "sentence" in linguistics. One is equivalent to what we have termed "clause" in this book, i.e., the highest node in a syntactic tree. The second definition of "sentence" is a structurally integrated combination of clauses. For example, a string such as *the director came in, closing the door behind her* may be considered one sentence consisting of two clauses.

serial verbs   Verbs that occur together in one verb phrase, e.g., *run go get me a newspaper*.

sound symbolism   When words sound like their meanings, for example *splash, thud, crash, bang, pop*, and *bow wow* are all sound-symbolic words in English.

specificity   A pragmatic feature of participants in the message world. A referent is specific if the speaker presents it as referring to a particular entity that exists in the message world. Non-specific expressions in English include *whoever, whatever, someone, anyone, and no one*.

state/stative   A situation type which involves no action or change, e.g., *to be red, to know, to see, to feel*.

stem An inflectable form of a word, often opposed to a root. A stem may be morphologically complex, but need not be.

stem change A morphological process that involves a regular, patterned change in a stem, e.g., *drive → drove*.

stress shift An autosegmental morphological process that distinguishes some noun–verb pairs, e.g., *permít* vs. *pérmit, recórd* vs. *récord*.

strong verbs Verbs that form their past tense and/or past participle with a stem change. These were the regular verbs in the Old English period, whence the name "strong" comes, e.g., *know → knew* and *sit → sat*.

structural ambiguity When a structure is ambiguous because it has two possible syntactic analyses. For example, *Lincoln wrote the Gettysburg address on a train.*

Subject A core grammatical relation, defined in English by the following properties: (1) immediately preverbal position in pragmatically neutral clauses, (2) Subject case pronouns, and (3) control of verb agreement.

Subject Complement A predicate Complement that in some sense "refers to" the Subject of the clause, e.g., *He looks <u>tired</u>.*

subjunctive There are two constructions that are traditionally known as subjunctive. These are semi-finite clause types that are used to express certain hypothetical or counterfactual modalities, e.g.: *<u>That he have a good place to stay</u> is very important to us* (present subjunctive = hypothetical modality), *<u>If I were a rich man</u> ...* (past subjunctive = counterfactual modality).

subordinating conjunction/subordinator Any of a set of forms that introduce clauses that usually express presupposed information. These include *because, after, before, while*, and others.

substitution One of the major "tests" for constituency. If a sequence of linguistic units can be replaced by a pro-form, the sequence is probably a constituent at some level.

suffix A morpheme that attaches to the end of a word, e.g., the past tense *-ed* or plural *-s* morphemes in English.

suppletion/strong suppletion When the two forms express different conceptual categories (exemplified by the pair *go/went* in English).

suprafix A regular morphological process involving an autosegmental feature such as pitch, tone, or stress. The structural difference between *convért* (a verb) and *cónvert* (a noun) is a suprafix.

syllable A phonological unit consisting of a vowel or other sonorant segment, plus potentially non-sonorant segments. For example, the English word *strength* consists of one syllable, *any* consists of two syllables, and *syllable* consists of three syllables.

syntactic categories A cover term for all the types of units that figure into a syntactic structure. Syntactic categories include lexical categories, phrasal categories, and, in earlier versions of Generative grammar, the category S, or Sentence.

syntactic function The structural relations between words in sentences. There are nine major syntactic functions as described in this text: Subject, Predicate, Direct Object, Indirect Object, Oblique, Complement, Head, Inflection, and Modification.

syntactic Head The element of a phrase that determines (or "projects") the syntactic properties of the whole phrase, e.g., *ridiculous big orange <u>cat</u>* or *<u>in</u> the willows*.

syntactic merger   When two elements in a syntactic structure "clump together" to form a constituent.

syntactic properties   How a word combines with other elements in constructions, e.g., whether it follows a preposition, heads a noun phrase, functions as a predicator, etc.

syntactic reflexive   A reflexive construction that employs a reflexive pronoun, e.g., *You are making yourself look creepy.*

syntactic typology   A way of categorizing the languages of the world according to the ways they characteristically order their syntax.

syntactic valence   The number of core arguments in a clause.

syntax   The study of how words "clump together" in phrases and clauses.

tag question   A yes/no question that consists of a statement, followed by a "tag," usually of opposite polarity, e.g., *You're almost finished, aren't you?*

TAM   An acronym for Tense, Aspect, and Mode.

telic   The inherent aspect (cf.) of a situation that has a logical endpoint, e.g., READING *WAR AND PEACE*, PLAYING A GAME. (See also "atelic.")

tense   Grammatical expression of the temporal orientation of an event with respect to a point of reference, usually the time of utterance.

terminal node   The lowest nodes on a syntactic tree.

time-stable   Something that doesn't change very much over time is said to be time-stable. This is a major semantic property that characterizes prototypical nouns.

topic   This term has many different uses in linguistics. The most general notion is "what someone is talking *about*." This is a pragmatic notion that sometimes relates to individual clauses and sometimes to longer spans of discourse.

transitive/transitivity   Traditionally, a clause that has more than one core argument, e.g., *they will never stop hunting you, the King's stinking son fired me*, and *you mock my pain!* However, more recent approaches tend to treat transitivity as a continuously variable property (Hopper and Thompson 1980).

translational motion   Movement that involves change in place, e.g., *exit, escape, ascend.* These notions are distinct from other motion concepts such as *turn, walk*, and *roll*.

trivalent   See "ditransitive."

truth-value focus   A special kind of construction that emphasizes the truth of a proposition, e.g., *I DID see a pussy cat!*

typological characteristics   The features of a language that give it its own unique "character."

typology   A division of any range of phenomena into types.

ungrammatical   A string of linguistic units is ungrammatical if it is not sanctioned by the grammatical patterns of the language. For example, the following strings are ungrammatical as linguistic units in English: *dog the, my you mock pain, fleas has dog my, turnips like I.*

unidentifiable   A referent is treated as unidentifiable if the speaker believes the audience cannot identify it.

univalent   See "intransitive."

valence   Valence can be thought of as a grammatical notion or a semantic notion; in both cases valence refers to a number. Grammatical valence refers to the number of arguments in a clause, whereas semantic valence refers to the number of core participants in a situation.

verb phrase   A "clump" in constituent structure that is headed by a verb, and which may or may not contain other elements. Verb phrases may be inflected, in which case they may be referred to as IPs, or "inflected verb phrases."

vernacular   Spoken language, in particular features of spoken language that distinguish it from a "standard," e.g., *ain't, init,* or *might could.*

verum focus   See "truth value focus."

vestigial   A remnant of an earlier functional system that currently has lost all or most of its function, e.g., verb agreement in English is vestigial.

voice   Constructions that adjust the relationship between semantic roles and grammatical relations are sometimes referred to as "voices" (see also "valence").

volition   Willingness, intention, purpose. A participant that acts with volition does so on purpose, e.g., *Mortimer changed the sheets.*

vowel reduction   The tendency for English vowels to be "reduced" (pronounced with less clarity) in unstressed syllables.

weak suppletion   A lexical process whereby a conceptual category is expressed by exchanging a root for another similar root, e.g., *buy~bought.*

weak verbs   English verbs for which the past tense is spelled *-ed.*

WH-questions   Questions that expect a response that involves a richer answer than simply "yes" or "no." Such questions usually contain a WH-pronoun, e.g., *Now why did you go and do that?*

WH-pronoun   One of several pronouns, all of which contain a "w" and an "h" that stand for some unknown, unspecified, or extracted piece of information, e.g., *what, who, whom, when, where, why, which, whence, whither,* and *how.*

word   A linguistic unit in syntactic structure that may be delimited by pauses in discourse.

word classes   Word classes are traditionally called "parts of speech." They are grammatically distinct classes of lexical items, such as nouns, verbs, adjectives, adverbs, etc.

yes/no question   A question for which the expected response is "yes" or "no," e.g., *Are you my mommy?*

zero pronoun   An anaphoric device that has no phonetic content. It can be thought of as the "conspicuous absence" of an audible form, e.g., *Calvin came in and 0 sat down.*

Endnotes

1. There is a large literature on sound symbolism and iconicity in language. Iconicity is the more general term referring to any respect in which the form of language is a "picture" (an icon) of its meaning. Sound symbolism is a type of iconicity that refers to how certain sounds seem to inherently evoke certain images in the minds of speakers.

2. A few verb-like expressions, such as *beware* and *daresay*, do not have acceptable past tense forms – **bewore/bewared/wasware *daredsay/daresaid*. These have arguably been "lexicalized" as fixed expressions, since they lack so many of the properties characteristic of good healthy verbs of English. See Chapter 3 for a discussion of lexicalization.

3. A tradition often used by linguists is to place as asterisk (*) before a form if it is not attested in the language. These are hypothetical forms that a speaker's internal grammar does not recognize or produce. Sometimes linguists will say that such forms are *ungrammatical*.

4. In spite of the spelling differences, the words *buy*, *cry*, and *die* all end in the same sound in modern English.

NOTES ON CHAPTER 1

1. The asterisk before these Indo-European roots means that these roots are hypothesized forms. There are no written records of the original Indo-European language, so all descriptions of this language are reconstructions based on forms in daughter languages from much later periods. This use of the asterisk is different from the use that means the form is ungrammatical in the modern language.

2. Sometimes the term "Vikings" is used to refer to all Scandinavian immigrants, whether they were invaders, traders, colonists, or settlers. Other times, "Vikings" refers only to the famous maritime invaders and pillagers who harassed coastal and riverene communities throughout Europe (and North America) between about 700 and 900 CE, whereas more neutral terms like "Scandinavian immigrants" are used to refer to those Scandinavians who came to settle. In this book we will employ the latter terminology.

3. This statement also applies to Eastern European languages, such as the Slavic languages, though less so than their Western cousins. The Eastern European languages, especially those that use a version of the Cyrillic alphabet (Russian, Ukrainian, Belo-Russian, Bulgarian, and others), have been more directly influenced by Greek. Since Latin was also heavily influenced by Greek, the Greek influence in the West is less direct, but still significant.

4. Some (notably Bailey 1996) claim that the emerging *lingua franca* that we now call Middle English was a version of Norman French infused with Old English calques and grammatical vocabulary. This view has the advantage of offering a consistent and reasonable explanation for Middle English as a descendent of the conquerors' language (as are, for example, the modern "Romance" languages descendents of the language of the Roman conquerors of South-western Europe). The opposite, and majority, view has the disadvantage of proposing a highly unlikely scenario in which the conquerors began to speak the language of the conquered people. This kind of event is nearly unprecedented in world history. The question boils down to whether Middle English was basically Norman French with a lot of grammatical influence from Old English, or basically Old English with a lot of lexical influence from Norman French. This question, it seems to me, is infused with politics and nationalism and is not really substantive to the endeavor of *understanding* English grammar today. I prefer the view presented here of the history of English as a tapestry, in which various threads intertwine, and together form a new and wholly self-sufficient tool for communication. There are major and minor threads, to be sure, but no one thread necessarily needs to be the basic or most important one.

5. This word comes from Hawaiian pidgin, meaning "quick." It may be Austronesian in origin, or it may be an adaptation of the English word *quick*. If the latter, it is an interesting case of a word being borrowed from one language, and then borrowed back into the original language with a new meaning. It first entered the mainstream of English vocabulary in 1995, when computer programmer Ward Cunningham invented the term "Wikipedia." Since then, thousands of "wikis" have arisen, and are in use by many organizations and individuals around the world.

NOTES ON CHAPTER 2

1. Such morphemes are sometimes termed "portmanteau" morphemes. We will see several other examples of portmanteau morphemes throughout this book.

2. "Accusative" isn't really a very precise term for the set of pronouns that includes *me, us, him,* and *them,* since this term is usually (in other language traditions) reserved for the case that marks only *Direct Objects.* This is only one of the uses of the "accusative" pronouns in English. In addition, these pronouns are used in all situations where neither the nominative nor the genitive is specifically called for, e.g., after prepositions, *We looked at them, She rushed over to them,* and in one-word answers to questions: *Who's coming? ... Me!* Thus these pronouns are perhaps better characterized as the "general" or "unmarked" case. However, the term accusative has been used extensively in the literature (see, e.g., Huddleston and Pullum 2002), so we will continue to use this term throughout this book.

3. The second person plural forms in Table 2.2 are "familiar" rather than formal. Most varieties of American Spanish do not employ the second person plural familiar forms, so this chart represents Iberian Spanish (the Spanish of most of Spain). The formal second person forms are the same as third person, both in Iberian and American Spanish.

4. These terms (Subject and Object) were not given very explicit definitions in early typological work – they were mostly taken for granted. For now we can consider the Subject to be the noun phrase that refers to the most active participant in the scene that a clause refers to, while O refers to the least active participant. If there is only one participant, then the noun phrase that refers to that participant is the Subject, even if it is not very active at all.

5. These Japanese examples are in the simple or "plain" form. There are at least two other politeness levels that may seem more appropriate in the context of a written work such as this textbook. However, all these examples are grammatical, and the syntactic generalizations are the same for all levels.

6. Remember that terms in capital letters, such as CAUSE or EAT, refer to meaning components, not particular verbs of English or any other language. When particular words are mentioned in the text, they are given in italics, e.g., the verb *eat* expresses the meaning component EAT. The verb *feed* expresses the meaning components ENABLE (or CAUSE) and EAT.

7. German also has a verb, *stehlen*, that is cognate with English *steal*. However, for a theft involving force or violence, such as grabbing someone's handbag, *rauben* is more appropriate. *Stehlen* simply means "gain control over someone else's property," with no sense of confrontation or force (Fernando Zúñiga, p.c.).

NOTES ON CHAPTER 3

1. Thanks to Radford (1997) for the building codes metaphor.

2. There are good arguments that in fact assemblies like *cats* are lexicalized (memorized as units) *to a certain extent*. Assemblies that are used often tend to become established in memory as inseparable units, and so effectively become individual lexical items.

3. Note that I refer here mostly to the large numbers of English speakers (perhaps two billion or more) who live in Africa, Southern Asia, the Pacific, and other parts of the world where multiple languages are spoken, but where English is a *lingua franca*. These multilingual speakers vastly outnumber monolingual English speakers, most of whom live in North America, England, Australia, New Zealand, and a few other enclaves (probably no more than about 500 million in total).

4. This usage of *for* as a conjunction is purported to occur 408 times in oral speech in the BNC. However, a cursory look makes it clear that most of these are actually the prepositional use that has been mistagged as conjunction. Another significant portion of these examples consists of quotes or near quotes from the Bible, and other familiar literature, e.g., "Forgive him for he knows not what he does."

5. There are some situations in English in which an adjective is used as a noun, e.g., *the poor will always be with you*, or in elliptical expressions, e.g., *Would you like to try the white or the red?*

6. See Chapter 8 for the difference between DPs (Determined Noun Phrases) and NPs (Noun Phrases).

NOTES ON CHAPTER 4

1. *Sect* "divide," *form* "shape," *duce* "lead," *fer* "carry," *spect* "look."
2. While *clothes* is obviously related to the word *cloth*, I do not consider the former to be the plural of the latter for at least two reasons. (1) They mean different things. A cloth is not an item of clothing in modern English. (2) *Cloth* has a different plural, *cloths* (187 examples in the BNC). There are several other words that appear exclusively or predominantly in the plural that also refer to clothing of various kinds, including *trousers, pants, vestments, habiliments,* and, *perhaps, outskirts.*
3. Huddleston and Pullum (2002:480–1) argue against the analysis of *-'s* as a clitic, in favor of treating it as an ordinary inflectional case marker. While it is true that the morphological properties of *-'s* are different from those of other clitics, it also must be acknowledged that *-'s* behaves differently from other suffixes, such as the plural *-s*, as outlined here. So, if it is not exactly a clitic, and not exactly a suffix, it must be something else that falls "in between" the classic definitions of these types of morphemes. This is yet another example of how the reality of language tends to slip out of the well-defined categories that linguists like to make, and is probably rooted in the gradual nature of historical change. The genitive *-'s* is just on its own path of historical development that is different than the ones the plural suffix, the articles, and the auxiliaries are on.
4. Unless the sibilant consonant happens to be the plural suffix *-s*, in which case the genitive *-s* is not, normally, pronounced: *The cars' headlights* (the headlights of many cars) [kʰarz] ?[kʰarzɨz].
5. This proportion compares the number of examples with root voicing, V, to the number of examples with no root voicing, F, in the BNC, as indicated by the spelling with *v* vs. *f* (V/F). It is impossible to obtain these proportions for roots ending in interdental fricatives, since the BNC only employs English spelling, and the spelling system does not distinguish voiced from voiceless interdental fricatives.
6. There is another *re-* prefix that is cognate with the one intended in this chart. This prefix is descended from Latin, and occurs in many words of Latin origin, like *refuse, require, reduce, resolve, refer, relax, resist,* and dozens of others. Try as I might, I cannot discern any consistent or even vaguely predictable pattern associated with this prefix in Modern English; therefore I am not considering it to be one of the derivational morphemes described in this chart. The *re-* intended here is quite productive, and consistently means "do over again."

NOTES ON CHAPTER 5

1. Note that the genitive case ending *-'s* does not constitute a morphological feature of nouns, but of phrases. This morpheme is discussed in some detail in Section 8.2.
2. The word *kine* is an archaic plural of *cow*. The nouns *flora* and *fauna* have some properties of collective plurals, but are different enough that they are best considered to be outside of this class.

3. The independent genitive form *its* seems to many speakers to be ungrammatical. However, it occurs several times in the corpora consulted for this book, e.g., *Singapore had persevered with a road pricing scheme, while Hong Kong had withdrawn its.*

NOTES ON CHAPTER 6

1. See Delancey (1990) for an alternative definition of AGENT. I believe Delancey's definition of AGENT as "the first CAUSE in the clause" is essentially compatible with Fillmore's definition plus the notion of "discourse stage." That is, the clause is the linguistic unit within which scenes on the discourse stage are perspectivized. Insofar as the "instigator of the action" is equivalent to the "first CAUSE," and the discourse stage is equivalent to the "clause," the two definitions become near restatements of one another. Foley and Van Valin (1984) describe a functional continuum between two "macroroles," ACTOR and UNDERGOER. The prototypical ACTOR is an AGENT and the prototypical UNDERGOER a PATIENT in the classic case grammar sense. This is their method of preserving an objective definition of AGENT and PATIENT while still accounting for variability in grammatical expression of these roles.

2. This sense of the term "argument" is borrowed from mathematical logic, in which an argument is an independent variable in a function, in other words, a thing that has a property, or has a relation to some other thing. A nominal that doesn't have a grammatical relation to some other word is called either a "nonargument" or an oblique.

3. In this chapter we are using the term "noun phrase" to refer in a general way to all noun phrases, including both undetermined and determined noun phrases. Arguments for treating these as two separate syntactic categories will be presented in Section 8.2.

4. The verb *agonise/agonize* is often used in phrasal verb constructions like *to agonize over* or *to agonize on*. These are arguably transitive prepositional verbs. However, the verb *agonize* on its own clearly has an intransitive use, and this is the use intended in these examples; cf. *I confess to having agonised all night to reach my conclusions* (BNC).

5. The transitive uses of these verbs are causatives. These are action-processes, described below.

6. Greenbaum and Quirk (2004) call the present participle the "*ing*-participle."

NOTES ON CHAPTER 7

1. Or *determiner phrase*. In our simplification of generative syntax, the terms *determiner phrase* and *determined noun phrase* are synonymous.

2. There are some Complements that are not, strictly speaking, obligatory, yet if a potential Complement is omitted a significantly different sense is communicated by the phase. Different kinds of Complementation are discussed in Chapter 9. *Prototypical* Complements, however, are obligatory phrasal elements that are also not the syntactic Head of the phrase.

3. This may be considered an example of "Object omission" described in Chapter 13.

4. Consistent with the use of capitalization throughout this book, capital letters refer to meanings. Since propositions may be considered meanings that underlie communicative acts, we will use capital letters to describe them. In the tradition of predicate logic, there are very precise mathematical formulae for expressing propositions (predicate calculus – see, e.g., Partee *et al.* 1990). For the purposes of this book natural English will suffice for expressing underlying propositions and other semantic content. The capital letters will be the only clue that meanings, and not necessarily actual English utterances, are in view.

NOTES ON CHAPTER 8

1. Including zero in certain cases, e.g., 0 *Trees were blown down, 0 cars were smashed and 0 Mary was injured.* We'll see some examples of categories other than articles serving a determining function in a minute.

NOTES ON CHAPTER 9

1. Notice, however, that semantic roles are still left out of this diagram. To specify semantic roles we need Argument Structure Diagrams, such as those introduced in Chapter 6. Box diagrams are very good at displaying the structural parts of utterances, but still lack specification of meaning and use.
2. In this book we are considering *be* in predicate nominal, adjectival, locational, and other clauses with Subject Complements to be an auxiliary rather than a lexical verb. This is contrary to most traditional approaches to English grammar, but is very consistent from a linguistic perspective. In Chapter 11 I argue in some depth that this approach significantly simplifies the conceptualization, teaching, and learning of English grammar.
3. This is a special transitive use of the verb *spoil*, meaning "pamper to an extreme." Usually the Complement is *rotten*, though other adjectives, such as *silly* and *to bits*, do occur in the corpora.

NOTES ON CHAPTER 10

1. Radford (1997:171) calls this node a QP "Quantifier Phrase," with the predeterminer as the Head and each of the two DPs within it functioning as conjuncts. This is a reasonable analysis as well. However, since the whole phrase *both the government and the industry* has the same distributional properties as a DP, I prefer to think of this syntactic element as a kind of DP.
2. However, *well child* and *well baby* seem to be acceptable as Modifiers themselves, as in *a well baby clinic.*
3. "Noun phrase" in this chapter is used as a cover term for all nominal elements, including pronouns, undetermined noun phrases, and determined noun phrases.

4. The words *today, yesterday, here, there, yonder,* and a few others are difficult to assign to a basic word class outside of a context. Of course, from the communicative perspective taken in this book, this is not a major conceptual problem – words are form–meaning composites that may or may not fall neatly into particular word classes apart from their use in particular discourse contexts. Dictionaries describe these time words as adverbs or nouns. There is no way to distinguish their categories when they function as IP Modifiers, since both adverbs and noun phrases may accomplish this task. For expository purposes I am treating them as adverbs, even though I am treating conceptually similar expressions like *this morning* and *last week* as noun phrases.

NOTES ON CHAPTER 11

1. The "semi-auxiliaries," including *be going to, ought to, have to,* and *used to,* are not prototypical in that they do not have all of these properties.
2. Expressions in which the verb phrase alone is emphasized do allow emphatic stress: *Yes she should EAT more kimchi* (rather than MAKE more kimchi). The property in question here is *verum focus,* when the truth of the whole proposition is emphasized. Only in this case may the Complement of the emphasized element be ellipted, as illustrated in the examples in (32).
3. There are also syntactic differences between passives and predicate adjectives (see Wasow 1977), just like there are syntactic differences between different kinds of adjectives. But again, there is no particular reason to ascribe the differences to a difference in word class between *be* in passives and *be* in predicate adjective constructions. Even within the class of adjectives there are significant syntactic differences, as discussed in Chapter 10.
4. Some languages actually do have distinct copulas that are used to express the range of semantics expressed by English *be.* Mandarin, for example, uses the form *shi* for attributive and equative clauses, *zài* for locational clauses, and *yǒu* for existential and possessive clauses. Spanish has two copulas, *ser* which occurs in predicate nominals and predicate adjectives describing permanent states, and *estar* that occurs in predicate locatives and predicate adjectives describing temporary states. But in both these languages, it is patently obvious that different copulas are involved. In English, the only evidence is different semantics, which is important, but not alone a reason to posit distinct syntactic categories. The distinctions among these meanings are very real, but they are just not strongly *grammaticalized* in English.
5. By the way, most American English speakers I have checked this example with agree that it makes sense that regularized *be* expresses an activity. Most, especially those who have children, can even provide additional examples. However, British English speakers I have consulted categorically reject regularized active *be.* It very well may be the case that this is a feature that distinguishes British and American English.

NOTES ON CHAPTER 13

1. Van Valin and LaPolla (1997:392ff) use the term "lexical reflexive" quite differently than we will be using it in this text. The use of the term here is consistent with the general three-way distinction between lexical, morphological, and syntactic expression types that is a major theme of the present book, as well as much work in descriptive linguistics in general. As all students who go on in linguistics eventually discover, linguistic terminology is constantly changing, and there are many terms and concepts that are used in different ways by different linguists.

2. Some other languages have specific verb forms that indicate that an Object has been downplayed. For these languages, "antipassive" is a useful gloss for such forms. However, in English the alternation is simply a matter of demotion of an Object to an Oblique role or omission, so few linguists feel the need to use a special term like "antipassive" to refer to these constructions.

NOTES ON CHAPTER 14

1. So-called "*to*-infinitives" are not really verb forms, but are bare infinitives preceded by the particle *to*. Traditionally, however, these particle+verb combinations are treated as though they were a single form, probably by analogy with infinitive verb forms in the classical languages. Since this is not too horribly misleading from a linguistic perspective, I have chosen to adopt this terminological quirk.

2. This example is from Huddleston and Pullum (2002:186).

3. The verbs *insist, demand, require, command, ask,* and others occur in mandative constructions (Huddleston and Pullum 2002:995–9). In a mandative construction, these verbs are not, strictly speaking, manipulative, since they mandate a state of affairs, but don't necessarily imply direct manipulation of another person. For example, *I commanded him to leave* is a manipulative construction. However, *I commanded that he leave* is "mandative" because it implies that the Subject issued a command, but not necessarily directly to the person expected to leave. The verb *insist* only occurs in the mandative, and not in a manipulative construction: **I insisted him to leave.*

4. What I am calling "implicative CTPs" are sometimes referred to as "factive verbs." Some linguists (e.g., Karttunen 1971) make a distinction between factive verbs and implicative verbs. Factive verbs are those that *presuppose* the truth of their Complements, while implicative verbs *imply* the truth of their Complements. Some examples of factive verbs include *know, realize,* and *regret.* Examples of implicative verbs include *manage, remember, bother, care, venture, condescend,* and others. This is a subtle distinction that has some grammatical consequences, but for our purposes the terms "implicative CTPs" and the related term "implicational constraints" will suffice. The important point is that the stronger the semantic constraints imposed on the Complement by the matrix predicate, the less grammatically finite the Complement tends to be.

5. The term "R-element" is not common in the linguistics literature, but there is no other generally accepted term. Keenan (2007) uses the term "NP$_{rel}$" or "Relativized Noun Phrase." This term has a number of problems, including the fact that the element in

question is seldom realized by a full noun phrase. I use the term "R-element" by analogy with "Q-element" used by Quirk and Greenbaum (1973) for the analogous part of a content question, e.g., the information requested in a question like *Whom did you see Ø?*

6. Note that in this book we are trying to be consistent in naming forms differently from their functions. Traditionally the term "gerund" is used for forms like *sleeping* in *I like sleeping during the day*, but "participle" for *sleeping* in *the sleeping woman*. These terms name distinct syntactic functions for a single verb form. We will continue to use the term "present participle" to describe all verbs suffixed with the derivational suffix *-ing*.

NOTES ON CHAPTER 15

1. In the tradition of generative grammar (see, e.g., Radford 1997:172, van Valin and LaPolla 1997:434), the term "topicalization" is often used for (26a). Here I do not adopt this terminology because I want to avoid using functional-sounding terms, such as topicalization, to describe morphosyntactic constructions. There are any number of pragmatic functions the clause initial position may be exploited to express in English. Making something into a topic may be one of them, but the function of topicalization does not determine what element comes first in a clause.

References

Aarts, Bas. 2008. *English Syntax and Argumentation* (3rd edition). Houndmills and New York: Palgrave MacMillan.

American Heritage. 2006. *The American Heritage Dictionary of the English Language* (4th edition). Boston and New York: Houghton Mifflin Company.

Austin, J. L. 1965. *How to Do Things with Words.* Oxford University Press.

Azar, Betty Schrampfer. 2002. *Understanding and Using English Grammar* (3rd edition). Pearson Longman.

Bailey, Charles James Nice. 1996. *Essays on Time-Based Linguistic Analysis.* Oxford: Clarendon Press; New York: Oxford University Press.

Baugh, Albert C. 1963. *A History of the English Language* (2nd edition). New York: Appleton-Century-Crofts.

Berk, Lynn M. 1999. *English Syntax: From Word to Discourse.* New York: Oxford University Press.

Binnick, Robert I. 2006. Aspect and aspectuality. *The Handbook of English Linguistics*, ed. Bas Aarts & A. M. S. McMahon, 244–68. Malden, MA: Blackwell.

Bošković, Željko & Howard Lasnik (eds.). 2007. *Minimalist syntax: The Essential Readings* (MIT Working Papers in Linguistics 27). Cambridge, MA: MIT Press.

Börjars, Kersti & Kate Burridge. 2001. *Introducing English Grammar.* London: Arnold Publishers.

Bragg, Melvyn. 2006. *The Adventure of English: The Biography of a Language* (paperback edition). New York: Arcade Publishing.

Brazil, David, Martin Hewings, & Richard Cauldwell. 1997. *The Communicative Value of Intonation in English.* Cambridge University Press.

Bresnan, Joan. 2001. *Lexical Functional Syntax.* Oxford: Basil Blackwell.

Brinton, Laurel J. 2000. *The Structure of Modern English: A Linguistic Introduction.* Amsterdam and Philadelphia: John Benjamins.

Brinton, Laurel J. & Leslie K. Arnovick. 2006. *The English Language: A Linguistic History.* Oxford University Press.

Brown, Gillian & George Yule. 1983. *Discourse Analysis.* Cambridge University Press.

Calude, Andreea S. 2009. *Cleft Constructions in Spoken English.* Berlin: VDM-Verlag.
    1872. *Through the Looking Glass, and what Alice Found there.* London: Macmillan and Company.

Carstairs-McCarthy, Andrew. 2002. *An Introduction to English Morphology.* Edinburgh University Press.

Celce-Murcia, Marianne, Donna Brinton & Janet M. Goodwin. 1996. *Teaching Pronunciation: A Reference for Teachers of English to Speakers of Other Languages.* Cambridge University Press.

Celce-Murcia, Marianne & Diane Larsen-Freeman. 1999. *The Grammar Book: An ESL/EFL Teacher's Course.* Boston: Heinle & Heinle.

Chafe, Wallace L. & Johanna Nichols (eds.). 1986. *Evidentiality: The Linguistic Coding of Epistemology.* Norwood, NJ: Ablex.

Chafe, Wallace L. 1970. *Meaning and the Structure of Language.* Chicago: University of Chicago Press.

1976. Givenness, contrastiveness, definiteness, subjects, topics and point of view. *Subject and Topic*, ed. Charles N. Li, 25–55. New York: Academic Press.

Chesterman, Andrew. 2005. *On Definiteness: A Study with Special Reference to English and Finnish* (Cambridge Studies in Linguistics 56). Cambridge University Press.

Chomsky, Noam. 1995. *The Minimalist Program.* Cambridge, MA: MIT Press.

Clancy, Patricia M. 1980. Referential choice in English and Japanese narrative. *The Pear Stories: Cognitive, Cultural, and Linguistic Aspects of Narrative Production*, ed. Wallace L. Chafe, 127–202. Norwood, NJ: Ablex.

Coleman, Linda & Paul Kay. 1981. Prototype semantics: the English word *lie*. *Language* 57: 26–44.

Comrie, Bernard. 1976. *Aspect: An Introduction to the Study of Verbal Aspect and Related Problems* (Reprinted with corrections 1978, 1981) (Cambridge Textbooks in Linguistics). Cambridge University Press.

1985. *Tense* (Cambridge Textbooks in Linguistics). Cambridge University Press.

1989. *Language Universals and Linguistic Typology* (2nd edition). University of Chicago Press.

Croft, William. 2002. *Radical Construction Grammar.* Oxford University Press.

2003. *Typology and Universals* (2nd edition). Cambridge University Press.

Croft, William & D. A. Cruse. 2004. *Cognitive Linguistics.* Cambridge University Press.

Davies, Mark. 2004. *The British National Corpus* (BNC). 100 million words, 1980–1993. Available online at corpus.byu.edu/bnc.

2008. *The Corpus of Contemporary American English* (COCA): 385 million words, 1990–present. Available online at www.americancorpus.org.

de Groot, Caspar. 2007. The king is on huntunge: on the relation between progressive and absentive in Old and Early Modern English. *The English Clause: Usage and Structure*, ed. M. Hannay and G. Steen, 175–190. Amsterdam: Benjamins.

DeLancey, Scott. 1990. Ergativity and the cognitive model of event structure in Lhasa Tibetan. *Cognitive Linguistics* 1, 289–321.

Dik, Simon. 1981. On the typology of focus phenomena. *Perspectives on Functional Grammar*, ed. Hoekstra, Teun, Harry Van der Hulst, & Michael Moortgat, 41–74. Dordrecht-Holland: Foris.

Dixon, R. M. W. 2005. *A Semantic Approach to English Grammar* (2nd edition) (Oxford Textbooks in Linguistics). Oxford University Press.

Dixon, R. M. W. & Alexandra Y. Aikhenvald (eds.). 2000. *Changing Valency: Case Studies in Transitivity.* Cambridge University Press.

(eds). 2002. *Word: A Cross-Linguistic Typology*. Cambridge University Press.

(eds.). 2006. *Complementation: A Cross-Linguistic Typology* (Explorations in Linguistic Typology 3). Oxford University Press.

Dreiser, Theodore. 2008. *Sister Carrie*. New York: Simon and Schuster.

Dryer, Matthew S. 1988. Object–verb order and adjective–noun order: dispelling a myth. *Lingua* 74: 185–217.

2007. Word order. In Shopen, Timothy (ed.) 2007a, 61–131.

Du Bois, John W. 1980. Beyond definiteness: the trace of identity in discourse. *The Pear Stories: Cognitive, Cultural, and Linguistic Aspects of Narrative Production*, ed. Wallace L. Chafe, 203–74. Norwood, NJ: Ablex.

Facchinetti, Roberta, Manfred G. Krug, & Frank R. Palmer (eds.). 2003. *Modality in Contemporary English* (Topics in English Linguistics 44). Berlin: Mouton de Gruyter.

Fanon, Frantz. 1952. *Peau Noire, Masques Blancs* [Black Skin, White Masks]. Paris: Seuil. Translation 2008 by Richard Philcox. New York: Grove Press.

Ferris, Connor. 1993. *The Meaning of Syntax: A Study in the Adjectives of English*. London: Longman.

Fillmore, Charles J. 1968. The case for case. *Universals in Linguistic Theory*, ed. Emond Bach & Robert T. Harms, 1–88. New York: Holt, Rinehart and Winston.

1976. Topics in lexical semantics. *Current Issues in Linguistic Theory*, ed. Peter Cole, 76–138. Bloomington: Indiana University Press.

1977. The case for case reopened. *Syntax and Semantics 8: Grammatical Relations*, ed. Peter Cole & J. M. Sadock. 59–81. New York: Academic Press.

1992. "Corpus linguistics" vs. "computer-aided armchair linguistics." *Directions in Corpus Linguistics: Proceedings from a 1991 Nobel Symposium on Corpus Linguistics*, 35–66. Stockholm: Mouton de Gruyter.

Fillmore, Charles J. & Collin F. Baker. 2001. Frame semantics for text understanding. *Proceedings of the NAACL-01 Workshop on WordNet and other Lexical Resources*. Available online at http://framenet.icsi.berkeley.edu/papers/FNcrime.pdf.

Fillmore, Charles J., Paul Kay, & Mary Catherine O'Connor. 1988. Regularity and idiomaticity in grammatical constructions. *Language*, 64, 3: 501–38.

Filppula, Markku, Juhani Klemola, & Heli Paulasto. 2008. *English and Celtic in Contact* (Routledge Studies in Germanic Linguistics 13). New York, London: Routledge.

Finnegan, Edward. 1994. *Language: Its Structure and Use*. Fort Worth: Harcourt Brace College Publishers.

Foley, William & R. van Valin. 1984. *Functional Syntax and Universal Grammar*. Cambridge University Press.

Givón, T. 1979. *On Understanding Grammar*. New York: Academic Press.

1980. The binding hierarchy and the typology of complements. *Studies in Language* 4:3, 333–78.

1983. Topic continuity in discourse: an introduction. *Topic Continuity in Discourse: A Quantitative Cross-Language Study*, ed. T. Givón (Typological Studies in Language 3), 1–42. Amsterdam and Philadelphia: John Benjamins.

2001. *Syntax: An Introduction* (vol. I). Amsterdam and Philadelphia: John Benjamins.

Goldberg, Adele. 1995. *Constructions: A Construction Grammar Approach to Argument Structure.* Chicago: University of Chicago Press.

Greenbaum, Sidney & Randolph Quirk. 2004. *A Student's Grammar of the English Language.* Harlow, England: Longman.

Greenberg, Joseph H. 1963. Some universals of grammar with particular reference to the order of meaningful elements. *Universals of Language*, ed. Joseph H. Greenberg, 40–70. Cambridge, MA: MIT Press.

Grice, H. Paul. 1975. Logic and conversation. *Syntax and Semantics* (vol. III): *Speech Acts*, ed. Peter Cole & J. Morgan, 41–58. New York: Academic Press.

1981. Presupposition and conversational implicature. *Radical Pragmatics*, ed. Peter Cole, 183–98. New York: Academic Press.

Hadley, Dawn M. 2006. *The Vikings in England: Settlement, Society and Culture.* Manchester University Press.

Haspelmath, Martin. 1993. *A Grammar of Lezgian* (Mouton Grammar Library 9). Berlin: Mouton de Gruyter.

Hawkins, John. 1994. *Comparative Typology of English and German: Unifying the Contrasts.* London and Sydney: Croom Helm.

Heath, Jeffrey. 1976. Antipassivization: a functional typology. Proceedings from the second annual meeting of the Berkeley Linguistics Society.

Higham, Nicholas J. 1994. *The English Conquest: Gildas and Britain in the Fifth Century.* Manchester University Press.

Hiltunen, Risto. 1999. Verbal phrases and phrasal verbs in Early Modern English. In *Collocational and Idiomatic Aspects of Composite Predicates in the History of English*, ed. Laurel J. Brinton & Minoji Akimoto. Amsterdam and Philadelphia: John Benjamins.

Hoey, Michael. 2001. *Textual Interaction: An Introduction to Written Discourse Analysis.* London: Routledge.

Hogg, Richard M. (ed.). 2001. *The Cambridge History of the English Language* (6 volumes). Cambridge University Press.

Hopper, Paul J. & Sandra A. Thompson. 1980. Transitivity in grammar and discourse. *Language* 56.2: 251–99.

Hopper, Paul J. & Sandra A. Thompson. 1984. The discourse basis for lexical categories in universal grammar. *Language* 60.4: 703–52.

Huddleston, Rodney & Geoffrey K. Pullum (with thirteen collaborators). 2002. *The Cambridge Grammar of the English Language.* Cambridge University Press.

Internet Movie Data Base (IMDB). www.imdb.com.

Jackendoff, Ray. 1986. Conceptual semantics. In *Meaning and Mental Representation*, ed. Umberto Eco, Marco Santambrogio, & Patrizia Violi, 81–97. Bloomington: Indiana University Press.

Jaggar, Philip. 1988. Discourse deployability and indefinite NP-marking in Hausa: a demonstration of the universal "categoriality hypothesis." *Studies in Hausa Language and Linguistics in Honour of F. W. Parsons*, ed. Graham Furniss, Philip J. Jaggar, & Frederick William Parsons, 45–61. London: Kegan Paul International Ltd.

Jones, Sir William. 1798. Third anniversary discourse: on the Hindus. *Asiatick Researches* 1: 415–31. (Delivered February 2, 1786.)

Karttunen, Lauri. 1971. Implicative verbs. *Language* 47.2 340–58.

Katz, Jerrold. 1990 *The Metaphysics of Meaning.* Cambridge, MA: MIT Press.

Keenan, Edward L. 2007. Relative clauses. In Shopen, Timothy (ed.) 2007c, 141–70.

Keizer, E. 2007. *The English Noun Phrase: The Nature of Linguistic Categorization.* Cambridge University Press.

Klein, Ernest. 1966. *A Comprehensive Etymological Dictionary of the English Language. Dealing with the Origin of Words and their Sense Development thus Illustrating the History of Civilization and Culture.* Amsterdam, New York: Elsevier.

Krapp, George P. & Elliot V. K. Dobbie. 1936. *The Exeter Book.* New York: Columbia University Press.

Lakoff, George 1987. *Women, Fire and Dangerous Things: What Categories Reveal about the Mind.* University of Chicago Press.

Lakoff, George and Mark Johnson. 1999. *Philosophy in the Flesh: The Embodied Mind and its Challenge to Western Thought.* New York: Basic Books.

Lambrecht, Knud. 1996. *Information Structure and Sentence Form: Topic, Focus, and the Mental Representations of Discourse Referents* (Cambridge Studies in Linguistics 71). Cambridge University Press.

Lambrecht, Knud. 2001. A framework for the analysis of cleft constructions. *Linguistics* 39.3: 463–516.

Langacker, Ronald W. 1987. *Foundations of Cognitive Grammar* (vol. I). Stanford University Press.

   1991. *Concept, Image, and Symbol: The Cognitive Basis of Grammar.* Berlin and New York: Mouton de Gruyter.

   1995. Possession and possessive constructions. *Language and the Cognitive Construal of the World*, ed. John R. Taylor & Robert E. MacLaury, 51–79. Berlin: Mouton de Gruyter.

   2008. *Cognitive Grammar: A Basic Introduction.* New York: Oxford University Press.

Larsen-Freeman, Diane. 1997. Grammar and its teaching [microform]: challenging the myths. *Washington*, DC: ERIC Clearinghouse on Languages and Linguistics, Center for Applied Linguistics.

Lass, Roger. 1995. *Old English: A Historical Linguistic Companion.* Cambridge University Press.

Lemmens, Maartin & Dan Slobin. 2008. How people move. *Discourse Across Languages and Cultures 2004*, ed. C. L. Moder & A. Martinovic-Zic (Studies in Language Companion Series 68), 195–210. Amsterdam: John Benjamins.

Levin, Beth. 1993. *English Verb Classes and Alternations: A Preliminary Investigation.* Chicago and London: University of Chicago Press.

Levinson, Stephen C. 1983. *Pragmatics* (Cambridge Textbooks in Linguistics). Cambridge University Press.

   2003. *Space in Language and Cognition: Explorations in Cognitive Diversity* (Language, Culture and Cognition 5). Cambridge University Press.

Li, Charles N. and Sandra A. Thompson. 1976. Subject and topic: a new typology of language. *Subject and Topic*, ed. Charles N. Li, 457–90. New York: Academic Press.

Livio, Mario. 2005. *The Equation that Couldn't be Solved: How Mathematical Genius Discovered the Language of Symmetry.* New York: Simon and Schuster.

Longacre, Robert E. 1983. *The Grammar of Discourse.* New York and London: Plenum Press.

Machan, Tim William. 2009. *Language Anxiety: Conflict and Change in the History of English.* Oxford University Press.

MacWhorter, John. 2009. *Our Magnificent Bastard Tongue: The Untold Story of English.* New York: Gotham Books.

Mahlberg, Michaela. 2005. *English General Nouns: A Corpus Theoretical Approach.* Amsterdam and Philadelphia: John Benjamins.

Mair, Christian. 1990. *Infinitival Complement Clauses in English: A Study of Syntax in Discourse* (Cambridge Studies in English Language). Cambridge University Press.

Mathesius, Vilém. 1939[1947]. *O takzvaném aktuálním členění větném* [On the so-called Functional Sentence Perspective]. Reprinted in *Čeština a obecny jazykozpyt* [The Czech language and general linguistics], 234–42. Prague.

Matthews, Peter H. 1991. *Morphology* (2nd edition). Cambridge University Press.

McCrum, Robert, Robert MacNeil, & William Cram. 2002. *The Story of English* (3rd edition). New York: Penguin.

Milne, A. A. 1956. The house at Pooh corner. In *The Complete Tales and Poems of Winnie-the-Pooh*, 2001, by the Trustees of the Pooh Properties. New York: Dutton Children's Books.

Minsky, Marvin. 1975. A framework for representing knowledge. *Theoretical Issues in Natural Language Processing*, ed. Bonnie Nash-Webber & Roger Schank, 118–30. Cambridge, MA: Yale University Press.

Mithun, Marianne. 1992. Is basic word order universal? *Pragmatics of Word Order Flexibility*, ed. Doris L. Payne, 15–62. Amsterdam and Philadelphia: Benjamins.

Nayuki, Ono. 2009. Cross-linguistic patterns of expressing complex events in English and Japanese. Paper presented at the Conference on Verb Typologies revisited: A Cross-linguistic Reflection on Verbs and Verb Classes, University of Ghent. Available online at www.verbtypology2009.ugent.be/index.php?id=92andtype=file.

Noonan, Michael. 2007. Complementation. In Shopen, Timothy (ed.) 2007c, 52–150.

O'Dwyer, Bernard. 2000. *Modern English Structures: Form, Function, and Position.* Peterborough, Ontario: Broadview Press.

Orwig, Carol. 2009. Workbook for independent language learners. Unpublished MS, available from SIL International (www.sil.org).

Palmer, Frank R. 2001. *Mood and Modality* (2nd edition) (Cambridge Textbooks in Linguistics). Cambridge University Press.

Partee, Barbara. 1977. John is easy to please. *Linguistic Structures Processing*, ed. Antonio Zampolli, 281–312. Amsterdam: North-Holland Publishing Co.

Partee, Barbara H., Alice ter Meulen, & Robert Wall. 1990. *Mathematical Methods in Linguistics.* Dordrecht: Kluwer.

Payne, Doris L. 1992. Nonidentifiable information and pragmatic order rules in "O'odham." *Pragmatics of Word Order Flexibility*, ed. Doris L. Payne, 137–66. Amsterdam and Philadelphia: John Benjamins.

Payne, Doris L. and Zhuo Jing-Schmidt. 2009. *A Cross-Language Typology of Lexical Transitivity*. University of Oregon colloquium, May 2009.

Piotrowski, Jennifer A. 2009. Information structure of clefts in spoken English. Unpublished University of Oregon master's thesis.

Plag, Ingo. 2003. *Word-Formation in English* (Cambridge Textbooks in Linguistics). Cambridge University Press.

Quirk, Randolph and Sidney Greenbaum. 1973. *A Concise Grammar of Contemporary English*. San Diego (*inter alia*): Harcourt Brace Jovanovich.

Radden, Günter and René Dirven. 2007. *Cognitive English Grammar* (Cognitive Linguistics in Practice 2). Amsterdam and Philadelphia: John Benjamins.

Radford, Andrew. 1997. *Syntax: A Minimalist Introduction*. Cambridge University Press.
     2004. *Minimalist Syntax: Exploring the Structure of English* (Cambridge Textbooks in Linguistics). Cambridge University Press.

Ramat, Anna Giacalone. (ed.). (2002). *Typology and second language acquisition*. Berlin: Mouton de Gruyter.

Reinhart, Tanya. 1982. *Pragmatics and Linguistics: An Analysis of Sentence Topics*. Bloomington: Indiana University Linguistics Club.

Roth, Eric. 2008. *The Curious Case of Benjamin Button* (Film).

Rudanko, Juhani and Lea Luodes. 2005. *Complementation in British and American English: Corpus-based Studies on Prepositions and Complement Clauses*. Lanham, MA: Rowman and Littlefield Pub. Inc.

Rushdie, Salman (ed.). 2008. *The Best American Short Stories 2008*. Boston and New York: Houghton Mifflin Company.

Russell, James. 1989. *Underground*. London: Victor Gollancz Ltd.

Sag, Ivan A., Thomas Wasow, & Emily Bender. 2003: *Syntactic Theory: A Formal Introduction* (2nd edition). University of Chicago Press.

Saussure, Ferdinand de. 1915. *A Course in General Linguistics*. Trans. C. Bally & A. Ferdlinger. New York: Philosophical Library.

Schank, Roger. 1972. Conceptual dependency: a theory of natural language understanding. *Cognitive Psychology* 3: 552–631.

Schank, Roger & R. Abelson. 1977. *Scripts, Plans, Goals, and Understanding*. Hillsdale, NJ: Lawrence Erlbaum.

Searle, John R. 1975. Indirect speech acts. *Syntax and Pragmatics* (vol. III): *Speech Acts*, ed. Peter Cole & Jerry L. Morgan, 59–82. New York: Academic Press.

Selinker, Larry. 1972. Interlanguage. *International Review of Applied Linguistics*, 10.209–241.

Selkirk, Elisabeth. 2002. Contrastive FOCUS vs. presentational focus: prosodic evidence from right node raising in English. *Speech Prosody 2002: Proceedings of the 1st International Conference on Speech Prosody, Aix-en-Provence*, 643–46.

Shibatani, Masayoshi. 1988. *Passive and Voice* (Typological Studies in Language 16). Amsterdam and Philadelphia: John Benjamins.

Shopen, Timothy (ed.). 2007a. *Language Typology and Syntactic Description* (vol. I): *Clause Structure* (2nd edition). Cambridge University Press.

(ed.). 2007b. *Language Typology and Syntactic Description* (vol. II): *Complex Constructions* (2nd edition). Cambridge University Press.

(ed.). 2007c. *Language Typology and Syntactic Description* (vol. III): *Grammatical Categories and the Lexicon* (2nd edition). Cambridge University Press.

Seuss, Dr. [Theodore Seuss Geisel]. 1950. *If I Ran the Zoo.* New York: Random House.

Slobin, Dan. 2006. What makes manner of motion salient? Explorations in linguistic typology, discourse, and cognition. *Space in Languages: Linguistic Systems and Cognitive Categories*, ed. Maya Hickmann & Stephen Robert, 59–81. Amsterdam and Philadelphia: John Benjamins.

Spencer, Andrew & Arnold M. Zwicky (eds.). 1997. *The Handbook of Morphology.* Oxford: Basil Blackwell Ltd.

Sperber, Dan & Dierdre Wilson. 1995. *Relevance: Communication and Cognition* (2nd edition). Oxford: Basil Blackwell Ltd.

Stannard, Russell. 2005. *Black Holes and Uncle Albert.* London: Faber and Faber.

Talmy, Leonard. 2007. Lexical typologies. In Shopen, Timothy (ed.) 2007c, 66–168.

Taylor, John R. 2006. *Possessives in English: An Exploration in Cognitive Grammar.* Oxford: Clarendon Press.

Teschner, Richard V. & Eston E. Evans. 2007. *Analyzing the Grammar of English* (3rd edition). Washington: Georgetown University Press.

Tesnière, Lucien. 1959. *Éléments de Syntaxe Structurale.* Paris: Klincksieck.

Thompson, Sandra A. 1988. A discourse approach to the cross-linguistic category "adjective." *Explaining Language Universals*, ed. John A. Hawkins, 167–85. Oxford and New York: Basil Blackwell.

1997. Discourse motivations for the core–oblique distinction as a language universal. *Directions in Functional Linguistics*, ed. Akio Kamio (Studies in Language Companion Series 36), 59–82. Amsterdam and Philadelphia: John Benjamins.

Thompson, Sandra A., Robert Longacre, & Shin Ja Hwang. 2007. Adverbial clauses. In Shopen, Timothy (ed.) 2007b, 237–69.

Tolkien, J.R.R. 1965. *The Two Towers.* New York: Ballantine Books. (Paperback edition of 1954 original George Allen and Unwin Ltd. London edition.)

Traugott, Elizabeth Closs & Bernd Heine (eds.). 1991. *Approaches to Grammaticalization* (vols. I and II). Amsterdam and Philadelphia: John Benjamins.

van Dijk, Teun. 1972. *Some Aspects of Text Grammars.* The Hague: Mouton.

van Gelderen, Elly. 2006. *A History of the English Language.* Amsterdam and Philadelphia: John Benjamins.

van Valin, Robert D., Jr. and Randy J. LaPolla. 1997. *Syntax: Structure, Meaning and Function.* Cambridge University Press.

Vendler, Zeno. 1967. Verbs and times. *Linguistics in philosophy*, ed. Z. Vendler, 97–121. Ithaca, NY: Cornell University Press.

Verstraete, Jean-Christophe. 2007. *Rethinking the Coordinate-Subordinate Dichotomy: Interpersonal Grammar and the Analysis of Adverbial Clauses in English* (Topics in English Linguistics 55). Berlin: Mouton de Gruyter.

Wagner, Jane. 1986. *The Search for Signs of Intelligent Life in the Universe.* New York: Harper and Row.

Wallace, Stephen. 1982. Figure and ground: the interrelationships of linguistic categories. *Tense and aspect*, ed. Paul J. Hopper, 201–23. Amsterdam and Philadelphia: John Benjamins.

Wanner, Anja. 2009. *Deconstructing the English Passive*. Berlin: Mouton de Gruyter.

Warner, Anthony. 1993. *English Auxiliaries: Structure and History* (Cambridge Studies in Linguistics 66). Cambridge University Press.

Wasow, Tom. 1977. Transformations and the lexicon. *Formal Syntax*, ed. Peter Culicover, Tom Wasow, & Adrian Akmajian. New York: Academic Press.

Wierzbicka, Anna. 1988. *The Semantics of Grammar* (Studies in Language Companion Series 18). Amsterdam and Philadelphia: John Benjamins.

Wittgenstein, Ludwig. 1981 [1958]. *Philosophical Investigations*. Oxford: Basil Blackwell Ltd.

Wright, Suzanne and T. Givón. 1987. The pragmatics of indefinite reference: quantified text-based studies. *Studies in Language* 11.1–33.

Index

CPSIA information can be obtained
at www.ICGtesting.com
Printed in the USA
LVHW020355170822
726060LV00005B/155